Canadian Society
in the Twenty-first
Century

Canadian Society in the Twenty-first Century

An Historical Sociological Approach

Trevor W. Harrison
University of Lethbridge

John W. Friesen
University of Calgary

Canadian Society in the Twenty-first Century
Edited by Trevor W. Harrison and John W. Friesen

Published by
Women's Press, an imprint of Canadian Scholars' Press Inc.
180 Bloor Street West, Suite 801
Toronto, Ontario
M5S 2V6

www.cspi.org

Canadian Scholars' Press Inc. gratefully acknowledges financial support for our publishing activities from the Government of Canada through the Book Publishing Industry Development Program (BPIDP).

Library and Archives Canada Cataloguing in Publication

Harrison, Trevor, 1952–
    Canadian society in the twenty-first century : an historical sociological approach / Trevor W. Harrison, John W. Friesen.

Includes bibliographical references and index.
ISBN 978-1-55130-371-0

    1. Canada —Civilization—Textbooks. 2. Canada —Civilization--21st century—Forecasting—Textbooks. 3. Canada —English-French relations—Textbooks. 4. Native peoples— Canada —Textbooks. 5. Native peoples— Canada —Government relations—Textbooks. I. Friesen, John W. II. Title.

FC95.5.H37 2010   971   C2010-902979-8

Cover design by Colleen Wormald.
Interior design by Aldo Fierro.

10 11 12 13 14   1 2 3 4 5

Printed and bound in Canada by Marquis Book Printing, Inc.

Dedicated to our wives:

*Terri Mae Saunders and
Virginia Lyons Friesen*

CONTENTS

ACKNOWLEDGEMENTS

As in the first edition, I want to thank first the many students whom I have instructed in courses on Canadian society, first at the University of Alberta and, since 2002, at the University of Lethbridge. Their keen interest and probing questions have led me to think hard about the nature of societies and Canadian society in particular.

Thanks go to Canadian Scholars' Press Inc., in particular Megan Mueller and Camille Isaacs with whom John and I worked closely in putting together this edition. I would also like to thank James MacNevin, Sarah Wayne, and Colleen Wormald with whom we worked in the final stages of the text's preparation.

Thanks go also to Gordon Laxer and Bob Brym for their strong support and advice leading to this edition's adoption by CSPI. I would be greatly remiss if I did not further thank Gordon, Bob, Claude Denis, William Ramp, and a host of other friends and academic acquaintances for their many contributions to my thinking about Canadian society, and my departmental colleagues for their general support over the years.

I would also like to acknowledge Dr. P.B. White for the use of his words quoted in Chapter 6 and John Robert Colombo for the use of various quotations from *Colombo & Company*.

Thanks also are due to James Falconer who, as my teaching assistant, worked on changes to the test bank and Paul Lawton who worked on the earlier version of the same.

Finally, I must also acknowledge the support of my wife, Terri, and my children, Jayna and Keenan. They are a constant source of inspiration and the cause of my dedication to a better Canada.

I apologize to any whose contributions I have unintentionally overlooked. I take sole responsibility for any errors or omissions contained in the text.

T.W.H.

To begin, I want to acknowledge the consistent support of my wife, Dr. Virginia Lyons Friesen, who shares my research interests and with whom I have co-authored more than a dozen books. Virginia shines in the areas of computer technology, Internet research, editing, and putting up with my whims. I owe her a debt that cannot be repaid in this life.

Second, I want to say thanks to the Aboriginal peoples who have graciously hosted us while we were conducting research through the years on reservations (reserves) from Alberta and Saskatchewan to Texas and Mexico. Locally, our gratitude must be extended to the Four Band Plains Cree, Siksika, Stoney (Nakoda Sioux), and Tsuu T'ina First Nations from whom we have learned a great deal. My own formal attachment to the Stoney First Nation as minister of the Morley United Church from 1986 to 2008 gave me the opportunity to be mentored by some of the most accepting individuals I have ever met. This includes a lengthy list, some of whom have since passed away. They are: Chief John and Alva Snow, Lazarus and Lily Wesley, Frank and Glenda Crawler, Ivan and Trudy Wesley, Rod and Reatha Mark, Lucy Daniels, Clara Rollinmud, Fred and Beatrice Powder, and Reba Powderface. There are many more people to list, but space will not allow, and I apologize for that. Still, I want to express my thanks for their influence on my life.

I also want to thank students at the University of Calgary and Old Sun College at Siksika who have enrolled in classes conducted by my wife, Virginia, and myself. The courses include Canadian Studies (CNST 311: Plains Indigenous History), CNST 313 (Native Art in Canada), and CNST 315 (Native Education in Canada). Our students deserve thanks because often we learn as much from them as they do from us. True learning is always a sharing process.

Finally, I want to thank my colleague,

Trevor W. Harrison, for the hard work he put into this project. He never seemed to weary of deadlines, but worked prodigiously and perseveringly to bring this production to its birth as a book. I only hope that our readers will appreciate the effort involved in producing this work.

J.W.F.

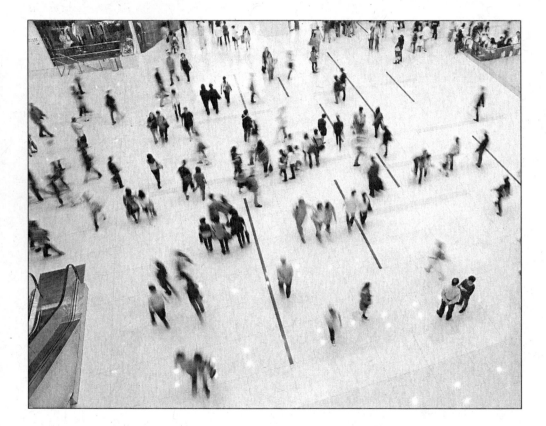

CHAPTER 1
WHAT IS SOCIETY?

In every generation Canadians have had to rework the miracle of their political existence. Canada has been created because there has existed within the hearts of its people a determination to build for themselves an enduring home. Canada is a supreme act of faith.

historian A.R.M. Lower, 1946

Ours is not the only nation which has out-travelled its own soul and now is forced to search frantically for a new identity. No wonder, for so many, the past Canadian experience has become not so much a forgotten thing as an unknown thing.

—novelist Hugh MacLennan, 1974

How could we have believed that there is such a thing as time, the self, or the nation?

—author John Gray, 1994

INTRODUCTION

Since its founding in 1867, Canada's imminent demise has been regularly predicted. Throughout much of the 19th and early 20th centuries, two threats were particularly prominent: the internecine battles between Canada's French and English communities, and the equally looming presence of the United States. The English-born journalist Goldwin Smith enunciated the first of these threats in 1891 with the publication of *Canada and the Canadian Question*, a text that somewhat too gleefully pronounced the conflict between English Canada and French Canada as intractable. The second threat, that of American absorption, found its voice in a duet sung across the borders, from the Canadian side by Sarah Jeannette Duncan in *The Imperialist* (1904) and from the American side by Samuel Moffett in *The Americanization of Canada* (1908). Later, as the western provinces were opened up for agricultural development, a

third peril reared its head—that of western alienation.

In one form or another, these same threats found an echo in later years. Quebec's escalating demands for recognition, if not outright sovereignty, after the 1960s resulted in a plethora of books predicting as before an end to Canada's national experiment. One of them, Peter Brimelow's *The Patriot Game* (1986), faithfully replicated Goldwin Smith's arguments of nearly a century previous. Similarly, changes in Canada's political economy after the Second World War caused some, like the philosopher George Grant in *Lament for a Nation* (1965), to decry the loss of British influence as a buffer against the American embrace. The adoption of free trade after 1988 heightened these warnings: Witness, for example, Lawrence Martin's *Pledge of Allegiance: The Americanization of Canada during the Mulroney Years* (1993). As before, these twin pillars of discontent were joined in the late 1980s by rising western discontent, then in the guise of the Reform Party (Harrison, 1995). These more traditional fears were joined in some quarters by warnings centred on Aboriginal demands for the redress of historic wrongs (Smith, 1995). Yet, amid the fears and doubts, a new confidence—even cockiness—has in recent years emerged. Writing in 2008, Lawrence Martin remarked that most of these threats "have significantly receded or been vanquished."

Canada still faces challenges, and always will. As Martin also noted, "battles won do not mean battles have ended." As with individuals, the scars that define nations are always ripe to be opened again. Likewise, Canada faces several other ongoing challenges: the need to integrate newcomers into a multicultural framework and to deal with the legitimate demands of Aboriginal peoples for historic redress and current inclusion, to name two. To these challenges and threats must also be added the growing and interrelated challenges of globalization, terrorism, resource scarcity, and climate change (especially global warming). These issues—some old, some new—and the processes by which Canadians have attempted to resolve them frame this text. In particular, this text deals with the thorny problem of Canadian society.

Given Canada's geographical vastness, its historical and cultural diversity, and its political and social complexity, one might ask how it is possible to grasp Canadian society. What sense does it make to even speak of "Canadian society" at a time when—we continue to be told—cultural, economic, and political borders are breaking down (Ohmae, 1990)? The vastness of the problem led one sociologist some years ago to comment that "the task of 'constituting society,' of creating knowledge about, and articulating a wholist account of, the total society, is no longer central to current concerns of sociologists in Canada" (Whyte, 1992: 313). To paraphrase Frisby and Sayer (1986: 121), Canadian society would seem "too grand an abstraction by far for modern sociological tastes."

The reader is thus forewarned: In opening this text, you begin the daunting task of journeying into a territory that many scholars avoid, where existing maps may be unclear, where the terrain is constantly shifting, where fact and myth coexist, and where abstractions run wild. To assist in this journey through Canadian society, this introductory chapter provides a set of rudimentary tools: terms, concepts, theories, and an explanation of historical sociology as a method of study. Learn to use these tools well. The chapter begins with an attempt at defining the object of study.

THE "PROBLEM" OF SOCIETY

What is society? At first, the question may seem strange. After all, we use the term *society* frequently. But try to touch it or point a finger to it. It cannot be done, of course, because—unlike a rock, for example—society is not a concrete thing; it is an abstract concept.

This comparison touches on the first problem with the concept of society. Abstract concepts are very powerful and necessary tools for assisting us to think about complex social phenomena. Abstract concepts become problematic, however, when we engage in **reification**: *the process of believing that our mental constructs actually exist materially.* Many of the terms we will deal with in this chapter, such as *state* and *nation*, share with *society* the frequent problem of being reified.

A second problem with the term *society* is its diverse meanings. Take, for example, the following definition of the term appearing in *Merriam-Webster's Collegiate Dictionary* (Merriam-Webster, Incorporated, 2003: 1115):

1 : companionship or association with one's fellows : friendly or intimate intercourse : COMPANY 2 : a voluntary association of individuals for common ends; *esp* : an organized group working together or periodically meeting because of common interests, beliefs, or profession 3 **a** : an enduring and cooperating social group whose members have developed organized patterns of relationships through interaction with one another **b** : a community, nation, or broad grouping of people having common traditions, institutions, and collective activities and interests 4 **a** : a part of a community that is a unit distinguishable by particular aims or standards of living or conduct : a social circle or a group of social circles having a clearly marked identity <literary society> **b** : a part of the community that sets itself apart as a leisure class and that regards itself as the arbiter of fashion and manners 5 **a** : a natural group of plants usu. of a single spe-

cies or habit within an association **b** : the progeny of a pair of insects when constituting a social unit (as a hive of bees); *broadly* : an interdependent system of organisms or biological units.

Such a definition is very broad. Clearly, Canada is not a society like that of a group of plants or the progeny of insects, or even that of individuals who believe in a flat earth. Moreover, the problem of definition is only partially remedied by adding a descriptive modifier, such as *Canadian*.

When sociologists refer to society, they often mean something more narrowly defined, yet conceptually larger. A popular introductory text in sociology (Brym, 2008: 49), for example, states that "A society involves people interacting socially and sharing culture, usually in a defined geographical area." Another introductory text (Kendall et al., 2007: 4) defines society as follows: "A society is a large social grouping that shares the same geographical territory and is subject to the same political authority and dominant cultural expectations." This definition suggests that a society's social boundaries are coexistent with its political boundaries. But which political boundaries are to be used: federal, provincial, or municipal?

This question points to a third problem with the concept of society: Where does one society end and another begin? Denis (1993) notes, for example, that while Canadian society courses are common throughout Anglo-Canadian universities, Quebec's francophone universities focus on Quebec society courses, while a popular anglophone text (Fournier et al., 1997) also deals with Quebec society. Add to this the fact that the University of Calgary has for some years offered an Alberta society course and we may acquire some understanding of the frustration voiced by Denis (1993: 255):

Where does it stop? If "English Canada" and Quebec can both be distinct societies within Canada, which is itself a distinct society relative to (or within?) the U.S., does this also mean that American society is within ... etc.? In this sociogeographic chain, shouldn't a number of statements be mutually exclusive?

A fourth problem with the concept of society is its conflation with several other concepts, notably those of country, state, and nation (see Denis, 1993). Note above, for example, the inclusion in *Merriam-Webster's* of *nation* in its definition of society, and Kendall's equation of the concepts of country and society. How can we distinguish among concepts such as country, state, and nation? And how are they related to the concept of Canadian society?

COUNTRY, STATE, NATION

Turning once again to our *Merriam-Webster's* dictionary, one of its definitions of *country* is as follows: "a political state or nation or its territory" (Merriam-Webster, Incorporated, 2003: 266). In other words, country *equals* nation *equals* state. There are problems with this formulation, as we will see. For now, however, we will define a **country** as *a territorial area, politically recognized as a country both by people within the territory and by governments outside it, on the basis of historical, material, and geographical factors* (see Lane and Ersson, 1994; Deutsch, 1980).

In these terms, Canada is a country consisting of 10 provinces and three territories, spanning a total land area of 9 984 670 square kilometres (*Time*, 2009: 268). This makes Canada the second largest country in the world, next to Russia, which spans 17 075 400 square kilometres, and just ahead of the People's Republic of China (9 572 900 square kilometres). Compared with Russia and China, however, Canada is quite sparsely populated, with roughly 33 million people (see Table 1.1). By comparison, Russia's population is 141 million, while China's population is 1.3 billion (*Time*, 2009: 462 and 276).

Defining Canada, Russia, or China as countries is unproblematic because each has diplomatic recognition of its sovereignty from the rest of the world. Contrast this reality with that of the Kurdish people, whose would-be homeland is divided among the countries of Iran, Turkey, Syria, and Iraq, or,

A term frequently employed offhandedly as synonymous with *country* is that of *state*. However, *state* is also often used when referring to issues of governance and the use of political power. In the former sense, an individual might argue that Canada *is* a state. In the latter sense, however, the same individual might ask what kind of state Canada *has* and what its characteristics are.

Table 1.1
Canadian Population, by Province and Region, 1851–2007 (in thousands)

Year	CANADA	Nfld[1]	PEI	NS	NB	Que	Ont	Man[2]	Sask[3]	Alta[3]	BC	YT	NWT	Nun[4]
1851	2 436	n.a.	63	277	194	890	952	n.a.	n.a.	n.a.	55	n.a.	6	n.a.
1861	3 230	n.a.	81	331	252	1 112	1 396	n.a.	n.a.	n.a.	52	n.a.	7	n.a.
1871	3 689	n.a.	94	388	286	1 192	1 621	25	n.a.	n.a.	36	n.a.	48	n.a.
1881	4 325	n.a.	109	441	321	1 360	1 927	62	n.a.	n.a.	49	n.a.	56	n.a.
1891	4 833	n.a.	109	450	321	1 489	2 114	153	n.a.	n.a.	98	n.a.	99	n.a.
1901	5 371	n.a.	103	460	331	1 649	2 183	255	91	73	179	27	20	n.a.
1911	7 207	n.a.	94	492	352	2 006	2 527	461	492	374	393	9	7	n.a.
1921	8 788	n.a.	89	524	388	2 361	2 934	610	758	588	525	4	8	n.a.
1931	10 377	n.a.	88	513	408	2 875	3 432	700	922	732	694	4	9	n.a.
1941	11 507	n.a.	95	578	457	3 332	3 788	730	896	796	818	5	12	n.a.
1951	14 009	361	98	643	516	4 056	4 598	777	832	940	1 165	9	16	n.a.
1961	18 238	458	105	737	598	5 259	6 236	922	925	1 332	1 629	15	23	n.a.
1971	21 962	531	113	797	643	6 137	7 849	999	932	1 666	2 241	19	36	n.a.
1981	24 820	575	124	855	706	6 548	8 811	1 036	976	2 294	2 824	24	48	n.a.
1991	28 031	580	130	915	746	7 065	10 428	1 110	1 003	2 593	3 373	29	61	n.a.
1996	29 672	561	136	931	753	7 274	11 101	1 134	1 020	2 781	3 882	32	68	25
2001	31 021	522	137	932	750	7 397	11 898	1 151	1 000	3 057	4 078	30	41	28
2004	31 995	517	138	938	752	7 549	12 420	1 171	995	3 208	4 204	31	43	30
2005	32 312	514	138	936	751	7 598	12 565	1 174	990	3 281	4 260	31	43	30
2006	32 649	510	138	935	749	7 651	12 705	1 178	988	3 371	4 320	31	42	30
2007	32 976	506	139	934	750	7 701	12 804	1 187	997	3 474	4 380	31	43	31
% (2007)	100	1.5	0.4	2.8	2.3	23.4	38.8	3.6	3.0	10.5	13.3	0.1	0.1	0.1

Notes:
1. Newfoundland figures before Confederation in 1949 are not included.
2. Population figures for Manitoba before 1871 are included in those of the Northwest Territories.
3. Population figures for Saskatchewan and Alberta before 1901 are included in figures for the Northwest Territories.
4. Population figures for Nunavut before 1996 are included in figures for the Northwest Territories.

Sources: Adapted from Statistics Canada, *Historical Statistics of Canada*, Catalogue no. 11-516, Series A2-14 (Ottawa: Statistics Canada, 1983); Statistics Canada, *Canada Year Book*, Catalogue no. 11-402, 2001, Table 3.2 (Ottawa: Statistics Canada, 2001a) and Statistics Canada On-line, *Annual Demographic Estimates: Canada, Provinces, and Territories—2007, Revised*, Catalogue no. 91-215-X 1, "Table 1-1: Annual Population Estimates, July 1, National Perspective—Population," http://www.statcan.ca/english/freepub/91-215-XIE/2007000/tablesectionlist.htm

for that matter, the small but militant Aryan Nations movement in the northwest United States. While the former have established a quasi-state within northern Iraq, there is no likelihood of the latter gaining a similar homeland in the foreseeable future.

The latter meaning of *state* is rendered even more diverse in scholarly accounts. For example, pluralist theorists tend to ignore the state altogether, choosing instead to narrowly analyze the formal institutions of government (such as parties, legislatures, bureaucracies), which they view as open to the influence of competing political interests (see Orum and Dale, 2008: 169–170). By contrast, neo-Marxist scholars, such as Miliband (1969) and Poulantzas (1973), have tended to view the state more broadly, the former seeing the state as an instrument of capital accumulation, the latter as a relatively autonomous ensemble of social and political institutions. For others, like Skocpol (1979), the state is a wholly autonomous actor with its own powers, goals, and interests.

In each of these interpretations, the state is described more or less as a thing. Recent definitions of the state, however, have taken a more radical turn. Beginning with Abrams (1988), the state has increasingly been described as an abstract concept, the reification of which is a weapon for enacting, legitimating, and ultimately condoning "violence" (Sayer, 1987; Denis, 1989).

Despite important differences, the definitions reviewed here agree that the concept of state has something to do with the exercise of political power. In this text, therefore, a **state** is defined as *a set of institutions successfully claiming a monopoly over political rule-making and the legitimate use of violence and coercion within a given territory, i.e., a country* (see Weber, 1958: 78; Lane and Errson, 1994: 30). The important question of globalization's impact upon states is taken up below.

The third term requiring definition is *nation*. Note, at the onset, how the terms *nation* and *state* are often linked together, that is, as *nation-state*. (Note also how the *Merriam-Webster's* definition above equates the concepts of country and nation.) We have looked at the meanings of *country* and *state*. What exactly is a nation?

A **nation** is defined as *a mass of individuals who define themselves collectively as a people.* But on what bases might individuals define themselves as a nation?

Scholars differentiate between two types of nations: civic nations and ethnic nations (Webber, 1994). Civic nationalism is determined by citizenship. Membership in the civic nation, at least in theory, is open to anyone. By contrast, ethnic—sometimes also termed *tribal*—nations are based on supposedly fixed biological (e.g., racial) and cultural (e.g., linguistic or religious) markers. Note, however, how malleable even these markers are. Biological descriptors are particularly uncertain measures of difference, and people can readily acquire a new language, convert to a different religion, or adopt new cultural practices.

Both civic and ethnic nations are tied to a specific territorial homeland. In the case of civic nations, however, the territorial referent is quite concrete: no territory, no citizenship. By contrast, ethnic nations may continue to exist, even thrive, after the territorial homeland has disappeared from political maps. Both civic and ethnic nations, however, constitute what Anderson (1983) terms "imagined communities." A person can never know all the other members of his or her nation. Rather, the other members are idealized figments, our relationship with them the product of collective stories that we tell each other.

As stated above, the term *nation* is often conflated with *state* to produce *nation-state*. This conjoining of these terms is both unfortunate and imprecise. The term *nation-state* suggests that every nation must be a state, and that every state must consist of only one nation. The actions of the Nazi regime in Germany (1933–1945) and the Balkan and African wars of the 1990s suggest the dangerous consequences that may result from such a belief. Beyond these extremes, however, the term *nation-state* is simply misleading in describing reality. As Hobsbawm (1992: 186) notes, no more than a dozen of today's 180-plus nation-states house only a single ethnic or linguistic group. Indeed, van den Berghe

(1992) argues that only Japan, Swaziland, and Somalia are genuine nation-states—and even these are, today, finding their "purity" challenged.

As Laxer (2000: 56) points out, most countries are heterogeneous and "cannot, even mythically, pretend all citizens are kith and kin." A lot of countries, in fact, are "state-nations," that is, nations organized—indeed, "created"—under the guidance of the state, while other nations are "stateless." In short, the assumption that country *equals* state *equals* nation is historically, politically, and socially constructed. Determining the exact fit between these terms in any particular case is a matter of empirical reflection. This point brings us to Canada.

A central thesis of this text is that, while Canada is indisputably a country, it is one founded on not one but three historic nations—English, French, and Aboriginal—and consequently requires a complex federal state structure. Efforts to make Canada conform to the European model—for example, repeated attempts by the English majority to coerce and otherwise assimilate either the French or Aboriginal peoples—have usually foundered, threatening Canada's continuance. The text's second thesis, however, is that these internal differences over nation and state, combined with external threats of absorption by the United States, have rendered Canada unique among 21st-century countries. The result, in turn, is a country in which civil and state relations are also unique; in short, something that we may consider a society.

BACK TO SOCIETY

The concept of society emerged in the nineteenth century. **Sociology**, meaning *the study of society*, arose at the same time. For early sociologists, the concept of society was meant to locate the site of the many changes wrought, both directly and indirectly, by the Industrial Revolution and the rise of capitalism. For Karl Marx (1818–1883) feudal relationships, based on tradition and fealty, were being replaced by capitalist relationships, based on private property and the cash nexus (Marx, 1977a). For Ferdinand Tönnies (1855–1936), rural and small-town life was being replaced by urban life, and kinship and tradition were being replaced by anonymity and self-interest (Tönnies, 1957). For Emile Durkheim (1858–1917), the changes were marked by a transformation in the basis of social solidarity from similarity-in-kind ("mechanical solidarity") to differentiation and, hence, greater interdependence ("organic solidarity") (Durkheim, 1964). For Max Weber (1864–1920), traditional authority was giving way to legal-rational forms of authority, reaching its apex in bureaucratic institutions (Weber, 1958).

Early on, however, the concept of society also came to define "one half of an antithetic tandem in which the other is the state" (Wallerstein, 1997: 315). Wallerstein adds:

> In this formulation, the state could be observed and analysed directly. It operated through formal institutions by way of known (constitutional) rules. The "society" was taken to mean that tissue of manners and customs that held a group of people together without, despite or against formal rules. In some sense, "society" represented something more enduring and "deeper" than the state, less manipulable and certainly more elusive.

This perspective is very much alive today. Consider, for example, how often you have heard someone—perhaps on a radio talk show—denounce the state or the government for doing something at variance with the interests of society. For many people, including some academics, society is an abstract concept defined by its opposition to another abstract concept, the state.

It was not always the case, however, that society and state were viewed as separate (and perhaps opposed). Knuttila and Kubik (2000) suggest, for example, that both Auguste Comte (1798–1857), who first coined the term *sociology*, and Durkheim, who held the first chair in sociology, viewed the state as an integral part—*but only a part*—of a functional modern society. From this perspective, society and state are not merely "coterminous" (Giddens, 1984); they are indivisible.

Denis (1989) has argued forcefully for a restoration of the links between the two concepts. For him, "'states' are a historically specific type of society, whose institutions take the legal-constitutional discursive form which has enabled capitalism to rise—*a state is not in (or above) society, a state is a society*" (Denis, 1989: 347–348, italics added). Similarly, Teeple (2000: 15) argues that the form of state that has emerged since the Second World War in most Western countries, the welfare state, "can also be seen as a capitalist society ... " (italics in original).

This formulation may seem at first extreme, positing that the capitalist state is everything, and everything is the capitalist state. Yet it is hard to think of any activity today that is not codified, regulated, and occasionally prohibited in some way by the state, often for the purposes of enabling markets and ensuring profits. This is true whether speaking of a state-capitalist country such as the "communist" People's Republic of China, the social democratic country of Sweden, or the laissez-faire capitalist country of the United States.

It is also true of Canada. The creation of Canada—of Canadian *society*—cannot be understood separate from the role of the state. A prime example of this is the National Policy of 1878 (see Chapter 7), which dramatically altered Canadian economic development and immigration policy. The real challenge in conceptualizing state and society as one thing involves determining which social actors have gained either influence or outright control of the state's machinery at given times and what this has meant, in turn, for defining and shaping socio-cultural, economic, and political relations within Canada.

What, then, is society? A **society** is defined as *the product of relatively continuous and enduring interactions, within a political territory, between people more or less identifying themselves as members of the society, these interactions being maintained by an ensemble of political, economic, cultural, and other institutions, the sum of such interactions being in excess of interactions occurring with similarly defined societies external to the given territory.*

This definition raises several points requiring elaboration. First, note that societies, like states and nations, are processes, not things. Whether any of these labels has substantive meaning for a group of people is dependent upon the maintenance of "relatively continuous and enduring interactions." We may presume further that, on balance, positive interactions are more fruitful than negative interactions. Second, note also that individuals may have either greater or lesser attachment to a society, just as they may have greater or lesser attachment to other social groups (such as the family) or may have different reasons for feeling they are part of a group. Third, note the important role of various institutions in acting as intermediaries between individuals, small groups, and society as a whole. Fourth, note that no society today is hermetically sealed off from external influences. This last point is brought home by globalization.

GLOBALIZATION, THE STATE, AND SOCIETY

The term *globalization* became popular in the late part of the 20th century as a shorthand means of describing global integration. But what does globalization actually mean? In brief, **globalization** is defined as *a series of interrelated economic, political, and cultural changes, sometimes contradictory and even opposed, occurring throughout the world* (see Harrison, 1999). Economically, globalization involves a complex series of worldwide exchanges in labour, trade, technology, and capital (Stubbs and Underhill, 1994; Laxer, 1995) and the reorganization over space of production itself (Mittelman, 1996; Lairson and Skidmore, 1997). Politically, globalization similarly manifests itself in increased interconnectedness and interdependence among countries, though not necessarily unification (Boyer and Drache, 1996). Culturally, globalization involves the spread of primarily Western liberal practices and notions of individualism and civil and political rights, as well as consumerism (Mittelman, 1996; Boyer and Drache, 1996; Sklair, 2002; Robbins, 2008).

A central debate surrounding globalization has been its impact upon the state. One school of thought holds that globalization has severely curtailed the power and capacity of states, if not actually signalled their outright demise. Economic historian Eric Heilbroner (1992: 60), for example, exclaims:

> The global market system stretches beyond the political authority of any single government. Faced with a network of connections that escape their powers of surveillance and regulation, national governments become increasingly unable to cope with the problems that arise from the intrusion of the global economy into their territories....

Or, in Daniel Bell's words, "the national state has become too small for the big problems of life, and too big for the small problems" (Bell, 1993: 362). In partial consequence, the state is being "decomposed" by globalization from above (by

transnationals, the World Bank, the International Monetary Fund, and so on) and the re-emergence of smaller communities from below (McDonald, 1994: 241). In effect, nation and state are viewed as decoupling (Paquet, 1997: 36), perhaps devolving into smaller, regional states (Ohmae, 1995). While hardly a case of peaceful devolution, the breakup of the former Yugoslavia in the 1990s may provide an example.

Note that not everyone views the state's supposed decline equally. Some applaud the decomposition of the state as allowing for greater economic efficiency and consumer choice (Ohmae, 1995) and the end of state-orchestrated violence (Rummel, 1994; van den Berghe, 1992). Others, however, fear that the state's eclipse will result in the sweeping away of 200 years of hard-won civil, political, and social rights (Teeple, 2000). Likewise, some believe that the fragmentation of states signals the decline of civic nationalism and its replacement by renewed forms of tribalism (Barber, 1996), perhaps even anarchism and terrorism as witnessed in the attacks on New York and Washington in September 2001. A few years earlier, the late Arthur Schlesinger, Jr. (1997: 10), historian and former special assistant to U.S. President Kennedy, remarked:

> The world today is torn in opposite directions. Globalization is in the saddle and rides mankind [*sic*], but at the same time drives people to seek refuge from its powerful forces beyond their comprehension.... The faster the world integrates, the more people will huddle in their religious or ethnic or tribal enclaves.

If traditional states are in decline, does this mean their powers of regulation and coercion have been dispersed? A second school of thought disputes this, arguing instead that the powers previously held by territorial states remains concentrated but has been transferred to undemocratic quasi-states—transnational corporations—and other unaccountable international organizations (see Robbins, 2008; Strange, 1996; Korten, 1995). From this perspective, the state itself is being globalized (Albrow, 1997: 172). In the words of David Korten (1995: 54), "Corporations have emerged as the dominant governance institutions on the planet...."

Clearly, either the outright demise of the state or its resurrection at the global level would have important implications for societies such as Canada's. What might be the fate of Canadian society in such a world? Malcolm Waters (1994: 233) provides a succinct answer: "If the nation-state is dissolving, or at least attenuating, then so too must national societies...." One logical extension of this dissolution is that national societies will be replaced by a global society, also known as "the global village." Is such a thing possible, or is this merely Utopian theorizing?

A third school of thought argues that the death of the state has been greatly exaggerated (Laxer, 1995). From this perspective, the world economy has not been globalized but rather "internationalized," with states themselves the architects reorganizing capitalist production. While many of the world's largest economies are not countries but corporations (Robbins, 2008: 134), the latter are not stateless, let alone "virtual." Most multinationals retain headquarters in the economically dominant states, especially the United States. Put another way, states peripheral to the world capitalist economy were weak before globalization and remain so now, while states that were central to that economy remain powerful actors, not merely despite, but as a *consequence of* globalization (Burbach et al., 1997: 19).

Finally, from an historical perspective, it should be noted that globalization is not a new phenomenon (Laxer, 1995). Of an earlier episode of capitalist globalization in the mid-19th century, Marx (1977a: 224) wrote: "The need of a constantly expanding market for its products chases the bourgeoisie over the whole surface of the globe. It must nestle everywhere, settle everywhere, establish connections everywhere." At the same time, however, capitalist expansion has not always proceeded in a straightforward manner; there have been periods of contraction, such as during the Depression of the 1930s. Faced with increasing challenges brought about by war, resource scarcity, and climate change, some argue the world may experience de-globalization and a return to localism (Bello, 2002). The credit crisis that spread like a virus through the world economy in the fall of 2008, leading to the widespread nationalization of banks and the overnight depreciation of stock values, bears witness to the negative side of global interrelatedness and dependency.

Whatever its final disposition, the recent period of globalization has not left states unscathed. Technological and organizational changes and the freer flow of capital associated with the growth of multinationals have had an impact on state roles, functions, and policies (see Jessop, 1993; Teeple, 2000). At the same time, states remain central actors, organizing economic life, providing political legitimacy, employing means of coercion, and generally exercising control over their populations (Boyer and Drache, 1996).

This fact remains true for Canada. Globalization has not left Canada and Canadian society untouched. As a wealthy but semi-peripheral country, Canada faces the additional challenge of residing next to the United States, the chief engine of recent globalization. Yet Canada also remains a sovereign country, its cultural symbols and political state intact. And within these geographic and political boundaries, Canadian society also continues to exist as an object worthy of study. Sociology is particularly suited for the task of carrying out this examination.

THEORIZING SOCIAL RELATIONSHIPS

Students approaching sociology for the first time are frequently confounded by an array of theories. This reaction is both unfortunate and unnecessary. Theories are like tools. A wrench is a poor instrument for hammering nails. Likewise, a hammer is useless for sawing wood. But, used properly, a wrench or a hammer can be very helpful.

The same goes for theories. Theories are neither good nor bad. They are either useful or not in assisting us to sort out and understand particular phenomena.

The sociological "tool box" contains several theories for understanding how individuals and groups (large and small) interact. For students at a beginning level of instruction, four theories, with their own perspective on human behaviour, are particularly useful: structural-functional, conflict, symbolic interaction, and post-structural theories.

Structural-functional theory has roots in the work of early anthropologists, including Herbert Spencer (1820–1895), an English sociologist, who adopted evolutionary theory for the study of human societies (the idea of Social Darwinism, e.g., the "survival of the fittest"). It was the American sociologist Talcott Parsons (1902–1979) who primarily codified the theory's tenets, however. Drawing upon earlier work by Weber and Durkheim (among others) and emerging ideas of systems theory and cybernetics, Parsons arrived at a grand theory of social action that emphasized the relationships among various institutions—the Church, family, schools, the state—each of which, he argued, fulfill specific functions necessary for the continuation and survival of a given society (Parsons, 1951). An institution's function may be *manifest* or *latent* (Merton, 1968). For example, schools are manifestly intended to educate students, but they also control young people and socialize them for later participation in the labour market.

Structural-functionalism draws our attention to how various social elements are interconnected. A change in one part of society—for instance, a downturn in the economy—may thus have unforeseen consequences for other parts (Merton, 1968), such as family structure. Where change in one sphere occurs, and other spheres are not able to adapt, or do so slowly, disequilibrium or *dysfunctions* may occur. In general, however, the theory suggests that the interconnectedness of functions slows the rate of social change.

The second perspective, **conflict theory**, has its roots in the work of Karl Marx and Max Weber. Marx, whose writings champion social revolution, argued that world history was the result of class struggle and, more widely, of structural contradictions. Weber's contribution to conflict theory was to suggest that conflict is not necessarily based on class alone, but also upon differences in status and power. Conflict theorists today recognize the many non-class bases of inequality and conflict, such as ethnicity, language, region, age, and gender, and that conflict frequently cuts across several lines (Curtis et al., 1999). For example, labour conflict at a bank may involve workers and owners/shareholders (class conflict). At the same time, it is likely that the majority of low-level employees are female while upper-level managers are male (gender conflict).

Within the Marxist stream of conflict theory, particular emphasis is given to the notion of **praxis**, defined as *purposeful action in contrast to abstract theorizing*. As Marx (1977b: 158) himself said, "The philosophers have only interpreted the world, in various ways; the point is to change it." This tradition of activism continues today in feminist and anti-oppressive approaches to research (see Box 1.1).

both conflict and structural-functional theories emphasize the structures within which action occurs or is constrained, symbolic interaction theory emphasizes that all human behaviour is meaningful, but that these meanings are collectively constructed and defined in the course of interaction. To give an example drawn from Durkheim (1978: 228), the flag for which a soldier dies represents symbolically more than a piece of cloth. In this sense, the methodological approach of Weber (1958), known as *verstehen*—that is, *an understanding of the meaning that others attach to events, symbols, and experiences*—is entirely congruent with this theory.

Structural-functionalism and conflict theory are generally viewed as the yin and yang of sociological perspectives (see Box 1.2). Nonetheless, both theories also share similarities. Both are macro theories, examining society as a whole using broad social categories, such as class, occupation, or gender. Both emphasize the interrelatedness of society's parts. Both also emphasize the social reality of the objects of study (e.g., class, family, etc.). By contrast, the other two theories examined here—symbolic interaction theory and post-structuralism—argue that social reality is largely constructed.

Symbolic interaction theory generally deals with interactions within small groups or organizations. Symbolic interaction is a sociological offshoot of social psychology. While social psychological concepts are embedded in the work of Marx, Weber, and Durkheim, symbolic interaction theory is chiefly a product of American pragmatism, particularly the work of George Herbert Mead (1863–1931) (see Morrow, 1994: 13; also Collins, 1982). Whereas

Box 1.2
The Essential Elements of Structural-Functional and Conflict Models

The Structural-Functional Model:

- Every society is a relatively persisting configuration of elements.

- Every society is a well-integrated configuration of elements.

- Every element in a society contributes to its functioning.

- Every society rests on the consensus of its members.

The Conflict Model:

- Every society is subjected at every moment to changes; social change is ubiquitous.

- Every society experiences at every moment social conflicts; social conflict is ubiquitous.

- Every element in a society contributes to its change.

- Every society rests on constraints of some of its members by others.

Source: R. Dahrendorf, "Toward a theory of social conflict," *Journal of Conflict Resolution* 2 (1958): 174.

Like symbolic interaction theory, **post-structural theory** deals with the social construction of meanings. Unlike the former, however, its origins lie in the structural linguistics of Ferdinand de Saussure (1857–1913), hence the theory's primacy of language as the medium by which reality is understood. Specifically, post-structural theorists argue that language operates through a system of signs that point not to a definite referent but gain their meaning through difference with other signs. In turn, any text (written or spoken) involves a combination, or string, of signs, each pointing to another sign, such that any "meaning" is both arbitrary and unstable. Put another way, there is an endless slippage between the words we use and the meanings (we think) we are conveying and the meanings that others derive. From a post-structural perspective, humans may engage in meaningful behaviour, but such meanings are not precisely decipherable.

At the extreme, post-structuralism would suggest "the impossibility of sociology" (Scott and Marshall, 2005: 512; see also Giddens, 1987). Especially as practised by theorists such as Jacques Derrida (1930–2004), post-structuralism questions the possibility of establishing taken-for-granted meanings (as suggested by symbolic interaction theory) or apprehending objective reality (as sought by structural functionalists and conflict theorists).

The work of theorists such as Michel Foucault (1926–1984) restores post-structuralism's radical potential, however. In a series of books, Foucault (1973, 1977, 1980) examined the discursive practices that define and categorize individual behaviour. Take criminal behaviour, for example. Rather than existing per se, Foucault argues it is a category produced by a social discourse produced within a set of social institutions (prisons, the criminal justice system) using a set of historical statements (theories, statistics, etc.). More important, however, post-structural theorists such as Foucault connect language with a rethinking of ideology and power (Fairclough, 1989: 15). Post-structuralism thus provides a link to structural-functionalism and conflict theory and to the work of theorists such as Antonio Gramsci and Noam Chomsky. To give an example, a post-structural analysis might question the role of data gathered by Statistics Canada (a source we will use throughout this text) in formulating our notion of Canadian society. Who decides what data will be gathered, how it will be analyzed, and finally distributed? Alternatively, what kinds of data are not gathered?

How might a sociologist use structural-functional, conflict, symbolic interaction, and post-structural theories? A typically Canadian example makes the case.

Box 1.3
The Essential Elements of Symbolic Interaction and Post-Structural Theories

The Symbolic Interaction Model:

- Human beings act toward things on the basis of meanings that things have for them.

- The meaning of such things is derived from, or arises out of, the social interaction that one has with one's fellows.

- These meanings are handled in, and modified through, an interpretive process used by the person in dealing with the things he or she encounters.

The Post-Structural Model:

- Social institutions are the product of discursive practices that manufacture knowledge.

- Knowledge is a means to ideological power.

- Ideological, social, and political power are mutually reinforcing.

THINKING THEORETICALLY: CANADA'S GAME

The theory you choose as your lens for examining a topic will provide you with particular questions and insights. Let's take hockey as an example. From a structural-functional point of view, a sociologist might examine the functions that hockey plays in our society. She or he might emphasize that hockey provides a source of national pride and cohesion, such as occurred in 1972 when Paul Henderson scored the goal that clinched Canada's defeat of the Soviet Union. Our sociologist might also remark on the role of hockey (and sports in general) in providing a safe outlet for male aggression, both at the interpersonal level and as a substitute for war between countries. (The 1972 series was widely viewed in the context of the Cold War as pitting the respective communist and capitalist systems against one another.) She or he might finally note that hockey has traditionally provided a means of social mobility for working-class youth.

A conflict perspective forces us to examine professional hockey quite differently. The National Hockey League (NHL) player lockout in 2004 highlighted a conflict between capitalist owners and workers (albeit very well-paid ones). Analyzing the events that led the Winnipeg Jets to move to Arizona in 1996 (see Silver, 1996) provides a similarly provocative view of corporate capitalism in an age of globalization. Alternatively, a conflict theorist might note that professional hockey seems stratified along ethnic lines. For example, most players in the NHL are White, whether Canadian, American, or European. The first Black player in the National Hockey League was Willie O'Ree with Boston in 1958. Since then, other Black players (such as Anson Carter and George Laraque), as well as some Aboriginal players (such as Jordan Tootoo), have entered the league, but ethnic minorities remain few and,

as in other arenas beyond sports, have often faced racist taunts from other players and fans.

Likewise, a conflict theorist employing a feminist critique might note how women's hockey remains marginalized (despite the Canadian women's team's gold-winning victories at both the 2002 and 2006 Winter Olympics) and how female players appear to receive publicity only when they are sexually attractive. The feminist approach might also draw our attention to how hockey, and sports in general, often enforce and reward a kind of male machismo whose aggressiveness is sometimes carried into the personal lives of players, with dire consequences for girlfriends, spouses, and children.

A symbolic interaction theorist might concentrate on the meanings that fans bring to hockey. What, for example, is the process by which an individual becomes a fan? How is it that people come to see their own success as reflected in a team? How do people at a hockey game learn to act like fans (and not like uninformed wannabes)? From the players' point of view, what is the process by which one becomes accepted as a team member? What is team bonding, and how is it achieved?

Finally, a post-structural theorist might begin by examining a set of binary elements surrounding hockey's place in fans' psyche (the individual vs. the team; play for fun vs. play for money; gentlemanly play—for which the NHL awards the Lady Byng Trophy—vs. often violent aggression) and how these are connected to other shifting signs. A post-structural theorist might also note the role played by sportswriters, cultural institutions (e.g., the Hockey Hall of Fame), and record keepers in lodging hockey within a series of classical tropes dealing with athletics, sport, and society.

Note that none of these theories is exclusive. For example, a sociologist might argue that fan disenchantment during the 2004 NHL lockout resulted from a specific set of cultural meanings (a symbolic interaction perspective) manufactured through a set of discursive statements within the institution of professional sports (a post-structural argument) that were upset by the increased corporatization of professional hockey (a conflict argument) and the subsequent breaking of the irrational—but very real—emotional bonds of solidarity (a structural-functionalist's concern) that male fans in particular (a feminist insight) have traditionally felt for their teams.

METHODOLOGY: SOCIOLOGY AND WHY HISTORY MATTERS

The methodological approach used in this text is termed **historical sociology**. Historical sociology combines historical detail with sociological generalization. Harrison (1995: 261) notes the following specific characteristics of the method:

- deliberate use of time as a variable

- the explicit use of narrative structure

- the tendency to deal simultaneously with events and processes at different levels

- the use of comparisons of distinct cases or between elements of a single case

Many students are familiar with sociology as the study of society, but often this understanding is focused upon society as it exists *at the moment*. This focus is comparable to that of a digital camera taking a single shot. By contrast, the focus of historical sociology is comparable to that of a video camera. An underlying assumption of historical sociology is that *our material institutions, actions, and beliefs are shaped, though not determined, by past events and our understanding (or misunderstanding) of those events.* As

shown in Box 1.4, the potential sources of historical material are nearly as vast as the researcher's imagination.

Box 1.4
Some Research Sources of Historical Sociologists

- official government and organizational records, including statistics

- newspapers and magazines

- public speeches and sermons

- private letters and diaries

- photographs, drawings, and audio recordings

- cemetery tombstones

- interviews with participants

For a time, the study of history fell out of fashion. At the end of the Cold War, the title of a bestselling book proclaimed "the end of history" (Fukuyama, 1992), meaning that the victory of capitalism over communism had resolved the major questions of how to organize society. About the same time, a line from a popular song spoke of "watching the world wake up from history." Some people appeared to view history as a kind of personal affront to their claims of individualism and self-achievement. Many agreed with Henry Ford, Sr. that "History is more or less bunk." Others, reflecting the legitimate concerns of post-structural theorists, questioned the "taken-for-granted" categories—men/women, black/white—that historians have traditionally employed in constructing their accounts (Mills, 2005).

History has made a recent comeback, however. The eminent historian, Margaret MacMillan (2008: 3) notes that history is "widely popular these days, even in North America where we have tended to look toward the future rather than the past."

To understand the value of historical sociology as a methodological approach, think for a moment about the role of history—and memory—in your own life.

Consider your own personal relations with others. Do you begin each meeting with your friends anew? Of course not. Your friendship is based on experiences, ideas, and feelings you have shared. In short, you have a history together. If you were to suddenly lose that history—if you contracted total amnesia, for example, like the protagonist in the film *Memento*—the friendship would also be lost.

Looking around us, we can see where history continues to play a role in shaping current events: long-simmering disputes in Ireland, the Middle East, and Kashmir provide ample evidence. Likewise, the echoes of history can be heard in the breakup of Yugoslavia in the 1990s. Not even the United States—surely the world's most proudly modern country—can escape history, as witness the plethora of Hollywood movies that continue efforts at coming to terms with *the* meaning of the Vietnam War, while several more recent movies about the Iraq War similarly appear designed to provide meaning, as history unfolds, to a catastrophe that most Americans and others find incomprehensible.

But what of Canada? In an oft-quoted remark, Prime Minister William Lyon Mackenzie King once stated regarding Canada: "If some countries have too much history, we have too much geography." As John Gray (1994: 124) notes, such arguments really mean that Canada "lacks *European* history," conveniently ignoring 50,000 years of Aboriginal existence in North America. But even by Eurocentric standards, the argument is false, as one glance at Quebec's licence plates will attest: "Je me souviens" (I remember). Remember what? History—though which particular historical events and how they are remembered often differs between groups of people.

We need not refer, however, merely to centuries-old history. Ask Aboriginal Canadians about the continuing impact of residential schools, some of which remained open until the early 1980s. Or ask Albertans about the National Energy Program of 1980–1986 and how it still colours a widespread understanding of political relations between that province and Ottawa (or at least the federal Liberal Party).

Note, however, that the facts of history often vary with people's understanding, valuation, and interpretation of history. People may agree on the former, but not on the latter. Alternatively, they may disagree about *both* the facts *and* the meaning of events.

The late Palestinian scholar, Edward Said (1993: xiii), remarked that "nations are narrations." But the history that makes up our narratives is often contested terrain (Francis, 1997: 12). History, in this sense, is not "dead" but, rather, a source of constant rediscovery, recreation, reinterpretation, and *power*. As George Orwell (2008: 37) wrote in his novel *1984*, "Who controls the past controls the future: who controls the present controls the past."

Every society possesses a dominant narrative. Always, however, there are also counter-narratives seeking expression. Among the questions an historical sociologist asks are the following: Who determines the "official" historical narrative? How does this narrative square with the facts? Are unofficial, alternative, and even multiple histories heard and respected within the society? What are the lessons—myths, really—that a people construct around their collective histories? In what forms (institutions, laws) is history enunciated in the present?

Of course, our historical narratives can sometimes trap us. It *is* possible for some countries to have "too much history," to be (as it were) stuck in the past, but not remembering—living in a state of amnesia—is also a trap.

History *determines* nothing (Carr, 1990). But our understanding—our *imagination*—of it locates us, both individually and collectively, in time in the same way that geography locates us in space. Put another way, our understanding of history organizes material in a manner that helps us interpret current events. Meaning and meaningful action are impossible without a temporal context (see Rickman, 1961; Dilthey, 1961).

Moreover, the consequences of historical events (as set down in institutions, treaties, laws, etc.), as well as our understanding and interpretation of these events, often set off chains of meaning and action long after the specific events themselves have ceased. Thus, in Canada, two lines can be drawn—one leading directly, the other indirectly—from the Royal Proclamation of 1763. The first of these lines leads to the Oka Crisis of 1990 and the passing of the Nisga'a treaty in British Columbia (Chapter 13). The second of these lines leads to the Meech Lake Accord and the Quebec referendum of 1995 (chapters 4 and 5).

One way to comprehend the role of history in shaping Canadian society is to employ a methodological technique termed **counterfactual history**, defined as *a simulation based on calculations about the relative probability of plausible outcomes* (Ferguson, 2003: 85).

What is counterfactual history? While often condemned as a parlour game, counterfactual history properly employed is not just history "made up." Rather, it is based on factual information and interpretive and extrapolative logic, held together by an historical sociologist's imagination.

The use of counterfactual history is not new (Honan, 1998). Recalling, for example, the events that led to the dissolution of the Austro-Hungarian Empire in 1918, Oscar Jaszi (1961: 380) wrote:

> Opposed to the materialistic point of view, I accept the ... reversibility of the historical process, and regard the chief utility of all historical and sociological investigations to be to admonish us of the alternative possibilities of history.

Counterfactual history provides a means of separating what is important in history from that which is merely incidental. It alerts us to the importance of history by asking the question: What if people involved in an event had made different decisions, or events had otherwise transpired in different ways? The reader is invited throughout this text to ask similar questions about Canada. What if New France had not been surrendered to the British in 1763 (Chapter 2)? What if the Meech Lake Accord had been passed in 1990 (Chapter 4)? What if the Liberals had won the 1988 election and not signed the Free Trade Agreement (Chapter 8)? What if Canada had entered the Iraq War in 2003?

Finally, counterfactual history also alerts us to the fact that individuals and the decisions they make matter; again, that history does not determine the present. For Canadians, repeatedly advised that globalization is inevitable and that the invisible hand of the marketplace cannot be resisted, reminders of personal efficacy are to be valued.

OUTLINE OF THE TEXT

The book is divided into three sections. These sections deal with what Canadian philosopher John Ralston Saul (1997: 81) argues are Canada's "three deeply rooted pillars, three experiences—the aboriginal, francophone, and anglophone." Each of these pillars is a kind of "master narrative" that is used to structure the overall text while, at the same time, dealing with other important relationships, based (for example) on differences of gender, ethnicity, race, and class.

Part 1 (chapters 2–5) examines francophone Quebec's relationship with the rest of Canada, while Part 2 (chapters 6–9) examines English Canada's relationship with the United States. In a manner calculated to disrupt the usual historicized narrative of Europeans' arrival and Aboriginal peoples' gradual disappearance from the scene, the

Aboriginal–non-Aboriginal relationship is dealt with in Part 3 (chapters 10–13). A final chapter situates Canada among the nations of the world and briefly summarizes some of the challenges it faces in the future.

CONCLUSION

Sociology is the study of society. But what is society? This chapter has established a framework and a set of theoretical and methodological tools for answering this question. The remainder of this text applies these tools to the study of a specific phenomenon—Canadian society.

In keeping with the narrative structure employed by historical sociologists, the story of Canadian society that follows enlists all the usual literary devices: myths (the Conquest); metaphors (are Quebec and Canada "two solitudes," in the phrase made famous by the novelist Hugh MacLennan [1998], or "Siamese twins," as described by Saul [1997]); symbols (Canadian hockey, the maple leaf, the fleur-de-lis); heroes, villains, and tragic figures (Louis Riel is all three, depending upon whom you ask); and recurrent subtexts (regional alienation, Americanization, ethnic divisions).

For hundreds of years—longer in the case of Aboriginal peoples—people in this part of North America have been creating, together and alone, a story as broad as the prairie landscape, as deep as the Hudson Bay basin, and as rich as ore from the Canadian Shield. It is a story worthy of many books. This is one of them.

KEY TERMS

conflict theory
counterfactual history
country
globalization
historical sociology
nation
patriarchy
post-structural theory
praxis
reification
sexism
society
sociology
state
structural-functional theory
symbolic interaction theory
verstehen

CRITICAL THINKING QUESTIONS

1. Is higher level thinking possible without employing abstractions?

2. In what concrete ways is the world both globalizing and becoming more localized?

3. Should sociologists strive to change the world?

4. How might you apply the four main theoretical perspectives discussed in this chapter to current issues in your community?

5. How does an historical sociological methodology help in studying a society such as Canada's?

RECOMMENDED READINGS

Anderson, Benedict. 1983. *Imagined Communities*. London: Verso.
   Imagined Communities remains a central book in nation studies, its title capturing a central idea of nationhood as less material than social-psychological.

Ferguson, Niall. 2003. *Virtual History: Alternatives and Counterfactuals*. London: Pan Books.
   This book provides a fun and interesting introduction to the idea of counterfactual history.

Knuttila, Murray, and Wendee Kubik. 2000. *State Theories: Classical, Global, and Feminist Perspectives*. Halifax: Fernwood.
   This book is an excellent review of theoretical perspectives on the state.

MacMillan, Margaret. 2008. *The Uses and Abuses of History*. Toronto: Viking.

MacMillan's short and very readable book is an excellent introduction to the importance of the historical perspective in social research and a warning regarding the improper uses of history.

Robbins, Richard H. 2008. *Global Problems and the Culture of Capitalism*, 4th ed. Toronto: Pearson.

Robbin's text provides a comprehensive sociological examination of globalization, including numerous case studies.

RELATED WEBSITES

Canadian Historical Association

www.cha-shc.ca

Founded in 1922, it is Canada's leading bilingual organization for the scholarly study of history.

Canadian Sociology and Anthropology Association

www.csaa.ca

Founded in 1965, it was renamed the Canadian Sociological Association in 2007.

Statistics Canada

www.statcan.gc.ca

Though census gathering in Canada dates back to New France, the first Dominion census was in 1871. In 1918, the Dominion Bureau of Statistics was created and, in 1971, renamed Statistics Canada. It is the Canadian government's central source of statistical data.

CANADIAN SOCIETY ON VIDEO

Postcards from Canada. 2001. National Film Board of Canada, 41 minutes, 20 seconds. A breathtaking photographic sweep of Canada, narrated by Peter Gzowski, from the frozen vistas of the Arctic to the frenzy of rush-hour traffic, from deep within the Canadian Shield to the orbiting Radarsat satellite.

PART ONE
CANADA AND QUEBEC

To many today, the threat of Quebec separating from Canada seems remote. This was not the case only a few years ago, however. For a brief moment, on the evening of October 30, 1995, it seemed the endless debates between English- and French-speaking Canada had reached a climax. Like deer caught in winter headlights, stunned Canadians watched the results of Quebec's referendum on sovereignty unfolding on their television screens.

In the end, the *No* side narrowly defeated the *Yes* side by less than a percentage point (50.6 percent to 49.4 percent), a mere few thousand votes. For supporters of sovereignty, the sadness of defeat was lessened by the true believers' faith that next time their side would win. For federalists, nervous relief dampened the ecstasy one would expect of victory. By the skin of its teeth, Canada had narrowly escaped a venture into unknown, uncertain, and, some argued, dangerous territory.

The time since the 1995 referendum has seen a different Quebec and a different Canada emerge. Much of what French-speaking Quebecers had demanded for decades has come to pass, including the Canadian House of Commons' recognition of the province in the fall of 2006 as a "nation." It would seem the issues that have historically aroused the separatist spirits have been rendered dormant. Nonetheless, many Canadians inside and outside Quebec believe separatism will re-emerge one day as an issue.

Part One examines the history of English-French relations in Canada, how those relations have structured both Quebec and Canadian society as a whole, and why a country reputed by many outsiders to be "the best in the world" has so often teetered perilously close to dissolving over the years.

CHAPTER 2

LIVING WITH THE CONSEQUENCES OF 1760

Valour gave them a common death / history a common fame / posterity a common monument.

> —words engraved on the Wolfe and Montcalm Monument, Quebec City

I expected to find a contest between a government and a people: I found two nations warring in the bosom of a single state.

> —Lord Durham's *Report*, 1839

[T]he human tragedy, or the human irony, consists in the necessity of living with the consequences of actions performed under the pressure of compulsions so obscure we do not and cannot understand them.

> —Hugh MacLennan, 1957; words later recorded by The Tragically Hip in their 1992 song "Courage"

INTRODUCTION

The Meech Lake Accord's failure in 1990 and the subsequent Quebec referendum on sovereignty in 1995 brought into sharp relief two very different views of Canada. Is Canada a partnership of two founding peoples, the French and English, or even a third, the First Nations peoples, as discussed in Part 3 of this text? Or is Canada a federation of 10 equal provinces, Quebec, and what has been termed "the rest of Canada" or ROC? Most francophone Quebecers believe the former, sometimes referred to as the "two nations theory." They further believe that as a minority nation within Canada, they have a historically distinctive patrimony that must be protected; that they constitute a "distinct society" within Canada.

Thanks to decades of political wrangling, many people in English-speaking Canada know something of the history of Quebec-Canada and French-English relations. But this knowledge is often partial or inexact. In any case, facts do not automatically produce meaning; even less do they constitute truths.

This chapter goes beyond the historic facts to explore the emotional and symbolic meaning of English and French relationships in Canada, and the early evolution of this unique relationship. Embedded in the discussion are important sociological questions regarding dominant-subordinate relationships and the responsibilities and consequences imposed upon conquerors and conquered alike by history.

THE AGE OF MERCANTILISM

Between 1689 and 1763, the French and the English fought a series of wars. The last of these wars (1756–1763) was known in Europe as the Seven Years War, but in British North America as the French and Indian War (Hofstadter et al., 1957: 64). North America was merely one outpost, albeit an important one, in these wars. To understand these wars, it is necessary to reflect briefly on the political economy of European expansion beginning in the 15th century.

Before that time, the basic structures of European society had remained fundamentally unchanged since (roughly) the collapse of the Roman Empire (see Manchester, 1992). In Thomas Hobbes's memorable phrase, life was "poor, nasty, brutish, and short." People lived predictable lives in small rural communities. Families were large, class structures and age and gender roles were fixed, trade was local, and barter was the chief means of exchange.

Slowly, however, European feudal society began to change. Central to the changes were the growth of states in which power was centralized and monarchs became all-powerful, a corresponding decline in the temporal power of churches (though religion itself remained important), and the emergence of a new merchant class. In earlier times, churches had frowned upon trade, especially such practices as the granting of monopolies, usury, and profiteering (Hofstadter et al.,

1957: 4). Between the 16th and 18th centuries, however, there arose a new economic arrangement. Now the new merchant class and the state encouraged commercial trade. Merchants paid the state levies and taxes, and even lent money at favourable rates to support the state's armies. In return, merchants induced states to enact policies, including war, designed to protect their business interests (La Haye, 1993: 534).

The new economic arrangement was called **mercantilism** (Hofstadter et al., 1957; La Haye, 1993; Norrie and Owram, 1996: 17–18). The chief aim of mercantilist policies was to preserve the mother country's supply of precious metals and to make it less vulnerable during times of war. Colonies were fundamental to mercantilist policy. In practice, because mercantilism and colonialism also meant the enrichment of one state and its merchant allies at the expense of other states and their business friends, conflict was a frequent result. In North America, the conflict primarily involved the English on the eastern seaboard and around Hudson Bay and the French in Nova Scotia and along the St. Lawrence, the colony of New France. The Aboriginal peoples of the region soon found themselves caught up in the conflict.

THE RISE AND FALL OF NEW FRANCE

The history of New France begins in 1534. That year, the French explorer Jacques Cartier (1491–1557) first made landfall on the shores of the Gaspé Peninsula (see Miller, 2000). Like the Spanish far to the south, Cartier came in search of gold. He was discredited, however, when the "gold" he brought back from his third voyage in 1541–1542 turned out to be iron pyrite. Diverted by a series of European conflicts, France temporarily forgot about North America (Morton, 1997: 24).

Early in the next century, however, France returned in the person of Samuel de Champlain (1570–1635). A "navigator, soldier, visionary," "a Protestant turned Catholic by conviction," and "a man of Renaissance curiosity and eternal fortitude" (Morton, 1997: 25), Champlain in 1608 founded a trading post at what is now Quebec City. Thus New France began.

From the beginning, the post's survival was perilous. Life was harsh. Champlain's efforts to forge alliances with the Huron Confederacy brought the colonists into conflict with the Huron's chief enemies, the tribes of the Iroquois Confederacy. Despite Champlain's efforts to build a colony, Quebec City in 1627 still had fewer than 100 people. In that year, France's chief minister, Cardinal Richelieu, formed a private company made up of 100 merchants and aristocrats. The *Compagnie des Cent-Associés* was given a monopoly over the fur trade in exchange for promises to colonize the territory (Moore, 2000).

Still the settlement did not thrive. Military threats continued. In 1629, an English trading company seized Quebec City; it was returned to France in 1632 only after diplomatic negotiations (Moore, 2000). The fact is, Quebec City and the surrounding area were far less politically and economically valuable to France than its posts in Cape Breton, Nova Scotia, and Newfoundland, which protected the valuable cod fishery. Dickinson and Young (2003: 16) note that, until 1760, "France imported far more cod than fur and the fishery employed many more seamen and ships than all other French colonial trade combined" (see also Eccles, 1993a: 163). By contrast, New France's fur trade economy was unstable. European demand fluctuated according to fashion. Supply was equally unpredictable. Weather conditions, the needs and good fortune of Aboriginal suppliers, the actions of middlemen (Norrie and Owram, 1996: 43), conflict between Aboriginal tribes, exacerbated by competition between the French and Dutch trading companies in Port Albany all affected supply. In

Box 2.1
State Terrorism, 1759

Terrorism is *the deliberate use of acts of violence or the threat of violence by individuals, groups, or the state for the purpose of furthering political ends.* We tend to think of terrorism as a recent phenomenon. In fact, terrorism—especially state terrorism—is quite old, as shown in the following excerpt from the written account of the Sergeant Major of the 40th Regiment's Grenadiers (part of the Louisbourg Grenadiers). The passage deals with Wolfe's campaign against New France in the summer of 1759, leading up to the Battle of the Plains of Abraham in September of that year.

The 15th of Aug. Captain Gorham returned from an Incursion, in which Service were employ'd, under his Command, 150 Rangers, a Detachment from the different Regiments, Highlanders, Marines, &c. amounting in the whole to about 300, an arm'd Vessel, three Transports, with a Lieutenant and Seamen of the Navy to attend him, of which Expedition they gave the following Account:

"That on the 4th of August they proceeded down to St. Paul's Bay, (which is opposite to the North Side of this Island) where was a Parish containing about 200 men, who had been very active in distressing our Boats and Shipping—At 3 o 'Clock in the Morning Capt. Gorham landed and forced two of their Guards; of 20 Men each, who fired smartly for Some Time; but that in two Hours they drove them all from their Covering in the Wood, and clear'd the Village which they burnt, consisting of about 50 fine Houses and Barns; destroy'd most of their Cattle, &c. That in this one Man was kill'd and 6 wounded; but that the Enemy had two kill'd, and several wounded, who were carried off.—That from thence they proceeded to Mal Bay, 10 Leagues to the Eastward on the same Side, where they destroyed a very pretty Parish, drove off the Inhabitants and Stock without any Loss; after which, they made a Descent on the South Shore, opposite the Island of Coudre, destroyed Part of the Parish of St. Ann's and St. Roan, where were very handsome Houses with Farms, and loaded the Vessels with Cattle; after which they returned from their Expedition."

The same Day 1 of our Schooners went from the Fleet below the Fall, and the French fir'd 8 or 9 Shot at her; but miss'd her. This Day a Party of young Highlanders came to the Island of Orleans from Gen. Monckton's Encampment; on Purpose to destroy all the Canada-Side.—The same Day our People set one of the Enemy's Floating-Batteries on Fire;—and in the Night General Monckton set the Town on Fire, (being the 4th Time) and the Flames raged so violently, that 'twas imagin'd the whole City would have been reduc'd to Ashes.

August 18th a Sloop and Schooner went below the Falls; the French hove Shot and Shells at them, but did 'em no Damage. The same Day the Enemy hove a Bomb from the Town, which kill'd one Man and wounded 6 more,—one Man had his Arm cut off by a Piece of the same Shell.

On the 20th the Louisbourg Grenadiers began their March down the main Land of Quebeck, in order to burn and destroy all the Houses on that Side.—On the 24th they were attack'd by a Party of French, who had a Priest for their Commander; but our Party kill'd and scalp'd 31 of them, and likewise the Priest, their Commander; They did our People no Damage. The three Companies of Louisbourg Grenadiers halted about 4 Miles down the River, at a Church called the Guardian-Angel, where we were order'd to fortify ourselves till further Orders; we had several small Parties in Houses, and the Remainder continued in the Church.—The 25th, began to destroy the Country, burning Houses, cutting down Corn, and the like: At Night the Indians fired several scattering Shot at the Houses, which kill'd one of the Highlanders and wounded another; but they were soon repulsed by the Heat of our Firing.—It was said that the Number of the Enemy consisted of 800 Canadians and Indians. Sept 1st we set Fire to our Houses and Fortifications, and marched to join the Grand Army at Montmorancy; the 3 Companies of Grenadiers ordered to hold themselves in Readiness to march at a Minute's Warning.

Source: Robert Henderson, *A Soldier's Account of the Campaign on Quebec, 1759,* taken from *A Journal of the Expedition up the River St. Lawrence,* originally published in 1759 (Manotick: The Discriminating General, n.d.), services@militaryheritage.com. Reproduced with the permission of The Discriminating General, www.militaryheritage.com.

the 1630s, disease decimated the Huron population, delivering a severe blow to the trade (Dickinson and Young, 2003: 20; Innis, 1962; Morton, 1997).

In 1650, about 1,200 French European colonists lived in New France (Dickinson and Young, 2003: 65). In theory, the Huron Confederacy's destruction opened up new opportunities to attract French immigrants into the fur trade and agriculture. However, war and the *Cent-Associés'* near bankruptcy prevented the colony from taking advantage of the changed circumstances (Moore, 2000: 121–122). In 1663, the colony's population was still only around 3,000 people. That year, Louis XIV dissolved the company and made New France a royal colony. An active immigration policy was pursued. Encouragement and financial inducements were given to disbanded military officers and their men, civilian workers, and—in an effort to redress a long-standing gender imbalance in the colonies—women. By 1681, the population of New France was 10,000. Most of Canada's francophone population today traces its roots to these original 10,000 inhabitants (Moore, 2000: 127–129; also, Dickinson and Young, 2003). New France's population thereafter increased primarily from births rather than immigration.

Growth and development create their own problems and natural contradictions. After 1663, the internal contradictions and conflicts facing New France mounted: the Catholic Church versus the state; rural versus urban; fur trading versus agriculture and industry. In the words of historian Desmond Morton (1997: 27), "Were the people of New France to be habitants, cultivating their small colony in the valley of the St. Lawrence, or were they to be voyageurs, carrying the fur trade, Catholicism, and French influence throughout the continent?" Yet the colony also began to develop. Visitors to New France in the mid-18th century regularly commented on its growing prosperity and cultural sophistication (Eccles, 1993b).

In 1756, however, New France faced a growing threat from England and its southern colonies. The 13 British colonies that eventually became the United States had a more developed and diverse economy than New France. Agriculture and commerce were thriving. The English colonists—roughly 1.5 million compared with New France's 75,000 (Eccles, 1993a: 171)—were eager to expand into the Ohio Valley. There however, they faced a belt of French forts constructed along the Ohio and Mississippi rivers, established both to support the fur trade and to hem off British expansion (Innis, 1962: 88–89; Morton, 1997: 30; Eccles, 1993a: 163). In 1754, a series of armed clashes occurred between British and French forces. These events partially set off the Seven Years War in Europe, which began two years later (Dickinson and Young, 2003: 46; Eccles, 1993a: 163).

As the war began, the English in North America possessed several advantages over the French. Besides a larger population in the colonies, the English also had a larger and more powerful navy, with which they could blockade the French colonies, and a larger standing army. In 1756, there were roughly 22,000 English regulars and militia in the colonies, to which were later added another 20,000 regular troops. By contrast, New France had no more than 7,000 regular troops, along with several thousand militiamen and Aboriginal allies (Dickinson and Young, 2003: 47; Moore, 2000: 185; but see also Eccles, 1993a: 171).

Despite these overwhelming odds, the French in the early stages successfully defended their colony, in part because the British had difficulty in marshalling their superior resources. Gradually, however, the British gained the upper hand. In 1758, the British seized the fort of Louisbourg in Nova Scotia. The following summer, a British fleet sailed up the St. Lawrence, while troops on the ground scorched the countryside (see Box 2.1).

Gradually, Quebec City was isolated from the surrounding territory, and the siege began. Throughout the following months, the British, led by General James Wolfe (1727–1759), conducted a constant bombardment of the city in hopes of forcing the French under the Marquis Louis-Joseph de Montcalm (1712–1759) out of their defensive position. Much of lower Quebec City was laid to rubble. The British also torched the surround-ing countryside (Dickinson and Young, 2003; Dufour, 1990; Moore, 2000), yet the French did not surrender.

Frustrated, Wolfe tried a final tactic. On the night of September 12, the British forces seized a path up the cliffs to west Quebec City, setting the stage for the historic battle of the next day, as related by Moore (2000: 188):

> On the Plains of Abraham, Wolfe's red-coated army formed one line, facing east towards the city. After some fierce skirmishing, Montcalm's troops in their white coats moved west towards them, drums beating, regimental banners flying. The two armies were roughly equal in numbers. These were precisely the conditions Wolfe had sought all summer, and in a battle that lasted barely fifteen minutes, the close-range volleys of his skilled regulars tore the French army apart.

Wolfe died that day in battle, Montcalm succumbed the next day to his wounds, and part of a national mythology was born (see Francis, 1997: 55–56). In effect, the war was over, although fighting continued for another year. In August 1760, Montreal capitulated, the French humiliation completed by a public surrender of arms (Dufour, 1990). The Treaty of Paris in 1763 formally ended the war. France ceded its former colony along the St. Lawrence to Britain.

THE ROYAL PROCLAMATION AND QUEBEC ACT

In 1760 New France, now known as Quebec, was in a state of ruin. Roughly a tenth of the colony's population had been killed (Moore, 2000: 188). Quebec City and the area around it were in ruins, the colony's economic infrastructure destroyed. Famine and disease were rampant. All in all, the war and its immediate aftermath were terrifying for the residents of the colony.

Adding to their abject circumstances was the French's fear of their conquerors. The French had good reason to fear the British. The torching of homes and villages along the St. Lawrence gave ample proof of the enemy's barbarity. The forced expulsion of roughly 7,000 Acadian people in 1754 from what is now Nova Scotia, without compensation for their land, was also fresh on French minds (Dickinson and Young, 2003: 47; Conway, 1997: 12). (Many of the Acadians resettled in Louisiana; hence, that region's "Cajun" culture.)

The French were surprised, therefore, by the generally courteous and respectful behaviour of the British. In the years between 1760 and 1764, Quebec was under martial law. Yet the British did little to interfere with French traditions, and indeed they helped in the province's reconstruction. In the words of Dufour (1990: 27), the conqueror's behaviour was "correct. Even exemplary."

The Royal Proclamation of 1763, however, gave the French a taste of the iron fist. Designed to assimilate the French, the Proclamation declared that Quebec henceforth would be governed by British institutions, with an elected assembly and British laws. British immigration would be encouraged. Finally, in an effort to head off further wars with Aboriginal peoples, the interior hinterland of the Ohio Valley was made a vast Native reserve (Innis, 1962; Dickinson and Young, 2003).

In an act of surprising civility, however, the British governor, James Murray (1721–1794), refused to enact many of the Proclamation's provisions. In part, Murray's actions were based on his recognition that the provisions were not enforceable. Eighty-five percent of the colony's inhabitants lived in rural areas beyond administrative control (Dickinson and Young, 2003). There was little likelihood soon of a wave of English immigration that might change the colony's predominantly French and Catholic character. Under existing British law, no Catholic could hold office, making impossible the notion of a representative legislative assembly. Montreal fur traders were already demanding that the Ohio Valley be reopened for business. Moreover, given growing unrest in England's southern colonies on the continent, the last thing the British needed was agitation in the north. But it is also true that Murray himself *actually liked and admired the French* and, setting a tradition followed for a time by his successors, acted, albeit paternalistically, as a protector of French interests (see Conway, 1997). Conqueror and conquered were mutually seduced (Dufour, 1990).

Thus, in 1774, the British passed the Quebec Act, which reversed much of the Royal Proclamation. The law was changed to allow Catholics to hold elected office. Seigneurial land tenure was confirmed. The colony's territorial boundaries were increased to include some of the First Nations territories. Catholics were given the right to practise their religion. The Catholic Church was once more allowed to collect tithes. And while English criminal law was retained, French law was allowed in civil cases (Dickinson and Young, 2003: 55).

In a curious sense, the Conquest seemed to have changed little. Nonetheless, its effects were real. In the most profound sense, the Conquest forged a people, a sociological—but not a political—nation.

BEING *CANADIEN*

A people somewhat distinct from the European French were arising in the colony even before the Conquest. In contrast to the town-dwelling French administrators, the peasant farmers—*habitants*, as they described themselves—were mostly rural. In their everyday lives, they experienced greater independence and social equality, including gender equality, than people living in France (Rioux, 1978: 17–18). This basic equality, combined with isolation, the harshness of their existence, and the constant fear of attack by Aboriginals, developed a strong sense of solidarity among the *habitants* over time (Dickinson and Young, 2003; Rioux, 1978). By the 1750s, visitors to New France "claimed that a new kind of French people was emerging along the banks of the St. Lawrence" (Morton, 1997: 28), a people distinguished by different beliefs, customs, behaviours, and even dialect (Rioux, 1978: 24–25; see also Eccles, 1993b; Thompson, 1995). They called themselves *Canadiens*, and their country Canada. There was no need to copyright the *Canadien* identity. By definition, *Canadiens* were French-speaking Catholics settled permanently along the St. Lawrence. Moreover, in their own minds at least, the territorial boundaries of their nation extended well beyond their colony's borders into areas traversed and imagined by French voyageurs and missionaries.

But distinctiveness, though necessary, is not a sufficient basis of nationalism. The Conquest transformed—though not all at once—New France's distinctiveness into nationalism (Cook, 1995: 86).

Try to put yourself for the moment in the shoes of a *habitant* after 1763. You have been conquered, not merely defeated, by the English (Dufour, 1990: 31). Equally, you have not been merely orphaned by the mother country, but, as the Treaty of Paris cruelly attests, abandoned. The past cannot be reversed. Finally, to add to your confusion, your enemy is actually magnanimous in victory. As a conquered subject, you welcome the difference; the fact that you are not tortured, raped, and killed is clearly important. Still, as Dufour (1990: 31) remarks, the conqueror's magnanimity changes nothing; indeed, it actually makes your subordinate status more humiliating because now you must also be grateful.

New France in 1760, like the British colonies to the south, was growing apart from France and no doubt one day would have sought independence, but the Conquest truncated this normal development. Quebec's sense of self-identity was not positive in the sense of one chosen by the people; rather, it was an identity thrust upon them, forged in war, trauma, and the torturous severing of the colony's umbilical cord from France. Time and circumstances conspired to make the Quebec's French population a distinct people—*les Canadiens*—before their time. By contrast, the few hundred British who occupied Quebec after 1763 remained, even to themselves, "the British."

The political circumstances were unstable, however. As the British feared, the American colonists in 1775 revolted. In the wake of the conflict, 40,000 United Empire Loyalists fled to the northern British colonies, about 10,000 of them settling in Quebec (Dickinson and Young, 2003). The contest for political, territorial, and economic power and national identity began again.

THE LOYALISTS AND THE CONSTITUTION ACT OF 1791

Imagine now that you are a United Empire Loyalist recently arrived in Canada. Your property in the 13 colonies has been stolen by the revolutionary leaders who have distributed it among themselves, their friends, and small farmers in order to garner their political support for the new republic (Zinn, 1995: 83). Your physical health, and that of your family, is poor. By contrast with the 30,000 Loyalists who arrived in Nova Scotia by ship, you came to Canada by horse cart overland and on foot, bearing little. You are bitter and angry; a historian will later remark that "quarrelsomeness" marked your character and that of your compatriots (Brown, 1993: 246). You were loyal to Britain (you say to yourself and anyone who will listen) and now have lost everything (Morton, 1997: 65; but also see Francis, 1997: 56). The free land, clothing, and farming utensils supplied by the British administration

(Dickinson and Young, 2003) do not assuage your bitterness.

Such, in part, was the view of the Loyalists as they arrived in the northern British colonies. Like the French, the Loyalists were a conquered people. In Canada, however, the roughly 10,000 who arrived found their humiliation increased by the fact that they were a minority surrounded by more than 70,000 French Catholics. For their part, the French were no more thrilled with their new neighbours, viewing them as an advance guard of future anglophone settlement. In an age when ethnic and religious bigotry were rife, the arrival of the Loyalists was like gasoline thrown on a fire.

Elsewhere, the arrival of Loyalists created similar tensions. In Nova Scotia, the Loyalists who arrived quickly swamped the existing population of 4,000 New Englanders and Acadians. The 1,000 Loyalists who arrived on the Island of St. John (renamed Prince Edward Island in 1799) equalled those already living there, while the 400 Loyalists who arrived on Cape Breton doubled that island's existing population (Brown, 1993: 241–242).

Anxious to prevent conflict, the British thus segregated the respective populations. Nova Scotia was divided and a new province, New Brunswick, created, while Cape Breton (temporarily) became a separate colony. The colony of Quebec, formally New France, likewise was divided.

The instrument of this latter division was the Constitution Act of 1791. The Constitution Act amended the Quebec Act, but left intact many of the latter's provisions protecting the French language, the Catholic Church, French civil law, and the seigneurial system. The Constitution Act, however, divided the colony into Upper Canada (where many of the Loyalists had settled) and Lower Canada (French Canada), the term *Canada* having historically been a loose synonym for New France. The Act further maintained strong executive power in the office of the governor, an executive council (made up of the governor's advisers), and a non-elected legislative council (a colonial House of Lords). But it also allowed, for the first time, popularly elected assemblies in both Canadas and extended the franchise. Finally, the Act envisaged the creation of a colonial aristocracy, a state church, and public education. The first idea was soon abandoned, but substantial land holdings were set aside for the Anglican Church and education (Careless, 1970: 119–121; Dickinson and Young, 2003: 59).

Even at the time, the Constitution Act pleased few people. The merchants of Montreal had not wanted Canada divided. The English in Lower Canada did not like being separated from the English in Upper Canada. The agrarians and rising bourgeoisie in both provinces did not like the Act's openly mercantilist bent. Democrats, believing that the elected assemblies did not go far enough, railed against oligarchic rule. But perhaps the major flaw in the Constitution Act was that it institutionalized ethnic conflict (Cook, 1995: 87). Thereafter, as Quebec premier Pierre Chauveau would later remark, the English and French met each other only "on the landing of politics," frequently in conflict.

THE CONQUEST'S IMPACTS

Social stratification is *the system by which a society ranks categories of people (e.g., by occupation, race, ethnicity, or gender) in a hierarchy involving inequalities of various sorts.* At the top of New France's stratification system before the Conquest were royal officials: the governor, the *intendant* (the business manager), and the senior military officers. The clergy were somewhat parallel to the royal officials, but after 1663 clearly subordinate in the final instance to the state. The *seigneurs*, some of whom came from the French nobility, came next in the social order, followed by a sizable middle class (composed of merchants and small vendors), the urban working class, then the *habitants* (Eccles, 1993a: 42). (Note that this stratification system does not include women or Aboriginal peoples.) The Conquest changed Canada's economic and political order. The degree and type of changes, however, are somewhat disputed.

One dispute involves the actual number of people who left New France. The articles of capitulation in 1760 gave inhabitants the right to return to France. Perhaps only a few hundred took advantage of the opportunity (Dickinson and Young, 2003: 49), perhaps 4,000 (Eccles, 1993a: 173). Most of those who left were French bureaucrats and soldiers (though some decommissioned soldiers remained), quickly replaced by British bureaucrats and soldiers.

A second, more important dispute arose during the 1950s and 1960s over the Conquest's impacts upon New France's economic classes and the colony's future. Early on, scholars of "the Montreal School" (Saul, 1997: 19)—Maurice Seguin, Guy Fregault, and Michel Brunet—developed the **decapitation thesis** (Cook, 1995: 92; Dickinson and Young, 2003) This thesis holds that the Conquest had destroyed New France's "embryonic bourgeoisie" (Brunet, 1993; also Rioux, 1978: 39; Conway, 1997: 15). The English and Scots merchants subsequently stepped into the void left by the French bourgeoisie, while the French who remained retreated to a rural existence. There, dominated by the Catholic Church, they espoused conservative values inimical to capitalist development (Norrie and Owram, 1996: 61; Dickinson and Young, 2003). Thus Lower Canada's economic development was truncated.

In direct refutation of the decapitation thesis, a second argument holds that New France in 1763 had no "viable business community" (Dickinson and Young, 2003: 51), no middle class (Hamelin, 1993) to be destroyed. More recently, a synthesis of both arguments has emerged.

This third argument suggests that the Conquest resulted in the departure of agents and merchants directly connected to France's trading companies, but that local merchants, storekeepers, and traders stayed. That is, the transatlantic French bourgeoisie was eliminated, but the local French bourgeoisie, albeit small, remained (Norrie and Owram, 1996: 63; also Dickinson and Young, 2003).

More broadly, these debates point to how historical interpretations can have current sociological and political significance. Reflecting on the political context within Quebec during recent decades, one can see that the decapitation thesis lent itself to support for the Quiet Revolution (Chapter 3) and sovereignty (Cook, 1995; Saul, 1997). By contrast, the second and third arguments provide much less support for the belief that the conquest held back Quebec's early development.

There is no dispute, however, that Canada's economy immediately after 1760 was in crisis. The war's devastation, the permanent disruption of its mercantile (metropolitan-hinterland) arrangements with France, and the outbreak of wars with Aboriginal tribes on the frontier were all contributing factors. Within a short time, however, Lower Canada's economy began to rebound. The colony was rebuilt; the Aboriginal wars ended in 1763 (see Chapter 10), restoring the Ohio Valley fur trade; and trade links were re-established, this time with Britain. Capital also began to enter Lower Canada from Britain and merchants in England's southern colonies.

The direct economic impacts of the Conquest should not be minimized. In the long term, however, the Conquest's social and political consequences were more important. After 1763 the English held the balance of **power**, defined as *someone's ability to impose his or her will upon others even against their resistance* (see Box 2.2). The imposition of English will was a fact of life in Lower Canada, despite the newcomers' frequent conciliations and sensitivity to the French majority. With the arrival of the Loyalists after 1775 (see Chapter 6), ethnicity came to play an even greater role in Canada's social structure. The effects of ethnicity, however, were mitigated somewhat by the granting of elected assemblies under the Constitution Act of 1791, which opened up opportunities for a nascent *Canadien* political class.

Box 2.2
Means of Exercising Power

Power can be exercised by three means. Each means may be effective depending on a particular situation, but each also has limits and none is effective in all situations. Often one means of power is used in combination with another. The three means of power are:

Force or the threat of force: The English expulsion of the Acadians in 1754, the Canadian government's use of the RCMP against protesters at Regina in 1935 (Chapter 7), the use of the Canadian military to deal with the FLQ Crisis in 1970 (Chapter 3), and the use of the military troops to deal with the Oka Crisis in 1990 (Chapter 12) provide examples of the use of force.

Reward: Whereas force involves use of the stick, reward involves the use of the carrot. Rewards may be material (e.g., money), but not always; status, for example, is also a form of reward. Because systems of social stratification differentially reward individuals and groups on the basis of class, race, ethnicity, gender, etc., such systems are themselves means of power. (Note that withholding instrumental rewards results in economic coercion—the use once more of force.)

Authority: Authority gains its power by being recognized as legitimate. Authority frequently coincides with the means of force and reward, but often includes elements of tradition, law, status, or prestige. The **dominant ideology** (see chapters 3 and 8) of any period tends to legitimize current power relations.

By the early 19th century, ethnicity had become a defining feature of Lower Canada's system of social stratification. The English controlled the executive and judicial branches in the political realm, but the French dominated the legislative branch. The English controlled the upper reaches of the economy: international trade, banking, and finance. The French business class was restricted to local trade. At the lower levels, British labourers, contractors, and producers—often favoured by British administrators—competed with their French counterparts (Dickinson and Young, 2003: 114; Innis, 1962; Norrie and Owram, 1996). Finally, the *habitant* majority occupied the bottom level of Lower Canada's social structure (Rioux, 1978: 35).

The ethnic division of Lower Canada was not merely social, but also demographic. Gradually, the English "captured" the urban portion of the colony, while the French retreated to the colony's villages and rural farms (Rioux, 1978). Early in the 19th century, 40 percent of Quebec City and 33 percent of Montreal were anglophone (Norrie and Owram, 1996: 98). In this context the Catholic Church, especially its parish priests, grew in importance.

By the 1830s, these social, political, and economic divisions, built on a foundation of Conquest, had nurtured among Lower Canada's French population a growing sense of grievance and a rising spirit of nationalism. Finally, the grievances boiled over.

THE REBELLIONS OF 1837–1838

In 1837, after years of political discord, and in the midst of a prolonged recession, rebellions broke out in both Upper and Lower Canada. The causes of the rebellions in the two Canadas were similar. Popular anger focused on the corrupt oligarchies that governed the provinces—the Chateau Clique in Lower Canada, the Family Compact in Upper Canada—and their political masters in London.

In Upper Canada, the rebels demanded "responsible government." They wanted real power to rest with an elected legislative assembly. The Upper Canadian rebels also wanted economic reform, believing—correctly—that current policies were designed to protect mercantilist interests. The rebels wanted instead increased immigration, greater access to capital, and more land opened up for agriculture (Careless, 1970; Norrie and Owram, 1996).

Though the movements in both Upper and Lower Canada were informed by liberal democratic ideals, inspired by the French and American revolutions (Rioux, 1978: 49; Cook, 1995; Conway, 1997; Romney, 1999), a fundamental difference existed between the two rebellions. In contrast with Upper Canada, the rebellion in Lower Canada was not only inspired by demands for representative democracy, but also nationalism (Conway, 1997: 22). In consequence, the conflict in Lower Canada could only be more serious—and bloody.

In Lower Canada, the rebellion's leader was Louis-Joseph Papineau (1786–1871), a member of the new middle class and speaker of the Assembly. The rebellion occurred in several stages. In October 1837, Patriote leaders issued a "Declaration of the Rights of Man," based on the American declaration of 1776 (Ouellet, 1993: 360). At St. Denis on November 23, 800 Patriotes defeated 200 British regulars. This was followed by a British victory two days later at St. Charles, then a massive British attack on the rebels at St. Eustache, north of Montreal, on December 14. Many of the rebels hid in the village church. The British, however, set the church alight and shot the rebels as they fled through the windows. Estimates of the number of Patriotes killed range from 58 to 100. The village of St. Eustache was razed. The fight continued into the countryside, where British irregulars left behind them a trail of scorched *habitant* homes, farms, and villages (Morton, 1997: 37; Dickinson and Young, 2003: 165; Conway, 1997: 29).

In the wake of the Lower Canada rebellion, martial law was declared, the Canadian constitution suspended, and a new governor of British North America, Lord Durham (1792–1840), was named (Dickinson and Young, 2003: 167). By now, Papineau had fled to the United States. The rebellion, however, soon flared anew.

A second uprising occurred in late November 1838, with its leader, a follower of Papineau, declaring Lower Canada a republic and issued a "Proclamation of Independence." The uprising was soon put down, however. While a degree of leniency followed the first wave of rebellions in Lower Canada, no leniency was shown after the second rebellion. Twelve Patriotes were hanged and 58 deported to Australia's penal colonies, while two more were banished (Dickinson and Young, 2003: 167; Conway, 1997: 29; Wynn, 2000: 211–212).

By contrast, the rebellion in Upper Canada was, in the words of historian Jack Granatstein (1996: 29), a "small-bore affair." There, William Lyon Mackenzie (1795–1861)—publisher, editorialist, social critic, *and* grandfather to a later prime minister—led the rebellion. Since the 1820s, he had fought against the Family Compact and for democratic reform, to no avail. Finally, emboldened by events in Lower Canada—Mackenzie was in frequent contact with Papineau—the rebels took up arms in December 1837. On December 7, after a night of heated discussion at Montgomery's Tavern, 800 of Mackenzie's followers (mostly farmers, small-town tradesmen, and some professionals) marched up Yonge Street in Toronto. There, untrained militia recruited by Upper Canada's elite met them. Shots rang out. The rebellion soon ended. Mackenzie fled disguised as a woman to the United States—he would return 12 years later and be elected to the legislature—but two of his lieutenants died on the gallows. Ninety-two more of Mackenzie's followers were sent to the penal colonies, while hundreds more, disenchanted with the rebellion's outcome, eventually left for the United States. As in Lower Canada, a few cross-border skirmishes occurred in 1838, led by groups trying to liberate Canada from "the British yoke." In 1840, Mackenzie supporters also burned a British steamship at the Thousand Islands and blew up General Brock's monument at Queenston Heights. These events were mere sideshows, however. Upper Canada's rebellion was over (Morton, 1997: 49; Dickinson and Young, 2003; Conway, 1997: 23–25; Wynn, 2000: 217).

Neither rebellion had widespread popular support. The movements were primarily middle class in origin (Morton, 1997; Ouellet, 1993; Trofimenkoff, 1993), no match for the power of the state and its allies. In Upper Canada, the rebels were easily tainted with the labels "American" and "republican" (Granatstein, 1996). In Lower Canada, the movement's avowed anticlericalism evinced even stronger condemnations from the Catholic Church (Trofimenkoff, 1993).

The rebels' final defeat in 1838 was decisive. French nationalism would not rise again with force until the 1960s (Cook, 1995). For Canada as a whole, defeat meant the throttling of liberal democracy (see Laxer, 1989; Trofimenkoff, 1993; Conway, 1997). Thereafter, conservatism, exercised both in the political-economic and religious realms, gained an increased hold on Canadian society.

LORD DURHAM AND THE ACT OF UNION

The new governor, Lord Durham, spent only five months in Canada before resigning in anger. On his return to England, he produced his analysis of the rebellions, based on his short time in Canada, which included a 10-day steamboat trip and conversations with a few close acquaintances (G. Martin, 1993: 444). Durham's *Report on the Affairs of British North America* condemned the ruling oligarchy, the abuses of land granting, and Anglican privileges in the colonies, while also dealing with a host of other issues, from immigration to canal building (see Careless, 1970: 195). It further made some of the most derogatory statements ever directed at the *Canadiens*, including this one, quoted in Colombo (1994: 38):

There can hardly be conceived a nationality more destitute of all that can invigorate and elevate a people, than that which is exhibited by the descendants of the French in Lower Canada, owing to their peculiar language and manners. They are a people with no history and no literature.

Finally, Durham's report included a particularly memorable paragraph (Colombo, 1994: 38):

I expected to find a contest between a government and a people: I found two nations warring in the bosom of a single state: I found a struggle, not of principles, but of races; and I perceived that it would be idle to attempt any amelioration of laws or institutions until we could first succeed in terminating the deadly animosity that now separates the inhabitants of Lower Canada into the hostile divisions of French and English.

Durham's analysis reflected European views of the time about the "necessary" relationship between state and nation (see Chapter 1); as such, it is a textbook example of material reality being shaped to fit theory and of the problems of biases in conducting research (see Box 2.3). Theories have consequences, and in this case two significant consequences resulted from Durham's report.

Box 2.3
Observer Bias: A Tale of Two Journeys

Lord Durham travelled through Upper and Lower Canada in 1838. Only a few years earlier (in 1830), Alexis de Tocqueville (1805–1859) journeyed to the United States. Both Lord Durham and Tocqueville were European aristocrats; both travelled in the respective countries for only a few months, yet the latter produced *Democracy in America*, still considered an accurate depiction of the United States' developing political culture, while the former's *Report* is viewed as biased and inaccurate. The result raises the question of why observer bias occurs and how it might be prevented.

Durham arrived with fixed notions of the situation in Lower Canada, and his informants were a relatively small number of the existing elite who supported his beliefs. By contrast, Tocqueville arrived in the United States to study that country's penal system, not U.S. society as a whole. As a result, he was relatively open to experiencing the new environment, and supplemented his observations by reading widely and interviewing a large number of Americans.

The tale of Durham and Tocqueville also raises the question of the proper distance researchers should have from the object of study. On the one hand, group members have an advantage over outsiders in understanding what is observed. On the other hand, insiders are sometimes too close to see what outsiders can observe.

Durham's report contained two major recommendations: first, that the British North American colonies be granted responsible government and, second, that Upper and Lower Canada be united (Careless, 1970: 195). In effect, the sundering of the two colonies by the Constitution Act of 1791 would be reversed. There was now, however, an important difference. In 1791, the French had been in the majority; it was to protect the English minority that the colonies had been split. By 1840, however, the demographics had changed. Lower Canada still had the larger population, between 600,000 and 650,000, compared with Upper Canada's population of 450,000 (Dickinson and Young, 2003: 183; also Conway, 1997). But virtually all of Upper Canada's population was anglophone, while approximately 150,000 people in Lower Canada were also of British heritage. Thus, the English could dominate in a united Canada. Moreover, Durham argued that English immigration should be strengthened to ensure over time the complete assimilation of the French, thereby blunting the nationalism that had fuelled the recent rebellions.

In 1840 the British government implemented much of Durham's report through the Act of Union, but what they did not implement was crucial. First, they denied outright responsible government, with the result that reformers in Upper Canada remained angry. Second, the union was not total. The Quebec Act's major provisions protecting French civil law, the rights of the Catholic Church, and local control of education remained extant. Even more importantly, the Act of Union meant that Canada would be governed by an elected legislative assembly in which Canada East (Lower Canada) and Canada West (Upper Canada) would equally hold 42 seats (see Conway, 1997).

The seeds for further crisis, leading ultimately to Confederation in 1867, were thus sown. The French population would not—could not—be assimilated; indeed, the legislative structure actually gave the French minority power disproportionate to its numbers, power that they sensibly used, voting *en bloc*, to protect their interests. The English in Upper Canada, meanwhile, complained bitterly that they had cast off the oligarchic power of the Family Compact only to find themselves now dominated by Lower Canada and a French-speaking minority that was Catholic to boot (see Romney, 1999).

The rebellions of 1837–1838 had seen French Canada conquered a second time. Both Papineau's dream of an independent French republic and Durham's hope of French assimilation were equally chimerical. Nonetheless, the conflicts remained. It would take the forces of modernity, a major depression, two world wars, and the rise of a new intellectual class before Quebec nationalism would again rise, but rise it would, in unexpected ways, with consequences for conquered and conqueror alike.

CONCLUSION

New France gave Canada its name, its history, and one of its languages; in the wording of Dufour (1990), its "heart." After 1840, however, the English increasingly put their stamp on the rest of Canada. A series of events symbolized the ongoing rejection of the French language and its near isolation to the province of Quebec: the hanging of Riel in 1885; the school acts adopted in several provinces, beginning with Manitoba in 1890; and, of course, the conscription crises of the two world wars.

Why does this matter? From the perspective of historical sociology, five later aspects of Canadian society derive, directly or indirectly, from these events. First, these events (beginning with the Conquest) help explain Canada's system of stratification until recent times, with those of English ethnic origin disproportionately occupying elite positions and people of French (and other) ethnic origins disproportionately occupying lower rungs (see Porter, 1965; Clement, 1975; Nakhaie, 1997). Second, they suggest why francophone Quebecers might feel a sense of grievance toward the rest of Canada (see Conway, 1997). Third, attention to historical and political contexts also sheds light on Quebec's continuing claims to linguistic, cultural, and religious distinctiveness.

A fourth, less obvious consequence of this early history is that no "strong national myth" could cement Canadian federalism, as in the United States (Balthazar, 1997: 45; see Part 2 of this text). In the words of political scientist Reg Whitaker (1987: 23), "Nationalism as legitimation is a weak, derisory ploy in Canada." Any attempt by political demagogues to "fly the flag" has quickly run aground on ethnic divisions and the Canadian tendency, perhaps inborn, toward skepticism.

Finally, a fifth related consequence (which we shall explore further) involves the complex nature of Canadian federalism. Some of the Fathers of Confederation no doubt wanted to create a strong, centralized government, leaving the provinces with only meagre powers. Quebec's presence, however, as well as that of the smaller Maritime provinces, made this impossible. Canada's flexible and significantly decentralized system of powers and responsibilities—sometimes a benefit, sometimes not—is a product of efforts to solve real problems and conflicts among Canada's constituent communities.

To a degree, political institutions and cultural traditions before the 1950s restrained conflict between Canada's English and French communities. Where these might have proved insufficient to reduce conflict, social isolation provided additional restraint. But the world would not let the two communities go on this way. War and the relentless forces of modernity—capitalism, industrialism, and secularism—were about to throw the separate worlds together.

KEY TERMS
decapitation thesis
dominant ideology
mercantilism
power
social stratification
terrorism

CRITICAL THINKING QUESTIONS

1. What are the similarities and differences between mercantilism and modern capitalism?

2. What are the processes by which social conflict between different groups emerges and is transformed over time?

3. Under what conditions are some means of power more effective than others?

4. Is it possible to overcome observer bias?

5. In what sense is nationalism always based on a myth?

RECOMMENDED READINGS

Dickinson, John, and Brian Young. 2003. *A Short History of Quebec*, 3rd ed. Montreal and Kingston: McGill-Queen's University Press.
This book provides an excellent social history of Quebec, from pre-European times up to the present.

Dufour, Christian. 1990. *A Canadian Challenge/ Le défi québécois*. Halifax: Oolichan Books and the Institute for Research on Public Policy.
In a Weberian manner, this book allows anglophones to understand the world from the point of view of francophone Quebecers, while also showing the unrecognized influence that each community has had upon the other.

Manchester, William. 1992. *A World Lit Only by Fire: The Medieval Mind and the Renaissance*. Boston: Little, Brown.
This book brings to life, in a very readable way, Medieval Europe and shows how very different it was from the present day.

Moore, Christopher. 1997. *1867: How the Fathers Made a Deal*. Toronto: McClelland & Stewart.
This book tells the engaging story of how the Fathers of Confederation arrived at making Canada.

Porter, John. 1965. *The Vertical Mosaic*. Toronto: University of Toronto Press.
Porter's book, *The Vertical Mosaic*, is a classic in sociology. It detailed, at the time, Canada's complex stratification system, paving the way for subsequent studies.

RELATED WEBSITES

Acadian Cultural Society
www.acadiancultural.org
This society is a non-profit, tax-exempt educational organization dedicated to preserving and promoting Acadian heritage among individuals of Acadian descent.

Canada: A People's History
http://history.cbc.ca
This 17-episode, 32-hour documentary television series, which first aired on the CBC, portrays the history of Canada.

Cangenealogy
www.cangenealogy.com/quebec.html
Quebec's demographic history is among the best recorded anywhere. Cangenealogy has a list of sites for those interested in genealogical history.

CANADIAN SOCIETY ON VIDEO

A License to Remember—Special Edition/Un certain souvenir—Édition spéciale. 2007. National Film Board of Canada, 121 minutes, 2 seconds. Examines the meaning of the words on Quebec licence plates, *"Je me souviens,"* at the heart of Quebec history and society.

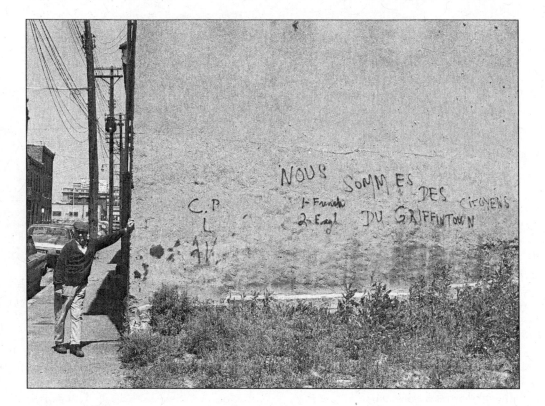

CHAPTER 3

A HUNDRED YEARS OF SOLITUDES

English and French, we climb by a double flight of stairs toward the destinies reserved for us on this continent, without knowing each other, without meeting each other, and without even seeing each other, except on the landing of politics.

—Pierre Joseph-Oliver Chauveau, first Quebec premier after Confederation, 1876

He shall hang though every dog in Quebec howl in his favour.

—Prime Minister Sir John A. Macdonald, refusing to pardon Riel, 1885

Society must take every means to prevent the emergence of a parallel power which defies the elected power.

—Prime Minister Pierre Trudeau, at the peak of the FLQ Crisis, 1970

INTRODUCTION

In the spring of 1955, Canadians were transfixed by television pictures of hundreds of hockey fans rioting in the streets of Montreal to protest the suspension, for the rest of the regular season and playoffs, of Maurice "Rocket" Richard (1921–2000). Store windows were smashed, cars overturned, and property looted, leading to the arrest of 37 adults and four juveniles. The Richard riot ended only when Richard went on radio and television the next day to ask the rioters to stop.

We noted in Chapter 1 the importance of symbols to societies. In 1955, Quebec was on the verge of *"La Revolution Tranquil,"* the Quiet Revolution. In this context, the Richard riot had little to do with hockey. Richard, the first player in NHL history to score 50 goals in a regular season, was hero to a French-speaking population dominated by an anglophone minority. For francophones, Richard's

suspension was symbolic of this unequal and discriminatory relationship. In turn, the riot was a symbolic protest against what many Quebecers viewed as 200 years of subjugation and humiliation. As we will see in this and subsequent chapters, however, symbols not only unite, they also divide. Indeed, much of French-English conflict in Canada can be viewed as a clash of symbols.

This chapter provides a necessarily short account of Quebec during the period between Confederation and the Second World War. It then provides a more detailed account of the events, individuals, and ideas that transformed Quebec, leading to the historic Quebec election of 1960 and the turbulent years of the Quiet Revolution, which ended with the October Crisis of 1970, a moment when, once more, English-speaking Canada watched transfixed by events on their television screens. Competing concepts of nationalism are discussed.

ENGLISH EXPANSION AND THE ISOLATION OF QUEBEC

Confederation in 1867 recognized Quebec as distinct, with its own majority French-Canadian population, Catholic religion, and civil law tradition, combined with autonomous political powers. For many French-Canadians, the historic province on the shores of the St. Lawrence was their homeland. At the same time, significant French-Canadian communities existed outside Quebec, especially in New Brunswick, but also in Nova Scotia, Prince Edward Island, Ontario, and the western territories (Silver, 1997). Confederation partially disentangled issues of Quebec's governance from those of the other, majority-English provinces. Confederation did not, however, separate French and Catholic sensibilities from the issue of how their compatriots were treated in the other provinces, indeed, from the issue of respect.

Some French Quebecers in 1867 no doubt viewed diaspora French as "dead ducks," to use Parti Québécois leader René Lévesque's expression of the 1970s. In their minds, only Quebec could provide security for French language and culture. Nonetheless, French-Canadians in general also viewed Canada as a bargain between French and English. Yes, Quebec for all practical purposes would always be the citadel of French culture in Canada, but the rights of French Catholics outside Quebec were also to be respected. By 1900, a broader understanding that "the two races" were not to be compartmentalized but rather forge a new nation had emerged within French Canada (Silver, 1997). Henri Bourassa (1868–1952), grandson of Louis-Joseph Papineau, was a chief spokesperson for this "pan-Canadian" view (Rioux, 1993).

Not all French-Canadians held this view; even less did English-Canadians. Alexander Muir's poem "The Maple Leaf Forever," written in the year of Confederation, says volumes about English Canada's view of the country just created:

> In days of yore, from Britain's shore,
> Wolfe the dauntless hero came,
> And planted firm Britannia's flag,
> On Canada's fair domain.

A hundred years of history had taught the English that the French could be neither defeated nor assimilated. However, the French could, it was believed, be contained. The French could have their separate language, religion, and civil laws, but only in Quebec. The rest of Canada would carry a distinctly British stamp.

These conflicting views of Confederation, and of the rights of minorities, inevitably met on the political landing. The rendezvous did not take long to occur. At Red River in the western territories in 1869, Canadian and American expansionism ran headlong into an established community of Métis (see chapters 7 and 10). Led by a young intellectual and visionary, Louis Riel (1844–1885), the Métis firmly rejected American efforts at annexation, but also demanded from the Canadian government full provincial status and protections for their French language and Catholic religion. The Conservative government of Prime Minister Sir John A. Macdonald (1815–1891) acceded to the demands. Thus, the Manitoba Act was passed in 1870, guaranteeing French-language rights in the legislature and schools and the right to a Catholic education in the new province of Manitoba.

The battle for French and Catholic rights outside Quebec was not over, however. The social conflicts and political intrigues of 1869 were repeated again in 1885, this time against the wider canvas of the entire western territories. This time, the demands of Riel and the Métis, not to mention the concerns of Natives and non-Natives, were rejected. The "rebels" were hunted down and tried. Louis Riel was hanged amid outcries from French-Canadian politicians and the Quebec press, who were convinced that he would not have been executed had he not been French and Catholic.

Riel's hanging was a blow to both French-Canadian and Métis hopes on the Prairies. For French Quebecers, Riel's hanging symbolized their exclusion from the rest of Canada. Incensed by Prime Minister Macdonald's refusal to pardon Riel (see quotation, above), French Quebec thereafter generally refused to vote Conservative, the two major exceptions being John Diefenbaker's landslide of 1958 and Brian Mulroney's equally massive electoral victories in 1984 and 1988 (appendices 1 and 2). More than ever, French Quebecers retreated behind their provincial walls, where the Catholic Church and conservative political leaders urged they remain (see Dufour, 1990; Rioux, 1993; Conway, 1997).

In the aftermath of 1885, immigrants quickly filled the West (see Chapter 7). In the early stages, many of these were from Ontario: English, Protestant, and often decidedly anti-Catholic. Soon they were a majority. In 1890, the English-speaking and Protestant legislature of Manitoba abolished Catholic separate schools and declared that French was no longer an official language (Careless, 1970; Conway, 1997). Declared unconstitutional by the Supreme Court in 1979, this legislative act nonetheless served its purpose: In the interim, French was reduced to a minority language in Manitoba. The legislature of the North-West Territories in 1892 passed similar language legislation. In 1912, Ontario eliminated French from its public education system. In 1916, Manitoba broke an agreement made with Sir Wilfrid Laurier (1841–1919) when he was prime minister and abolished French and any other language except English from its schools (Conway, 1997: 400; Silver, 1997: 244).

Throughout the 20th century, the minority status of French-Canadians and the political impotence of Quebec within Confederation were thus reinforced again and again. Symbolically, French-Canadians were "put in their place," that is, the place of a vanquished people. Canada was British.

The maintenance of British constitutional symbols, such as the monarchy and the Union Jack, was particularly grating to French-Canadians. For nationalists, such symbols were constant reminders of defeat. For pan-Canadianists, such symbols revealed English-Canadians as slavish colonials unable or unwilling to get on with the task of creating a new nation. Tensions heightened in 1903 with the Boer War, leading to Bourassa's break with the Laurier government. French-English conflict escalated into a full-blown political crisis during the First World War (see also Chapter 7).

Many French-Canadians viewed the First World War as not Canada's fight, and were offended that English-Canadians had allowed themselves and the country to be dragged into the conflict. By contrast, many English-Canadians were still emotionally tied to the British Empire and could not understand the lack of a similar French-Canadian need to defend France. That the umbilical cord between French-Canadians and France had been severed in 1763 entirely escaped most people in English Canada, who viewed French-Canadians en masse as disloyal, if not cowardly.

As the war dragged on, the need for fresh troops (and British demands that Canada "pull its weight") caused the Unionist government of Prime Minister Sir Robert Borden (1854–1937) to intensify its efforts at recruitment. These efforts were botched and led in 1916 to anti-recruitment riots in several Quebec towns. Amid continued Quebec opposition, the next year Borden introduced the Military Conscription Bill, and called an election on the issue. Though many Canadians opposed conscription, farmers and labourers among them, the election results revealed a particularly massive fissure between Quebec and the rest of Canada (see appendices 1 and 2). Borden's government won, but there were no French-Canadians from Quebec or Acadia among his MPs (Silver, 1997: 248). The will of the English majority ruled over the French minority, and the Conscription Bill was passed. The riots resumed throughout Quebec (Careless, 1970; Conway, 1997).

In the end, only 60,000 men were actually drafted. A large number of French recruits—as many as 40 percent—did not report (Dickinson and Young, 2003: 254). Few of the conscripts reached the front before the war ended. Bitterness lingered, however, between the French and English communities.

The Conscription Crisis of 1917 was reprised during the Second World

War. In 1940, the Liberals, under Prime Minister William Lyon Mackenzie King (1874–1950), won re-election, partly on a promise made to Quebec that he would not bring in conscription. Two years later, however, as casualties again mounted, he sought political absolution from his promise through a national referendum. Since the promise had been made to them alone, French Quebecers viewed the matter as one that should have been resolved only with them, not all of Canada (Silver, 1997). Nonetheless, the referendum was held. The outcome was quite predictable. Once again, Quebec was isolated. Quebec voted 73 percent against releasing King from his promise, while the rest of Canada voted 80 percent in favour of the release and, thereby, conscription (Conway, 1997: 47).

In the end, King's adroitness—some would say dithering—forestalled the sort of flare-up that had occurred in 1917. Though anti-conscription riots did occur in parts of Quebec, their intensity was less than in the previous war (see Fraser, 1967: 14). Most Quebecers understood King had gone the extra mile in attempting to meet their objections to conscription.

For many French Quebecers, the hanging of Riel, Canada's ongoing British connection, the conscription crises, and the school controversies symbolized their minority status within Confederation. Too often, when conflicts arose, Quebec's views and interests were ignored. By the late 1940s, the idea of a pan-Canadian, French and English Canada had all but retreated from Canada's political map. More than ever, Canada consisted of "two solitudes."

By then, however, the consequences of two world historical events were rapidly pushing the French and English communities together. The first event was the world wars of 1914–1918 and 1939–1945. The second event was the intervening economic depression (see Chapter 7). Both of these events had the consequence of enlarging and centralizing state power, the first in making Canada a giant war factory, the second in creating the liberal welfare state (Rice and Prince, 2000). A further consequence was the emergence from the Second World War (in particular) of a new spirit of nationalism in English-speaking Canada. The stage was thus set for a clash over the nature of Canada and Quebec's place within it. These changes in English-speaking Canada cannot be understood, however, without reference to the profound social, economic, and, ultimately, political changes also occurring inside Quebec.

SOCIAL AND ECONOMIC CHANGE IN QUEBEC, 1867–1960

Quebec's population grew from 1.36 million in 1881 to 2.36 million in 1921, then 5.25 million in 1961. Its percentage of the Canadian population declined from 31.4 percent in 1881 to 26.8 percent in 1921, but rebounded to 28.8 percent by 1961 (see Table 1.1). In part, this decline during the middle period resulted from decreased birth rates. Quebec's birth rates fell from a pre-industrial high of 50 per 1,000 to 41.1 in 1884–1885 to 29.2 during the period 1931–1935 when Quebec was rapidly industrializing (Dickinson and Young, 2003: 202). Birth rates in rural areas remained higher than in urban areas, but high death rates, especially infant deaths, reduced overall population growth. During and after the Second World War, however, birth rates once more rebounded—part of the broader Canadian phenomenon known as the baby boom (Chapter 8)—while life expectancy gradually increased.

The larger reason, however, for Quebec's relative decline in population during this period, compared with the rest of Canada, lay in immigration and emigration. The early 20th century witnessed massive European immigration into Canada, especially the West (see

Chapter 7). At the same time, despite the exhortations of church leaders and politicians, many francophone people left the boundaries of Old Quebec. Fearful of their treatment elsewhere in Canada, but finding themselves unable to survive farm life economically, some were convinced to move into the Shield country north of the St. Lawrence. Thus began Quebec's period of northern expansion. Work in New England's lumber mills, however, proved a far greater attraction. Between 1840 and 1930, perhaps 900,000 Quebecers, along with many francophone people from Nova Scotia, moved (in particular) to the New England states (Cook, 1995: 91; see also Dufour, 1990).

Of course, immigrants also came to Quebec. This was not a new occurrence. The potato famine of the 1840s, for example, saw the arrival in Quebec of large numbers of Irish, many of whom as orphaned children were welcomed into francophone families (Dufour, 1990). Immigration intensified during the period 1911–1915, however, resulting in large and thriving Italian and Jewish communities arising in Montreal (Dickinson and Young, 2003: 206). As in the rest of Canada, immigration declined during the two world wars and the intervening Depression years. After 1945, however, as immigrants streamed into Canada, many again located in Quebec. Indeed, the percentage of immigrants to Canada settling in Quebec increased steadily, from 13.6 percent in 1946 to 23.7 percent in 1951 and 23.6 percent again in 1961 (GRES, 1997: 97). Nonetheless, Quebec remained about 80 percent francophone, while the actual number of anglophones declined and became more confined to the Montreal region.

These demographic changes were accompanied by other social and economic changes. For example, agriculture was still an important element of Quebec's economy in 1891, employing 45.5 percent of Quebec's labour force. Even then, how-ever, Quebec was rapidly industrializing. Quebec's transition from a rural and pre-industrial society to an urban, industrial society intensified in the early 20th century, fuelled by the flow of foreign (mainly American) capital into Canada (see Chapter 7). By 1941, agriculture in Quebec employed only 19.3 percent of the workforce (Dickinson and Young, 2003: 213). As noted, some of the "surplus" workers left Quebec. Many more, however, found employment in manufacturing (based on Quebec's abundant hydro power) and resource extraction (especially timber and mining).

The decline in rural Quebec was matched in both relative and absolute terms by growth in urban Quebec. In 1901, 36.1 percent of Quebec's population lived in urban areas; by 1931, the figure was 63.1 percent (Dickinson and Young, 2003: 203). Montreal was the hub of much of this urban growth, spurred by the presence of the head offices for the Bank of Montreal, Sun Life, the Canadian National Railway, and the Canadian Pacific Railway. Other urban centres, many of them resource towns, sprang up across the province.

Again, however, the interrelated social and economic changes that Quebec experienced after Confederation and up until the end of the Second World War were not particularly unusual. Industrialization, urbanization, and assorted social changes occurred throughout Canada (see Chapter 7). What made Quebec's situation different was that the changes it experienced brought into sharp relief the social, political, and ideological structures that had arisen around the Conquest.

As we have seen, Quebec after 1760 was stratified (among other things) along ethnic lines. Whether an individual was French or English influenced his or her occupational status, class position, chances for social mobility, and even the town and neighbourhood in which he or she lived. Curiously, the arrangement "worked"—if that term can be used—after 1837–1838 precisely because French and English did live in separate worlds.

Industrialization and urbanization disrupted this arrangement, forcing French and English into renewed contact and conflict. For example, industrialization created a (largely) **francophone proletariat**. At work sites, francophone workers found themselves in regular conflict with their anglophone bosses. Class conflict merged with ethnic conflict, creating a dangerous mix that finally exploded at the company town of Asbestos in 1949 (Finkel, 1997: 74). The Asbestos strike became a symbolic rallying point for opponents of the conservative government of Maurice Duplessis (1890–1959) and an economic structure that favoured anglophone-dominated corporations.

Likewise, industrialization, mass communication, and rising levels of literacy also gave rise to new occupations and professional groups. Quebec's new francophone middle class felt thwarted in its aspirations for social and economic advancement (Taylor, 1993: 8–9; Rioux, 1993: 82).

Inevitably, these changes resulted in challenges to the old political order. These challenges came from trade unionists, progressive intellectuals (including some within the Catholic Church), and members of the new middle class and were directed first at replacing Duplessis's Union Nationale government, but the challengers also had broader goals of changing Quebec's role within Confederation.

The challengers were not homogeneous, however. In particular, each possessed a different ideological notion of Quebec's identity and its relation to the rest of Canada.

IDEOLOGY AND IDENTITY

What is ideology? **Ideology** is *the set of assumptions, beliefs, explanations, values,* *and unexamined knowledge through which we come to understand reality* (Marchak, 1988: 1). As we have seen (Chapter 2), the dominant ideology tends to legitimize existing power relations; as Marx (1977a: 236) stated, "The ruling ideas of each age have ever been the ideas of its ruling class."

Throughout the late 20th century, federalists and sovereigntists in Quebec argued strongly about Quebec nationalism and its future (see below). They agreed, however, on one thing: Quebec's past (Couture, 1998: 48), in particular that Quebec had been governed, in the words of Rioux (1993), by an "ideology of conservation"—alternatively "conservative nationalism" or (reflecting the influence of the Catholic Church during this period) "**clerico-nationalism**" (Cook, 1995: 91). After the rebellions of 1837–1838, they argued, Quebec had been in a 100-year "time warp," dominated by the Catholic Church, a bourgeois and anglophone business establishment, and an anti-democratic and authoritarian state, resulting in a reactionary and backward society (Trudeau, 1996).

Conservative nationalism stressed French Quebec's unique cultural heritage. The past and rural life were glorified. Engaging in business or seeking material rewards, by contrast, was denounced. So also were Quebecers warned against leaving their homeland, either for the United States (though many did so) or for Canada's opening West: there, the dragons of certain assimilation waited. Furthermore, French Quebecers were charged with a historic and sacred mission to defend and preserve their culture against the English, the last bastion, moreover, of "true" Catholic France. (It was viewed as providential that Quebec had been saved from the radicalism and anticlericalism that had befallen the mother country after the French Revolution of 1789.) Large families were applauded. Catholic, French-speaking, agricultural, and traditional: These were the idealized traits, federalists and sovereigntists both agreed in the 1950s, that marked Quebec society in the second half of the 19th century and continued largely unchallenged until the end of the Second World War (Rioux, 1993).

There frequently is a kernel of truth in generalizations. The Catholic Church *did* grow more powerful after the failed rebellions, as was reflected in the Ultramontane movement, and continued to exercise considerable influence over Quebec society until the 1950s (Dickinson and Young, 2003). Anglophones *did* dominate Quebec's increasingly capitalist economy after 1880, especially its financial and manufacturing sectors. Quebec's political culture *was* strongly conservative, as represented by the Catholic priest, teacher, and historian Lionel-Adolphe Groulx (1878–1967), whose fierce nationalism also mixed with anti-secularism and, some argue, anti-Semitism. Its political system likewise *did* have anti-democratic and authoritarian aspects. Women, for example, did not get the vote until 1940, civil rights were sometimes abridged, and the state's coercive powers were frequently abused, particularly under the reign of Maurice Duplessis in 1936–1939 and again in 1944–1959 (see Black, 1977), against labour and in defence of private property (Dickinson and Young, 2003: 292–295).

Nonetheless, dominant ideologies rarely go unchallenged. Recently, Couture (1998) has argued that pre-1960s Quebec was never entirely homogeneous. Equally important, he points out that Quebec was not much different from other Canadian provinces of the period. The Ultramontane movement had its counterpart in the Orange movement, which swept Ontario and much of the West (see also Saul, 1997: 32). Into the 1960s, Canada as a whole was socially conservative and highly religious. With the exception of Saskatchewan after 1944 (see Chapter 7), Canadian governments at all levels were business-oriented and, on occasion, authoritarian. Likewise,

the economic and social changes (such as urbanization and industrialization) occurring in Quebec during the 20th century were similar in broad terms to those in the other provinces. In short, while displaying some distinct features, Quebec historically was neither entirely monolithic nor dissimilar from much of the rest of Canada.

In the early 1950s, however, the dominance of conservative ideology in Quebec declined in the face of two other ideological views of Quebec's future.

The first of these ideologies was liberal, federalist, and anti-nationalist. Its leaders were Pierre Trudeau (1919–2000), a lawyer and political economist who rose to political prominence during the Asbestos strike, and Gérard Pelletier (1919–1997), a long-time friend, journalist, and social activist. They founded a radical magazine, *Cité libre*, in 1950 to articulate their vision of Quebec's future in Canada. The magazine denounced the insularity and conservatism of Quebec. Though Catholic, the editors also denounced the power of the Catholic Church. Finally, taking a stance that marked his later adult life, Trudeau also denounced Quebec nationalism—indeed, all forms of nationalism, new and old—as retrograde, a reversion to tribalism. Trudeau's vision of Quebec and Canada was essentially liberal, ostensibly valuing the individual over the collective (but see Couture, 1998). He and Pelletier argued that Quebec had all the powers it needed under the British North America Act. What was needed to address Quebec's rising demands was for increased democracy within the province and greater power in Ottawa (McCall-Newman, 1982; Clarkson and McCall, 1990; Balthazar, 1993).

The second ideological strain challenging conservative Quebec was sovereigntist and nationalist. Quebec's intellectual class, especially historians, provided early impetus for the nationalist cause by reinterpreting the history of Quebec in light of neo-Marxist notions of class and colonial oppression. But other members of the new middle class, such as journalists, broadcasters, and teachers, also were prominent (Rioux, 1993; Cook, 1995). The old Quebec nationalism was cultural rather than political; largely unconcerned with economic development; based on a set of mainly Catholic values; inward looking and defensive; and rejecting of newcomers. By contrast, while the new nationalism shared with the old a belief in the French language and was perhaps even more dedicated to preserving the French fact in North America, it was otherwise opposed, even scornful, of Quebec's traditional culture.

Like the liberal anti-nationalists, the new nationalists favoured modernization and political reform. Unlike the liberals, however, the new nationalists were often stridently anticlerical and highly secular, and their reforms extended into the economy. Most importantly, the new nationalists argued that French culture could survive only if Quebec had the powers of an autonomous state (Balthazar, 1993; Taylor, 1993; Conway, 1997: 52–53). These powers could be exercised within a loose federal arrangement, if not, however, within an independent country.

Embedded in this idea was an important transformation in identity. Prior to the Second World War, Canada's two identities, French-Canadian and English-Canadian, had existed (distantly) side by side. The war, however, fuelled a new sense of nationalism in English-speaking Canada and, by the close of the 1950s, increasing demands for an end to "hyphenated" Canadianism (see Chapter 7). In Quebec, however, these demands and the federal government's increasing encroachment into areas of provincial jurisdiction were viewed as threats. Quebec's long isolation and rejection by the rest of Canada produced finally an identity coincident with the new nationalism. The old nationalism identified with the French language and the Catholic faith; its people were *French-Canadian*. By contrast, the people of the new nationalism were Québécois (Webber, 1994: 49).

Revolutions require not only symbols but ideological justifications and blueprints. Quebec's *Tremblay Report* of 1956 provided both of these. The report became a bible for the Quiet Revolution. In four volumes, it "gave ideological and statistical support to provincial autonomy and to the idea that the Quebec government was the primary defender of a threatened culture" (Dickinson and Young, 2003: 296). In some ways profoundly traditional and nostalgic, the report nonetheless contained two ideas important to debates about Canada and Quebec ever since. First, the report gave voice to a belief already existing in Quebec that Confederation involved a pact between two equal peoples, French and English. Quebec was not "just one" of several provinces. Second, the *Tremblay Report* argued that Quebec was distinct from the other provinces and required continued jurisdictional autonomy in some areas into which the federal government was moving (Cook, 1995: 162).

When Maurice Duplessis died in 1959, the last vestiges of conservative nationalism died with him. The Liberals, led by Jean Lesage (1912–1980), defeated Duplessis's Union Nationale government the next year. Quebec's Quiet Revolution had begun.

CLASHING NATIONALISMS AND QUIET REVOLUTIONS

Lesage's Liberal Party contained elements of both the new liberal and new nationalist factions. In time the marriage would break down. At first, however, the goals of replacing the Union Nationale and modernizing Quebec provided sufficient cement to hold the coalition together.

The Liberals, in their first mandate, moved to bring Quebec's public services (health, education, labour laws, social welfare) up to the level of the other provinces (Conway, 1997). Political changes were also made. The voting age was lowered from 21 to 18, new laws governing election expenses were passed, and patronage and gerrymandering were attacked. Much of English Canada applauded these steps. Two years later, however, Lesage won re-election using the slogan *"Maîtres chez nous"* ("Masters in our own house"). English Canada grew more wary.

In 1962 the Liberals called an election seeking a mandate to nationalize Quebec's private electric companies. The idea was that of René Lévesque (1922–1987), a former journalist and prominent television commentator, now Lesage's minister of natural resources. Like many Québécois, Lévesque believed Quebec's distinctiveness could be protected only if francophone Quebecers had control over the economy, a belief that in time caused him to leave the Liberal Party and head a nationalist party favouring independence.

In the meantime, however, the Liberals created Hydro-Québec, which quickly became a symbol of Quebec nationalism. Other measures followed, such as the creation in 1965 of the Caisse de Dépôt et Placement du Québec, made responsible for Quebec's own pension plan. These actions were popular among Quebec francophones who saw in economic nationalism a means of addressing entrenched inequalities between themselves and the English minority. Quebec's English-dominated business community viewed these actions with alarm, however.

The fears of English-speaking Canadians within Quebec were matched by their counterparts outside the province who were concerned that Quebec nationalism threatened their ideal of "One Canada." Few Canadians were yet travelling across their country; the Trans-Canada Highway was not formally opened until the summer of 1962. Television and radio provided a kind of link, but also reinforced regional and cultural divisions. Indeed, French television in Quebec after 1950 became a chief breeding ground for cultural nationalism (Balthazar, 1993). In consequence, Canadian nationalism exhibited what Rotstein (1978) described as **mapism**, *the tendency of English-speaking Canadians to identify with the shape of Canada as learned in school by looking at the map, but to know nothing about the history or culture of their fellow citizens, especially those in Quebec.* They knew only that Quebec was geographically at Canada's heart, and that Quebec nationalism now seemed to be a dagger pointed at that heart.

For most Quebecers, Canada outside Quebec also remained a mystery; more than a century of parochial education had ensured that. The new nationalists did not harbour any hatred toward English Canada. (This could not be said regarding the dominant anglophone minority within Quebec, especially the business class.) In the main, French Quebecers were simply indifferent to the rest of Canada.

For a few Quebec nationalists, however, the pace of social and political change was too slow. In the early 1960s, the *Front de Libération du Québec* (FLQ) was formed for the sole purpose of taking Quebec out of Canada, by force if necessary. The FLQ and many of its sympathizers drew their revolutionary ideals from broader social currents of the time, in Canada and abroad. While in English Canada, anti-establishment politics focused upon opposition to the U.S., in Quebec the spirit of revolution focused on anglophone symbols and institutions and their supporters. In the revolutionaries' view, Quebec was still a colony. In the blunt words of the nationalist writer Pierre Vallières (1971), francophone Quebecers were "White Niggers." They needed to be liberated.

In 1963, the FLQ began a terrorist campaign directed at symbols of English privilege and power. Banks were robbed, weapons were stolen, bombs exploded. The campaign began with the bombing of the Wolfe monument in Quebec City— what more symbolic target could there be? Over the next seven years the FLQ proceeded to other targets: McGill and Loyola universities; the Westmount district of Montreal; the Eaton's department store and the Montreal Stock Exchange; the RCMP and the Black Watch Regiment; a monument to Queen Victoria and the Queen's Printer. Six lives were lost. Some of the terrorists were caught, tried, convicted, and sentenced (Conway, 1997: 57).

The FLQ's tactics never had strong support in Quebec; indeed, they were denounced. The bombings served a purpose, however, in garnering English-speaking Canada's attention. Thus began English-speaking Canada's education on Quebec and the history of French-English relations.

COMMISSIONS AND THE "THREE WISE MEN"

In the context of growing civil strife in Quebec and rising angst elsewhere, Liberal Prime Minister Lester Pearson (1897–1972) created the Royal Commission on Bilingualism and Biculturalism (Government of Canada, 1963) in 1963. In its preliminary report of 1965 and a final report, encompassing six books, the commission detailed the second-class status of francophones within Quebec and Canada's federal structures. In 1961, for example, unilingual anglophones had the highest average income in Quebec ($6,049), followed by bilingual anglophones ($5,929), bilingual francophones ($4,523), and finally unilingual francophones ($3,107) (Webber, 1994: 45; see also Conway, 1997). Most of Quebec's private sector economy was owned by anglophone Canadians or non-Canadians. Francophones were similarly disadvantaged in the federal civil service,

significantly underrepresented and concentrated in the lower tiers of administration. Both inside and outside Quebec, English was the language of work in the federal service. Francophone hospitals, schools, and universities were inferior to those of anglophones (see also Porter, 1965). In short, the pattern of social stratification in Quebec, set in motion by the Conquest, seemed largely unbroken 200 years later.

Even before the commission's final report, acting on its preliminary recommendations and spirit, the Pearson Liberals took several steps. There was never any intent that all of Canada could or should become a completely bilingual country. At the level of federal institutions, however, an intensive French and English language training program was instituted for civil servants. In keeping with its demands for greater control over internal economic affairs, Quebec was allowed to opt out of the Canada Pension Plan (Webber, 1994). And a new Canadian flag also was created (see Chapter 7), one that broke with Canada's long-standing fealty to Britain (Conway, 1997: 60).

These measures had their critics, both among Quebec nationalists who viewed the commission as obscuring their demands, and some in English-speaking Canada who were unsympathetic to francophone demands for equality. Yet, many English-speaking Canadians also accepted, even embraced, the administrative and linguistic changes.

More problematic was the commission's vision of Canada, specifically, the idea that Confederation involved a partnership of the French and English "nations." Very quickly, some academics, including the eminent historian Donald Creighton, denounced this **two nations theory** (a.k.a., **compact theory**) as revisionist (Creighton, 1970). For them, Canada was not a partnership between the French and the English, but rather a partnership of equal provinces (see Romney, 1999). In Weberian terms, French- and English-speaking Canadians had a very different understanding of the basis of their relationship with the country. The resultant disagreement has continued to frame Canada-Quebec relations and constitutional debates into the present (see Chapter 5).

Jean Marchand (1918–1988) was a prominent member of the Royal Commission on Bilingualism and Biculturalism. Already a well-known labour leader who had fought against the Duplessis regime and worked with Lesage's provincial government, Marchand was approached by Prime Minister Pearson to run for the Liberals. He agreed, but only on condition that his long-time friends Pierre Trudeau and Gérard Pelletier join him. They did, and the three were soon referred to as Quebec's "three wise men." Marchand, Pelletier, and Trudeau believed Quebec's demands for cultural protection could best be met by securing representation within Ottawa. For the Liberal Party, Marchand and his associates also represented the resurrection of an old idea that Canada was the home of both English and French. In English Canada, however, another message was frequently understood: that Quebec's new ministers would stop the nationalist agitation and put Quebec back in its place.

The year 1967 was Canada's centennial. English speaking Canada was optimistic, its cheery enthusiasm captured by Bobby Gimby's song, "Canada." All Canada and much of the world seemed to congregate that summer in Montreal, home of the "Man and His World" exhibition, to celebrate. But France's president, Charles de Gaulle (1890–1970), came to Canada in July on a state visit. Steaming up the St. Lawrence on a French cruiser, he disembarked at Quebec City and proceeded by cavalcade to Montreal. There, overcome by the occasion, speaking from the balcony of city hall, de Gaulle shouted *"Vive le Québec libre!"* The Canadian government was not amused with this break in diplomatic protocol— Quebec and Quebecers did not, in its view, require liberation—and quickly insisted on de Gaulle's exit (see Clarkson and McCall, 1990: 103–104). Nonetheless, for English-speaking Canadians the Quebec "problem" had reared its head once more.

In 1968, Pierre Trudeau succeeded Lester Pearson as leader of the Liberal Party and prime minister. As justice minister in the previous Cabinet, Trudeau had reformed Canada's divorce laws and made liberal amendments to Criminal Code laws on abortion and homosexuality (Clarkson and McCall, 1990: 107). Now, in 1968, Canadians experienced "Trudeaumania" and became familiar for the first time with the word *charisma*, a term coined by Max Weber (1958: 295), meaning *an extraordinary quality of a person, regardless of whether this quality is actual, alleged, or presumed.*

As prime minister, one of Trudeau's first acts was to bring in the policy of official bilingualism. Following in the footsteps of Henri Bourassa, Trudeau held a pan-Canadian vision of the country, one in which French and English were equal from sea to sea. Quebec nationalism, he believed, would wither as francophones came to feel at home in the rest of Canada. Two years later, however, the Canadian state and society faced a serious challenge from those in Quebec who believed Trudeau did not understand their demands and was selling the rest of Canada a false vision.

THE OCTOBER CRISIS AND ITS AFTERMATH

On October 5, 1970, members of the FLQ kidnapped James Cross (1921–), a British trade commissioner. The terrorist cell quickly made seven demands in exchange for Cross's release. The Quebec and Canadian governments rejected all demands at first. They soon relented, however, granting one request: the broadcast and publication of the FLQ's manifesto.

Few Quebecers supported the FLQ's actions. Nonetheless, the manifesto, a broadly Marxist polemic laced with invective and dark humour, drew much applause. In its way, the FLQ touched on real frustrations and angers felt by francophones in the province.

Faced with unexpected public support within Quebec for the FLQ's position, the Quebec government declared on October 10 that no further concessions would be made to the kidnappers. A few hours later, the crisis escalated. Pierre Laporte (1921–1970), Quebec's labour minister, who had only months before nearly been elected provincial Liberal leader, was kidnapped by another FLQ cell acting independently.

René Lévesque, union leaders, and some others demanded negotiations with the FLQ for Cross's and Laporte's lives. Rejecting, however, the notion of a "parallel government," Pierre Trudeau ordered Canadian troops be positioned in Ottawa and the province of Quebec. On October 16, the federal government declared the War Measures Act (WMA). Under this act, all civil rights and liberties in Canada were technically suspended. Those suspected of criminal offences were arrested without charge and held without bail and without trial. The focus was upon Quebec and those suspected of being FLQ supporters, but the Act's application was wider. Under the WMA, 465 Quebec "supporters" were arrested, 403 of whom were released without charge. Of the remainder, 32 were charged but not prosecuted, while 18 were convicted of minor offences (Conway, 1997: 77).

The day after the WMA was declared, Laporte's kidnappers murdered him. The killing intensified feelings of fear and panic, both inside and outside Quebec. Support for the Trudeau government rose, especially in English-speaking Canada.

Feelings were more mixed in Quebec, but many also accepted the presence of tanks and the suspension of civil liberties without question.

Laporte's killers were eventually caught, tried, and convicted using regular police methods. Shortly thereafter, in early December, Cross was located and freed in return for his kidnappers' safe passage to Cuba. Over time, all of Cross's kidnappers voluntarily returned to Canada, where they too were tried, convicted, and sentenced (*Maclean's*, 2000).

Thus, the October Crisis—and the Quiet Revolution with it—came to an end. Today, the crisis and the imposition of the War Measures Act remain controversial (see Gagnon, 2000), though replaced in 1988 by the Emergencies Act. Was invoking the WMA necessary? Or was it an overreaction? What is the best way to protect civil society from threat? When is state coercion justified, and what are its limits?

In the short term, Trudeau's government was praised for its handling of the situation, while the use of violence to achieve sovereignty, never widely supported in Quebec, was thoroughly repudiated. Yet, if invoking the WMA was meant to render Quebecers fearful of pursuing nationalism, it utterly failed. Within a few years, support for Quebec nationalism among francophones was stronger than ever.

CONCLUSION

The story of Quebec in the 20th century is one of sociological change. These changes occurred early in the period, but became more obvious (especially to English-speaking Canada) after 1945. Still largely Catholic and conservative at war's end, Quebec only 25 years later was essentially secular and liberal. Birth rates fell remarkably and divorce rates rose. Likewise, sexual mores and social views changed, with Quebecers becoming more generally liberal in these matters than people elsewhere in North America.

Industrialization, long a fact in Quebec, also continued apace and expanded into the province's north, bringing Quebec society into increasing contact and conflict with its Native population, but economic development also remained uneven. After 1960, social stratification along French-English lines began lessening, and a new francophone bourgeoisie emerged. Rural-urban and gender differences remained, however.

At the same time, these changes were not dissimilar to changes elsewhere in Canadian society during this period. What made the changes occurring in Quebec particularly cogent was that they occurred against the historic backdrop of French-English relations starting with the Conquest. Moreover, Quebec's demands also coincided with and reinforced changes occurring in English-speaking Canada's structure, beliefs, and identity. Sometimes, English-speaking Canada even changed in response to demands it *imagined* French Quebec had made (for example, bilingualism). Throughout the 1960s, Canada and Quebec danced together, each reacting to the other, tailoring their steps, measuring the other's performance. Yet, as the fall of 1970 ended, they were seemingly more separate than ever. Ironically, conflict increased between the French and English groups as the two communities became more functionally integrated and more similar as, to continue the metaphor, their steps became more synchronized. In 1970, no one could be certain how or when the dance would end.

KEY TERMS
charisma
clerico-nationalism
francophone proletariat
ideology
mapism
two nations theory (a.k.a., compact theory)

CRITICAL THINKING QUESTIONS

1. In what ways did English expansion during the 19th and 20th centuries lead to Quebec isolation and a strengthened nationalism in that province?

2. How might structural functionalists and conflict theorists view both differently and similarly the political, economic, cultural, and social changes that occurred in Quebec during the 20th century?

3. Why is symbolism so important in shaping human relations?

4. In what ways do maps help or hinder our ideas about what is real?

5. Does charisma exist within individuals or is it something that their followers "read into" them?

RECOMMENDED READINGS
Conway, John. 1997. *Debts to Pay*. Toronto: James Lorimer & Company.
Written with passion, this book calls upon English-speaking Canada to discover its real history and thereby to understand the legitimate grievances of French-speaking Canada.
Couture, Claude. 1998. *Paddling with the Current: Pierre Elliott Trudeau, Etienne Parent, Liberalism, and Nationalism in Canada*. Edmonton: University of Alberta Press.
This book provides an alternative construction of the career of Pierre Trudeau, liberalism, and nationalism in Canada.
Romney, Paul. 1999. *Getting It Wrong: How Canadians Forgot Their Past and Imperilled Confederation*. Toronto: University of Toronto Press.
This book tells the story of how Confederation came about and holds lessons for Canadians today who seek constitutional reform.

Saul, John Ralston. 1997. *Reflections of a Siamese Twin: Canada at the End of the Twentieth Century.* Toronto: Penguin Books.

Saul's book outlines the complicated relationship that has arisen between Canada's "two solitudes," creating the kind of society Canada has today.

Silver, A.I. 1997. *The French-Canadian Idea of Confederation 1864–1900,* 2 vols. Toronto: University of Toronto Press.

Silver's book examines how French-Canadians understood the bargain struck at Confederation between their community and English-speaking Canada.

RELATED WEBSITES

CBC Digital Archives (October Crisis)
http://archives.cbc.ca/war_conflict/civil_unrest/topics/101-618/
The archive also contains useful footage of the "October Crisis: Civil Liberties Suspended."

CBC Digital Archives (Richard Riot)
http://archives.cbc.ca/sports/hockey/clips/13341
This archive contains numerous video clips of important events in Canadian history, including the Richard riot, shown here.

Manitoba Métis Federation
www.mmf.mb.ca

This non-profit organization was founded in 1967 to give an independent voice to Métis people.

CANADIAN SOCIETY ON VIDEO

The Champions Series, Part One: Unlikely Warriors. 1978. National Film Board of Canada, 57 minutes, 27 seconds. Examines the lives of Pierre Trudeau and René Lévesque from the early 1950s through to 1967, the year Lévesque left the Liberal Party and Trudeau became the federal minister of justice.

The Champions Series, Part Two: Trappings of Power. 1978. National Film Board of Canada, 55 minutes, 44 seconds. Examines the period from 1967 to 1977, during which Pierre Trudeau won three federal elections, the October Crisis occurred, and the Parti Québécois under Rene Levesque came to power.

The Great Resistance. 2008. National Film Board of Canada, 77 minutes, 22 seconds.

In the 1930s, in the throes of the Great Depression, the government relocated more than 80,000 citizens to found a new settlement in the virgin forests of Quebec's Abitibi region. After enduring back-breaking work to clear the land, however, many left, seeking a better life in the city or as labourers for the large corporations that came to exploit the North's valuable resources.

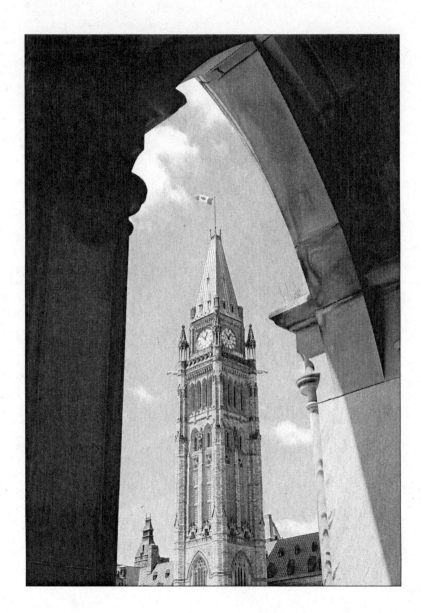

CHAPTER 4

THE CONSTITUTIONAL YEARS

The Magnificent Obsession.
—subtitle to Clarkson and McCall's 1990
examination of the Trudeau years and efforts
at constitutional reform

Quebec constitutes, within Canada, a distinct society.
—the Meech Lake Accord, 1987

The process of constitutional reform in Canada has been discredited.
—Quebec premier Robert Bourassa after the failure of the Meech Lake Accord, 1990

INTRODUCTION

Goa is a former Portuguese colony on India's western coast. In a country predominantly Hindu, Goa's population is largely Catholic, and much of its small population bears decidedly non-Indian names, like de Jesus. In other words, despite being surrounded by a dominant majority population, Goa, like Quebec, retains its distinct cultural identity.

One of this book's authors was travelling in Goa in the fall of 1976 when he heard that the separatist Parti Québécois, led by René Lévesque, had been elected to govern Quebec. Because he was a young, unilingual, and politically unaware westerner, the significance of the event escaped him then. He remembers, however, two francophone Québécois in their late twenties, also visiting Goa, who were elated by news of the PQ's victory and celebrated long into the night.

This chapter examines events in Quebec and the relationship between Canada and Quebec during the 20 years that followed the FLQ Crisis of 1970. As noted in the previous chapter, the FLQ crisis ended the Quiet Revolution in Quebec. Thereafter, nationalist and separatist impulses within the province took a less violent but, in the long term, potentially more lethal turn, alternating between efforts to reform Canada's Constitution and threats of referenda on Quebec's independence. The period ended with the failure of the Meech Lake Accord in 1990 and the referendum defeat of the Charlottetown Accord two years later, events whose aftershocks can still be felt today. The chapter begins with a discussion of sociology and its relationship to political constitutions.

SOCIOLOGY AND THE CANADIAN CONSTITUTION

The events of the 1960s, culminating in the FLQ Crisis in 1970, set off a profound rethinking of Canada's Constitution. Sociology and sociologists played a major role in this rethinking. This should not surprise us. After all, one of sociology's main interests involves **social norms**, *the more or less agreed-upon societal rules and expectations specifying ways of behaving in society.*

Constitutions fall under a specific type of norm: **laws**. The term **constitution** *refers both to the institutions, practices, and principles that define and structure a system of government and to the written document that establishes or articulates such a system* (taken from Hemberger, 1993: 189). A constitution defines a state's sphere of authority, the means of its governance, and claims that may be made in the political realm, broadly defined and contested. More broadly, constitutions represent symbolically a statement of spirit or intent, for example, that "all people are created equal." Beginning with the American and French revolutions, constitutions arose as a means of formally specifying the relationship between individuals and groups and their relationship to the modern state, a chief interest of early sociologists such as Tönnies, Weber, and Durkheim (see Chapter 1). Finally, while some constitutions are more easily changed than others, none are written in such a way that they can be changed at whim. Constitutions are meant to represent a more or less firm statement of a country's legal foundation. By comparison, the American Constitution is relatively "fixed" while the Canadian Constitution is sometimes referred to as a "rolling compromise." Beginning in the 1960s, the compromise picked up speed.

Until 1982, Canada's key constitutional document, of course, was the British North America (BNA) Act (later renamed the Constitution Act, 1867), creating the Dominion of Canada (Dunn, 1995) (see Chapter 6). Long before 1867, however, Canada's existence was structured by a series of constitutional acts: for example, the charter of the Hudson's Bay Company in 1670, the Royal Proclamation of 1763, the Quebec Act of 1774, the Constitution Act of 1791, and the Act of Union of 1841 (see Chapter 2). The BNA Act repealed some elements contained in these previous legal documents. Other commitments, however, remain in effect; for example, current Native land claims date from the Royal Proclamation Act (see Chapter 13).

The BNA Act was repeatedly altered after 1867 to meet changing conditions and demands. A partial list of these changes includes the various acts that incorporated the lands of the Hudson's Bay Company and the North-West Territories into Canada, made Manitoba, British Columbia, Alberta, and Saskatchewan provinces, established the Yukon Territory, and brought Newfoundland into Confederation.

Constitutional reform stalled, however, after the 1920s, even as the need for it became greater. The Statute of Westminster in 1931 declared Canada (along with Australia, New Zealand, and South Africa) sovereign and equal to Britain. Canada, however, declined at that time to take control over the Constitution because the federal and provincial governments could not agree on how the Constitution would be amended in future.

Why was the issue of an amending formula problematic? It was problematic because it dealt with issues of power between levels of government and between government and individual citizens. For example, would the federal government be able constitutionally to make changes unilaterally? Or would provincial consent for constitutional changes be required? If so, how many provinces and would all provinces, large and small, be equal? If not provinces, would Canadian citizens have the ultimate say over constitutional changes through, for example, a Canada-wide referendum? How would the rights of smaller provinces and, in the case of Quebec, minorities be protected against the majority provinces or population? Would some elements of the Constitution be more easily changed than other elements? These were only some of the constitutional questions facing Canadian politicians after 1931. With no clear answers in sight, the Constitution remained "housed" in Britain, even as Canada symbolically distanced itself from Britain in other ways. (In 1950, for example, the British Privy Council ceased to be Canada's Supreme Court.)

Constitutional questions would not go away, however. Two issues with constitutional implications dominated federal-provincial relations in Canada during the 1950s. The first was the ongoing search for an amending formula. The second was fiscal relations between the two levels of government (Webber, 1994: 93), the latter a by-product of the federal government's control of revenues and the expansion of welfare state programs after 1945 (see Chapter 7). With the Quiet Revolution of the 1960s, a third issue was added to the mix: Quebec's historical relation to the rest of Canada. Was Canada a confederation of 10 equal provinces, or was it a bargain between two nations, French and English (Chapter 3)?

The events of the Quiet Revolution, culminating in the October Crisis of 1970, made obvious the necessity of resolving these issues. Quebec, however, was not the sole impetus for demands for constitutional change. In particular, the western provinces in the 1970s also demanded constitutional changes in two areas: first, "control over the taxing and marketing of natural resources" and, second, "reform of federal institutions, especially the Senate" (Webber, 1994: 103) (see chapters 8 and 9). Quebec and many of Canada's "hinterland" provinces demanded *both* a greater devolution of federal powers and, concomitantly, more inclusion at the centre of federal decision making.

The Trudeau government's interpretation of Canada's "problem" was quite different. Among developed countries, Canada was significantly decentralized already. The problem was not an excess of power at the centre, but too much power in the regions. Giving in to Quebec's nationalist demands would only encourage more demands. Already other provinces were piggybacking on Quebec's demands, threatening further weakening of the Canadian state. The solution to Canada's problems, in Trudeau's eyes, lay in constitutional reforms that would bring Quebecers and Quebec into the "Canadian nation" (see Balthazar, 1997).

By 1971, both the federal and provincial governments were seeking constitutional reform. At a federal-provincial meeting held in Victoria, the two levels of government appeared at last to have reached an accord on some principles for renewing Confederation. Quebec Premier Robert Bourassa (1933–1996) faced strong opposition from nationalists, unionists, business groups, and the media, however, upon his return to Quebec. These opponents feared the agreement would enhance federal authority while reducing Quebec to the status of just another province. Constitutional reform thus was put on hold. In the absence of a constitutional solution to Quebec's demands, new coalitions of social and political forces soon arose in Quebec, proffering different solutions to the Quebec-Canada "problem."

THE ELECTION OF THE PARTI QUÉBÉCOIS

On November 15, 1976, René Lévesque's Parti Québécois became Quebec's governing party, taking 71 of 110 seats and 42 percent of the popular vote (Conway, 1997: 86). The election was a startling turnaround for the PQ, which in 1973 had won only six seats (though they won 30 percent of the vote) in losing to Bourassa's Liberals. Much of English Canada panicked. The business community was particularly stunned, fearing equally the PQ's avowed separatism—Levesque promised to hold a referendum on sovereignty sometime during his party's electoral mandate—and social democratic platform. What had happened?

In part, the PQ's election was the Liberal government's rejection. Bourassa's personal image had never fully recuperated from his handling of the FLQ crisis of 1970, when he was widely seen by francophone Quebecers as weak and ineffectual in defending their interests. More broadly, however, the PQ's election reflected a further evolution in Quebec society itself and in Quebec nationalism. By the 1970s, the economic changes undertaken during the Quiet Revolution were bearing fruit. New middle and entrepreneurial classes were emerging, dominated by francophone Quebecers. Labour unions, long suppressed in Quebec, were also growing in power, and labour militancy was on the rise, exemplified in an extreme manner by workers' intentional destruction of the James Bay hydroelectric site in 1974. Quebec culture and arts, no longer insular or defensive, were also thriving. The PQ's positive message of creating a more autonomous, social democratic, and modern society appealed to a wide cross-section of francophones within the blue- and white-collar, intellectual, and cultural communities.

Like all Quebec political parties, going back to the previous century, the PQ was nationalist, but the PQ's nationalism was fundamentally different from that of previous Quebec governments. First, reflecting changes among Quebecers themselves, the PQ's nationalism was more positive and future-oriented than in the past (Dufour, 1990; Thompson, 1995). Second, where Quebec governments in the past had defended the French "nation"—albeit with its obvious homeland in Quebec, still within Canada—the PQ rejected both the notion of allegiance to Canada and to a broader pan-Canadian French nation (Webber, 1994: 101). For the PQ and many of its followers, there was only a Québécois nation, its interests represented by Quebec's quasi-state, on the verge of becoming a sovereign country. All that was needed to make Quebec sovereign was a decision by its people to assert their rights of self-determination.

Third, where the Union Nationale had been authoritarian and conservative, and the Liberals classically liberal, the PQ was unabashedly democratic socialist as reflected in several progressive policies enacted during its first term in office. Labour laws were amended, outlawing strikebreaking and adopting the Rand formula (see Chapter 8) for deducting union dues. Reflecting the strength of emergent feminism within the party, the rights of women also were extended (see Dickinson and Young, 2003). Finally, Quebec's minimum wage became the highest in Canada, and the sales tax was removed on shoes, clothing, and furniture (Conway, 1997: 92). The PQ's most important moves, however, were in defence of the French language.

THE LANGUAGE OF QUEBEC NATIONALISM

Language is perhaps the chief element of national identity as it represents continuity with the past and future (see Chapter 5). It is also central to much sociological thought. From a symbolic interaction perspective, for example, language is the chief vehicle for understanding and expressing a group's history, beliefs, and values, but from a post-structural perspective, language and its putative efforts at defining a precise "meaning" is tied up with issues of power. Likewise, while structural-functionalists view language as a means of facilitating mutual exchanges, conflict theorists view it as a contested terrain between the dominant culture and minority groups.

Until the Constitution Act of 1982, only the BNA Act of 1867 (later renamed the Constitution Act of 1867) dealt constitutionally with language, and then only in Section 133 and in a limited context. Section 133 states that either French or English can be used in the legislatures of Canada and Quebec and courts under their authority, and that records and journals of both Parliament and the Quebec legislature must be bilingual. Section 23 of the Manitoba Act of 1870 replicated the Quebec provisions of the BNA Act (Dunn, 1995: 340–342), as did arrangements in the North-West Territories in 1874 (Cook, 1995: 153).

The cultural wars of the 1890s and early 20th century saw English majorities abuse French language protections, however. Meanwhile, the majority French in Quebec found their social and cultural status gradually declining against the minority and unilingual anglophone population. In effect, where constitutional bilingualism existed, it provided greater protection for English speakers, minority or otherwise, than it did French speakers.

By the 1960s, survival of the French language and culture in Quebec was further threatened by a combination of declining birth rates and rapidly increasing immigration into the province (Dickinson and Young, 2003; Fournier et al., 1997). Many of the new arrivals spoke neither French nor English. Surrounded by a North American sea of English, however, and experiencing the economic and social benefits of English within the province, most immigrants were choosing to speak English. Moreover, schools were pressed into the debate as immigrants demanded their children receive education in English. For many francophones, their ancestral homeland and culture were once more under siege. Official bilingualism, enacted in 1969, did not address these fears. Indeed, official bilingualism was the answer to a question most francophone Quebecers had not asked, satisfying only Canadian nationalists outside the province. In 1968, violence broke out in Montreal between francophone nationalists and immigrant Italians over language instruction in schools (Dickinson and Young, 2003: 323–324; Thompson, 1995; Fournier et al., 1997).

The Bourassa government in 1974 attempted to deal with the issue through the Official Languages Act (Bill 22). Bill 22 made French Quebec's official language in certain key areas, such as business, labour, education, some professions, and public administration (Conway, 1997: 88). It did not demand the exclusive use of French, however. Education matters, for example, were left largely untouched, with immigrant parents still able to enroll their children in English-language schools.

After its election, the Parti Québécois moved quickly to remove any ambiguity concerning the status of French in Quebec. The Charter of the French Language of 1977 (Bill 101) made French the official state language and the "normal language of work, education, communications, and business." Bill 101 also restricted English instruction to those whose parents were educated in English in Quebec. (An exception was granted to Aboriginal peoples, especially in the case of Aboriginal languages.) Bill 101 further placed limits on bilingual signs and restricted the use of English in business and government (see Fournier et al., 1997: 242–259; Dickinson and Young, 2003: 324; Webber, 1994: 100–101).

Anglophones within Quebec, many of whom had deep ancestral roots, felt themselves under attack. Their anger found support outside Quebec among English-speaking Canadians who could not understand the Quebec government's moves to make the province predominantly French at a time when they were (grudgingly) accepting bilingualism. Anger outside Quebec was aided and abetted by some English-Canadian politicians pandering to anti-French, anti-Quebec sentiment in search of cheap votes.

Supporters of Bill 101 pointed out, however, that its provisions dealt solely with Quebec's public and symbolic realms, not with cultural institutions (e.g., McGill University) or private interactions (Webber, 1994: 101). They further pointed out the failure of governments elsewhere to protect and promote the French language (see Conway, 1997: 96–97). However, few in English-speaking Canada listened to such arguments. Following the passage of Bill 101, Sun Life announced it was moving its headquarters from Montreal to Toronto. Other businesses soon followed. Many young anglophone Quebecers also left the province during this period (Morton, 1997).

By 1979, the Parti Québécois was entering the bottom half of its electoral mandate. It had been elected on a promise to hold a referendum on sovereignty that would make the Quebec state the political embodiment of that expression. Now time was running out to fulfill the promise. The stage was set for the 1980 referendum and one of the most compelling political rivalries of the late 20th century.

A STUDY IN PERSONAL AGENCY: THE 1980 REFERENDUM

One of sociology's ongoing central debates involves the relationship between individual behaviour and the constraints and imperatives of social structure. Do individuals really make a difference, or are we merely creations of our time and place? In a famous passage, Marx (1977b: 300) once wrote that people "make their own history, but they do not make it just as they please, they do not make it under circumstances chosen by themselves, but under circumstances directly encountered, given, and transmitted from the past." The American sociologist C. Wright Mills (1961: 6) viewed agency and structure as a meeting place for what he termed the **sociological imagination**, *the ability "to grasp history and biography and the relations of the two within society."* From this perspective, Pierre Trudeau and René Lévesque can be seen as products of pre-war 1939 Quebec society and the political and ideological struggles of their time.[1] Yet each also influenced the shape and manner of those struggles (Cook, 1995: 138).

Trudeau and Lévesque are often viewed as opposites: Trudeau the reasoned intellectual and committed federalist, Levesque the passionate "man of action" and Quebec nationalist. Certainly, their public styles were at odds (Clarkson and McCall, 1990: 198–200), yet they were both children of the post-First World War French-Canadian bourgeoisie, had fought to end the Duplessis regime, and were social liberals dedicated to modernizing Quebec. Both believed in a "large role for the state in public affairs" (Chodos and Hamovitch, 1991: 195). Moreover, each in his way represented a form of Quebec nationalism (see Dufour, 1990: 81), Trudeau as passionately as Lévesque, Lévesque in as calculated a manner as Trudeau. In their time, each elicited mixed public responses. Loved by francophone Quebecers, loathed by their anglophone counterparts, Lévesque was at the same time both respected and feared in English-speaking Canada. For his part, Trudeau likewise was loathed and hated, admired and respected, often by the same people. (The late poet Irving Layton once wrote: "In Pierre Trudeau, Canada has at last produced a political leader worthy of assassination.") Yet Lévesque's death in 1987 resulted in a profound outpouring of grief in Quebec (Conway, 1997: 126), while Trudeau's death in September 2000 was mourned by much of Canada, his funeral perhaps the largest attended and watched in Canadian history (*Maclean's*, 2000).

In 1979, Trudeau and Lévesque's visions of Quebec's relationship to Canada were on a collision course. Trudeau believed in a strong Quebec, but as a province among other provinces, within a bilingual Canada. As already noted, Trudeau held a pan-Canadian vision of a bilingual Canada, a vision with deep roots in Quebec (Chapter 3), but his idea of a strong central state and constitutionally equal provinces was also very European, as well as American (see Dufour, 1990; Balthazar, 1997).

For many Quebecers, this vision of Canada was at odds with the historic reality of Quebec's relationship with the rest of Canada, going back at least to the Quebec Act of 1774. Perhaps worse, Trudeau's vision created a kind of straitjacket for constitutional change (Dufour, 1990). Many francophones supported Lévesque's vision of a strong Quebec with unique powers within a decentralized Canadian federation. By 1979, a sizable number of Quebecers believed the only option, if their nation could not be protected within Canada, was Quebec independence.

Lévesque's vision of the Canadian federation was neither radical nor recent. Debates about how centralized or decentralized Canada should be, or about jurisdictional responsibilities, had gone on since before Confederation and were a key aspect of discussion at Charlottetown and Quebec leading up to 1867 (Moore, 1997; Romney, 1999) (Chapter 6). Beginning with the Depression and the Second World War, however, Ottawa's role had increased in Quebec and Canada at large (Balthazar, 1997; Thompson, 1995). In the wake of Quebec's separatist threat, and faced with a stagnating economy in 1970s, the Trudeau Liberal government attempted to reassert federal authority both politically and economically. These actions elicited hostility from Quebec, as well as other provinces, especially in the West (see Chapter 8).

In this context of renewed constitutional conflict, the federal government created the Task Force on Canadian Unity (Government of Canada, 1979). The Task Force's report was tabled in early 1979 and called for a more decentralized and flexible federation, including the replacement of the Canadian Senate by a House of the Provinces that would bring the provinces and regions into the national decision-making process. The Trudeau government immediately dismissed the report, however. Faced with increasing economic problems of rising unemployment and a skyrocketing debt, the Trudeau Liberals feared that meeting Quebec's demands would result in similar demands from the other provinces (see Clarkson and McCall, 1990; Webber, 1994). Decentralization would spur on centrifugal forces that would further delegitimize and weaken the Canadian state. The Trudeau government's rejection of the Task Force's recommendations set the stage for further constitutional confrontations.

The Ottawa-Quebec, Trudeau-Lévesque showdown was briefly postponed by the Liberal Party's defeat in the 1979 federal election by the Progressive Conservatives, led by Joseph Clark (1939–). A few months later, however, Clark's minority government was defeated and the Liberals, led by a rejuvenated Trudeau, returned to office in the subsequent election (see appendices 1 and 2). In the meantime, Lévesque's government had called for a sovereignty referendum to be held on May 20, 1980.

The PQ worded the referendum question strategically to embrace the twin notions of increased sovereignty with which to defend and assert Quebec's nationhood and, at the same time, a continuing "association" with Canada, thus mitigating the economic, political, and social uncertainties of independence. The question also seemed to put off the hard step of actual independence. After all, the government was asking only for a "mandate to negotiate," while still giving separation a push (see Conway, 1997: 93).

The debates and speeches leading up to the referendum vote were impassioned, occasionally nasty. Families were divided, friendships dissipated (Chodos and Hamovitch, 1991: 193). In the end, 60 percent of Quebecers voted No in the referendum. Why did the first Quebec referendum result turn out as it did?

In part, for older francophone Quebecers, the question represented a kind of "Sophie's choice" between two heritages, Canada and Quebec, and, for that matter, between two respected "sons," Trudeau and Lévesque. Many Quebecers in general also feared the economic consequences of sovereignty, a fear magnified by the No side throughout the campaign. But the reasons for the referendum's outcome also were reflected in the demographics of the voters. Quebec's anglophones and allophones, making up roughly 20 percent of the population, voted nearly en masse for the No side, meaning that francophone voters were split 50/50. In short, half of Quebec's large francophone population had publicly voiced their displeasure with their place in Canada's constitutional arrangements. Moreover, Yes supporters could take hope from the fact that the young and the educated among francophones had voted overwhelmingly in favour of sovereignty (Conway, 1997: 105). The future seemed theirs to grasp.

For the moment, however, the referendum outcome left Yes supporters with a sense of bitterness and gloom, feelings of "collective trauma," and a mood of "political exhaustion" (Chodos and Hamovitch, 1991: 107). For *No* supporters, the predominant feeling was one of relief (Conway, 1997). They understood too well that, in the words of Balthazar (1993), Quebecers had said *no* to sovereignty but had not said *yes* to Canada.

In the closing days of the referendum campaign, Trudeau repeated promises that if the *No* side won, he would work to revitalize Confederation (Clarkson and McCall, 1991: 236–239; Conway, 1997). The vote was not likely swayed by these promises, vague in any case. The referendum was fought "on the ground" by individuals and groups on both sides of the debate. Nonetheless, Trudeau's pledge, repeated the day after the referendum, set the stage for the most substantial revision of Canada's Constitution since 1867.

THE 1982 CANADIAN CONSTITUTION

Trudeau's statements before and immediately after the referendum were not clear, occasionally suggesting changes to federal institutions and a redistribution of powers. His only certain statement was that the patriated Constitution must contain a Charter of Rights and Freedoms. Such a charter had long been one of Trudeau's dreams. In February 1968, before announcing his run at the Liberal leadership, he had tabled a white paper in the House of Commons entitled "A Canadian Charter of Human Rights." Now, more than ever, he viewed the proposed charter as a means of ensuring the individual equality of all Canadians, especially against the "collective assaults of Quebec nationalism" (Conway, 1997: 108).

By long-standing tradition, however, Quebec held a veto over constitutional changes. Quebec did not oppose per se the constitutional entrenchment of individual rights; after all, Quebec had passed its own Charter of Human Rights

and Freedoms in 1975 (see Fournier et al., 1997: 260–267). Quebec nationalists, however, feared Trudeau's Charter could be used against Quebec's national interests, for example, in attacking Quebec's language laws.

Quebec's possible veto was not the Trudeau government's only problem. Many Conservative premiers also feared the Charter's application, believing that judicial activism would replace legislative supremacy. Several provinces also wanted changes in other areas. The western provinces wanted institutional reforms, notably dealing with the Senate. They also wanted clarification over provincial control over resources.

Finally, new actors also were appearing on the scene. Aboriginal Canadians, women's groups, and other social organizations also wanted input into constitutional changes.

In September 1980, the premiers and the federal government announced they had failed to agree on an amending formula. Not deterred, however, Trudeau announced his government's intention to proceed with unilaterally patriating the Constitution. A joint Commons-Senate committee held hearings throughout November and December on the proposed Charter of Rights and Freedoms.

In September 1981, however, Canada's Supreme Court ruled that, while the federal government could unilaterally patriate the Constitution, doing so "offended the federal spirit" (*Maclean's*, 2000; Clarkson and McCall, 1991). It was a strong judicial rebuke to Trudeau's plans. Thus, the federal government and provinces returned to talks in the fall of 1981.

As talks began that November, only the provinces of Ontario and New Brunswick supported the federal plans. The other premiers, known as the "gang of eight," posed a seemingly solid front, but the Trudeau government held a winning card. The public at large liked the idea of the Charter and wanted Canada's

Constitution "brought home." In the negotiations that followed, the alliance of provincial premiers slowly began to crack. Equally important, Lévesque had agreed in the course of negotiations to give up Quebec's traditional constitutional veto. When the final agreement was reached on the Constitution, Levesque stood alone, Quebec—in the eyes of nationalists—defenceless (Clarkson and McCall, 1991; Conway, 1997).

The new Canadian Constitution, proclaimed on April 17, 1982, has six parts (Government of Canada, 1982; Webber, 1994, Dunn, 1995). Part One deals with the Canadian Charter of Rights and Freedoms. These rights and freedoms include the fundamental freedoms of conscience, religion, thought, belief, opinion, expression, peaceful assembly, and association, as well as democratic, mobility, legal, equality, and language rights. Part One makes French and English the official languages of Canada. It further designates New Brunswick Canada's only officially bilingual province. The Charter of Rights and Freedoms, however, also includes a "notwithstanding" clause that allows provinces to opt out of a provision if they choose.

Part Two of the Constitution Act, 1982, recognizes Aboriginal rights, including those existing by way of land claims, and formalized the holding of conferences between first ministers and Aboriginal peoples (Chapter 12). Part Three commits governments to promoting equal opportunities for all Canadians, reducing regional disparities, and providing essential public services. Part Four commits the government to holding two future constitutional conferences on Aboriginal peoples and the representatives of Yukon and the Northwest Territories, since held. Part Five sets out a procedure for future amendments to the Constitution. Amendments may henceforth be done with the agreement of Parliament and seven provinces totalling 50 percent of the population. Part Six amends the British North America Act of 1867, renaming it the Constitution Act of 1867.

By and large, English-speaking Canadians seemed happy with the new Constitution. A Gallup poll in May 1982 found that 57 percent of Canadians viewed it positively, ranging from a high of 65 percent in Ontario to a low of 49 percent in Quebec, the latter figure skewed by overwhelming anglophone support in that province for the new act. The political elite outside Quebec were also generally pleased. The new Constitution clarified provincial powers over natural resources, a key sticking point for provinces such as Alberta. The Charter's application had been limited by the insertion, demanded by some western premiers of the "notwithstanding clause."

The PQ government and francophone nationalists in Quebec were embittered, however. For them, the promises of constitutional renewal had been hollow. Ottawa and the rest of the provinces had gotten what they wanted. What had Quebec gotten? Quebec had been "humiliated," "betrayed," "stabbed in the back." Quebec had lost its traditional veto, and now was constitutionally defenceless against Canada's anglophone majority. The Charter of Rights and Freedoms, it was feared, could and would be used to advance anglophone rights and attack French language laws. Thus, the Constitution Act of 1982, meant to heal the rifts of past years, became yet another source of Quebec grievances. Lévesque's government refused to put Quebec's signature on the Constitution and did not participate in the ceremonies marking the occasion.

Whether the PQ would ever have signed a constitutional agreement is a moot point. Trudeau, the provincial leaders, and most Canadians outside Quebec doubted that a government dedicated to separatism would ever have signed. Yet, the referendum defeat had left the PQ with few options and Lévesque himself was viewed as a "soft" separatist.

As for the PQ, though re-elected in 1981, the period after 1982 saw the party's fortunes decline. Beset by a faltering economy, the PQ floundered, at odds with its union supporters, slowly withdrawing from its social-democratic ideals. Lévesque himself, his health diminished, seemed increasingly erratic. Age, disappointment, humiliation, and the shock of discovering just prior to the First Ministers meeting in 1981 that his chief adviser and colleague, Claude Morin, had long been an RCMP adviser finally took their toll (Conway, 1997: 116).

By 1984, Lévesque seemed to have abandoned his commitment to either social democracy or sovereignty. Lévesque's old nemesis, Trudeau, had retired, replaced as Liberal leader by a former finance minister, John Turner (1929–). The Tories, meanwhile, also had a new leader, Brian Mulroney (1939–), a bilingual Quebecer and lawyer with strong ties to American business. When Mulroney promised Quebecers a deal that would allow them to sign the Constitution "with dignity," Lévesque and Quebec nationalists as a whole threw their support behind the Tories.

QUEBEC, MULRONEY, AND THE MEECH LAKE ACCORD

The Mulroney Tories in 1984 routed the widely discredited Liberals, taking 211 (of 282) seats, 58 (of a possible 75) seats in Quebec (see appendices 1 and 2). It was the largest number of seats ever won by a federal party, reflecting the broad sweep of Mulroney's electoral coalition, which featured at its core western Canadian conservatives, pro-business advocates of free trade, and Quebec nationalists.

No sooner was the election over than Mulroney moved to make good his promise to Quebecers on constitutional reform. By the spring of 1987, informal discussions had proved sufficiently positive that a federal-provincial meeting was held at Meech Lake, a resort a few miles outside Ottawa. Much to everyone's surprise, that meeting ended in a formal agreement signed by the federal government and all the premiers. Five elements made up the Meech Lake Accord's proposed amendments to the Canadian Constitution (Balthazar, 1997: 54). These elements were:

- restoring and enshrining in the Constitution Quebec's historical veto

- enshrining the convention that Quebec holds three of nine appointments to the Supreme Court

- limits on federal spending in provincial jurisdictions

- increased powers over immigration

- recognition of Quebec as a **distinct society**

Signing the Meech Lake Accord did not immediately change the Constitution, however. Both Mulroney and the premiers were required to take the Accord back to the people, in the form of passage through their respective legislatures. The time frame for doing so was three years from the date when any one legislature passed the Accord, failure by any legislature (federal or provincial) to do so resulting in the Accord's rejection. Quebec passed the Accord quickly. The clock hence began ticking on its acceptance by the various levels of government.

Opposition to the Meech Lake Accord was slow in mobilizing, in part because the impact of constitutional changes is not always apparent and such documents are far from easy or enjoyable reading. Slowly over the next few years, however, opposition mounted. Three years after its signing, the

Accord collapsed, dividing Canada more than any time since the FLQ crisis. At the extremes, anti-French bigots in English-speaking Canada attacked the Accord as Ottawa's "sellout" to Quebec, while nationalists in Quebec condemned the agreement as the Bourassa government's "sellout" of the French historical "fact." Lit by well-televised burnings of the Quebec flag in Ontario and the Canadian flag in Quebec, passions flamed brightly throughout the fall of 1989 and spring of 1990.

Opposition to the Accord was quite diverse and even, at times, contradictory, making defence of the Accord doubly difficult. In general, however, opposition centred on five main points (see Cohen, 1990; Smith et al., 1991; Webber, 1994). First, the Accord came under attack for "how" it was created, a process viewed by an increasingly aware, sophisticated, and less deferential public (Nevitte, 1996; Adams, 1998) as elitist. Second, federalists, led by Pierre Trudeau, denounced the Accord as dangerously decentralizing, threatening Canada's further balkanization. Third, opponents argued the Accord's granting of a veto to Quebec would prevent further constitutional reform, for example, of the Senate, or to grant eventual provincial status to the northern territories. A fourth complaint was lodged against what the Accord did not contain. For example, minority groups, particularly Aboriginals and women, complained that the Accord neglected their concerns and further entrenched inequalities.

The fifth and most politically important argument against the Meech Lake Accord, however, revolved around its distinct society clause. Why was the notion of Quebec as a distinct society so controversial in 1990?

IS QUEBEC A "DISTINCT SOCIETY"?

At least on the surface, few could seriously argue that culturally, Quebec is a province comme les autres. This is widely acknowl-edged not only in Quebec, but outside as well, especially among sociologists (see Box 4.1). Two measures of culture, language, and religion, support this point.

Box 4.1
Quebec Sociology and Quebec Society

Marcel Fournier argues that Quebec sociology developed over three particular periods: (1) a pioneering stage before 1939, when Quebec scholars focused on the province's ethnic particularity, often as a handicap or historicized artifact; (2) an institutional period between 1940 and 1969 when academic scholars, including many from the United States, examined the province's transition (according to a modernization theory) from a traditional to a modern society; and (3) the nationalization period of Quebec sociology, beginning in 1970 and continuing today, during which descriptions of Quebec as a "distinct society" or even sociological nation became de rigueur. His central argument is that sociological studies over the decades have made "significant contributions to the formation of national identity," attributing such characteristics as race, ethnic, group, society, and nation.

What contributions might sociology make to your community?

Source: Marcel Fournier, "Quebec sociology and Quebec society: The construction of a collective identity," Canadian Journal of Sociology 26(3) (2001): 333–347.

Linguistically, Quebec is the only domain in Canada and in North America in which the French language dominates, although New Brunswick is Canada's only officially bilingual province (see Table 4.1 below). In 2006, French was the primary language of nearly 80 percent of Quebecers, but of only 3.9 percent of people outside Quebec, a decline from 4.7 percent in 1991. Indeed, the use of French is down in every individual province since 1999, though rising slightly in the Yukon and remaining static in the Northwest

Territories. On the other side, English was the primary language of only 7.7 percent of Quebecers in 2006, down from 8.8 percent in 1991, but was the primary language outside of Quebec for nearly 73 percent of Canadians. In this sense, terming Canada a "bilingual country" is misleading. Canada is marked at the federal level by **institutional bilingualism**. At the level of everyday usage, however, **territorial bilingualism** predominates, much as it does in Belgium or Switzerland (Dunn, 1995: 368–369). For francophones inside and outside Quebec, the general pattern of decline reinforces fears of assimilation and suggests their worsening position within Confederation. If language remains a significant marker of cultural difference, religion historically has also played such a role. As indicated in Table 4.2, nearly 44 percent of Canadians in 2001 identified themselves as Catholic. As with the French language, however, this figure is misleading. The largest majority of Catholic identifiers are located within Quebec, with nearly 84 percent of people describing themselves, at least nominally, as Catholic. By contrast, many people outside Quebec define themselves as Protestant, though there has been a steady decline in religious identification generally and other religions have also made gains.

Table 4.1
Population with English, French, or English and French Mother Tongue, Canada, Provinces, and Territories, and Canada Less Quebec, 1991 and 2006 (in thousands and percent)

	1991						2006					
	English	%	French	%	Both	%	English	%	French	%	Both	%
Canada	16 169.9	59.9	6 502.9	24.1	91.9	.3	17 882.8	57.2	6 817.7	21.8	98.6	.3
Newfoundland	555.6	99.0	2.7	.5	.2	.1	488.4	97.6	1.9	.4	.3	.1
Prince Edward Island	120.6	94.1	5.6	4.4	.3	.2	125.3	93.3	5.3	4.0	.5	.4
Nova Scotia	830.1	93.2	36.6	4.1	1.7	.2	832.1	92.1	32.5	3.6	2.1	.2
New Brunswick	460.5	64.3	241.6	33.7	4.2	.6	463.2	64.4	233.0	32.4	4.5	.6
Quebec	599.1	8.8	5 556.1	81.6	39.5	.6	575.6	7.7	5 877.7	79.0	43.3	.6
Ontario	7 380.4	74.0	485.4	4.9	31.4	.3	8 230.7	68.4	488.8	4.1	32.7	.3
Manitoba	784.2	72.7	49.1	4.6	3.0	.3	838.4	74.0	44.0	3.9	2.6	.2
Saskatchewan	807.1	82.7	20.9	2.1	1.5	.2	811.7	85.1	16.1	1.7	1.1	.1
Alberta	2 031.1	80.6	53.7	2.1	5.4	.2	2 576.7	79.1	61.2	1.9	5.4	.2
British Columbia	2 545.5	78.4	48.8	1.5	4.6	.1	2 875.8	70.6	54.7	1.3	5.9	.1
Yukon	24.4	88.3	.9	3.1	.1	.2	25.7	84.9	1.1	3.7	.1	.4
Northwest Territories	31.1	54.2	1.4	2.4	.1	.2	31.5	76.8	1.0	2.4	—	.1
Nunavut*	—	—	—	—	—	—	7.8	26.5	.4	1.3	—	.1
Canada less Quebec	15 570.7	77.1	946.8	4.7	52.4	—	17 307.2	72.7	940.0	3.9	55.3	.2

Note: Figures for Nunavut for 1991 are included in Northwest Territories.
Sources: Adapted from the Statistics Canada publication, "Mother Tongue—20% sample data," The Nation, Catalogue no. 93-333, 1992, Table 1, pp. 10–11; and from "Population by mother tongue, by province and territory (2006 Census)," the Statistics Canada website http://www40.statcan.gc.ca/l01/cst01/demo11a-eng.htm. Last modified December 11, 2007. Downloaded September 15, 2008.

Clearly, however, Quebec is distinct in terms of both language and religion from the rest of Canada. Moreover, this distinctiveness is historically and constitutionally grounded. (Remember, for example, that the Quebec Act of 1774 granted Quebec control over language and religion, and a distinctive legal system.)

Most English-speaking Canadians, inside and outside Quebec, acknowledge that the province of Quebec is distinct. Some even embrace Quebec's difference as a corner of their identity. So why did the notion of "distinct society" lead to the failure of the Meech Lake Accord in 1990 and threaten Canada's survival?

Much of the furor revolved around the vagueness of society as a concept (Cook, 1995), previously discussed (Chapter 1). For example, does the phrase mean that Quebec is distinct? Or does it refer to the francophone community within Quebec?

Opponents, like Pierre Trudeau, and the newly created Reform Party, led by Preston Manning (1942–), successfully argued that the Meech Lake Accord's "distinct society" clause went against the notion of equality of the provinces, granting Quebec powers or claims to a status not held by others (Denis, 1993; Harrison, 1995). They further argued that "distinct society" status implied something greater than mere difference, that it could be used later on by Quebec governments to leverage further demands for nationhood and, perhaps, separate statehood.

Table 4.2
Population by Religion, Canada, Provinces, and Territories, and Canada less Quebec, 2001 (in percent)

Affiliation	Catholic(1)	Protestant(2)	Christian Orthodox	Other Christian	Muslim	Jewish	Other Religions(3)	No
Canada	43.6	29.2	1.6	2.6	2.0	1.1	3.3	16.5
Newfoundland/ Labrador	36.9	59.7	—	.5	—	—	.2	2.5
Prince Edward Island	47.4	42.8	.2	2.4	.1	—	.2	6.7
Nova Scotia	36.6	48.8	.4	1.1	.4	.2	.6	11.8
New Brunswick	53.6	36.6	.1	1.1	.2	.1	.3	8.0
Quebec	83.3	4.7	1.4	.8	1.5	1.3	1.1	5.8
Ontario	34.7	34.9	2.3	2.7	3.1	1.7	4.3	16.3
Manitoba	29.3	43.1	1.4	4.0	.5	1.2	1.9	18.7
Saskatchewan	31.7	46.6	1.5	2.8	.2	.1	1.3	15.7
Alberta	26.7	38.9	1.5	4.2	1.7	.4	2.9	23.6
British Columbia	17.5	31.4	1.0	5.2	1.4	.5	7.2	35.9
Yukon	21.1	33.3	.5	3.5	.2	.1	2.7	38.6
Northwest Territories	45.8	31.3	.4	2.5	.5	.1	1.7	17.8
Nunavut	23.3	66.7	.1	3.1	.1	—	.5	6.2
Canada less Quebec	31.1	37.0	1.7	3.2	2.1	1.1	4.0	20.0

Source: Adapted from the Statistics Canada publication "Population by religion, by province and territory (2001 Census)." http://www40.statscan.ca/101/cst01/demo.30b.htm Downloaded August 25, 2008. Some percentages may not add to 100 due to rounding.
1. Includes Roman, Ukrainian and other Catholics. By far the largest group, however, are those belonging to the Roman Catholic Church.
2. Includes United Church and Anglican (the two largest denominations) as well as Baptist, Lutheran, Pentecostal and smaller religious groups based in the Protestant faith.
3. Includes Buddhist, Hindu, Sikh, Eastern, and other religions.

Interestingly, hardline separatist factions in Quebec argued just the opposite. For them, Quebec was not merely a distinct society, but a sociological nation. The vapidity of "distinct society" was underlined when then B.C. Premier Bill Vander Zalm commented that Canada was made up of "ten distinct societies" (see Bourgault, 1991: 35). In this context, Denis (1993) argued that "distinct society" seemed merely a clever way of avoiding the "two nations" concept fundamental to many Quebecers' understanding of Canada.

At the more general level, the passions unleashed in English-speaking Canada by the notion of a "distinct society" can be traced to the fragility of Canadian identity itself. The author Joseph Conrad once wrote that underlying every great emotion is a great fear. What is English-speaking Canada's great fear? Just as Quebec's overarching fear has been assimilation into English Canada, Canada's fear has been a fatal embrace by the United States. For many Canadians, Quebec's assertions of difference and its refusal to unreservedly become Canadian nationalists threaten Canada's integrity. In the spring of 1990, English Canada's demands for uniformity, swelling in the aftermath of the recently signed Free Trade Agreement with the United States, ran up against Quebec's long-standing demands for respect and recognition of its differences.

THE DEFEAT OF THE MEECH LAKE AND CHARLOTTETOWN ACCORDS

The Meech Lake Accord unravelled under increasing pressure in the spring of 1990. The unravelling occurred simultaneously from both the top and the bottom, attacked at one end by Trudeau, Manning, and the premiers of New Brunswick, Newfoundland, and Manitoba, and at the other end by popular, grassroots elements (Conway, 1997: 127). In the end, despite last-minute efforts to save it, the Accord died on the order paper, the three-year time frame for its ratification (June 23) having passed. An Aboriginal member of Manitoba's Legislative Assembly, Elijah Harper, delivered the decisive blow when he refused to allow that province's legislature to fast-track debate on the measure before time elapsed (see Chapter 12) (see Cohen, 1990; Conway, 1997).

The short- and long-term consequences of Meech Lake's failure were immense. Support for Quebec separatism increased (see Bourgault, 1991). The Bloc Québécois, formed in the spring of 1990 by a breakaway faction of Mulroney's government when it became apparent the Accord would fail, received an immediate boost (Cornellier, 1995). Elsewhere, in the context of fear and anger, the fortunes of the western-based Reform Party also rose (Harrison, 1995). Three years later,

the federal Tory party—its political coalition of westerners and Quebecers having evaporated—was dismembered, suffering the greatest electoral defeat by any government in Canadian history. In Quebec, the Tory limbs were torn off by the separatist Bloc, which, in a moment of supreme political irony, rose to the position of loyal Opposition to the victorious Liberals. The Reform Party led the slaughter in the West (see Appendix 1).

In the medium and longer terms, the failure to ratify the Meech Lake Accord left three principle concerns unresolved—(1) Quebec's role in Canada, (2) western Canada's growing sense of alienation, and (3) Aboriginal self-government (Meekison, 1993)—and with no clear means of resolution. Thus Canada entered a time of constitutional fumbling, culminating in a historical footnote known as the Charlottetown Accord.

The Charlottetown Accord arose out of a meeting of English Canada's nine premiers in July 1992. It was meant to appease the various interests who had opposed the Meech Lake Accord. The Charlottetown Accord gave widespread new powers to the provinces, while limiting those of the federal government. It further proposed entrenchment of Aboriginal rights and creation of a Triple-E (equal, elected, and effective) Senate. Finally, the Charlottetown Accord relegated the notion of "distinct society" to a new proposed Canada clause, whereby its constitutional meaning would be constrained by commitments to "equality of the provinces" and "linguistic duality" (Conway, 1997: 140). The new Accord did not offer Quebec much. Nonetheless, Quebec Premier Robert Bourassa reluctantly accepted the agreement, with a few minor changes.

Like its predecessor, however, the Charlottetown Accord also failed. Stung by previous criticisms that the public had largely been excluded from ratifying the constitutional changes, politicians submitted the Charlottetown Accord to a rare Canada-wide referendum, held on October 24, 1992. The referendum's wording was standard throughout Canada, except in Quebec, where that province enacted its own (though similar) referendum question. Seventy-five percent of Canadians turned out to vote, 55 percent voting *No* to the Accord, and 45 percent voting *Yes*. The *No* side won in nearly every province, including Quebec, British Columbia, Manitoba, Saskatchewan, Alberta, and Nova Scotia, as well as Yukon. The *Yes* side only barely prevailed in Ontario.

Why did the Charlottetown Accord fail? In part, after Meech Lake the chalice of constitutional reform was already poisoned. In part also, Charlottetown failed because it was too unwieldy. It attempted to do too much, to address all issues, and be all things to all people at the same time. In the end, the best thing that could be said about the referendum result was that the Accord had been rejected throughout Canada, though the reasons for its rejection varied from person to person, and between Quebec and the other provinces.

The Charlottetown Accord's rejection thus ended for a time formal constitutional change in Canada. Many Canadians heaved a sigh of relief. Quebec's relationship with Canada still remained unresolved, however.

CONCLUSION

The history of societies, like that of individuals, is one of roads both taken and not taken. The failure of the Meech Lake Accord and its Charlottetown successor put an end to the era of formal constitutional change in Canada begun with the Quiet Revolution, but it did not end change. Canada was much different at the end of the constitutional years than it had been at the beginning, in part because of the Charter of Rights and Freedoms and promises made to

Aboriginal peoples. But Canadians and Quebecers in 1992 also saw themselves differently from how they had in 1970. Meanwhile, new and different pressures for change were coming from forces beyond the political sphere and even beyond Canada's borders. The old issues were dying or being recast. In time, the old warriors themselves would disappear. Before then, however, one more battle was to be fought, one more reprise of the referendum wars.

NOTE

1. It is now known that Trudeau, in his youth, admired the corporatist (and fascist) regimes of Francisco Franco in Spain and Benito Mussolini in Italy (Nemni and Nemni, 2006). Trudeau's later conversion to liberalism shows that early socialization is reversible.

KEY TERMS

Constitution
distinct society
institutional bilingualism
laws
social norms
sociological imagination
territorial bilingualism

CRITICAL THINKING QUESTIONS

1. Why are constitutions important for understanding societies?

2. How might symbolic interaction theorists and post-structural theorists view the importance of language, particularly its ability to arouse strong emotions?

3. To what extent do individuals effect change? To what extent are they products of their time and place?

4. What did Joseph Conrad mean when he said that underlying every great emotion is a great fear?

5. From the perspective of counterfactual history, what might have happened had the Meech Lake Accord been enacted?

RECOMMENDED READINGS

Clarkson, Stephen, and Christina McCall. 1990. *Trudeau and Our Times,* vol. 1: *The Magnificent Obsession.* Toronto: McClelland & Stewart. This book is the definitive work on Pierre Trudeau's "obsession" with constitutional reform.

Cohen, Andrew. 1990. *A Deal Undone: The Making and Breaking of the Meech Lake Accord.* Vancouver: Douglas & McIntyre. Cohen's book details the making and breaking of the Meech Lake Accord.

Fournier, Marcel, Michael Rosenberg, and Deena White (eds.). 1997. *Quebec Society: Critical Issues.* Scarborough: Prentice-Hall Canada. Though somewhat dated, this book provides essential material for understanding Quebec society during the critical period after the Quiet Revolution leading up to the two referendums on sovereignty.

Harrison, Trevor. 1995. *Of Passionate Intensity: Right-Wing Populism and the Reform Party of Canada.* Toronto: University of Toronto Press. This book examines the rise of the Reform Party in western Canada in 1987 and its impact in mobilizing opposition to the Meech Lake Accord.

Mills, C. Wright. 1961. *The Sociological Imagination.* New York: Grove Press. This book is essential reading for any beginning sociologist, outlining Mills's idea of the "sociological imagination."

RELATED WEBSITES

Canadian Constitution Acts, 1867 to 1982. Department of Justice website: laws.justice. gc.ca/en.const/index.html This act fundamentally reshaped Canada. In the eyes of some, it also led to Quebec's increased isolation from the rest of Canada.

Official Bilingualism in Canada: History and Debates www.mapleleafweb.com/features/official-bilingualism-canada A useful summary of the history of bilingualism in Canada can be found on the Mapleleafweb.

Province of Quebec www.gouv.qc.ca The government of Quebec's website.

CANADIAN SOCIETY ON VIDEO

The Champions Series, Part Three: The Final Battle. 1986. National Film Board of Canada, 87 minutes, 2 seconds. Examines the period from 1978 to 1986, including the divisive 1980 referendum on independence and the repatriation of the 1982 Constitution.

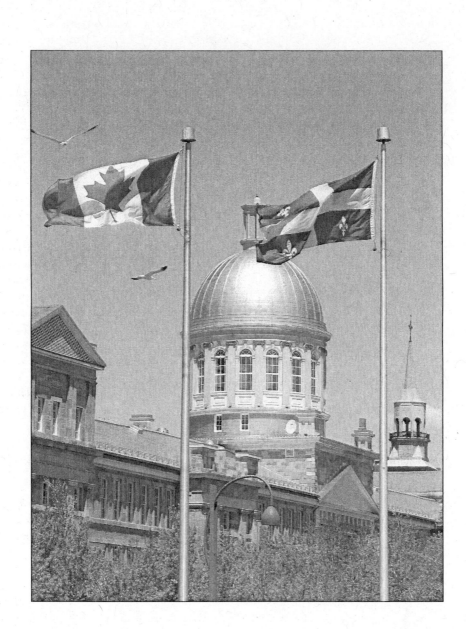

CHAPTER 5

THE RETURN OF THE NATION

Canada suffers in many respects from the same ailments as Québec. In fact, Canadian nationalism is also in the process of congealing under the weight of myths and dogmas that are becoming obstacles to the country's evolution.

—journalist Alain Dubuc, LaFontaine-Baldwin Lecture, 2001

That this House recognize that the Québécois form a nation within a united Canada.

—motion passed by the House of Commons, November 27, 2006

We coexist by recognizing the volatility and not wanting to disturb it.

—John Wright, Ipsos Reid polling, 2008

INTRODUCTION

Since 1970, Quebec and Canada had held constitutional negotiations designed to address Quebec's grievances and resolve their different visions of the country. The defeat of the Meech Lake and Charlottetown accords removed constitutional change, at least for a time, as a means of doing so. What options now remained? Effectively, there seemed only two options. Either Quebec could accept the status quo and perhaps sign the current Constitution, or it could reject the status quo and push for independence.

This chapter begins with an examination of the 1995 Quebec referendum, through which the Parti Québécois government sought a mandate to pursue this second option, and events since that time, including the House of Commons' recognition of Quebec as a nation in 2006. The chapter also examines sociological questions regarding individual and collective identity, the power exerted by symbols and metaphors in shaping

group solidarity and conflict, and the issue of minority rights within a multicultural society. Finally, in anticipation of the book's next section, the issues of nation and state are reconsidered in the context of globalization and the threat posed by the United States to both the Québécois nation and English Canada.

A NEAR-DEATH EXPERIENCE: THE 1995 QUEBEC REFERENDUM

On October 30, 1995, Quebecers once more voted in a referendum on sovereignty. Canadians watching on their televisions saw their country come within a few thousand votes of being fundamentally changed, perhaps disintegrating altogether.

The referendum was presaged by three major events. First, the separatist Bloc Québécois elected 54 members to Parliament in the 1993 federal election, suggesting widespread support for independence within Quebec (Appendix 1). Second, the BQ's provincial counterpart, the Parti Québécois, led by Jacques Parizeau (1930–), won the Quebec provincial election in September 1994 with a commitment to pursue sovereignty. Third, the PQ tabled a draft bill on sovereignty, following by public consultations throughout Quebec during the early part of 1995 (Balthazar, 1997; Conway, 1997).

It was clear from the beginning the vote would be close. Polls conducted since the 1994 Quebec election showed support for sovereignty stable at 45 percent (Conway, 1997: 214), a significant base upon which to build. Moreover, the sovereigntist camp believed the referendum question was sufficiently benign as to attract "soft" voters. By contrast, federalists were hamstrung by the fact they appeared to have nothing concrete to offer Quebecers. The defeat of the Meech Lake Accord (Chapter 4), in which Canada's Prime Minister Jean Chrétien again had been instrumental, had foreclosed the possibility of constitutional renewal, at least for a time. All Chrétien and Canada's other leaders could offer was the status quo, liberally sprinkled with threats should the *Yes* side prevail (Conway, 1997: 219).

Moreover, even these threats were bound to be less successful than in 1980. First, Quebec's economy in 1995 was far more developed, and Quebecers felt more secure. Second, francophones made up a larger proportion of Quebec's business class in 1995 than in 1980. Though not stridently nationalist, many remained at least neutral in the 1995 sovereignty debate. Third, English-speaking Canada's constant reminders that Quebec is a net beneficiary of federal transfer payments fell on deaf ears, partly because such reminders are insulting and partly because many Quebecers do not believe this to be the case (Valaskakis and Fournier, 1995). (Many Quebecers outside the Montreal area do not directly see the benefits of transfer payments, which often go to large corporations; in consequence, the alleged economic downside of separation is lost on people in the rural areas of Quebec, who often face double-digit unemployment.)

As referendum day approached, many ordinary Canadians outside Quebec felt fearful, angry, bewildered, and powerless. On October 27, a unity rally was held at Canada Place in Montreal. The *No*-sponsored rally attracted between 30,000 and 150,000 people, many of them from outside the province, loudly declaring their love for Quebec. No doubt, these expressions of affection were sincere. But, as Balthazar (1997: 58) notes, "Since those Canadians had nothing to offer but their words of love, they gave Quebecers the image of an all-inclusive Canada that did not allow for the recognition of Quebec's uniqueness."

The impact of these events upon the referendum's outcome is uncertain. A study of polls conducted during the period suggests voting intentions remained fairly stable throughout and that the impact of

Bouchard's increased prominence during the latter part of the campaign was negligible (see Fox et al., 1999). Likewise, the pro-federalist Montreal rallies may have made those in attendance feel better, or may have driven undecided voters into the *Yes* camp, or may have had no impact at all.

Few televisions in Canada were silent on referendum night 1995. The *Yes* side took a seemingly commanding lead in the early stages, and jubilation reigned among its supporters. Gradually, however, the outcome turned as results came in from Montreal Island. Nearly all of Quebec's eligible voters—90 percent (4.7 million people)—cast ballots, the final result being that 50.6 percent voted *No* while 49.4 percent voted *Yes* (Morton, 1997: 340). A swing of less than 30,000 votes would have changed the referendum's outcome (Young, 1998).

As in 1980, the 1995 referendum split not only Canada but also Quebec. The *Yes* side won strong support from francophones, about 60 percent of eligible francophone voters (compared with 50 percent in 1980). The *Yes* side also won strong support in Quebec City and rural Quebec, from middle-class and better-educated voters, and from union supporters. In contrast to 1980, the *Yes* side also received some support from business, though business in general remained on the sidelines of the sovereignty debate (Conway, 1997: 217). Polls conducted prior to the referendum also suggested that sovereignty appealed especially to those 35–44 years of age and males slightly more than females, though the gap had lessened (Trent, 1995). By contrast, the *No* side fashioned its close victory from about 40 percent of francophones and almost all anglophones and allophones, mostly located in Montreal (Fox et al., 1999), not to mention northern Quebec's small but politically powerful Cree and Inuit peoples (Conway, 1997: 219), thus opening up new and important ground for discussing the future of Aboriginal peoples within Canadian society (see Part 3).

MULTICULTURALISM, SECULARISM, AND CIVIC NATIONALISM

On referendum night in 1995, an obviously distraught Quebec Premier Jacques Parizeau remarked that the pro-sovereignty side had been defeated by "money and the ethnic vote" (quoted in Conway, 1997: 220; see also Balthazar, 1997; Morton, 1997). Reproached by colleagues and opponents alike for his divisive remarks, a remorseful Parizeau resigned the next day and was succeeded shortly thereafter as Quebec premier by Lucien Bouchard.

In broad statistical terms, Parizeau's observations leading to his resignation were correct. Francophones in Quebec *do* disproportionately favour sovereignty; non francophones *do not*. His remarks, however, were divisive in singling out all members of Quebec's allophone community as being opposed to Quebec nationalism—indeed, being unpatriotic (Balthazar, 1997: 59). As such, Parizeau's comments unearthed debates within Quebec and the Parti Québécois itself about who is a true Québécois and the nature of Quebec nationalism.

As noted in Chapter 3, traditional Quebec nationalism was cultural and inward looking. It traced its ancestry through bloodlines to the original 10,000 *Canadiens* of the St. Lawrence. Old Quebec nationalism was anti-modern, tribal, and *Catholic*. Vestiges of it still exist today, expressed linguistically through descriptions of people as either "*Québécois pur laine*" (literally, "pure wool") or "*Québécois de souche*" ("later arrivals") (Ignatieff, 1993: 172).

But Quebec, like the rest of Canada, has changed a great deal since the 1950s. The new nationalism that arose then was modern, democratic, territorial, pluralistic, and secular even if (as previously noted) most Quebecers still nominally declare themselves members of the Catholic faith. In theory, the new nationalism welcomes anyone living within Quebec's borders willing to accept the values of Quebec society. In practice also, this is the case. Most Quebecers today view their nationalism as civic, not ethnic (Ignatieff, 1993: 169; also Smith, 1998).

In this context, the Bloc Québécois released a policy document in 1999 suggesting that language, culture, and history define Quebec identity, but that anyone living in an independent Quebec would enjoy equal rights (*Edmonton Journal*, 1999a). Nonetheless, the debate over who is a Québécois continues in Quebec.

An important element of this debate is the role of secularism. As already noted, the transformation from old to new nationalism in Quebec was tied to the decline of the Catholic Church's authority. Shortly after this transformation occurred, however, Quebec also began dealing—as did the rest of Canada—with the arrival of new immigrants, many from neither francophone nor anglophone countries who still hold strong religious beliefs.

The concern expressed by many Quebec francophones is not simply whether new immigrants will support sovereignty (a specifically nationalist concern), but how immigrants can be successfully integrated into modern—and *secular*—Quebec society. These concerns arise always around specific incidents that take on larger symbolic meaning, such as a court ruling on one occasion that a Sikh student could carry a *kirpan* (religious dagger) to school and in another instance when a youth belonging to the Islamic faith wanted to wear a *hijab* (head scarf) while playing soccer, which was against league rules. Some Quebecers viewed the new immigrants as trying to fundamentally change the province's traditional culture and reacted with anger, the response garnering the most notoriety when the small town of Herouxville established a policy saying that immigrants must conform to local culture.

In search of an answer to the perceived rise of cultural and religious divisions, in February 2007 the Quebec government established the Consultation Commission on Accommodation Practices Related to Cultural Differences (Government of Quebec, 2007). The commission's mandate was to examine accommodation practices in Quebec; to examine similar experiences in other societies; to conduct extensive public consultations on the issue; and "to formulate recommendations to the government to ensure that accommodation practices conform to the values of Québec society as a pluralistic, democratic, egalitarian society" (Government of Quebec, 2008: 7).

Co-chaired by a sociologist, Gerard Bouchard, and a liberal philosopher, Charles Taylor, the commission travelled throughout Quebec through the fall of 2007, garnering submissions on the question of **reasonable accommodation**, *defined as a form of arrangement or relaxation aimed at ensuring respect for the right of equality ... which, following the strict application of an institutional standard, infringes on an individual's right to equality* (Government of Quebec, 2008: 7) of minority cultural and religious rights. In the end, the commission made 37 recommendations based on the notion not of multiculturalism but of "*interculturalisme*," what Saul (2008: 147) describes as "the intercultural dovetailing relationship among four groups: the francophone majority, the anglophone minority, the Aboriginal minority, and *the cultural communities*, that is, the newcomers, with French as the central convening language of all four."

Among the commission's specific recommendations were greater cultural awareness, improved intercultural relations, better integration of migrants, and greater effort on the part of government and its institutions to deal with racism and inequality. Its broadest thrust, however, was to recommend Quebec's adoption of **open secularism** based on four principles: (1) the moral equality of persons; (2) freedom of conscience and religion; (3) separation of church and state; and (4) the state's neutrality with respect to religions

and deep-seated secular convictions (Government of Quebec, 2008: 45).

Quebec's anxieties, fears, and successes in accommodating cultural difference have their mirror in the rest of Canada. This is ironic, for Canada's mirror is in fact larger, embracing Quebec itself. Quebec's struggles to incorporate minority cultural differences within a framework of civic nationalism are a subset of Canada's struggle as a whole to fashion a coherent national community that embraces three nations—the English, the French, and the Aboriginal—and an assortment of other ethnic groups (Saul, 1997, 2008).

THE SOVEREIGNTY QUESTION TODAY

How strong is the appeal of Quebec sovereignty today? Data conducted since 1995 are consistent on four points (Trent, 1995; *Edmonton Journal*, 1999b, 2000b; Johnson, 1999; Macpherson, 2000; Dubuc, 2001). First, the vast majority of Quebecers—as many as 80 percent in one poll—oppose holding another referendum. Second, few Quebecers believe a referendum on sovereignty would pass if held today. Third, support for sovereignty during "normal" periods averages about 42 percent (Leger Marketing, 2008). Support for sovereignty rises above this only when Quebec feels attacked or rejected by English Canada, as during the Meech Lake crisis or in late 2008 when Bloc Québécois support for a Liberal-New Democrat coalition to defeat the minority Conservative government led to anger directed at Quebecers at large (see Chapter 9), or when the idea of sovereignty is presented in the abstract or its definition unclear. Fourth, a large number of Quebecers hold the apparently contradictory belief that Quebec and Canada have reached an impasse *and* that federalism can be renewed.

Looked at another way, about a third of Quebecers are consistent federalists. Another third are hard-core *indépendantistes* who identify with the Quebec state. The remaining third of Quebecers are torn between choosing the Quebec nation or the country of Canada, a predicament captured in the oft-quoted joke of Quebec comedian Yvon Deschamps that "All we want is an independent Quebec within a strong and united Canada" (Colombo, 1994: 224). It is on this third of Quebecers that the outcome of any future sovereignty referendum would hinge, should such a vote be held.

At the same time, most analysts agree that compared with the 1960s and 1970s, sovereignty today invokes little passion in Quebec. Why is this the case? In part, the reason is that most of the political, economic, and cultural grievances expressed during the Quiet Revolution have been addressed (Ignatieff, 1993).

In consequence of this fact, both the Bloc Québécois and Parti Québécois have soft-pedalled independence instead of more provincial autonomy in specific areas.

Politically, francophones since the 1960s have used their strength in Quebec particularly to make gains within Canada's political and labour sectors (Nakhaie, 1997). (Between 1968 and 2008, three of eight Canadian prime ministers held ridings in Quebec, while a fourth—Paul Martin Jr.—had strong Franco-Ontario roots.) By contrast, while those of British background continue disproportionately to dominate elite positions within Canada, they do not do so unopposed; indeed, it can be argued that British Canada as a sociological construct no longer exists (Gwyn, 1996; Igartua, 2006). The object of francophone Canada's wrath—White Anglo-Saxon Protestant (WASP) Canada—is today largely a historical artifact.

Economically, French-Canadians in general, and francophone Quebecers in particular, no longer experience the second-place status relative to English-Canadians once identified by Porter (1965) and the Royal Commission on Bilingualism and Biculturalism (1963).

Table 5.1
Median Earnings, 2005 Constant Dollars, Full-Time Earners, Canada, Provinces, and Territories, 1980–2005

	1980	1990	2000	2005	% Canadian 1980(1) Median	% Canadian Median 2005(1)	% 1980–2005(1)	+/−
Canada	41,348	40,778	40,443	41,401	—			0.1
Nfld. and Lab.	37,510	38,153	36,079	37,429	90.7		90.4	0.3
PEI	37,405	33,441	33,561	34,140	78.4		82.5	4.1
NS	36,532	38,237	36,165	36,917	88.4		89.2	.8
NB	36,436	36,848	34,763	35,288	88.1		85.2	2.9
Que.	39,938	38,325	37,836	37,722	96.6		91.1	5.5
Ont.	41,395	42,354	44,440	44,748	100.1		108.1	8.1
Man.	37,247	36,564	35,425	36,692	90.1		88.6	1.5
Sask.	38,804	34,082	33,785	35,948	93.8		86.8	7.0
Alta.	43,732	40,711	40,782	43,964	105.8		106.2	0.4
B.C.	47,605	42,173	43,715	42,230	115.1		102.0	13.1
Yukon	52,942	49,410	47,611	49,787	126.6		120.3	6.3
NWT(2)	50,353	54,759	56,122	60,119	121.8		145.2	23.4
Nun.(2)	46,140	49,701	50,542	58,088	111.6		140.3	28.7

Notes: (1) Percentages and percentage change calculated by authors.
 (2) The territory of Nunavut was created in 1999. Data for Nunavut and the Northwest Territories for 1980 and 1990 have been adjusted to reflect the new boundaries.
Source: Statistics Canada. 2008. "Earnings and incomes of Canadians over the past quarter century, 2006 census," 14. Cat. # 97-563-x. Ottawa: Statistics Canada. http://www.statcan.gc.ca/bsolc/olc-cel/olc-cel?lang=eng&catno=97-563-X2006001.

In 2005, the average nominal wage in Quebec was $32,074 compared to the Canadian average of $35,498, or about 90 percent (Statistics Canada, 2006b). As shown in Table 5.1, the median income in Quebec (constant dollars) for the same year was $37,722, only 91 percent of the Canadian median income and down in terms of percentage from 1980.

Today, much of Quebec's bourgeoisie is francophone and, like the Canadian bourgeoisie at large, wedded to breaking down rather than defending national borders. Moreover, among workers, those of French ethnicity (in Canada as a whole) actually earned significantly more than workers of British ethnicity in 1991 (Lian and Matthews, 1998).

Clearly, there remains considerable inequality in Canada in terms of both income and wealth; indeed, the gap between rich and poor has increased in recent decades (see Chapter 9). Education and occupation are key factors in inequality, but opportunities and outcomes in both these areas are in turn highly correlated with several other demographic factors. Among these factors are racial and ethnic discrimination (Fleras and Elliott, 2007), especially with regard to Aboriginal ancestry (see Chapter 13), as well as gender, marital status, region of residence, and age. Income and poverty rates are particularly high for single-parent female-headed families and single, widowed, or divorced female seniors (Morissette and Zhang, 2001). Recent immigrants also have lower earnings, even when education is controlled, than long-term immigrants or Canadian-born individuals (Statistics Canada, 2003).

Quebec's success in stemming the cultural threat is harder to measure. Though the percentage of French-speaking people in Quebec has stabilized at roughly 80 percent (see Chapter 4), many francophone Quebecers remain "linguistically insecure" (Thompson, 1995: 78). They fear particularly the impact of allophone immigrants to Quebec who might choose English rather than French as their adopted language, a fear that ties into concerns about cultural differences generally as discussed above. Still, the level of insecurity concerning language is lower among younger Quebecers, who are used to the protections provided by Quebec's language laws. Moreover, recent census figures suggest that in fact allophone immigrants are today actually strengthening the French language in Quebec by opting to adopt that language (*Globe and Mail*, 2002), an outcome likely the result of powers obtained by the provincial government over immigration that allow for the recruitment of immigrants from francophone countries.

Beyond Quebec, the world has also changed dramatically since the time of the Quiet Revolution. Liberation politics, drawn from Third World experiences and the writings of Franz Fanon and Che Guevara, have little appeal today. Few Quebecers today, especially young people, see their province as a colony. In this time of increased global connectedness, as the world seems drawn closer and closer together by economics, technology, cultural exchanges, and trade deals, the very notion of sovereignty seems unclear. (What does independence mean? What would Quebec gain through sovereignty that it does not already possess?) Meanwhile, recent examples of ethnic nationalism gone wrong (in Yugoslavia, for example) provide stinging counterpoints to the ideal of independence. (What would an independent Quebec lose?) Finally, many young Quebecers increasingly see themselves—not unlike young people elsewhere—as individual consumers and mobile workers. A CROP/Environics poll conducted in the fall of 2002 found that 63 percent of Quebecers aged 18–44 identify with neither federalism *nor* sovereignty (*Edmonton Journal*, 2002).

For two centuries English-speaking Canada has believed that Quebec nationalism would disappear. Federalist politicians have fuelled these beliefs for the past 30 years, often after yet another crisis has shaken the Canadian federation, yet Quebec nationalism and the idea of an independent homeland continue to stir within Quebec. Why is this the case? The answer lies in the fact that the issue of French-English, Quebec-Canada relations within the country cannot be addressed solely by material or even constitutional changes alone. The basis of the issue lies in such intangible, but immanently sociological, issues as self-identity, mutual respect, and the need for recognition.

SOCIETY, NATION, MODERNITY, AND "SELF"

Who are you? That is, what are the elements that shape who you are and speak to you and others of your "self"? This is a distinctly sociological question, one that emerged in the 19th century with modernity. Riesman et al. (1950) note, for example, that notions of individual identity make little sense in pre-modern, feudal societies, where ideas, norms, behaviours, expectations, and outcomes are fairly rigidly controlled by tradition. In the Middle Ages, to use the popular phrase of the 1960s, no one would have sought to "find himself or herself." People of that era were told directly and indirectly who they were from the time they were born. By contrast, in modern societies, individuals not only *seem* to be freer of social restraints, they are also expected to find and express their particular uniqueness.

What are the building blocks used in this construction? For Marx, writing in the mid-19th century, class was the primary factor in a person's identity kit; for Durkheim, occupation was central. For feminist scholars today, gender is a chief source of one's identity as well as one's world view, but other factors, such as religion, ethnicity, or education may also provide salient materials informing

an individual's self-identity. For people growing up in modern societies, the cache of materials from which to make a "self" is seemingly endless, drawn from television, the Internet, magazines, and so on.

Sociologists view this construction critically, however. First, individual and collective identities are mutually constructed. In a real sense, no one simply chooses an individual identity. Rather, an identity arises out of membership in a group (Tajfel and Turner, 1986). Second, both individual and collective identities are highly malleable (Cook, 1995: 235). The importance of an identity may lessen over time for a person or group, or events may lead an individual or group to rediscover and reassert their roots. Third, individual identities are neither singular nor exclusive. A person may simultaneously see himself or herself as Italian, a doctor, a soccer player, a conservative, and gay or lesbian.

What does the issue of individual and collective identity have to do with Quebec and Canada? Simply this: Quebec's national culture, broadly conceived, provides many Quebecers with essential materials for their personal identities. Writing in 1951, André Laurendeau (1985) noted that: "Except for the stateless (and even then!) every being carries the mark of a particular culture. The richer it is, the more it nourishes him [sic]."

This notion is at odds (at least on the surface) with dominant Western culture, where private and public spheres are viewed as separate, the individual is sacrosanct, and "the state and civil society are typically understood as facing off against each other" (White, 1997: 22). Pierre Trudeau's denunciations of Quebec nationalism as tribal (Chapter 4) were rooted in a supposed separation of individual self and society (Couture, 1998), hence his desire to entrench the Charter of Rights and Freedoms in the 1982 Constitution as a means of protecting individuals from collective oppression.

Separating the spheres is difficult, if not impossible, however. Note, for example, that the Charter of Rights and Freedoms deals with both individual and collective rights (Cook, 1995: 234). Likewise, the policies of official bilingualism and multi-culturalism enacted by Trudeau similarly protect collective rights over language and culture (Webber, 1994; Couture, 1998).

It is therefore inaccurate to argue that a necessary opposition exists between the rights of collectives and those of individuals, represented by Quebec and English-speaking Canada, respectively. Repeated surveys show Quebecers have at least as much deep regard for individual rights as other Canadians. Indeed, Quebecers are generally quite liberal in their acceptance of individual differences (Denis, 1993). At the same time, English-speaking Canadians also possess a sense of collective identity, albeit understated, as evidenced quickly if someone tells them they are "just like" Americans.

If the sociological (and political) problem between Quebec and Canada does not lie in an opposition between individual and collective rights, it lies even less in an absolute separation of the French and English cultures. French and English identities (and others) in Canada include elements of each other (Dufour, 1990; Webber, 1994; Saul, 1997). Notes Dufour (1990: 81): "Almost by definition, the Quebec identity comprises a more or less significant, more or less conscious, Canadian component." And again: "English is a deeply ambivalent and perturbing element of the Quebec identity" (1990: 97). A majority of Quebecers (though less among francophones) still see themselves simultaneously as Quebecers *and* as Canadians (see Smith, 1998), though the former generally takes precedence in their identity structures.

What, then, underlies the conflict? Simply that *the right of Quebecers to possess a distinct identity be recognized and respected by the rest of Canada* (Taylor, 1993; Coulombe, 1998).

There is an apparent paradox in this demand for, as Taylor (1993) and Ignatieff (1993) note, Canada and Quebec have never been closer. Quebec was "more distinct" before the Quiet Revolution than it is today. Throughout Canada, regional differences on social factors and values have been lessening for decades (see Goyder, 1993; Baer et al., 1993), a product of modernization. The paradox of diminishing differences and escalating demands for recognition is partly explained, however, if we consider globalization's impact upon states and nations (see Chapter 1).

On the one hand, globalization has accelerated the process of homogenizing cultures. On the other hand, it has left many national groups feeling uneasy and compelled to overemphasize and protect remaining distinctions. The weakened capacity of states, especially multinational states such as Canada, to protect them, has further pressed national cultures to seek shelter in smaller units. In line with Bell's (1993: 362) contention that national states today are both too big and too small to deal with important issues, supporters of sovereignty argue that an independent Quebec would be better able to adapt to the demands of the global marketplace (see Bourgault, 1991; Parti Québécois, 1994).

Such claims are debatable but ultimately beside the point. The question is: Is it possible for English-speaking Canada to acknowledge Quebec's distinctiveness in a meaningful way; to grant recognition and respect for Québécois identity; and to give Quebec sufficient powers for its survival within Canada's existing state structures (see Taylor 1993; Denis, 1993; Coulombe, 1998)? Or does the flow of history lead inexorably to Quebec sovereignty?

THE RETURN OF THE NATIONAL QUESTION

Suddenly, in the fall of 2006, Canada caught up with its history and, one might argue, with sociology. In an act unimaginable only a few years before, on November 27, 2006, the Canadian House of Commons passed the following motion (by a vote of 266 to 16, the rest abstaining or absent): "That this House recognize that the Québécois form a nation within a united Canada."

How did this turn come about? And, to what extent, does it represent a "turn" in French-English relations? To unpack the meaning of the Common's resolution, we need to briefly return to previous discussions.

We have seen how, depending on the time and place, since 1763 Canada's dominant anglophone elite have employed various policies (from coercion and subjugation, to isolation, and subtle assimilation, to tentative efforts beginning in the 1960s at accommodation and recognition) of dealing with the smaller, but nonetheless significant and distinct francophone minority. The prevailing issue underlying these policies is that of the nation.

Chapter 1 noted the conflation of nation, state, country, and society. Canada is a textbook case of this conflation in practice. The "problem" with which Canada has struggled since its founding is in every sense a modern one: Can it survive as a country administered by a state that accommodates several nations within its territory? As noted in Chapter 2, Lord Durham's Eurocentric background led him to conclude that every nation must have a state, and that no state must have more than one nation, a situation that led to the failed Act of Union of 1841, which led finally to Confederation.

The years after 1867 saw the French "fact" in Canada largely isolated (and thus strengthened) within Quebec, while the rest of Canada took on a decidedly English stamp. By the 1960s, arguments about the nature of Canada focused on whether it was a confederation of 10 provinces (of which Quebec was merely one) or a marriage of "two nations," with separatists in Quebec arguing for a third option: that the marriage be dissolved (Chapter 3).

The constitutional discussions of the 1970s and 1980s failed to resolve Quebec's place within Canada. Subsequent efforts to revise the constitution also failed and even heightened the crisis. English-speaking Canada's rejection in 1990 of the Meech Lake Accord, based primarily on the Accord's recognition of Quebec as a "distinct society," increased many Quebecers' sense that they were not accepted by the rest of Canada; the result was a rise in support for sovereignty and the nearly successful vote for separation in 1995 (Chapter 4).

Fast-forward to the fall of 2006. Earlier that same year, the governing Liberal Party was defeated in a federal election by the Stephen Harper-led Conservative Party, a party rebuilt from the ruins of the former Progressive Conservative Party and Reform-Alliance parties). In the course of the subsequent race to replace Paul Martin as Liberal leader, one of the contenders, Michael Ignatieff (see Chapter 9), suggested that Quebec be recognized as a "nation" in the Constitution. Though endorsed by the federal party's Quebec wing, the other Liberal candidates and much of English-Canada's media quickly denounced Ignatieff's proposal, which went against not only the Trudeau legacy of opposing Quebec nationalism in favour of a dual, pan-Canadian, but went further than any previous constitutional effort, including the failed Meech Lake Accord, in recognizing Quebec's distinctiveness (Fidler, 2006).

Sensing an opportunity to divide the Liberal Party, however, the Bloc Québécois, which had elected 51 members in the 2006 election, proposed a parliamentary motion along the lines of Ignatieff's position, that Quebec constituted a nation within Canada. Likewise, sensing the chance to build support in Quebec while blunting the Bloc Québécois motion,

Prime Minister Stephen Harper proposed the motion (above) that the House of Commons subsequently adopted.

At first glance, the proposal appears to be a major step in recognizing Quebec's distinct identity, something that the Reform Party, of which Harper was a prominent member, had vehemently opposed two decades earlier.

Fidler (2006), however, argues that:

> [T]he original Bloc motion, which had identified the "Québécois" as a nation, referred to them in English as "Quebeckers." That is, a territorial concept, encompassing everyone who inhabits Quebec irrespective of first language or ethnic origin. This is now the common definition of "Québécois" in Quebec. [Prime Minister] Harper's motion, in contrast, used the term "Québécois" in both French and English versions, an ethnic connotation implying that only those whose first language is French qualified as a "nation."

In short, the House of Commons motion recognized an ethnic definition of the nation, while the Bloc version recognized a civic definition of the nation tied to territory (see Chapter 1).

Mere semantics? Perhaps. Linguistic meanings are slippery at the best of times, especially when moving between two languages. Nonetheless, Fidler raises important questions about the exact meaning of the House of Commons resolution. Quoting journalist Pierre Dubuc, Fidler argues that recognition of the Québécois nation is designed to prepare for the partition of Quebec should that province ever vote *Yes* to a referendum on sovereignty. That is, while the Québécois (francophone) nation might vote to separate, likewise the English-speaking areas could also vote to remain in Canada. Such a stance would be commensurate with that of previous Canadian governments, both Liberal and Conservative.

But Fidler (2006) also notes something further, the phrase "a nation within a united Canada":

> One would think that if the "Québécois" are a nation within Canada, then surely they are a nation without Canada. Ah, but there's the rub. Whoever says "nation" says ... self-determination. The right of nations to self-determination has long been a fundamental concept of international law and diplomacy.

In short, the resolution passed by the House of Commons appears to thwart the Bloc Quebecois' motion by giving symbolic (but not constitutional) recognition to the Quebecois nation, while simultaneously denying the territorial nationhood of Quebec with all its political implications. Likewise, while the Bloc version would have given particular power to the provincial state as representing and perhaps even constituting the Quebec nation and society, the House of Commons version reserved considerable political power for the Canadian state in this regard. Ultimately, was the House of Commons motion of 2006 too clever by half? Does it offer Quebecers the appearance of recognition, but provide something much less? Does it in consequence represent another failed opportunity to recognize Quebec's specific identity and needs?

How do Canadian people view Canada's "nations," not merely that of Quebec, but otherwise? A poll of 1,500 Canadians, conducted by Leger Marketing for the Association of Canadian Studies shortly before the vote on the House of Commons motion, found that 93 percent of those polled, both anglophone and francophone, agreed that Canada is a nation. When asked, however, if Quebecers are also a nation, only 38 percent of anglophone Canadians agreed compared with 78 percent of francophone Canadians. The results suggest that anglophones are more likely to recognize ethnic definitions of nation-hood while francophones hold a more territorial or civic definition of nation-hood. Moreover, while francophone Quebecers overwhelmingly believed that they constitute a nation, they also sup-ported recognition of Aboriginal peoples and Acadians as nations (see Table 5.2).

Table 5.2
Percent of Anglophone and Francophone Respondents Viewing Various Groups as Nations within Canada, 2006

Group	Anglophones	Francophones
Aboriginal peoples	61%	79%
Métis	46%	59%
Acadians	37%	74%
Quebecers	38%	78%

Source: Adapted from Jack Jedwab, The Association for Canadian Studies, available at: http://www.acs-aec.ca/oldsite/CurrentEvent/Face%20the%20Nations%20_2_.pdf.

A more recent survey suggests these different views have not changed. An online survey of 2,505 adults (including 932 Quebecers) conducted by Ipsos Reid in the summer of 2008, amid the celebra-tions of the founding of Quebec City in 1608, found that 70 percent of Quebecers view themselves as "a nation within a united Canada," while only 36 percent in the rest of Canada agree. Likewise, half of Quebecers subscribe to the "two nations" concept of Canada, compared with only one-third in the rest of Canada. Instead, more than 40 percent of those outside Quebec see Canada as "a nation with one dominant culture and several equal minorities," a view held by only 20 percent of Quebecers (figures in the *Edmonton Journal*, 2008).

In short, Canada's French and English communities continue to view each other from quite different promontories.

QUEBEC "SOLUTIONS"—AND CANADA'S PROBLEM

In the aftermath of the events of 1995, the federalist forces led by Jean Chrétien's Liberal government adopted two strate-gies to counter Quebec sovereignty's appeal. These strategies were referred to as "Plan A" and "Plan B" or, as Conway (1997: 227) describes them, the carrot and the stick.

Plan A involved attempts to show Quebecers that Confederation works and perhaps, in time, to win Quebecers' hearts and minds. At the symbolic level, the House of Commons passed a motion one month after the referendum that recognized Quebec as a distinct society (Balthazar, 1997: 59). This was followed two years later by the premiers' Calgary Unity Declaration acknowledging the "unique character of Quebec society." At the more practical level, the federal gov-ernment transferred administrative pow-ers over immigration to Quebec (one of the Meech Lake Accord's five demands); launched a series of programs, especially in higher education; promoted a national, private French television network, and expanded French usage online. Finally, as in the past, the federal government enticed federalist Quebecers such as Stéphane Dion and Pierre Pettigrew to Ottawa.

By contrast, Plan B involved a "tough love" approach to Quebec (Conway, 1997; Balthazar, 1997). Politically, the centrepiece of Plan B is Bill C-20 (the Clarity Act). Passed by the House of Commons in March 2000, the Clarity Act allows federal MPs to vote on both the clarity of the wording of any referendum question on sovereignty introduced by the Quebec National Assembly and the clarity of any victory in a referendum before beginning negotiations on Quebec sovereignty. In short, the Clarity Act renders a vote in favour of sovereignty in any future referendum null until debated and passed by the House of Commons. Quebec nationalists, and sovereigntists in particular, view the Clarity Act as an infringement on Quebecers' rights to self-determination and the jurisdiction of Quebec's National Assembly. The Clarity Act further suggests that Quebec's boundaries would be up for negotiation if Quebecers ever vote *yes* to sovereignty (*Edmonton Journal*, 2000a), something that Fiddler (2006) argues is repeated in the House of Commons' "nation" motion of 2006. For many Quebecers, in general, Plan B repeats an all-too-familiar pattern of trying to coerce French Canada into accepting the rules of Confederation.

Even before the sovereignty vote, however, a third strategy, Plan C, was already being proposed in several quarters. Less mentioned than either Plan A or Plan B, this strategy had as its aim a radical **decentralization** of Canada whereby Quebec's demands would be applied throughout the federation; that is, whatever powers Quebec obtained would be automatically given to every other province. In the words of Gordon Gibson (1994), a former Liberal and Social Credit politician and conservative policy adviser, Plan C would see Ottawa reduced to a "service centre," a relatively powerless clearing house for functions residual to those of the provinces.

The idea of decentralization (or devolution) has been around for a long time and appeals to several distinct constituencies albeit for different reasons. To rigid formalists, decentralization meets Quebec's demands while also maintaining a strict equality of the provinces. To provincial rights advocates, especially in western Canada, decentralization means a return to the division of powers written into the 1867 Constitution, before the Great Depression and two world wars meant the growth of federal powers. To political leaderships in the "have" provinces, it means more money and power that need not be shared with other jurisdictions. To pro-business think tanks (such as the Fraser Institute) and corporations (and their lobbyists, such as the Canadian Council of Chief Executives), decentralization means dealing with only one level of government—smaller and more compliant—regarding, for example, environmental and labour regulations. To some mainstream economists, decentralization embraces the principle of **subsidiarity** *that unless there is a valid reason to the contrary, state functions should be exercized by the lowest level of government* (Courchene, 1997). Finally, in the years leading up to the financial crisis of 2007–2008, some viewed decentralization as an inevitable and perhaps even positive adaptation to globalization (Courchene, 1998; Resnick, 2000; Ibbitson, 2001) that might ultimately strengthen Canadian federalism through greater co-operation.

Decentralization also has critics, however. First, it is argued, Canada is already the world's most decentralized federation (Valaskakis and Fournier, 1995), a situation that slows responses to crises. Second, most Canadians still believe in a strong role for the federal government, particularly in areas of health and social policy. Further decentralization would result in large corporate interests playing regions and provinces off against each other, endangering national standards and programs, such as medicare (Laxer and Harrison, 1995). Third, the federal government provides one of the few "checks and balances" to provincial power, and vice versa (see Taylor, 1993), an equilibrium that decentralization would alter (Romanow, 2006). Fourth, as more power flowed to the provinces, people's identification with

Canada as a whole would lessen, threatening national unity.

Many of these same critics offer a different solution: **asymmetrical federalism** (Laxer, 1992; Taylor, 1993). Asymmetrical federalism begins from the premise that Quebec is not like the other provinces, that the needs of both Quebec and the other provinces are different, and that federalism cannot be practised in the manner of treating all provinces the same.

How would asymmetrical federalism work? Laxer (1992, 2001) and Webber (1994: 230) suggest that Quebec be given constitutional powers over areas it views as necessary for preserving its national identity, while these same powers for Canadians elsewhere remain "housed" in Ottawa. In effect, Quebec would have more powers than the other provinces, but it would not have powers over the citizens of other provinces, nor would Quebecers have more powers than other Canadians. The change would require two sittings of the House of Commons: an all Canada sitting, in which Quebec MPs would participate, and a separate sitting in which Quebec MPs would not participate, dealing with those areas delegated to the Quebec provincial government (see also Resnick, 1991).

In a more complex development of this argument, Resnick (2000) suggests Canada be reconfigured as a country with three tiers that include six provinces (the four Atlantic provinces, Manitoba, and Saskatchewan); three region-provinces (Ontario, Alberta, and British Columbia) with large populations and significant resources; and one nation-province (Quebec). These changes could be combined with other political reforms, such as reform or abolition of the Senate, fixed electoral dates, and the replacement of Canada's first-past-the-post electoral system with proportional representation (Resnick, 2000; Conway, 1997: 245).

Asymmetrical federalism also has its critics, however (see Cook, 1995: 242–245;

also Valaskakis and Fournier, 1995). First, such a change is politically unacceptable to the other provinces and most Canadians, as attested by English-speaking Canada's response to the Meech Lake Accord, which, in effect, had attempted to "codify" the existing practice of asymmetry (Gregg, 2005: 53). Second, Canadian federalism is already asymmetrical in certain respects. Like decentralization, further asymmetry would weaken Canada's federal principle as other provinces quickly sought the same powers. Third, by making the government in Quebec City more important to Quebecers, an action not wholly endorsed by many Quebecers themselves (*Edmonton Journal*, 2000b), the path could be set for further separatist agitation in that province.

Whether asymmetrical federalism could work is debatable. In any case, its program has little support outside of the academic community. By contrast, as noted, Plan C—decentralization—is supported by a number of powerful constituencies. In consequence, some observers suggest after 1995, Canada embarked on a steady, slow, and largely invisible course of decentralization (see Gregg, 2005; Griffiths, 2008). Plans A and B got all the press, but Plan C had the greatest impact.

Gregg (2005) identifies decentralization's start with the 1995 federal budget. Canada was then dealing with a growing national debt. Canada's then Liberal finance minister, Paul Martin, made deep cuts to the federal budget to deal with the problem. The cuts were particularly deep to shared-cost welfare-state programs (see Chapter 8). In effect, the federal government opted out of its share of paying for national programs it had been instrumental in founding. But those who pay the piper get to call the tune; in consequence, the provinces demanded more control over these programs. The province of Quebec saw the opportunity, suggests Gregg, to enlist the other provinces to join in calls for greater autonomy. (Gregg notes that the

Calgary Unity Declaration in 1997 stated: "If any future constitutional amendment confers powers on one province, these powers must be available to all provinces.") The provincial premiers' demands also coincided with the impact of the free trade agreement (implemented in 1989) upon economic relations, which shifted traditional east-west exchanges with north-south exchanges, thus making the provinces less interdependent (see Courchene, 1998; see also Chapter 9). The effect of these changes was that, while the federal government over the next decade succeeded in eliminating its fiscal deficits and paying off much of the national debt, control over programs was increasingly delegated to the provinces. Decentralization, whether planned or not, became a *fait accompli*.

For critics of decentralization, the insistence of dealing with the "Quebec problem" through a rigid adherence to symmetrical powers poses the risk that Canada will not end with a bang—the cataclysmic result of Quebec's separation—but with a whimper; with the slow dismantlement of Canada into a number of incoherent fiefdoms. In the words of former Saskatchewan Premier Roy Romanow, "the soil has been tilled for the sprouting of views at odds with shared destiny, and today there is a palpable momentum toward decentralization, individualism, and privatization, all peddled as a means to forge a stronger nation" (Romanow, 2006: 50).

Yet, one does not exclude the other. The dissolution of all does not render impossible the separation of one. What if Quebec were to separate? What would it mean for Quebec and for the rest of Canada?

THINKING THE UNTHINKABLE: SEPARATION

Countries, states, nations, and societies change. Though Canada's dissolution would astound and dismay much of the world—as Ignatieff (1993: 147) remarks, "If federalism can't work in my Canada, it probably can't work anywhere"—no country is ordained to last forever.

What would Canada and Quebec look like if they separated? In descriptive terms, Canada would cover 8.4 million square kilometres, nearly 85 percent of its previous size, though the Atlantic provinces would be separated from Ontario (Young, 1995: 9; Scowen, 1999), and have a population of more than 25.3 million, roughly 50 percent of which would be located in Ontario. Quebec would cover 1.5 million square kilometres and have a population of about 7.7 million people (see Table 1.1 for these figures). The economies of both Canada and Quebec would still be large. For Canada, *sans* Quebec, in 2007 real (constant 2002 dollars) **gross domestic product** (GDP)—*the total value of all goods and services produced by a country in a year*—was $1.053 trillion, while that of Quebec was nearly $266 billion (Statistics Canada, 2007b). Indeed, Quebec today ranks among the world's 30 leading economies (Ramonet, 2001). These figures, however, assume no massive transfers of land either way, no large movements of population, and no disruptions to either economy resulting from political unrest. These are big assumptions.

Setting aside the real possibility of violence (see Gibson, 1994; Monahan, 1995; Martin, 1999), with which authorities would have to deal, several key issues would need to be addressed immediately and involve likely bitter negotiations. These issues would include territorial boundaries (Reid, 1992: 37–66); division of public assets and the national debt, which was $508 billion as of March 31, 2007 (Statistics Canada, 2007b; see also Valaskakis and Fournier, 1995; Scowen, 1999); and determination of citizenship (Bourgault, 1991; Scowen, 1999). A further key issue would be jurisdiction over and responsibility for Aboriginal peoples (Bourgault, 1991; Parti Québécois, 1994; Gibson, 1994; Conway,

1997; Scowen, 1999). These issues would only scratch the surface, however. Deeper questions would remain for the citizens of both new countries.

Canada and Quebec would both require new constitutions. Quebec could achieve this task more easily than Canada (Parti Québécois, 1994). By contrast, constitutional renewal in Canada would require far more actors and a fundamental rethinking of the country's purpose and structure.

Both countries also would have to refashion their international relations. Quebec's task in this case would likely be more difficult than Canada's, though Quebec sovereigntists assume that international recognition, a seat at the United Nations, and partnership in all agreements previously signed by Canada would be automatically forthcoming (Bourgault, 1991; Turp, 1993; Parti Québécois, 1994). Finally, both Canada and Quebec would need to consider their changed relationship with the United States.

By far, however, the most wrenching adjustment for people in both countries would be psychological. Only a minority of people within Quebec desire outright independence; most hold strong feelings of attachment for Canada. Outside of Quebec, while there is an element of anti-French, anti-Quebec sentiment, and in recent years a hefty dose of fatigue with separatist threats leading to some remarking that it is time to "say goodbye" (Scowen, 1999; see also Brimelow, 1986; and Bercuson and Cooper, 1991), the vast majority of Canadians want Quebec to remain within Canada. A breakup would be difficult for both communities, though likely more so for English-speaking Canada. While Quebecers have had longer to prepare for the event and to define themselves as Québécois, English-speaking Canadians have not prepared themselves for such an eventuality. Their sense of identity includes Quebec, even if many refuse to acknowledge this. Quebec remains at the heart of most Canadians' psychological map of their country (as noted in Chapter 3).

QUEBEC AND THE "OTHER" ANGLOPHONE STATE

Bourgault (1991: 24) notes: "In Quebec, pro-American feeling is probably stronger than in the rest of Canada." At first, this may seem curious given the virulent antipathy between New France and the New England states in the years prior to the American Revolution (Chapter 2). After this time, however, Quebec's contacts with the United States gradually became more positive. The American Revolution's ideals appealed to Quebec's intellectual class and fuelled the rebellions of 1837–1838 (Conway, 1997). From Louis Papineau to Louis Riel, French-Canadian "rebels" repeatedly sought safe haven across the border. Nor were they alone. Throughout the 19th and 20th centuries, francophone emigrants, too, chose the eastern United States over the Canadian West.

Meanwhile, American capital also streamed into the province, stimulating Quebec's industrialization (Chodos and Hamovitch, 1991). The fact Prime Minister Brian Mulroney grew up in a Quebec town built by American investment and was president of an American branch plant before entering politics (Sawatsky, 1991) is symbolically significant.

The rise of English nationalism in the 1960s (Chapter 8) in counterpoint to Quebec nationalism further pushed (unwittingly) many Quebecers into the American embrace. Anglo-Canadian desires for a strong central government found little support among Quebecers, who viewed the concept of One Canada and the federal state with suspicion. Closer economic links with the United States were furthered by economic development after the Quiet Revolution, especially the expansion of hydroelectric power during the 1970s, and by the sovereigntist argument that less dependence upon Canada enhanced the separatist project. Thus was premised in part Quebec's support of the Free Trade Agreement in the 1988 federal election, or so thought some of English-speaking Canada's nationalists (see Resnick and Latouche, 1990).

Like people everywhere, Quebecers are large consumers of American culture. Likewise, many Quebecers, including many of its elite, also spend considerable time in the U.S., especially Florida (Cook, 1995: 229). For them, visits to the rest of Canada hold little attraction, though this sometimes changes when Quebecers do venture into the other provinces.

Quebec's unconscious relationship with the United States raises interesting questions. As André Laurendeau (1985) argued, "the homogenizing influence of the United States put in question the very existence of both Canadian [French and English] cultures." Unlike English-speaking Canadians, few Quebecers seem concerned about this influence. Some have argued, however, that Quebec's distinct culture has survived against American influence precisely because of its protected place within Canadian Confederation (Dufour, 1990; Resnick, 1991; Valaskakis and Fournier, 1995). More recently, Brunelle (1999) and Ramonet (2001) have further suggested that the sovereignty question has distracted Quebecers from examining the impact of neo-liberal globalization and Americanization upon Quebec society, and the problems it might face after separation. (One interesting sidelight to the American-led invasion of Iraq in March 2003 was the sudden rise of anti-American sentiment in Quebec, which, of all Canadian provinces, most opposed the war.)

Interestingly, many of the same arguments can also be made regarding English-speaking Canada: that it has insufficiently valued the role of the French language and culture in differentiating Canada from the United States. Could either Quebec or Canada alone long withstand the assimilating influences of the American giant? This question and others are addressed in Part 2.

CONCLUSION

Canada and Quebec have travelled a long way since 1960, let alone since 1763. Sometimes in conflict more often than in co-operation, each has shaped the other. Canada's institutions, its decentralized system of governance, its tolerance of cultural differences (not to be overstated), and much of its identity are built upon French foundations. For its part, Quebec—the territory in which the French "fact" was suppressed and contained, and therefore incubated—also contains a hidden English element. Together, Canada's French and English "nations" have withstood absorption into the United States and built, by nearly any standard, one of the best societies on earth.

Canada, it is often said, is an experiment (Bernard, 1996; Conway, 1997; Saul, 1997). Is it possible to break the European model of nation *equals* state *equals* country *equals* society? Is it possible to conceive and create a state structure in which two nations—three, counting the Aboriginal peoples—exist harmoniously and prosper, housed within a single country? A society in which majority, minority, and individual differences are embraced and respected, and yet political and social coherence are maintained? I leave the last words to Conway (1997: 252):

> If we can continue our unique experiment in seeking unity through diversity, if we can retain the two great cultures [French and English] together in one federal or confederal structure, Canada could yet become a model for all the world.... [I]f we fail, it will not be a disaster. Life will go on.... But the Canada we could have become ... will be lost, perhaps forever.

The world watches.

KEY TERMS
asymmetrical federalism
decentralization
gross domestic product (GDP)
interculturalisme
open secularism
reasonable accommodation
subsidiarity

CRITICAL THINKING QUESTIONS

1. Is secularism a kind of modern "religion"?

2. Is it possible to differentiate between individual and collective identities?

3. Why do anglophone and francophone Canadians hold such differing views about the meaning of "nation"?

4. Why do many francophone Quebecers view the United States, another anglophone country, more positively than English-speaking Canada?

5. Does globalization increase or decrease the likelihood of independence movements in Quebec and elsewhere in the world? Why?

RECOMMENDED READINGS

Courchene, Thomas. 1997. *The Nation State in a Global/Information Era: Policy Challenges.* Kingston: John Deutsch Institute for the Study of Economic Policy, Queen's University.
One of Canada's best-known economists, Courchene outlines in this book some of the difficulties faced by states in the era of globalization.

Griffiths, Rudyard. 2008. *We're Prying French and English Canada Apart.* Ottawa: The Dominion Institute.

Written by the head of Canada's Dominion Institute, this book argues that recent federal initiatives are tearing apart the country's historic relationship between French and English.

Igartua, Jose E. 2006. *The Other Quiet Revolution: National Identities in English Canada, 1945–1971.* Vancouver: University of British Columbia Press.
This book examines the enormous transformation that occurred in English-speaking Canada during Quebec's Quiet Revolution.

Ignatieff, Michael. 1993. *Blood and Belonging: Journeys into the New Nationalism.* Toronto: Penguin.
Ignatieff's book examines several nationalist movements, including Quebec's.

Riesman, David, with Reuel Denney and Nathan Glazer. 1950. *The Lonely Crowd: A Study of the Changing American Character.* New Haven: Yale University Press.
Don't let the year of publication put you off. This book remains a classic examination of individualism and the construction of personal identity in modern society.

RELATED WEBSITES

Bouchard-Taylor Commission Report
www.accommodements.qc.ca
In an effort to address perceived cultural and religious divisions, in February 2007 the Quebec government established the Consultation Commission on Accommodation Practices Related to Cultural Differences, otherwise known as the Bouchard-Taylor Commission.

CBC Digital Archives (1995 Sovereignty Referendum)
http://archives.cbc.ca/politics/federal_politics/topics/1891/
A useful video clip dealing with the 1995 sovereignty referendum, *Separation Anxiety: The 1995 Quebec Referendum.*

Statistics Canada (Language Usage in Canada)
http://www12.statcan.ca/census-recensement/2006/as-sa/97-555/p13-eng.cfm
Derived from the 2006 census, Statistics Canada has a useful report on language usage in Canada, *The Evolving Linguistic Portrait of Canada.*

CANADIAN SOCIETY ON VIDEO

The Black Sheep: Ten Years Later. 2003. National Film Board of Canada, 82 minutes. In 1992, filmmaker Jacques Godbout made *The Black Sheep*, a film about rising discontent in Quebec after the failure of the Meech Lake Accord. This sequel deals with the new Quebec emerging today.

PART TWO
CANADA AND THE UNITED STATES

Part One of this book examined conflict and co-operation between Canada's French and English cultures, and how this relationship has shaped—often unbeknownst—Canada's political, economic, and cultural landscape. Part Two examines Canada's—especially English-speaking Canada's—equally complex, troubled, and often ambivalent relationship with the United States.

The chapters that follow trace the political, economic, and cultural moments defining this relationship. Sometimes, such as during the development of the Canadian economy in the 19th century or at the time of Roosevelt's New Deal in the 1930s, the United States has been considered a positive model for Canadian society. At other times, however, such as the turbulent period of the 1960s and the recent War on Terrorism, the United States has been seen as a negative model. The result has been a relationship that, if traced, would show two ships occasionally running parallel, and occasionally tacking quite differently into the future.

The chapters do not focus solely on this external relationship, however. They also examine Canada's internal development and deal with such issues as regionalism, the evolution of corporate capitalism, and the development of the Canadian welfare state. Along the way, other changes in Canadian society are also detailed, such as Canada's class structure, the role of women in Canadian society, and immigration policy.

Finally, Part Two examines the recent period of neo-liberal globalization and its impact upon Canada, from issues of free trade and market liberalization to the terrorist attacks upon New York and Washington in September 2001 and the subsequent wars in Afghanistan and Iraq.

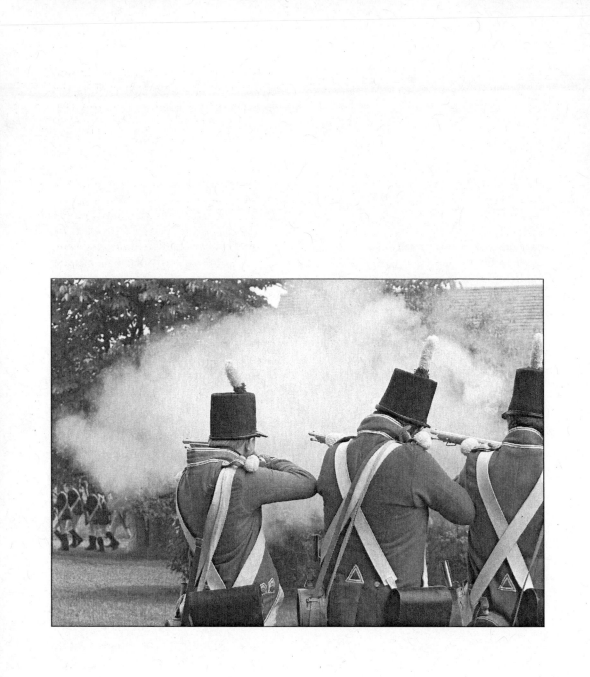

CHAPTER 6

THE MAKING OF ENGLISH CANADA

[T]he American continents, by the free and independent condition which they have assumed and maintain, are henceforth not to be considered as subjects for future colonization by any European power.... [W]e should consider any attempt on their part to extend their system to any portion of this hemisphere as dangerous to our peace and safety.

—U.S. President James Monroe, Annual Message to Congress, 1823

It is our Manifest Destiny to overspread the continent allotted by Providence for the free development of our multiplying millions.

—newspaper editor John O'Sullivan, *United States Magazine and Democratic Review*, 1845

When the experiment of the "dominion" shall have failed—as fail it must—a process of peaceful absorption will give Canada her proper place in the great North American Republic.

—publisher Horace Greeley, *New York Tribune*, 1867

INTRODUCTION

The phrase "the world's longest undefended border" is an overused metaphor for describing Canada's relationship with the United States. No Canadian prime minister, American president, or accompanying journalist leaves home without some variation on it. While the phrase is not entirely incorrect—though who can say, given events since the terrorist attacks of September 2001—it is historically misleading.

Canadians and Americans forget that their mutual relationship began less cordially, with a war. The American Revolution spawned not only the

United States but also Canada (Lipset, 1990). From then on until 1871, the threat of American invasion was real and Canadians had frequent cause to anticipate war (Winks, 1998: 3). Even after, until at least 1936, the American Department of Defense regularly updated invasion plans for Canada (Rudmin, 1993).

This chapter traces the development of English-speaking Canada from 1775, when the American Revolution began, until Confederation in 1867. The chapter concentrates on the early troubled history of relations between Canada and the United States and how events in the United States helped spawn the creation of Canada in 1867. Specifically, this chapter shows that Canadian society has developed socially, economically, and politically both for internal reasons and as a defensive response (see Aitken, 1959) to the American threat. Finally, the chapter begins the process of defining English Canada's identity.

THE BIRTH OF TWO NATIONS

The American War of Independence, popularly known as the American Revolution, began at Lexington, Massachusetts, on April 18, 1775, and ended with the Treaty of Paris in 1783. Why did the American colonists revolt in 1775?

The American Declaration of Independence of 1776 (*Time*, 2009: 584–585) provides a useful starting point for answering the question. Like all revolutionary tracts, the Declaration does not shy away from rhetoric: "The history of the present King of Great Britain is a history of repeated injuries and usurpations, all having in direct object the establishment of an absolute Tyranny over these States." The Declaration lists a series of specific complaints: the general suspension of natural and constitutional rights, unjust trials, press ganging, the denial of political representation, unlawful taxation, the prevention of trade, the growth of colonial bureaucracy, general harassment of the people, and the "quartering of large bodies of armed troops."

Many of these complaints were justified. The American colonists believed strongly that a paternalistic and authoritarian British monarch and his administration had breached constitutional rights guaranteed by the English Bill of Rights (1689).

Taxation was a particularly vexing issue. From the late 17th century on, the English Crown and Parliament had imposed a series of taxes on the colonies. At first purely regulatory in nature, after 1763 taxation became a means of generating revenues (Hofstadter, 1958: 3–4). The colonists were unaccustomed to paying revenue-raising taxes and, in any case, viewed them as potentially ruinous. The colonists also believed that the taxes had been imposed without their consent, given either directly or indirectly, through the will of Parliament (Hofstadter et al., 1957: 42).

The British viewed taxation differently. "The empire was expensive; costly wars had been fought to acquire and defend it; still more money would have to be laid out in the future to garrison it" (Hofstadter, 1958: 3). In short, it was time for the colonists to shoulder their fair share of state expenses.

Though frequently the tax measures were withdrawn under protest, or otherwise circumvented by the industrious colonists (see James, 1997), taxes were certainly a major sore point leading up to the revolution. Anti-tax protests were common. In several instances, such as Boston in 1770, there was violence between British troops and civilians. These confrontations invited further repressive measures. Troops were posted, and dissenters were dealt with harshly.

Nonetheless, as James (1997: 107–109) notes, "Americans in 1774 enjoyed considerable freedom," including a free press, rights of assembly, and the right to travel.

Indeed, these freedoms provided much of the basis for the revolution's success. While the issues listed in the Declaration were important, they were not intractable before 1775. There was little support for independence, even less for war (Zinn, 1995: 76).

The reasons for this lack of support are easy to discern. The American Revolution was less a nationalist fight against foreign oppression than a family squabble. Nine-tenths (James, 1997: 101) of the colonies' 2.5 million people were of British descent, many of them "excessively proud of their Britishness" (James, 1997: 100). At least a third of the American colonists were staunch Loyalists to the Crown, while another third were probably neutral throughout the conflict (Zinn, 1995: 76). Many of the colonists were not sure why they were fighting (Hofstadter, 1958).

Why, then, did the American colonies revolt? The general answer is, ironically, that the conclusion of the war with France in 1763 removed a major threat to the colonies. In simple terms, the British Empire had outlived its usefulness. But this explanation only provides a context, not a substantive cause for the revolution.

More to the point, the consequences of managing the peace created enormous and unexpected conflicts between the British and certain colonists, especially in New England (see Orchard, 1998). The colonies that would become Canada were integrally involved in these disputes. Two sections of the Declaration of Independence make clear this connection (*Time*, 2009: 585). One of the two sections reads:

> For abolishing the free System of English Laws in a neighboring Province, establishing therein an Arbitrary government, and enlarging its Boundaries so as to render it at once an example and

fit instrument for introducing the same absolute rule into these Colonies.

The second important section of the Declaration reads:

> He [the King] has excited domestic insurrections amongst us, and has endeavoured to bring on the inhabitants of our frontiers, the merciless Indian Savages, whose known rule of warfare is an undistinguished destruction of all ages, sexes and conditions.

The reference in both quoted sections is to the Quebec Act of 1774. As we've seen (in Chapter 2), the Quebec Act restored to the French-Canadians and the Catholic Church certain privileges removed in 1763 by the Royal Proclamation Act. The resurrection of French Catholicism in North America provoked hysterical alarm among the overwhelmingly Protestant colonists whose memories of sectarian conflict were fresh. James (1997: 105) notes that, in early 1775, "the New England backwoods buzzed with rumours that Popery was about to be imposed...." Among the colonists, papal fears alone might have seemed sufficiently provocative. But the Quebec Act also extended the boundaries of Quebec into the Ohio-Mississippi Indian Territory, thereby limiting the expansionist ambitions of American agrarians, investors, and land speculators (among them, George Washington, Thomas Jefferson, and Benjamin Franklin) (see Orchard, 1998: 14).

Why did the British extend Quebec's boundaries? In part, they did so under pressure from merchants in the Montreal-based fur trade (Innis, 1962: 176). But the British also extended the boundaries in hopes of reasserting control over lands designated in the Royal Proclamation Act of 1763 as specifically "reserved" for the Indians: the lands west of the Appalachian Mountains (see Chapter 12). The expansion-minded colonists had consistently ignored the Royal Proclamation Act, resulting in renewed conflict with the Indians of the Ohio Valley. The British meant through the Quebec Act to curtail settlement in the volatile region. In the minds of the colonists, however, the Quebec Act had merely incited further conflict with the Indians, whom the colonists hated and wanted removed from the territory, hence the Declaration's rather florid statements quoted above.

The Quebec Act was passed in the summer of 1774. Shortly thereafter, in September 1774, a Continental Congress was convened to devise a slate of measures in retaliation to the Quebec Act (James, 1997: 105). Events thereafter continued apace. The revolution's first volleys were fired only days before the Quebec Act was to have come into effect (May 1, 1775).

The war dragged on for six years. It was fought by unconventional means by untrained colonists and conventional means by the trained British troops. Long periods of idleness and boredom were punctuated by brief battles of horrific savagery on both sides.

In June 1775, the Americans launched a two-pronged attack on Canada. One American army went along Lake Champlain and captured Montreal, forcing Governor Guy Carleton (1724–1808) to flee to Quebec City. A second American army landed in Maine and proceeded to the shores of the St. Lawrence, where both armies then joined in an assault upon Quebec City. The siege failed the following May, however, when a flotilla of British troops arrived. The American forces withdrew (Conway, 1997; James, 1997; Orchard, 1998).

Thereafter, the war never seriously threatened Canadian territory. Nonetheless, the American colonists believed throughout that Canada would soon join them in open revolt. The invasion of Canada in 1775, for example, was "advertised as a war of liberation" (James, 1997: 113). When the American Articles of Confederation were written in 1777, a special Canada provision (article 11) was even included, which read:

> Canada, according to this confederation, and joining in the measures of the United States, shall be admitted into, and entitled to all the advantages of this Union: but no other colony shall be admitted into the same unless such admission be agreed to by nine states.

The idea that Canada might join the rebellion was not far-fetched. The people in Nova Scotia, linked by trade and family connections to the New England states, briefly considered joining the cause (Winks, 1998: 3). Likewise, many within Montreal's English-speaking business class supported the revolutionary cause (Morton, 1997). The larger French-Canadian community—clergy, seigneurs, and merchants alike—remained neutral, however. As the British had hoped, the Quebec Act ensured French neutrality.

Which side would emerge victorious was not quite certain until 1778, when France, ever desirous of revenge upon Britain for losses suffered in 1763, joined the conflict. With French assistance in the form of both troops and a naval blockade, the Americans won the last great battle of the war at Yorktown, Virginia, in October 1781 (Hofstadter et al., 1957: 108–109; Zinn, 1995: 79).

The Treaty of Paris saw England recognize American independence. The treaty further set America's borders at the Mississippi River on the west, the 31st parallel (just above Florida) in the south, and the Great Lakes in the north. The treaty also acknowledged American rights to Newfoundland's fisheries. England, however, retained joint privileges with America in navigating the Mississippi. The Americans further agreed to compensate British creditors for private debts owed them and to recommend that individual states restore Loyalist property (Hofstadter et al., 1957: 109–110).

In 1783 many Americans viewed Canada as a natural extension of their colonies, and wanted to remove British influence entirely from the continent. The United States, however, was not strong enough, politically or militarily, to press such demands (Horsman, 1993). Moreover, at least some Americans may have viewed a continuing British presence in North America, for all its drawbacks, as a kind of bulwark against possible French and Spanish expansion (James, 1997: 119). For these reasons, Canada remained standing, but it was a Canada quickly changing, and soon facing renewed threats from its American neighbour.

THE WAR OF 1812

The Treaty of Paris did not end disputes between Britain and its former American colonies. A major source of conflict was ended with the signing in 1794 of Jay's Treaty, which saw Britain evacuate the forts it had maintained in the Ohio Valley in defence of the Montreal fur interests (Horsman, 1993: 297). Setting a pattern that would repeat itself again in 1814 (the Treaty of Ghent) and in 1846 (the Oregon Treaty), trade—and good relations—with the United States was far more important to Britain than trade with Canada. The interests of Montreal's fur traders, and Canada generally, were expendable.

Still, irritants remained and were heightened after 1793 by the outbreak of yet another war between Britain and France. In their zeal to defeat the French (this time in the person of Napoleon), the British were soon seizing American ships that traded with France, arresting escaped British seamen, and pressing American seamen into Royal service (Berton, 1980; Horsman, 1993). Understandably,

Americans viewed Britain as not only harming American trade but also breaching American neutrality and sovereignty (Bowler, 1993). America's still fragile honour was at stake (Horsman, 1993: 279).

Once more, the Aboriginal peoples also featured prominently among American complaints. The British, it was alleged, were encouraging their Indian allies, led by the Shawnee chief Tecumseh (see Chapter 10), to attack American settlers (Bowler, 1993: 298; Hofstadter, 1958: 227; Berton, 1980; Morton, 1997; Granatstein, 1996).

As such "provocations" mounted, war fever gripped the United States. During the American congressional debates of 1811 and 1812, legitimate complaints gave way to overblown rhetoric that Canada must be liberated. Finally, President Madison declared in June 1812 the beginning of a second War of Independence (Morton, 1997: 42).

Once again, the Americans believed Canada would be an easy conquest. Former President Thomas Jefferson stated confidently that "The acquisition of Canada this year ... will be a mere matter of marching" (Colombo, 1994: 29).

As in 1775, such confidence was well placed. In 1812, there were only half a million people in British North America compared with 7.5 million in the American states (Morton, 1997: 33). Moreover, two-thirds of Upper Canada's population were newly arrived Americans (Bowler, 1993: 302), largely indifferent to the war. The British themselves were occupied in fighting Napoleon. In short, the War of 1812 seemed like one that the British colonies could not win, yet they did.

The War of 1812 was fought almost entirely in Upper Canada, though it strayed occasionally into Lower Canada, spawned a few memorable sea battles, and touched off a mini-boom in maritime smuggling (Bowler, 1993). Along Upper Canada's main front, the war began in a gentlemanly fashion, continuing indifferently at times—along the invisible border, truck, trade, and personal contacts continued largely unabated—but became more savage as time progressed (Berton, 1980). In April 1813, the Americans sacked and burned York (now Toronto). In revenge, in August 1814 British forces captured and burned the U.S. Capitol building and the presidential mansion at Washington.

In the end, a combination of three things saved Canada from American takeover: American military ineptness, French and Indian support at key moments, and the end of the Napoleonic Wars in Europe, which freed regular British troops to come to Canada (Berton, 1980: 27; Morton, 1997: 42; Horsman, 1993).

The Treaty of Ghent in 1814 formally ended the war. The pre-existing borders were restored; the problems that began the war were forgotten or soon disappeared. In the words of historian Desmond Morton (1997: 43), "The war changed no boundaries, brought no reparations, avenged no wrongs." The Battle of Waterloo and Napoleon's subsequent banishment to St. Helena ended Britain's need to seize ships and impress seamen. The severely weakened Aboriginal tribes were no longer a threat to the Americans or an impediment to settlement.

The War of 1812 gave English Canada its first heroes: Major-General Sir Isaac Brock (1769–1812) and Chief Tecumseh (1768–1813), who both died in battle, as well as Laura Secord (1775–1868) (Morton, 1997; Bowler, 1993; Orchard, 1998). The war also strengthened British resolve to protect its North American colonies. It further solidified the alliance of the French, English, and Aboriginal peoples, who had fought side by side against the Americans, though the last of these received the least reward for their sacrifices (see Chapter 10). Finally, and most importantly, the War of 1812 forged a sense of English Canada as a community and the beginnings of its distinct identity.

THE MAKING OF ENGLISH-CANADIAN IDENTITY

We have briefly to reacquaint ourselves with the Loyalists (Chapter 2), especially those 10,000 or so who settled in Canada and caused its division in 1791. Our first impressions were not favourable. Contemporaries used the words "quarrelsome" and "bitter" to describe them. It is time, however, to revisit the Loyalists and ask: Who were they? and, more importantly: What became of them?

To the first question: The Americans portrayed the Loyalists as an "elite of Anglican clergy, bureaucrats, and merchants living off government favours" (Dickinson and Young, 2003: 69), an image the Loyalists themselves later encouraged. The image was incorrect, however. The Loyalists were not fundamentally different from the Americans who stayed behind. Most were subsistence farmers, disproportionately young, often poor and illiterate. While most were recent immigrants from Britain, the Loyalists also included various other religious and ethnic minorities (Dickinson and Young, 2003: 69; Brown, 1993: 244, 247; Granatstein, 1996: 15). They also included approximately 3,000 escaped Black slaves, who settled in Nova Scotia, and almost 2,000 Iroquois, who settled north of the Great Lakes, where the city of Brantford today commemorates the name of their leader, Joseph Brant (Wynn, 2000: 220).

The American Revolution did not merely create two nations; it also created two myths. Not *all* Americans were democrats; not *all* Loyalists were monarchists. Most people on both sides were indifferent, confused, and scared, caught up in events beyond their control (see Granatstein, 1996: 13).

Yet the Loyalists quickly began to believe their own myths, which brings us to the second question: What became of them? A couple of quotations will point us toward an answer.

The first is taken second-hand from Christian Dufour (1990: 54), who cites a Canadian history text used in English high schools in the 1930s as it concludes the episode of the American invasion of 1812: "Once again, the American invaders were repelled, as in 1776, as in 1690." But, asks Dufour, "How can the British Canada that drove back the Americans in 1812 be linked to the New France that stood up to the English in 1690?" Put another way, who were the "Americans" in 1690? They were, of course, the English. (The specific date 1690 refers to a famous incident in which Governor General Louis Frontenac defeated the invading army of the Bostonian Sir William Phips.)

The second quotation is from historian P.B. Waite, recalling his days as a schoolboy in Belleville, Ontario, in the early 1930s. In the quote, Waite (1997: 13) remembers situating his identity within Canada's history:

> We mapped the voyages of Champlain, of La Salle.... We rejoiced in the story of Phips' demand ... and Frontenac's reply.... Thus did we English-*Canadiens* fight the Americans and their British allies. And we continued to be *Canadiens*....
>
> Then suddenly, oddly, sharply we became English. It was something of a wrench. Wolfe had laid siege to Quebec in the summer of 1759 and all that summer we stayed with Montcalm fighting off the British. Then, early on the morning of 13 September 1759, we changed sides. We crossed the St. Lawrence with Wolfe and the British in the dark, silent boats, we fought with the British regulars on the Plains of Abraham; and though we mourned both Montcalm and Wolfe, by the time of Montcalm's death the next morning we were already on our way at last to being English-Canadians.

What became of the Loyalists? Upon their arrival, they were defeated and humiliated, indeed, not unlike the French they found in the new land. But they found in the French something of particular value: The French had an identity, one ready-made for appropriation, an identity, moreover, shaped by being the first anti-Americans. Thus, the Loyalists became *Canadiens* and Canadians became (by Loyalist definition and thereafter) anti-Americans.

Of course, we cannot lay the whole weight of appropriation upon the Loyalists. In most provinces, the Loyalists soon found themselves a minority (they never were a majority in Quebec). The sole exception was New Brunswick. Even there, however, after 1812 the Loyalists found themselves engulfed by other immigrants. In 1812, only one-fifth of Upper Canada's population of 100,000 was Loyalist in origin (Brown, 1993: 247; see also Wynn, 2000: 221). Nonetheless, the Loyalists' myth of rejecting American takeover and their incorporation of French Canada into their identity structure began the process of forging in English Canada a distinctive identity (Brown, 1993; Granatstein, 1996). After 1812, the people of British North America at last had something in common: British and French alike, Aboriginal and Black, they were *not* Americans.

THE MONROE DOCTRINE, MANIFEST DESTINY, AND AMERICAN EXCEPTIONALISM

The Treaty of Ghent did not end tensions between the United States and Britain's North American colonies. Conflict was blunted, it is true, by the signing in 1817 of the Rush-Bagot Convention, which prohibited large warships on the Great Lakes, and by the 1818 Convention, which clarified somewhat the boundary lines. The existing line was extended westward from the Lake of the Woods to the Rocky Mountains along the 49th parallel (Careless, 1970: 134–135).

American expansion continued unabated, however, fuelled by the demands of a growing population (9.6 million people in 1820) (*Time*, 2009: 648) and a changing economy. But American expansion also invoked as its justification the notion of "liberating" land and people from the foreign and colonial yoke, even when the people involved did not want to be liberated and viewed the Americans as aggressors. Thus, President James Monroe, in his message to Congress in December 1823, coined what become known as the **Monroe Doctrine** (see opening quotation above), *the doctrine that declares that the Americas are to be free of foreign influence and that the United States will act to prevent such influence.* American expansion also was justified by the notion of **Manifest Destiny**, a term coined in 1845 by John O'Sullivan, that held *the new country was divinely ordained with a special mission to cover North America* (see quotation above). In turn, such beliefs paved the way for what is often termed **American exceptionalism**, *the belief held by many Americans that the United States cannot be judged by the same standards as other countries* (see Chapter 9).

America expanded steadily across the continent throughout the first half of the 19th century. The process was always similar. American trade with and exploration of new territories was soon followed by immigration. Soon the American land speculators, merchants, and settlers would complain about the actions of local government officials (usually Spanish in origin); then they would lobby Washington to intervene. Covert aid would follow. In time, the existing government would be dethroned (sometimes with the help of American troops), the populace would "ask" to be annexed, and the United States would oblige. Thus, Florida was seized from Spain in 1819; Texas, after years of internal intrigue inspired by the American government, also from Spain in 1845; and New Mexico and California, following an American-provoked war, from Mexico in 1848 (Hofstadter et al., 1957: 181–182 and 279–281; Orchard, 1998: 32–33). The war with Mexico doubled the size of the United States, not incidentally, on the eve of the California gold rush.

Canada was not immune from American intrigues and claims. War nearly erupted in the 1820s after Maine's governor declared New Brunswick's timberlands part of the state and ordered U.S. troops to seize the territory (Orchard, 1998: 30). In a prelude to the Mexican wars, in 1844 the United States also claimed, by dint of biblical injunctions, the Oregon territory. The dispute was settled in 1846, again under threat of war, on grounds favourable to the Americans. This dispute was followed in 1859 by the so-called Pig War over the San Juan Islands in Puget Sound, which ended in 1873 with the United States gaining sole ownership of the islands (Lower, 1983: 66–88, and 75). By the 1850s also, American settlement in the Red River Valley was pressuring for annexation to the United States.

In these ventures, the biggest losers were the Aboriginal peoples (see Chapter 10), who were vilified, pacified, assimilated, and often hunted down, sometimes to extinction. Before becoming American president in 1832, Andrew Jackson (1767–1845) earned a well-deserved reputation for savagery directed at Aboriginal peoples, whom he terrorized and killed by the thousands, before taking more than 2 million acres in northern Alabama (Wright, 1993: 211–212). Another future president, Abraham Lincoln (1809–1865), while sympathetic to the situation of Blacks, thought the Indian people unredeemable and fought briefly as a young man in the vicious Illinois Black Hawk wars of the 1830s.

By 1853, the United States had nearly achieved its present territorial size. Alaska was added in 1867 and Hawaii in 1898. The only territory in North America unincorporated into the United States was what the French author Voltaire once called "a few acres of snow": Canada (quoted in Colombo, 1994: 18).

THE POLITICAL ECONOMY OF BRITISH NORTH AMERICA, 1800–1866

To the unreflecting eye, the British colonies in 1800 must still have seemed not much more than a frozen wasteland. The combined population of the five British North American provinces in 1805 was about 360,000. Of this total, about 230,000 resided in Lower Canada, 46,000 in Upper Canada, 54,000 in Nova Scotia, 25,000 in New Brunswick, and 5,000 or so in Prince Edward Island (Careless, 1970: 122; Norrie and Owram, 1996: 84, 119; Dickinson and Young, 2003). Newfoundland's total population in 1805 was just short of 20,000, but this number included a large number of semi-permanent residents engaged in the seasonal fisheries (see Norrie and Owram, 1996: 75).

The end of the Napoleonic Wars, however, saw Britain hit by a depression and rising unemployment. Thus, after 1815 the colonies—except Newfoundland, which itself entered a period of stagnation until the 1850s (see Norrie and Owram, 1996)— experienced a massive wave of immigration that lasted four decades. Between 1815 and 1850, nearly 800,000 mainly British immigrants arrived in Canada: "discharged soldiers and half-pay officers from Wellington's armies, Irish weavers and paupers, Scottish artisans and dispossessed crofters, English country labourers and factory workers" (Careless, 1970: 147).

Few British immigrants settled permanently in Lower Canada. Those who did settled mainly in the Eastern Townships and the growing cities of Montreal and Quebec. Elsewhere, however, British immigration left a permanent mark.

Scottish immigration especially filled Nova Scotia, competing with the settled Loyalists and pre-Loyalist New Englanders, and Prince Edward Island, while the Irish, especially after the 1840s, filled New Brunswick (Careless, 1970: 148).

Immigration effects were felt most, however, in Upper Canada. There, British immigration rose steadily after 1820, dropped in the mid-1830s due to cholera and the province's political troubles, then rose again sharply during the 1840s. Though all elements of British society— "English, Welsh, Lowland and Highland Scots and Catholic and Ulster Irish" (Careless, 1970: 149)—arrived, it was perhaps the Irish who left the greatest impression. Driven from their homeland by poverty, overcrowding, and, finally, the potato famine, the Irish soon found employment building canals and, later, the railways (Morton, 1997: 54; also Pentland, 1991; Norrie and Owram, 1996).

American immigration to the British colonies generally declined during this period due to American westward expansion. A sole exception to this pattern was the relatively large influx into the Maritimes and Upper Canada of American Blacks escaping slavery during the 20 years leading up to that country's Civil War (see below). By 1861, there were about 60,000 Blacks in British North America (Winks, 1998: 8; also Kelly, 1997).

As a consequence of immigration and births, British North America's population by 1851 had grown to over 2.4 million; by 1861, 3.2 million. Upper Canada now had the largest population—nearly 1.4 million—followed by Lower Canada (1.1 million), Nova Scotia (331,000), New Brunswick (252,000), and Prince Edward Island (61,000) (see Table 1.1).

Immigration to the colonies, however, began declining in the early 1850s, and by the 1860s was actually outpaced by people leaving Canada. Indeed, from 1851 to 1901, for example, while 1.9 million people entered Canada, 2.2 million left, primarily for the United States (McKie, 1994: 26).

The British colonies' problem in attracting and retaining people was simple: Their economies were unable to compete with the expanding and rapidly industrializing neighbour to the south. Though economic development occurred, the British colonies generally lacked investment capital; their transportation systems were substandard and internally not integrated; and their separate economies exhibited many of the instabilities characteristic of staple-based, export-driven economies.

Newfoundland, for example, remained an imperial outpost, not even a colony, until 1824. And, though the granting of responsible government in 1855 coincided with a period of growth lasting until the mid-1880s, its economy remained dangerously one-dimensional. In 1858, for example, 89 percent of Newfoundland's labour force worked in the fishery, a statistic that remained relatively constant over the next decade, indicating a single-industry dependence that would sink the Newfoundland economy two decades later (Norrie and Owram, 1996: 78–79, 350–351).

The situation elsewhere in the colonies was less bleak but still no cause for optimism. The American Revolution spurred a short-lived economic boom. Nova Scotia's timber industry developed around producing pine masts for the British navy; shipbuilding, formerly concentrated around local markets, also grew to service trade with the West Indies; and internal markets, especially for agricultural products, arose around the province's increased population, inspired in part by Loyalist immigration. Subsequently, the Napoleonic Wars produced a second Maritime boom, as Britain increased its colonial imports. The fisheries remained important, but forestry also now developed in New Brunswick and spurred forward economic linkages:

sawmills and (especially) shipbuilding. By 1860, the Maritimes were one of the world's premier shipbuilding centres. Other important industries developed included Nova Scotia's trade in coal and agricultural produce (Norrie and Owram, 1996: 79–80, and 86).

The years, especially after 1815, were not kind to Lower Canada. The fur industry entered a period of decline following the signing of Jay's Treaty in 1794 and left the St. Lawrence Valley altogether following the merger in 1821 of the North West Company with the Hudson's Bay Company. Wheat became a major export item to Britain and the West Indies during the late 18th century, but early the next century it too entered a period of permanent decline occasioned by recurrent crop failures (see Trofimenkoff, 1993: 384) and increasing competition from Upper Canada (see below).

These losses were partially offset by other sources of economic growth, notably timber (Norrie and Owram, 1996) and power generation. Also, the two major urban centres of Quebec City and Montreal increased in size and importance, the former economy based on shipping, the military, and services; the latter on industry and finance. But much of the province remained rural—indeed, became even more disproportionately so during the century (see Chapter 3)—and underdeveloped, while the benefits of industrialization went almost entirely to the anglophone bourgeoisie.

By contrast, Upper Canada's situation grew decidedly more hopeful as the 19th century progressed. The province was at first economically dependent on British administrative expenditures in the form of direct handouts: subsidies and claims to Loyalists and military and civil construction. In the words of Norrie and Owram (1996: 123), "the British government subsidized the initial stages of settlement in Upper Canada." The arrival of the "late Loyalists" (Americans newly arrived

in the early 1800s) and of British immigrants after 1820 provided both labourers and consumers. Local domestic markets developed and the timber industry grew. But wheat was Ontario's real story.

Small amounts of wheat were already being shipped down the St. Lawrence as early as 1794 (Norrie and Owram, 1996: 124). During the War of 1812, however, wheat became a major export to Britain. Though wheat sales declined after the war, a new market was soon found in Lower Canada, then later again in Britain and the United States. Wheat exports from Upper Canada rose by 500 percent during the 1840s and then doubled again, peaking in 1861 (McCallum, 1991: 11).

The importance of wheat to Upper Canada's economy cannot be overestimated. In 1820, over 95 percent of the province's population was still rural (Norrie and Owram, 1996: 126). Locally produced wheat thus fed Upper Canada's population without resort to imports. Capital acquired through exports of surplus wheat, especially after 1840, later fuelled industrial development (McCallum, 1991).

Instances of economic development and diversification aside, in the mid-1850s the British colonies were marked by uneven development and export dependency. Nova Scotia's export trade was spread between the other British North American colonies, the United States, and the West Indies. New Brunswick's export trade was heavily tied to Britain. Prince Edward Island's export trade was moderately tied to the other colonies. The Province of Canada's economy was based on agricultural and forestry exports, primarily to Lower Canada and the United States. All of the colonies imported a larger percentage of their manufactured goods (Norrie and Owram, 1996: 91).

The colonies' resultant economic instability fuelled ongoing political demands, particularly from the Province of Canada's business class, for either annexation by the United States or (at the very least) a reciprocity agreement with the U.S. that would ensure stable markets. In 1854, they got their wish.

Understanding how the Reciprocity Treaty of 1854 came about requires a brief discussion of changes in economic thinking that had occurred since the 18th century. As the reader will remember (Chapter 2), Canada was founded primarily as a mercantilist adventure. Two centuries later, however, mercantilism was under increasing attack. Adam Smith (1723–1790) launched the first attack in his classic text *The Wealth of Nations*, which, fittingly, came out in 1776, the same year as the American Declaration of Independence. The latter stated a liberal interpretation of political freedom. Smith's text similarly argued for a liberal interpretation of economic freedom.

Smith directed three specific arguments against mercantilism. First, he argued that free trade among countries was mutually beneficial. Second, he argued that trade enhanced specialization in production, leading to increased efficiency. And third, Smith denounced mercantilism on the basis of the "collusive relationship" it encouraged between governments and the merchant classes (La Haye, 1993: 535).

Smith's arguments found fertile ground in Britain during the American Revolution. Many British already viewed the colonies as expensive to maintain, administratively and militarily. Now they were a political headache as well.

The outbreak of the Napoleonic Wars in 1793 brought mercantilism a temporary reprieve as Britain became dependent upon its colonies for food and materials, for example, Maritime fish and timber. After 1814, however, Smith's ideas—now augmented by a young economist, David Ricardo (1772–1823)—gained momentum. Slowly at first, then with greater alacrity, mercantilism's regulatory walls collapsed. In 1833, Britain abolished colo-

nial slavery, thus creating "free labour." "Free trade" followed in the 1840s with the repeal of timber duties, the Navigation Acts, and the Corn Laws (Norrie and Owram, 1996: 173). Britain's policy of preferential trade with the North American colonies ceased after 1846.

Free trade made perfect sense from the British point of view. Britain, after all, was the first modern industrialized capitalist country. Moreover, it was still a great empire possessing the world's most powerful fleet.

Elsewhere, including the United States, Smith's and Ricardo's ideas had far less appeal (Laxer, 1989; Watkins, 1991) (see Chapter 7). The ending of free trade-protected markets was viewed with especial fear in Britain's North American colonies. How did this affect the security of the colonies' exports? The panic climaxed in April 1849.

The Canadian government had been moved the previous year from Kingston to Montreal, the site of Canada's business establishment. In 1849, the Reform government of Baldwin-Lafontaine passed a bill compensating Patriotes and innocent victims of the rebellions of 1837–1838 (see Chapter 2) for losses suffered during the conflict. Montreal's English business class, already feeling abandoned by the British government's adoption of free trade and fearing a recession, stormed and burned the new Parliament buildings, and threatened the governor general, Lord Elgin (1811–1863) (Careless, 1970: 203; Morton, 1997: 56–57). A manifesto circulated in favour of annexation to the United States. In Chatham, New Brunswick, meanwhile, inhabitants "marched through the streets on July 4, 1849, firing pistols in the air and singing 'Yankee Doodle'" (Wynn, 2000: 207).

Annexation was not very popular anywhere. Within weeks, talk of joining the United States subsided. By then, gold had been discovered in California, and the North American economy entered a period of growth that continued until the early 1870s. Nonetheless, many in the colonies remained concerned to secure access to the large American market.

The Reciprocity Treaty of 1854 was the result. The treaty came into effect in 1855 and lasted until 1866, when the United States terminated it. Specifically, the treaty eliminated the tariff on natural products, including fish.

The signing of the Reciprocity Treaty blunted Montreal merchants' demands for annexation (Winks, 1998: 4). The following decade witnessed rapid economic growth throughout the British colonies (Aitken, 1959). This period featured the increased economic integration of the St. Lawrence lowlands, the extension of the agricultural area of southern Ontario, the beginning of manufacturing in Ontario and Quebec, and the development of a railway from the Detroit River to the Atlantic seaboard.

How responsible was the Reciprocity Agreement for this period of prosperity? The question is not easily answered. On balance, however, reciprocity seems to have increased the overall volume of trade between the two countries and specifically to have benefited British North American trade in wheat, oats, and flour (Norrie and Owram, 1996: 184–185; see also Careless, 1970; Laxer, 1989).

By the 1860s, however, Americans increasingly viewed reciprocity with alarm. Business interests pressured the American government to abrogate the agreement. American politicians noted, with some accuracy, that Canada was doing very well by the agreement. Ultimately, however, the Reciprocity Agreement collapsed for reasons political—and military—rather than economic.

CANADA AND THE AMERICAN CIVIL WAR

As the debate over the Meech Lake Accord and "distinct society" heated up in 1989,

Reform Party leader Preston Manning repeatedly borrowed American President Abraham Lincoln's phrase warning of the perils of a "house divided" (see Harrison, 1995: 173). In the overheated aftermath of the 1995 Quebec referendum, parallels between Canada's situation and events leading up to the American Civil War in 1861 were again advanced (McPherson, 1998). The discerning of Canadian parallels, or parables, in the American Civil War was not new. The war was very much on the minds of Canadian politicians in 1864 as they began deliberations on Confederation.

The American Civil War (1861–1865) previewed wars soon to come, introducing trench warfare, advanced weaponry (for example, the Gatling gun), and calculated terrorism against civilians. To this day, the number of Union and Confederate deaths during the American Civil War (563,000) is larger than the number of American deaths in any other war (*Time*, 2009: 642). As in later wars, a modern invention— the camera— "brought home" the Civil War to those far removed, including the people of British North America.

British North America was affected by events in the United States even before the war began. In the months leading up to the conflict, some American officials suggested that a war with Britain over Canada might prove a useful diversion and unite the squabbling states. Other Union officials argued that, in the event of losing the South, the conquest of Canada would make for an adequate replacement (Morton, 1997: 61; Winks, 1998; see also Marquis, 2000).

In the beginning, most people in the British colonies supported the North, believing that the war was intended to abolish slavery (Winks, 1998). As the war went on, however, sympathies in the colonies became more conflicted. It became apparent that ending slavery was incidental to the Union's crusade. The war's first purpose was to save the

Union (Hofstadter, 1958). The South's argument that individual states had voluntarily entered into a Confederacy in 1776 and therefore retained the right of self-determination, including the right of exit, struck a more responsive chord in the British colonies than did the North's federalist alternative.

Inevitably, the British colonies also found themselves caught up in the war's actual dynamics. To the North's displeasure, the British continued to trade with the South. The South also used the colonies as a staging ground for raids against the Union, both by land and sea (Winks, 1998; Marquis, 2000). In retaliation, and much to British annoyance, northern forces also breached the Canadian border in pursuit of the rebels. Throughout the American Civil War, many in Canada feared, and some in the Confederacy actively hoped, that Britain would be dragged into war with the Union (Winks, 1998).

Nor did fears lessen with the conflict's end. British and colonial officials noted the United States had a battle-tested army of 2.3 million men, nearly equal to the entire population of the province of Canada (G. Martin, 1993b: 560), which now could be turned north. Facing the American army was a regular military force of a little more than 19,000 (Winks, 1998: 282) and perhaps another 10,000 militia. Elaborate plans were made and discussed throughout 1864–1865 concerning Canada's defence (see Winks, 1998: 351–352). These plans became more urgent when Irish raiders, known as the Fenians, invaded Canada (with tacit American support) in 1866 (McCue, 1999).

Most British officials, including Prime Minister William Gladstone (1809–1898), accepted the obvious: Canada ultimately was not defensible against American attack. So, to avoid provocation, in 1871 Britain removed all its troops from Canadian soil. But

the American Civil War, and the threats of invasion that followed, provided the psychological context (G. Martin, 1993b: 559) for getting on with a task long debated: Confederation (see also Winks, 1998: 379; and Moore, 1997).

CONFEDERATION

Confederation in 1867 was intended to address three problems. First, Confederation was meant to provide an "effective defence" against the threat of American invasion. (The fact that such a defence was no more possible after Confederation than before is incidental.) Second, Confederation was meant to create an economic union. Economic union was made necessary by the American government's suspension of the Reciprocity Treaty in 1866 in response to British support for the South during the Civil War. Third, Confederation was meant to deal with French-English political instability in the Province of Canada, where 12 governments had fallen in 15 years (see Moore, 1997; Romney, 1999).

Confederation began as a discussion of Maritime union at Charlottetown, Prince Edward Island, in June 1864. Almost immediately, however, these discussions expanded to include plans for a broader union of all British North America. A follow-up meeting at Quebec City in October that same year drafted the union's essential features. The Quebec Resolutions were then taken back to the individual colonial legislatures for debate and ratification (see Careless, 1970: 243–249; Norrie and Owram, 1996: 207–209; Moore, 1997; Silver, 1997; Romney, 1999).

Confederation's blueprints, and the British North America (BNA) Act of 1867, which legally constituted the federation, drew heavily from "British precedent and practice" (Norrie and Owram, 1996: 210), including an elected federal Parliament and a system of jurisprudence based on the British model. Also, the British monarch remained the formal head of state, and the highest court for judicial appeals remained in London. But Confederation also drew upon practices already employed in the Province of Canada and the American model.

From the Province of Canada was adopted the idea of tariffs, an important element of the National Policy soon devised (see Chapter 7). Likewise, many of the Dominion's banking regulations copied legislation developed in the Province of Canada (Norrie and Owram, 1996: 211).

From the American model came the idea of the Senate. Like the American Senate, which represents individual states (Hofstadter, 1958: 76–77), the Canadian Senate was meant to represent the provinces (Moore, 1997: 108–109). Unlike American senators, however, Canadian senators were not to be elected. Why not? In part, the reason is that the Canadian Senate was modelled also on the British House of Lords; in part it was also that an appointed Senate left obvious opportunities for patronage, a current criticism. But the Fathers of Confederation also feared that elected senators would possess legitimacy equal to the elected members of Parliament, threatening the principle of "one person, one vote" (see Moore, 1997: 108; Romney, 1999).

The Fathers of Confederation also discerned in the American experience, specifically the recent Civil War, an object lesson (Winks, 1998) on the perils of decentralized government. Here, however, the perceived lesson could only partially be applied (Moore, 1997; Silver, 1997; Romney, 1999). Certainly, Sir John A. Macdonald desired to construct a strong central government, but this was not possible. Neither the Maritime provinces nor (especially) Quebec would accept a strongly centralized federation.

The result was a Confederation in which jurisdictional powers were divided between the federal government and the provinces. The federal government was given powers over national defence, postal services, the census and statistics, currency and banking, navigation and shipping, fisheries, criminal law, the regulation of trade and commerce, weights and measures, bankruptcy and insolvency, and taxation. Provincial governments were given powers over two areas that would become particularly important later on, health and education, as well as generally local matters, such as property and civil rights, civil law, municipal governments, licences, and the chartering of companies, as well as direct taxation for government costs. All residual powers lay with the federal government. Finally, the federal government was further charged with responsibility to ensure equitable fiscal assistance to all the provinces to meet their constitutional functions (Careless, 1970: 254–255; Norrie and Owram, 1996: 209–210).

There was no great outcry of public support in 1867 for Confederation; in some quarters there was significant opposition. Newfoundland and Prince Edward Island rejected Confederation (Careless, 1970: 246; Norrie and Owram, 1996: 208), while New Brunswick and Nova Scotia were only slowly brought on side (Careless, 1970; Moore, 1997). In Canada East, opposition remained high despite the implicit and explicit promises of the Conservatives and their leader, George Cartier, that Confederation offered the French a sovereign homeland within a federated state (see Silver, 1997; Romney, 1997). Only Canada West—festering under the Act of Union, demanding separation from entanglements with Canada East and a system of "Rep by Pop," its gaze fixed on westward expansion—greeted Confederation with something like passion.

Thus, on July 1, 1867, the Dominion of Canada was proclaimed, made up of four provinces: New Brunswick, Nova Scotia, Quebec (formerly Canada East), and Ontario (formerly Canada West). Housing roughly 4 million people—mainly French and English, Catholic and assorted flavours of Protestant—the new country covered 370,045 square miles (958,416.5 square kilometres), a tenth of British North America. Small clusters of minority populations were growing, however, presaging Canada's multi-ethnic mix of the next century.

Montreal, the site of trade and finance, was the country's largest city, with more than 100,000 people, followed by Quebec City (59,699), Toronto (56,092), Halifax (29,582), and Saint John (28,805) (Morton, 1997: 12–19), but the majority of people still lived and worked on rural farms and in small villages.

A significant manufacturing base was developing (Laxer 1989), but most manufactured goods were still imported and staple exports (fish, wheat, and trees) still ruled Canada's economy (Norrie and Owram, 1996: 208). Indeed, the new Dominion remained largely pre-industrial, even pre-capitalist. Probably few people realized immediately they had become subjects of a new country. Even less did the Aboriginal peoples of the West and the North know that they too would soon be absorbed into something called Canada (see chapters 10 and 11).

CONCLUSION

English Canada was born as a fragment cast off by the American Revolution. The United States became English Canada's "Other," a place of attraction, mystery, awe, and fear. Where few differences marked the Loyalists from other Americans in 1775, war, politics, and economics erected borders that, in time, also took on a cultural and psychological reality. Separate histories make separate peoples: Attempts to unite East and West Germans after the Cold War provide a contemporary example.

Confederation made concrete the idea of Canada. Shortly thereafter, American efforts at conquering Canada militarily ceased almost entirely. As Governor General Vincent Massey (1887–1967) later noted, "the disparity of population has made armaments for one country futile and for the other superfluous." Yet Canada's future remained uncertain beside the American behemoth that, on the shores of the 20th century, was flexing its muscles. Much remained to be done if the new country was to thrive.

KEY TERMS

American exceptionalism
Manifest Destiny
Monroe Doctrine

CRITICAL THINKING QUESTIONS

1. How might North America look different today had the American colonies not revolted in 1775?

2. Why did the notion of Manifest Destiny arise in the United States and what is its continued impact today?

3. Why did Canada expand more slowly than the United States?

4. Why did beliefs in free trade arise in England?

5. Why did the Fathers of Confederation choose the particular elements they did in fashioning Canada's Constitution in 1867?

RECOMMENDED READINGS

Berton, Pierre. 1980. *The Invasion of Canada, 1812–1813*. Toronto: McClelland & Stewart.
Written by one of Canada's great popularizers of history, this book details the events of the somewhat ambiguous War of 1812.

Granatstein, Jack. 1996. *Yankee Go Home? Canadians and Anti-Americanism.* Toronto: HarperCollins Publishers.
This book examines the history of anti-Americanism in Canada.

Norrie, Ken, and Douglas Owram. 1996. *The History of the Canadian Economy*, 2nd ed. Toronto: Harcourt Brace and Company, Canada.
This book details the economic history of Canadian development, from resource extraction to industrialization.

Winks, Robin. 1998. *The Civil War Years: Canada and the United States,* 4th ed. Montreal and Kingston: McGill-Queen's University Press.
Winks examines the complex relationship between Canada and the United States during the latter's civil war, 1861–1865.

Zinn, Howard. 1996. *A People's History of the United States 1492–Present.* New York: Harper Perennial.
One of the United States' best-known radical historians, Zinn provides a historical account of that country's development significantly at odds with conventional narratives.

RELATED WEBSITES

American Declaration of Independence
http://www.archives.gov/exhibits/charters/declaration.html
The Government of the United States' Archives contains the American Declaration of Independence.

Library and Archives Canada
http://www.collectionscanada.gc.ca/confederation/index-e.html
This archives also contains valuable documents on Confederation.

Reciprocity Agreement, 1854
http://www.collectionscanada.gc.ca/confederation/023001-2996-e.html
Library and Archives Canada holds Canada's national collection of books, historical documents, government records, photos, films, maps, music, etc. The archives contain a full text of the Reciprocity Agreement of 1854.

CANADIAN SOCIETY ON VIDEO

Canada: A People's History, Episode 5: "A Question of Loyalties." 2000. Canadian Broadcasting Corporation, 120 minutes. Covers the period 1775–1815 dealing with the arrival of the United Empire Loyalists during the American Revolution and the American invasion of Canada in 1812.

Canada: A People's History, Episode 8: "The Great Enterprise." 2000. Canadian Broadcasting Corporation, 120 minutes. Covers the period 1850–1867 and the events leading to Confederation.

CHAPTER 7

ENGLISH CANADA IN TRANSITION

We often say that we fear no invasion from the south, but the armies of the south have already crossed the border. American enterprise, American capital, is taking rapid possession of our mines and our water-power, our oil areas and our timber limits.
—Sara Jeanette Duncan, *The Imperialist*, 1904

I am for [reciprocity] because I hope to see the day when the American flag will float over every square foot of the British North American possessions clear to the North Pole.
—Champ Clark, speaker of the U.S. House of Representatives, 1911

Air force operations from a base in the Great Lakes area would be capable of dominating the industrial heart of Canada, the Ontario peninsula.
—American commander of the Army-Air Force, in secret testimony to the U.S. Congress supporting the building of a border air base, 1935

INTRODUCTION

Despite Confederation, immediately after 1867 Canada faced two great challenges: constructing a viable national economy and securing the western region from American advances. Between 1867 and 1905, two internal wars were fought, the economy was transformed, immigrants entered the country in droves, and five new provinces joined the Dominion: Manitoba (1870), British Columbia (1871), Prince Edward Island (1873), and Saskatchewan and Alberta (both 1905). Over the following 40 years, Canada fought in two world wars and suffered through a major economic depression. Canada also changed structurally. Cor-

porate capitalism took hold, mass consumerism flourished, and class conflict intensified. Canada became more urbanized. Women entered the workforce as never before. Slowly a fledgling sense of Canadian nationalism began emerging from the broad shadows cast by Britain and the United States. This chapter examines these and other events, ending with the Second World War.

THE "AMERICAN SYSTEM" AND THE NATIONAL POLICY

Confederation in 1867 was meant in part to deal with Canada's recurrent economic problems and the threat of American expansion (Chapter 6), but the new nation still faced the question of what specific policy to adopt to meet these goals.

Looking around the world today, models of economic and social development are dominated by "globalization," based on economic liberalism and free trade. In the 19th century, however, several models competed. The British system, with ideas similar to current neo-liberalism—*a belief in free markets and limited state involvement in the economy* (see Chapter 9)—provided one model, but outside England it was widely rejected. A European system of economic development existed, based on activist government policies, investment banks, and technical education (Watkins, 1991), but it was largely unknown and culturally distant from the Canadian experience. A third model, however, known as the American system, existed next door and was therefore more familiar to Canadian business and political leaders.

The American system employed three elements: (1) high tariffs to protect domestic manufacturers, therefore making it cheaper to buy domestically than to import products, a policy often referred to as **import substitution**; (2) expanded transportation systems (especially railways), built through federal contracts and guaranteed loans to private operators, and designed to bring products to market; and (3) immigration to supply domestic markets (Hofstadter, 1958: 250; also Laxer, 1989; Watkins, 1991). In 1878, the Conservative government of John A. Macdonald ran on a platform of economic development based on the American system and renamed the National Policy.

The National Policy's specific elements were not new to Canada. Tariffs, for example, were already an established tradition in Upper and Lower Canada by the time of Confederation. Thus, in 1879, tariffs were raised from 17.5 percent to 29 percent on a host of manufactured and agricultural goods, and in 1887 they were raised again, especially on iron, steel, farm machinery, and textiles (Norrie and Owram, 1996: 249). Likewise, railway construction was by then another Canadian tradition going back to the boom years of 1850–1859 (Norrie and Owram, 1996: 191). What was fundamentally different about the National Policy, compared with previous economic policies, was its broader aim of nation-building, specifically incorporating the western territories into Canada.

Canadian politicians and the people of Ontario specifically had long viewed the lands west to the Pacific as theirs to occupy. By the 1860s, however, competing notions of Manifest Destiny were evident along the 49th parallel. In British Columbia, 30,000 people were attracted to the Fraser Valley and Cariboo regions by the discovery of gold in 1857 (Norrie and Owram, 1996: 213; see also Easterbrook and Aitken, 1988). Many of these immigrants were Americans, veterans of the recent California boom, who began pressing for annexation to the United States (see Morton, 1997).

Similar pressures were exerted at Red River (later Winnipeg). Between 1850 and 1860, the population of Minnesota, just south of Manitoba, increased by 2,730 percent (Winks, 1998: 4). As arable land filled up, Americans pushed further northward

into the Red River area, where in 1869 they too pressed for statehood. Caught between the Canadian and American visions for the West were the Aboriginals and Métis (see Chapter 10). In both cases, Sir John A. Macdonald's vision won out, aided by the use of force in Manitoba and the promise of a railway in British Columbia.

Between the two newest provinces lay the vast North-West Territories. The Territories had long been the Hudson's Bay Company's preserve. Especially after its merger with the rival North West Company in 1821, the entire region, including British Columbia, had fallen under the company's control. By the 1860s, however, the fur trade was dying, and the West was coveted by Canadian politicians, for whom the National Policy was already a gleam in the eye, not to mention Americans with their own plans for the Territories.

In 1870, the Hudson's Bay Company formally transferred the Territories to Canada, and settlement of the western region slowly began. Immigrants began settling in the "postage stamp" province of Manitoba, so-called because of its shape. When the best land was taken, later settlers pushed further westward into the Territories. In 1883, however, land prices soared, the CPR faced bankruptcy, and immigration stopped (see Morton, 1997). The word "secession" was heard in British Columbia (Conway, 1994: 25).

The hard times were even harder for the West's Aboriginal and Métis people. The buffalo were disappearing, the fur trade no longer provided a secure living, and unscrupulous traders were wreaking havoc on the people. In 1885, rebellion in the Territories provided the Canadian government with justification to send in troops (see Chapter 10). The long-promised rail link to British Columbia was completed in time to facilitate their arrival.

Thus, by 1885, Canada had expanded to fill the top shelf of North America from sea to sea. The National Policy's alleged economic benefits, however, had yet to be realized: public debt was rising, markets were failing, and immigration stalled. Why was the National Policy slow in delivering expected results?

Several factors limited Canada's economic takeoff. First, beginning roughly in 1873 and lasting for six years, the increasingly integrated world economy entered a prolonged slump that reduced demand for Canadian commodities and hindered the necessary flow of investment capital into Canada (Hobsbawm, 1995: 86–87; Lairson and Skidmore, 1997; Saul, 1969). Second, the National Policy depended upon the development of western agricultural land, specifically for wheat exports. But development of the Canadian West could not proceed until the more productive lands of the American West were "used up" (Morton, 1997) and new strains of wheat were developed to meet the Canadian Prairies' harsh climate and short growing season (Norrie and Owram, 1996: 227; also Laxer, 1989). Third, public debt acquired throughout the early 19th century meant that after 1867 the Canadian government employed private interests to build railways by granting them monopoly rights and free land (Laxer, 1989). The companies, however, restricted railway construction to areas of profitability and limited land development to keep prices high, with the result that the massive immigration necessary to make the National Policy viable never occurred.

By 1890, the mood in Canada was sour. Many felt the National Policy had failed. Demands were renewed for a reciprocity treaty with the United States; some called for outright annexation.

The federal election of 1891 was held in this context of uncertainty. The Liberal Party under Wilfrid Laurier ran on a platform of unrestricted reciprocity with the United States (Morton, 1997; also Norrie and Owram, 1996). By contrast, the Conservatives under Sir John A. Macdonald appealed to anti-American and pro-British sentiments (see Granatstein, 1996) in successfully arguing that free trade

would inevitably lead to Canada's political annexation, and won.

Canada's first free trade election occurred just as the world economy was rebounding. After 1896, investment capital was freed up and circulated throughout the world at an unprecedented rate (Dunning, 1983). Internationally, consumer demand increased, while production also expanded in the wake of the second industrial revolution (Norrie and Owram, 1996: 223).

At last, the National Policy had its desired result. Fuelled by the Yukon gold rush (see Chapter 11), increased mining in the Canadian Shield, the development of the newsprint industry, and large-scale hydroelectric developments on the Great Lakes and the St. Lawrence, between 1900 and 1913 Canada (especially southern Ontario) experienced its second economic boom (Aitken, 1959). While Canada's real GNP grew at a compound rate of only 2.38 percent during the period 1870–1896, between 1896 and 1913 it grew at a rate of 6.48 percent (Norrie and Owram, 1996: 218).

Integral to this growth was a change in Canada's labour market. Though still dependent upon primary sector employment (for example, resource extraction industries such as agriculture, mining, and forestry), employment in the secondary sector (manufacturing, construction, and the like) also grew under the National Policy, as did employment in the tertiary or service sector, where the commodities exchanged have no tangible form (e.g., teaching, retail trade, hotels, and finance). By 1891, 49 percent of Canada's labour force worked in primary industry, 20 percent in secondary industry, and 31 percent in the service sector.

But the benefits of economic growth were unevenly shared: Aboriginal peoples were particularly left out (see Part 3), but others outside the industrialized region of southern Ontario soon also felt the sting of colonization.

Box 7.1
What Is a Region?

A **region** is *a territory defined physiologically, geographically, climatically, culturally, politically, or economically.* This definition is not as straightforward as it seems, however. Even using the same definition, two people may recognize different regional boundaries. Thus, regions do not exist as physical things. Rather, they are "read into" the landscape, socially constructed (as symbolic interaction theory argues), and then reified (Chapter 1).

The concept of **regional differences** refers to *observable variations between two or more regions.* For example, the West Coast is wet, while the Prairie provinces are dry. Likewise, Ontario is home to much of Canada's manufacturing, while Alberta is a major producer of oil.

Regionalism refers to *an individual's personal identification with a region.* In this sense, regionalism provides a sense of who we are, much as nationalism does.

Regional alienation refers to *a sense of grievance based on the belief that regional differences are not "natural" but result from the actions of individuals or groups residing outside the region.*

Sources: Janine Brodie, *The Political Economy of Canadian Regionalism* (Toronto: Harcourt Brace Jovanovich, 1990); William Westfall, "On the concept of region in Canadian history and literature," in D. Taras, B. Rasporich, and E. Mandel (eds.), *A Passion for Identity: An Introduction to Canadian Studies* (Scarborough: Nelson Canada, 1993); William Wonders, "Canadian regions and regionalism: National enrichment or national disintegration?" in D. Taras, B. Rasporich, and E. Mandel (eds.), *A Passion for Identity: An Introduction to Canadian Studies* (Scarborough: Nelson Canada, 1993).

REGIONS AND REGIONALISM

Sociological concepts, such as class and gender, condition the way we see social relations. Within Canada, the concept of region is particularly persuasive as the lens through which Canadian society is often viewed. Such an emphasis is not misplaced, even if the definition of "region," like so many concepts, and a host of terms that stem from it, is unclear (see Box 7.1).

Regional (and sub-regional) divisions were already present at the start of Canada. Quebec and Ontario are obvious examples, each with different cultures, histories, and economies, but there were also differences among Canada's three Maritime provinces of Prince Edward Island, Nova Scotia, and New Brunswick, and between the people of this region and the two larger provinces over issues of political control and economic development.

Nova Scotia provides a useful example. Important early on for its geopolitical and military position on the Atlantic coast, by 1867 Nova Scotia was a major economic player with a diversified economy that sported the building of ships and the manufacture of steel, glass, and rope. At the same time, however, the businesses were small, often family affairs. Moreover, they were not well integrated into the British North American economy, instead remaining dependent upon exports to Britain. In consequence, much of the province's business and political elite opposed joining Canada, fearing that Confederation would negatively impact the region's (and their) prosperity, a fear that within decades proved correct in the years after 1885 as the direction of economic flows changed to benefit Ontario's larger manufacturing sector. In effect, Nova Scotia and much of the Maritime region exchanged its status as a colony of Britain for that of being a colony of central Canada.

Canada's fourth Atlantic province, Newfoundland, provides another example. Sparsely populated and less diversified than Nova Scotia, economic development in Newfoundland nonetheless increased into the late 19th century, built upon the inshore fisheries and St. John's as a port city. As in Nova Scotia, however, the island experienced a major downturn after 1880 as the importance of the island on shipping routes declined.

Each of these regions faced developmental problems common to the rest of Canada, and responded with similar policies. Economically, they were geographically far from markets, hence subsidies and other inducements were given to private developers to build transportation systems (roads, railways, and canals). Lacking also investment generally, generous inducements were given to companies to settle in areas. Likewise, land was opened up cheaply to encourage immigration.

Often, however, people in these regions found that development was uneven and centred on a single commodity—the fishery in Newfoundland, for example—resulting in recurrent cycles of boom and bust (Norrie and Owram, 1996). (Amid the Great Depression and facing bankruptcy in 1933, the Newfoundland

legislature voted to suspend its operations and reverted to a Crown colony of Britain in the following year.) In turn, economic instability often resulted in political unrest with its own distinctive regional characteristics (Clark et al., 1975; Brym and Sacouman, 1979). This unrest has national consequences. As many scholars have pointed out, Canada does not have a national economy, nor even national policies of development, but instead regional policies that too often pit one region against another (see Clement and Williams, 1989; Laxer, 1991), a situation no more evident than in the history of western Canada.

Table 7.1
Immigration to Canada 1852–2008

Year	Immigrants	Year	Immigrants	Year	Immigrants	Year	Immigrants	Year	Immigrants	Year	Immigrants
1852	29,307	1878	29,807	1905	141,465	1931	27,530	1957	282,164	1983	89,192
1853	29,464	1879	40,492	1906	211,653	1932	20,591	1958	124,851	1984	88,276
1854	37,263	1880	38,505	1907	272,409	1933	14,382	1959	106,928	1985	84,346
1855	25,296	1881	47,991	1908	143,326	1934	12,476	1960	104,111	1986	99,353
1856	22,544	1882	112,458	1909	173,694	1935	11,277	1961	71,689	1987	152,084
1857	33,854	1883	133,624	1910	286,839	1936	11,643	1962	74,586	1988	161,582
1858	12,339	1884	103,824	1911	331,288	1937	15,101	1963	93,151	1989	191,554
1859	6,300	1885	79,169	1912	375,756	1938	17,244	1964	112,606	1990	216,456
1860	6,276	1886	69,152	1913	400,870	1939	16,994	1965	146,758	1991	232,818
1861	13,589	1887	84,526	1914	150,484	1940	11,324	1966	194,743	1992	254,818
1862	18,294	1888	88,766	1915	36,665	1941	9,329	1967	222,876	1993	256,702
1863	21,000	1889	75,067	1916	55,914	1942	7,576	1968	183,974	1994	224,397
1864	24,779	1891	82,165	1917	72,910	1943	8,504	1969	161,531	1995	212,873
1865	18,958	1892	30,996	1918	41,845	1944	12,801	1970	147,713	1996	226,073
1866	11,427	1893	29,633	1919	107,698	1945	22,722	1971	121,900	1997	216,039
1867	10,666	1894	20,829	1920	13,824	1946	71,719	1972	122,006	1998	174,198
1868	12,765	1895	18,790	1921	91,728	1947	64,127	1973	184,200	1999	189,954
1869	18,630	1896	16,835	1922	64,224	1948	125,414	1974	218,465	2000	227,458
1870	24,706	1897	21,716	1923	133,729	1949	95,217	1975	187,881	2001	250,639
1871	27,773	1898	31,900	1924	124,164	1950	73,912	1976	149,429	2002	229,049
1872	36,758	1899	44,543	1925	84,907	1951	194,391	1977	114,914	2003	221,348
1873	50,050	1900	41,681	1926	135,982	1952	164,498	1978	86,313	2004	235,825
1874	39,373	1901	55,747	1927	158,886	1953	168,868	1979	112,093	2005	262,241
1875	27,382	1902	89,102	1928	166 783	1954	154,227	1980	143,140	2006	251,643
1876	25,633	1903	138,660	1929	164,993	1955	109,946	1981	128,642	2007	236,754
1877	27,028	1904	131,252	1930	104,806	1956	164,857	1982	121,179	2008	247,243

Sources: Citizenship and Immigration Canada. 1996. *Citizenship and Immigration Statistics 1996*, Cat. no. MP22-1/1996, Ottawa: Citizenship and Immigration; and Citizenship and Immigration Canada. 2008. Facts and Figures – Immigration Overview: Permanent and Temporary Residents. http://www.cic.gc.ca/english/resources/statistics/facts2008/permanent/index.asp

IMMIGRATION AND THE WEST

Pre-Confederation, in 1861, 3.2 million people lived in British North America. Canada's population stood at only 4.8 million (Table 1.1) 30 years later. By contrast, the population of the United States during this period rose from 31.4 million to nearly 63 million (*Time*, 2009: 648). Nature and geography, mercantilist policies, and American competition held Canada's population growth at bay. Indeed, so unattractive was Canada relative to its southern neighbour during the 50-year period 1851–1901 that only 1.9 million people entered Canada while 2.2 million left, most of them for the United States (McKie, 1994: 26).

By 1896, however, the American West was virtually filled and the depression over. In Ottawa, the new minister of the interior, Clifford Sifton, fervently pursued immigration. By 1900 the West's Aboriginal peoples had largely been pushed aside (see Chapter 10). Now the prohibitive land regulations (Laxer, 1989) were changed, the railways were forced to open up land for settlement, and irrigation construction was proceeded with, especially in the arid region known as the Palliser Triangle (see Norrie and Owram, 1996: 227). Above all, Canadian immigration was promoted as never before. The result was the largest influx of immigrants in Canadian history. More than 1.5 million immigrants entered Canada between 1901 and 1911 (McKie, 1994: 28; Hall, 1977), another 375,756 arrived in 1912, and 400,870 more in 1913 (see Table 7.1).

The immigrants came primarily from three main areas: the United States, Great Britain, and Europe. Of these groups, the first two were viewed as particularly desirable. American immigrants had capital, goods, and Prairie farm experience, and they could "fit in" ethnically into Canada. Thus, the number of American immigrants to Canada increased from 2,400 in 1897 to 12,000 in 1899. Between 40,000 and 50,000 Americans annually entered Canada during the years 1902–1905 (Hall, 1977: 70). For their part, British immigrants, with the exception of the Irish, were viewed as loyal to the Crown. The immigration boom attracted large numbers of people from the rural areas of England and Scotland. By 1901, however, the great wave of British immigration, fuelled in the early 19th century by a population boom in the Old Country, was already declining. Thus, Canadian immigration officials hesitantly expanded their search for immigrants beyond the traditional Anglo countries, into northern and eastern Europe.

Certain ethnic groups, however, remained restricted from entering Canada. These groups included "Negroes," "Orientals" (including East Indians), "Galicians" (meaning eastern Europeans), Italians, and Jews whom, it was argued, were urban people who could not adjust to the demands of Prairie life and who, in any case, would not fit into Canadian culture. In the case of the Chinese, government policies were explicitly racist. Good enough to be employed as cheap labour in building the railways, then later in British Columbia's mines and forestry industry (Morton, 1997: 122), Chinese immigrants were not considered good enough, however, to become citizens. The first of several "head taxes" was enacted on the Chinese in 1885 to prevent workers from being able to afford bringing over family members (Hall, 1977: 78).

Immigration moved in waves across the Prairies, leaving distinctive cultural traces that remain today in every province. Between 1871 and 1891, Manitoba's population increased from 25,000 to 153,000, rising to 461,000 by 1911 (see Table 1.1). The early days saw Anglo farmers and expatriate elements of Ontario's upper class settle in southern Manitoba (Lower, 1983: 195), though a sizable Icelandic contingent also moved to Manitoba in

1873, settling north of Winnipeg. Later, European immigrants who arrived, finding the best land already taken, settled in the north and west of the province, while Anglo-Americans moved into the southwest (Widdis, 1997). But these waves of immigrants to Manitoba were not only ethnically distinct. Over time, they also transformed Manitoba's class structure and political culture. By the start of the First World War, Winnipeg had developed a strong working-class culture, the product of British and eastern European immigrants, paving the way for the strike of 1919 (see below) (Wiseman, 1993).

The combined population of the entire Territories in 1871 was about 48,000 (not including Aboriginal peoples). By 1901, Saskatchewan's population alone had risen to 91,000, while that of Alberta stood at 73,000. Ten years later, these provinces' populations had risen to 492,000 and 374,000, respectively (Table 1.1). Before the turn of the century, there were significant francophone populations in Saskatchewan's north and southwest. Like western Manitoba, however, the early 20th century saw Saskatchewan settled by the second wave of Anglo and European immigrants, not to mention (in the province's southwest) American immigrants (see Wiseman, 1993; Widdis, 1997)

Alberta, too, at the turn of the century had a large francophone population, located mainly in the northeast. In the late 19th century, however, Anglo-American immigrants moved into southern Alberta, bringing with them populist notions of direct democracy, as well as strong beliefs in possessive individualism (Harrison, 2000) that remain part of the province's political culture today (see Chapter 9). American influence in the south was further strengthened after the discovery in 1914 of oil at Turner Valley, a harbinger of events to come. But other ethnic groups also arrived. The mining communities of the southern Crowsnest Pass, for example, filled with southern (especially

Italian) and eastern Europeans, while the province's north similarly experienced an influx of central and eastern Europeans.

British Columbia's population growth was slower, but steadier. Approximately 36,000 people (not including Aboriginals) lived in B.C. at Confederation in 1871, rising to 179,000 by 1901 and 393,000 by 1911. Much of this non-Aboriginal population was English and Scottish in origin, via Canada's Atlantic region; others were American. In the early stages, settlement was tied to the coastline and Vancouver Island. Later, settlers spread inland, along paths set by the railways. These late arrivals, employed in construction and resource extraction, brought a distinctive working-class consciousness (see Robin, 1993). At the same time, sizable numbers of Chinese and Japanese immigrants also came.

There were other distinctive populations throughout the West who were unable or unwilling to be "fitted" easily into the dominant British mould. Black communities developed early on, for example, in Breton, Alberta, and around Maidstone, Saskatchewan. Catholic, Anglican, and other Protestant religious orders dominated Canadian religious and cultural life. Nonetheless, some persecuted religious minorities also found a home in the West. With the moral and financial support of Count Leo Tolstoy, some 7,400 Doukhobors arrived in Canada between December 1898 and April 1899, settling near Yorkton and Prince Albert, Saskatchewan (Mayes, 1999). Other religious minorities— Mennonites in southern Manitoba, Hutterites throughout western Manitoba and southern Alberta, and Mormons in southern Alberta—also arrived.

National concern focused on how best to assimilate the "new Canadians" whom James S. Woodsworth (1874–1942), a Methodist minister and later first leader of the Co-operative Commonwealth Federation, in 1909 called the "strangers within our gates" (Woodsworth, 1972). Outside Quebec, Canada's immigration and other policies (for example, education) at the time enforced **Anglo-conformity**—*the requirement that subordinate group members express outward compliance with the values and practices of the dominant British group*—and reflected broad public sentiment and fears of social discord.

In the early 1900s, "Canadians were more provincial than cosmopolitan, more openly biased than politically correct, and each social grouping more protective of its niche in society" (Lyon, 1998: 26). Small differences, even the neighbourhood one lived in, were magnified in importance. Thus, there was a recognized pecking order even within the British "tribes." (Those of Irish Catholic descent were decidedly last.)

In extreme cases during the period 1901–1911, **racism** (*the belief that one racial category is innately superior or inferior to another*) and **xenophobia** (*the fear of what is strange*) resulted in anti-immigrant riots in several cities (see Palmer, 1982). Anti-Oriental riots broke out in Vancouver during the recession year of 1907 (Whitaker, 1991), for example. In most cases, however, public reaction took the form of occupational or social exclusion, or snickering at the new immigrants' "exotic" and "peculiar" lifestyles. Groups kept to their own turf. Finally, we should keep in mind the well-meaning, if often paternalistic, efforts of many individuals, voluntary agencies, and church groups who assisted the new immigrants' adjustment to Canadian life.

The immigration boom ended in 1913. That year, more than 400,000 immigrants landed on Canada's shores. The world economy was slowing down, however, and the war that followed ended immigration almost entirely. In 1914, only 150,484 immigrants entered Canada, and the number declined further during the war years (see Table 7.1, above).

The wartime decline in immigration was presaged in May 1914 by the arrival in Vancouver harbour of a former collier ship, the *Komagata Maru*. Immigration officials met the ship, which carried 376 East Indians, mainly Sikhs, and refused the migrants entry. The ship was held in port for two months, its passengers detained while a Canadian warship kept watch. Finally, 21 of the migrants were allowed to disembark. The rest, however, returned to India on the ship. Arriving there in September, they were greeted by British gunfire. Eighteen died (Jensen, 1988).

BETWEEN TWO EMPIRES

Why did many in English Canada view new immigrants as such threats during this period? First, English Canada in 1900 certainly was parochial and ethnocentric. Second, however, English-Canadians remained anxious over the country's future. As we have seen, Canada's hesitant economic development after 1867 raised questions not only about the National Policy but Confederation generally. While some, such as the liberal historian and journalist Goldwin Smith, positively embraced the idea (see Smith, 1891), many others feared what annexation by the United States would bring.

A group of eminent intellectuals argued for strengthened ties to the British Empire. These "Canadian imperialists"— among them novelist Sara Jeannette Duncan, Presbyterian minister and educator George Monro Grant, humorist and political economist Stephen Leacock, and educator Sir George Robert Parkin— idealized the Loyalist legacy, especially elitism and anti-Americanism. Nostalgic for a simpler life and opposed to the raw materialism, industrialism, and urbanism represented by the United States (Cook, 1995), the imperialists saw Canada as having a kind of religious "mission" on earth (Berger, 1976; Romney, 1999).

Canadian imperialism and its organizations had some successes in pressuring the Canadian government to increase ties with the Crown. In 1897, Prime Minister Wilfrid

Laurier re-established preferential trade with Britain (Norrie and Owram, 1996: 249). In 1899, to the chagrin of his French-Canadian supporters, Laurier also sent Canadian soldiers overseas to fight alongside Britain in the Boer War (Miller, 1999).

After 1900, however, American influence upon Canada increasingly replaced that of Britain. Trade and investment figures from these early decades highlight America's increased influence.

Throughout the late 19th century, Canada's trade with the United States and Britain steadfastly shifted toward the former. While British import and export trade with Canada continued to grow during this period, its overall importance to the Canadian economy declined relative to that of the United States. By 1891, Canadian imports from the United States surpassed those from Britain and thereafter never looked back. Export trade took longer to shift, picking up additional steam during the First World War as Canadian industry met British wartime demand. By 1921, however, Canadian exports to the United States, like imports, also surpassed those to Britain (Marchildon, 1995; see also Alford, 1996: 38–39).

This shift in trade was in part reflected in the amount and form of British and American investment in Canada. Canadian economic development historically has relied upon massive amounts of foreign capital. The boom after 1896 involved especially huge investments, with foreign capital flows into Canada increasing from 2.1 percent of GNP in 1897 to a high of 17.7 percent in 1912 (Norrie and Owram, 1996: 241). Until 1922, Britain was Canada's chief source of investment capital. That year, however, American investment totalled $2.6 billion (50 percent of total foreign investment), compared with $2.5 billion (47 percent) from the U.K. (Norrie and Owram, 1996: 324; also Marchildon, 1995; Li, 1996). Thereafter, American investment in Canada, both in actual dollars and as a percentage of foreign capital, was never overtaken.

From early on, there was an important difference between American and British foreign investment. Foreign investment takes two forms: portfolio investment (for example, long-term investments, such as bonds and loans) and direct investment (the actual ownership of productive property). British investment took predominantly the portfolio form. By contrast, American investments abroad were predominantly direct in nature. In Canada, direct investment involved buying up Canadian resources and firms or establishing branch plants. This meant, in practice, that American capital had greater control than British capital over the Canadian economy as a whole, but especially in certain areas of the economy—automobiles, newsprint, metals, and petroleum—that would become important in the 20th century. The increasing number of American firms in Canada also helps explain the rising level of exports to, and imports from, the United States: American firms were trading with themselves.

As always, Canada's need for capital and the prospect of jobs were balanced against the fears of American control leading to annexation (see the Sara J. Duncan quotation above). These fears reached a symbolic climax in 1911.

In 1910, Laurier became the first Canadian prime minister to visit western Canada. There, he heard repeated complaints from farmers regarding the National Policy's tariff. Remembering his defeat in 1891, but still dedicated to the liberal notion of open markets, Laurier's government worked out a limited reciprocity agreement with the United States (Norrie and Owram, 1996: 250). Laurier believed the Conservatives under Robert Borden would not seriously oppose the agreement as they had for years held out hopes of gaining a similar agreement.

The American House of Representatives and Senate gave the agreement swift passage, but the outspoken remarks of several congressmen that the agreement would hasten Canada's annexation (see Champ Clark quotation above) soon became front-page news in Canada. The election that followed saw Laurier's Liberals defeated by a potent mixture of fear, anti-Americanism, and protectionism (see Granatstein, 1996; Orchard, 1998; Norrie and Owram, 1996). The issue of free trade hence disappeared from public debate, revived only in the late 1980s by the Conservative government of Brian Mulroney (Chapter 9).

Outside Quebec, Canada in 1914 remained decidedly British, but American economic, cultural, and geopolitical influence over Canada was gradually increasing. The war that followed reinforced this emerging pattern.

A WORLD INTERRUPTED: CANADA AND THE FIRST WORLD WAR

In 1914, years of political posturing, unbridled jingoism, and imperial competition resulted in war. Estimates for the number of people killed in the First World War (1914–1918) range between 8.5 and 16 million; the number of wounded is estimated at more than 21 million (Stearns, 1975: 277–278). Russia's casualties were the greatest, made even greater by the revolution and the famines that followed, but Germany, France, and Britain also suffered enormous costs, including in effect the wasting of an entire generation. Many who returned bore wounds that were not always obvious. In strictly monetary terms, the total direct costs of the war were $180 billion, the indirect costs $151 billion, substantial amounts for the time (Langer, 1948: 951).

Canadian wartime losses amounted to 60,661 Canadian troops dead, among them a host of "war poets," such as John McCrae. Another 1,600 people were killed (6,000 more wounded) at Halifax harbour on December 6, 1917, when an ammunition ship collided with a freighter, exploding with the force of an atomic bomb and destroying much of Halifax. The year following war's end saw nearly as many Canadians die as a result of a worldwide influenza epidemic, caused indirectly by the war.

European places like Ypres, Passchendaele, and Vimy Ridge entered Canada's history, while a small number of individuals—mainly "air aces" like Billy Bishop, William Barker, and A. Roy Brown (who shot down the "Red Baron," von Richthofen)—became household names for a time. Small towns and villages throughout Canada erected monuments to the dead that still stand, augmented later by more names from other wars. Some towns were named after the battles (such as Vimy, Alberta); however, Berlin, Ontario (founded by people of German ancestry, but now afraid to admit their heritage), was renamed in 1916 after a British war hero, Field Marshall Lord Kitchener, who had died at sea.

Beyond the obvious losses of men, money, and material, the war had several major impacts on Canada, some more immediate than others.

First, the war altered Canada's position relative to other powers within the international state system. The Russian, German, Austro-Hungarian, and Turkish empires were destroyed; the British Empire was hobbled. By contrast, the United States, already the world's leading economy in 1914 (Norrie and Owram, 1996: 223), ended the war as the world's leading creditor country (Palmer, with Colton, 1957: 691), second only to Britain as the world's chief direct investor (Dunning, 1983), and in military matters an increasingly formidable power. A series of invasions and military coups after 1898, underpinned by the Monroe Doctrine, had ensured that, in the Americas especially, the United States reigned largely unopposed (Zinn, 1995: 399).

Second, the war discredited old institutions and traditional authorities, especially in Europe but also in Canada, paving the way for the rise during the 1920s and 1930s of new political ideologies and parties.

Third, at the same time, the role of the state in Canadian society (as elsewhere) expanded. Canadian government spending on goods and services, for example, rose from 10 percent of GDP in 1913 to 14.5 percent of GDP in 1914, remaining at that level throughout the war (Norrie and Owram, 1996: 300). The bureaucratic infrastructure of government also expanded. On the revenue side, the Canadian government introduced business and personal income taxes, a temporary wartime measure that soon became a permanent part of Canada's fiscal landscape.

Fourth, the First World War accelerated in all countries a series of social changes. Women, for example, entered the labour force, especially the growing public bureaucracies (Lowe, 1987). As in most combatant countries, women in Canada also gained the vote (1918). In the previous year, Louise McKinney was elected to the Alberta legislature, becoming the first woman to hold such an office in the British Empire. But there were other social changes, notably the continued decline in rural life and the growth of cities (see below), a gradual shift from primary production to secondary manufacturing and services, and the expansion of wage labour.

Fifth, the Conscription Crisis (see Chapter 3) became part of the panoply of grievances dividing the French and English in Canada. Sixth, the war slowed immigration to Canada—indeed, killing off many who might have come—thus cutting off an important leg of Canada's National Policy.

Finally, the war also sparked in English Canada a fragile sense of independent nationalism. In 1914, Canada was still very much a British colony. Britain's declaration of war meant that Canada was itself immediately at war, its troops under British command. By 1918, however, there was a distinct Canadian Corps led by Canadian officers. Canada's separate signing of the Treaty of Versailles in 1919 and garnering of a seat in the newly founded League of Nations further symbolized the country's growing independence from Britain.

CANADA, 1919–1929

The troops returning in 1919 were greeted with high unemployment, rising inflation, declining wages, and mounting anxiety. In the spring of 1919, a dispute in Winnipeg between labourers in the metal and building trades and management over collective bargaining rights, better wages, and working conditions escalated into a General Strike of 30,000 workers that lasted 40 days. The strike encouraged sympathy strikes (particularly in the West) involving another 88,000 workers. It ended on June 25, amid lingering images of the RCMP on horseback charging into a crowd of strikers at the corner of Portage and Main, causing 30 casualties and at least one death, and federal troops occupying the streets of Winnipeg (Conway, 1994: 90–93).

There was also anxiety in rural Canada, especially in the West. Mass immigration between 1901 and 1911 (see above) had transformed the Prairie landscape and, in less than two decades, had led to Ontario's being supplanted as Canada's wheat growing region (see Morton, 2000: 28; Norrie and Owram, 1996: 233). This transformation came at a cost, however.

The West, reliant upon a single commodity, was particularly at the mercy of world markets. When wheat prices collapsed at the end of the war, Canada's agrarians revolted at the ballot box. The United Farmers of Ontario were elected in 1919. Subsequently, the United Farmers of Alberta gained office in 1921, and the United Farmers of Manitoba in 1922. Meanwhile, at the federal level, the newly founded National Progressive Party in 1921 elected 65 MPs, the most successful showing by a federal "third party" until the Reform Party in the 1990s (see Chapter 9). Among Progressives elected was Canada's first woman parliamentarian, Agnes Macphail.

Why the widespread discontent following the war? The explanation lies in a series of social and economic trends that, beginning in the early 20th century, were rapidly transforming Canadian society.

Think for a moment about life in mid-19th-century Canada. Family and community were the focal point around which people's lives revolved. Except for arriving immigrants, people travelled little in their lifetime. Much of Canada was still rural (80 percent in 1871). The family was still the site of production and consumption, gender roles were largely fixed, markets were mainly local, and few people were full-time wage labourers. Well into the late 19th century, small, paternalistic, family-operated businesses—what Marx termed the "petite bourgeoisie"—dominated the Canadian economy, while family farms were the norm.

After 1900, however, a new form of capitalism emerged: corporate capitalism. Moving beyond the limitations of either petit bourgeois or mercantile or industrial capitalism, corporate capitalism (sometimes also termed "monopoly capitalism") is large-scale, highly capitalized, centralized, and non-competitive (Heron and Storey, 1986; Li, 1996). Between 1900 and 1920, for example, the number of manufacturing units in Canada fell from 76,000 to 22,000 (Li, 1996: 16; also Morton, 2000: 29). Similarly, the number of Canadian banks went from 36 in 1900 to 22 in 1914 to 10 in 1928 (Li, 1996: 20). Canada was quickly transformed from a society of petit bourgeois agrarians and nascent small-time industrialists into one in which large-scale manufacturing (especially in the automobile industry) and services began playing an increasingly large role. At the same time, industrialization and economic development were unevenly distributed and thus increased regional divisions in Canada.

The rise of corporate capitalism had particular impacts in shaping Canada's labour market. Demand for labour grew. Thus, the number and percentage of wage labourers in the overall labour force grew rapidly (see Li, 1996: 34). As in the past, labour demand was met in part by new immigrants, but immigration during the 1920s did not recover to pre-war levels. Instead, labour demand was met largely through natural population growth, rural migration—hence, in part, the farmers'· revolts of 1919–1922—and a largely untapped source: women.

The period leading up to the 1920s saw increasing numbers of women entering the workforce. Between 1911 and 1921, the participation rate for females of 14–65 years of age rose from 16.6 percent to 19.9 percent, compared with a rise from 82 percent to 89.7 percent for males in that age group during the same period. By 1931, the participation rate of females in the labour force was 23 percent, compared with 87.2 percent for males (calculated from Denton, 1983).Women's jobs, however, were mostly in the low-paying clerical occupations that arose in the burgeoning bureaucracies of the state and corporations (Lowe, 1987; Krahn et al., 2007).

The situation of women was changing at the political level, too. In 1929, five women—Irene Parlby, Louise McKinney, Henrietta Muir Edwards, Emily Murphy, and Nellie McClung—won an especially important legal battle when the Judicial Committee of the Privy Council in Britain (then Canada's highest court) overturned an earlier ruling by the Supreme Court of Canada and declared that women were "persons" under the law and therefore could hold public office (Bellamy and Irving, 1981).

Meanwhile, corporate capitalism was also changing Canada's workplaces and workplace relations in important ways. This period saw the introduction to the workplace of new forms of organization. Bureaucratic principles and management techniques based on Frederick Taylor's principles of scientific management (see Box 7.2) were introduced into factories and soon also into white-collar work. These organizational forms increased managerial control over workers and deskilled workers in the name of efficiency and higher profits (see Krahn et al., 2007).

> **Box 7.2**
> **The Six Elements of Scientific Management**
>
> 1. Shift the decision-making responsibility for doing a job from workers to managers.
>
> 2. Use scientific methods to determine the most efficient way of executing a job and redesign it accordingly.
>
> 3. Provide a detailed description of how to perform each step in a job.
>
> 4. Select the best worker to perform the job.
>
> 5. Train workers to execute the job efficiently.
>
> 6. Closely monitor workers' performance.
>
> *Source:* From KRAHN/LOWE/HUGHES. *Work, Industry, and Canadian Society*, 5E. © 2007 Nelson Education Ltd. Reproduced by permission. www.cenage.com/permissions.

In the long run, concentrated capitalism also meant concentrated labour, resulting in the rise of trade and industrial unions. In the short run, however, these changes led to growing alienation and intensified class conflict, as occurred in Winnipeg.

Technology, the war, the increasing role of the state, and the rise of corporate capitalism changed Canada in other ways during this period. Canada gradually became more urbanized. In 1901, 62 percent of Canadians still lived in rural areas. By 1921, however, an equal number of Canadians lived in urban and rural areas (see Table 7.2). Canada's urbanization had begun.

In 1901, Montreal (population 328,172) and Toronto (population 209,892) were still Canada's largest cities. The next largest city was Quebec City, with 68,840 people. Over the next 10 years, however, Winnipeg grew from 42,340 to 136,035 people, while Vancouver increased from 29,432 to 120,847. By 1921, Hamilton and Ottawa also exceeded 100,000 people, joined in 1931 by Quebec City (see Norrie and Owram, 1996: 334).

Table 7.2
Canadian Rural and Urban Population, 1871–2006 (in thousands)

Year	Canada	Urban					Rural			
		Total	%	Non-farm	%	Farm	%		Total	%
1871	3,689	722	19.6	n.a.	n.a.	n.a.	n.a.		2,967	80.4
1881	4,325	1,110	25.7	n.a.	n.a.	n.a.	n.a.		3,215	74.3
1891	4,833	1,537	31.8	n.a.	n.a.	n.a.	n.a.		3,296	68.2
1901	5,371	2,014	37.5	n.a.	n.a.	n.a.	n.a.		3,357	62.5
1911	7,207	3,273	45.4	n.a.	n.a.	n.a.	n.a.		3,934	54.6
1921	8,788	4,352	49.5	n.a.	n.a.	n.a.	n.a.		4,436	50.5
1931	10,377	5,469	52.7	1,670	16.1	3,238	31.2		4,908	47.3
1941	11,507	6,271	54.5	2,123	18.4	3,113	27.1		5,236	45.5
1951	14,009	8,817	62.9	2,423	17.3	2,769	19.8		5,192	37.1
1961	18,238	12,700	69.6	3,465	19.0	2,073	11.4		5,538	30.4
1971	21,962	16,410	76.1	3,738	17.3	1,420	6.6		5,158	23.9
1981	24,820	18,436	75.6	4,867	20.0	1,040	4.3		5,907	24.3
1991	28,031	20,907	76.6	5,583	20.5	807	3.0		6,390	23.4
2001	30,007	23,908	79.7	6,371	21.2	727	2.4		6,098	20.3
2006	31,512	25,298	80.3	5,571	17.7	643	2.0		6,214	19.7

Notes: Urban is defined as people living in a built-up area having a population of 1,000 or more and a population density of 400 or more per square kilometre. *Rural* is defined as people living outside "urban areas." *Rural farm* is defined as persons living in rural areas who are members of households of farm operators. *Rural non-farm* is defined as people living in rural areas who are not members of households of farm operators.

Sources: Calculated from the Statistics Canada publication *Historical Statistics of Canada*, Cat. 11-516, 1983, Series A67-69 and A75-77; and *Population and Dwelling Counts (On-line)*; the Statistics Canada website at www12.statcan.ca/english/census01/products/standard/popdwell/Table-UR-PS.cfm; Statistics Canada, *Canada at a Glance 2008*, Table 35: "Farm population"; and Statistics Canada, 2006c. *Canada's Farm Population: Agriculture-Population Linkage Data for the 2006 Census* (95-633-XWE), Table 1, http://www.statcan.gc.ca/ca-ra2006/agpop/article-eng.htm

Mass consumption became a reality in the 1920s (Bell, 1996: 66; Robbins, 2008). The automobile was the chief symbol of the new consumer society. Cars had been around for decades. By the 1920s, however, mass production technology, low cost, and easy credit made it possible for more people to own a car. The number of cars registered in Canada increased from 275,000 in 1918 to 1.9 million in 1929 (Norrie and Owram, 1996: 327), a growth rate far outstripping even the United States (see Hofstadter et al., 1957: 642).

By the 1920s, British influence, though still strong, was waning; the pull of American culture was increasing. Many of Canada's corporations were American-owned. Faintly, however, a more independent Canadian culture was stirring within English-speaking Canada, spearheaded by artists such as Emily Carr and the Group of Seven. Prints of these artists' paintings soon appeared in banks and magazines across the country, promoting images of their land that few Canadians had actually seen.

The first half of the 1920s in Canada, as elsewhere, began with a recession. By contrast, the years between 1925 and 1929 were a time of prosperity, marked by illegal gin, Charleston-dancing flappers, Model T Fords, and jazz. Then, suddenly, the prosperity ended.

THE DEPRESSION YEARS, 1929–1939

In October 1929, the New York stock market crashed. Stock values on the New York Stock Exchange alone fell by 40 percent (Palmer, with Colton, 1957: 780), and 10 percent of private wealth vanished, virtually overnight (Norrie and Owram, 1996: 296). Despite repeated statements by government officials in Canada, the United States, and elsewhere that the economy was sound, the crisis soon spread. As industrial and finance capital collapsed, production fell and unemployment rose, resulting in more uncertainty,

a further decline in consumption, and yet more layoffs occurred throughout the industrialized, capitalist world.

During the Depression's worst period (1932–1933), the **unemployment rate**, generally calculated as *the number of people out of work and actively looking for work divided by the total number of labour force participants, including the unemployed* (Krahn et al., 2007: 76), reached 23 percent in Britain and Belgium, 24 percent in Sweden, 27 percent in the United States, 29 percent in Austria, 31 percent in Norway, 32 percent in Denmark, and no less than 44 percent in Germany (all rates from Hobsbawm, 1995: 90–93). Canadian unemployment officially peaked in 1933 between 25 and 30 percent (Rice and Prince, 2000: 48). How much official statistics underestimate the problem is open to question, however.

Canada suffered uniquely in the Depression because, first, its economy was export dependent; second, its range of exports was small and lacked diversification; and third, its chief export market was the United States, a country that became highly protectionist during the Depression (Norrie and Owram, 1996: 354). Canada's economy was insufficiently developed, self-contained, and integrated to withstand the shocks. In consequence, during the period 1929–1933, Canadian industrial production fell by half, exports by two-thirds, and construction by 90 percent (Rice and Prince, 2000: 48).

Within Canada, the Depression hit the West hardest. The region's economy was particularly dependent on wheat for export. Additionally, much of the West experienced a long, harsh drought. The worst-hit area was southwest Saskatchewan, resulting in an estimated quarter of a million people abandoning their farms during the 1930s (Berton, 1991: 291). For the Maritimes, in semi-permanent recession since the 1880s, the Depression hardly seemed a change (see above).

The Depression halted, even reversed for a time, years of social change in Canada.

Barter, for example, partially replaced the money economy. Cars morphed into horse-drawn carriages, nicknamed (after Prime Minister R.B. Bennett) "Bennett buggies." The process of urbanization slowed. Immigration to Canada all but ended; indeed, for the first time since the 19th century, more people left Canada than entered (McKie, 1994). Most Canadians did not mind, however. Anti-immigrant sentiment in the 1930s was high. The Canadian government took special steps to halt the entry of people viewed as communist agitators and "trouble-makers," or people who were deemed as not fitting in. In a replay of the *Komagata Maru* incident, in 1939 the Canadian government refused the embarkation of 907 Jews aboard the liner *St. Louis*, resulting in their return ultimately to Nazi Germany's death camps (Abella and Troper, 1982; Whitaker, 1991).

The Depression damaged Canada's social fabric. Crime rates rose. The year 1931 witnessed an "unprecedented wave of bank holdups" (Berton, 1991: 88). Fuelled by Prohibition south of the border, booze became a growth industry throughout Canada, from the Maritime ports to the cities of southern Ontario to the Crowsnest Pass region of Alberta. Suicide rates climbed while birth rates, already dropping in the 1920s, declined further to 3.0 per 1,000 in 1936 and 2.8 in 1941 (see Li, 1996: 155), figures not seen again until the 1960s. In the 1930s, few people wanted to have children, not knowing if they could care for them.

Yet Canadians' sense of being part of a larger society also expanded during the Depression. Some young Canadians experienced the country first-hand, hopping freight cars and travelling from community to community in search of work (Berton, 1991). Others learned about Canada and the world at large through the cinema, though in the main the silver screen provided not access to but an escape from reality. By contrast, radio played a major role in incorporating Canadians into society.

Bennett's government recognized in the early 1930s the importance of radio in nation-building and so created the Canadian Radio and Television Commission. Radio manufactured an "imaginary collective," creating and sharing common experiences for Canadians from coast to coast, related to a host of events, from Foster Hewett's hockey broadcasts to disasters both real and fake (the "War of the Worlds") to human interest stories (the Dionne quintuplets).

Bennett's government expanded the role of the state in other ways, notably the creation of the Bank of Canada and the Wheat Board. In areas of economic and social concern, however, during the early years of the Depression Bennett followed the policies of his American counterpart, President Herbert Hoover, in steadfastly arguing that governments could not—*should* not—do anything to interfere in the economy. In both countries, problems of the poor, the hungry, and the unemployed were thrown back on local authorities and charities. The role of governments was to balance budgets, protect private property, and maintain social order.

In Canada as in the United States (Zinn, 1995), there were strikes and protests by workers throughout the decade. The state did not hesitate to use coercive force to deal with them. At Estevan, Saskatchewan, in 1931, low wages, poor living conditions, and unsympathetic management led to a confrontation between striking mine workers and police in which three strikers were killed, 11 more injured, and five policemen sent to hospital (Berton, 1991: 126–127).

As the Depression continued, Canadian governments grew increasingly wary of worker unrest—the mining town of Blairmore, Alberta, twice elected a communist town council in the mid-1930s, which promptly erected Karl Marx Park—and took further steps to curtail political unrest. One such step involved setting up work camps in remote rural areas. Before being shut down in 1936, Canada's relief camps housed 170,248 men and provided 10.2 million worker-days of relief (Howard, 1999: 2408), but the food was poor and predictable, the clothing of army issue and distinctly prison-like, and camp control was authoritarian and punitive (Berton, 1991: 176). The camps became breeding grounds of hopelessness and anger.

In June 1935, 1,500 young men of different racial and ethnic backgrounds, refugees from the British Columbia camps, set off from the Vancouver waterfront by train, headed for Ottawa, picking up supporters along the way. They were forcibly halted at Regina, however, on Dominion Day. Under orders from Prime Minister Bennett, the RCMP and local police moved into an unsuspecting crowd of 1,500 people on Regina's Market Square to arrest the trek leaders. A panic ensued. By the time it was over, 12 trekkers and five Regina citizens were hospitalized for gunshot wounds, 39 RCMP officers had been hospitalized for injuries (none from gunfire), and one plainclothes detective lay dead. Over 100 people were arrested. Twenty-eight went to trial; eight were eventually convicted and sent to jail (see Berton, 1991).

In the main, unrest in Canada during the Depression paled in comparison with other countries where strikes, protests, civil violence, and state repression were daily news. Still, it was a time of serious political unrest. Both communism and fascism gained converts in Canada. The authorities treated communists, or those suspected of being communists, far more harshly than fascist sympathizers, who garnered at least tacit support from some members of Canada's political, business, and religious elite (see Robin, 1991; Berton, 1991: 22).

Two less politically extreme alternatives to communism and fascism arose in western Canada. Like the agrarian parties of the early 1920s, both of these were **populist** parties, that is, parties *built around mass political movements, mobilized around symbols and traditions congruent* *with the popular culture, which express a group's sense of threat, arising from powerful "outside" elements and directed at the group's perceived "peoplehood."*

In Saskatchewan, the Co-operative Commonwealth Federation (CCF), built around a broad coalition of farmers, labourers, religious activists (mainly Protestant), and university-trained intellectuals (mainly economists), melded traditional Prairie populism with democratic socialism. Its leader was J.S. Woodsworth (see above), a former Methodist minister, who had been among those arrested in the 1919 Winnipeg Strike and later elected as a National Progressive in 1921. In 1944, another minister, Tommy Douglas, led the CCF to success in Saskatchewan, bringing to power the first socialist government elected in North America. In 1961, the CCF became the New Democratic Party (Lipset, 1968a; also Conway, 1994) (see Chapter 8).

In Alberta, Reverend William Aberhart, a radio evangelist, adopted the economic ideas of a British engineer, Colonel Douglas, in founding the Social Credit Party. In 1935, Aberhart's party was elected, defeating the tired and scandal-ridden United Farmers of Alberta. Broadly supported by farmers and workers alike (Bell, 1993), the party at first mixed populist rhetoric and evangelical zeal, demanding protection against bankruptcy, unemployment insurance, and public health care. Following a series of legislative setbacks, Aberhart's death in 1943, and the discovery of oil in the late 1940s, however, Social Credit became a fairly conventional conservative party opposed to government intervention in the economy (Finkel, 1989).

Government policies in Canada in the 1930s were shaped by events in the United States. In 1932, Franklin Delano Roosevelt became U.S. president. Soon Canadians as well as Americans were hearing Roosevelt over the still-new medium of radio. Canadians liked what they heard. Like Canada, the United States was faced with massive unemployment, civil unrest, and populist agitation. Unlike Bennett, Roosevelt offered solutions to the crisis, embarking on a series of economic and social reforms between 1933 and 1938 that protected farmers, regulated banking, gave relief to the unemployed, extended labour rights, and fuelled the economy through public works projects (Langer, 1948: 1053–1056; Hofstadter et al., 1957: 650–675; Zinn, 1995: 382–384).

Facing political pressures, in 1934 Bennett's government launched its own version of Roosevelt's "New Deal": unemployment insurance, minimum wages, legislation dealing with hours of work, marketing legislation, and laws against price-fixing (Langer, 1948: 1060; Morton, 1997: 205–206). The reforms came too late, however, to save Bennett's government from defeat in 1935 at the hands of William Lyon Mackenzie King's Liberals.

Under King, as under Bennett, the state's role in building Canada grew stronger. The Canadian Radio and Broadcast Commission became the Canadian Broadcasting Corporation, and government-owned Trans-Canada Airlines was launched (Morton, 1997: 207). The economy, however, continued to languish. After a short period of recovery, both Canada and the United States entered recession again in 1937. Labour and civil unrest continued. A strike in 1937 by General Motors' workers in Oshawa, Ontario, over poor wages and union recognition led to violence. Meanwhile, ties to the United States grew, symbolized by the signing of a limited reciprocity agreement in 1935, King's almost fawning relationship with Roosevelt, and the latter's comments at Queen's University in 1938 pledging American support in the event of war (Martin, 1982).

CANADA AND THE SECOND WORLD WAR

On September 1, 1939, what English poet W.H. Auden once referred to as a "low, dishonest decade," ended as Germany invaded Poland. Within days, much of the world, except the United States and Russia, was at war.

It is impossible to overstate the war's human devastation. Hobsbawm (1995: 43) notes that the "losses are literally incalculable" because many of those killed were civilians and "much of the worst killing took place in regions, or at times, when nobody was in a position to count...." Gilbert (1991: 746) estimates the total of civilian and military deaths for China, Japan, the Soviet Union, Germany, Poland, and Yugoslavia, and assorted Jewish populations within Europe as "in excess of forty-six million," suggesting that the total figure for all countries is at least 50 million deaths (Keegan, 1990), and perhaps much more.

More than a million Canadian men and women (out of a total population of only 11 million people) joined the army, navy, or air force during the Second World War. In total, 42,042 Canadian military personnel were killed and 53,145 wounded. Canada's financial expenditures rose from $118 million in 1939–1940 to $4.5 billion in 1943–1944 (Stacey and Hillmer, 1999: 2552). Public debt rose from $5 billion in 1939 to $18 billion by 1945 (Norrie and Owram, 1996: 378), resulting in a net federal public debt of nearly 107 percent of GNP in 1946–1947 (Chorney, 1989: 43).

Journalist Blair Fraser (1967: 14) later wrote: "The most that could be said was that World War II had done less damage to the fabric of the nation than World War I did." The lasting effects of the Conscription Crisis of the Second World War were less—no "gaping wound," merely "a bruise." There were "no jobless veterans begging or rioting in the streets," no "counterpart of the Winnipeg General strike," though a strike at Windsor in 1945 proved significant for labour relations. Canada's liberal self-image, however, did take a beating for its treatment of ethnic minorities, notably the expulsion and internment of men, women, and children of Japanese extraction.

Yet there had also been positive gains. Dragged from their towns and farms, many Canadians saw their own country for the first time; many also gained a sense of their own and Canada's place internationally. Likewise, skills were developed that paid dividends in the postwar years.

The Canadian economy benefitted as a whole. The war dragged Canada and the world out of the Depression and set off Canada's third great period of economic growth, a period that continued into the early 1960s (Aitken, 1959). Enormous investments in economic infrastructure had turned Canada into a gigantic armaments factory, producing thousands of aircraft, tanks, anti-aircraft guns, tracked vehicles, and machine guns (James, 1997: 509). These plants were soon refitted to meet peacetime consumer demand. Likewise, Canada ended the war with a huge and disciplined navy and the world's fourth largest merchant marine, important to export trade. At the same time, however, Canada's military and economy were more integrated than ever into the American orbit.

CONCLUSION

Within a few short decades of Confederation, the world of 1867 had ceased to exist except in memory and old photographs. The basic contours of Canadian society in the second half of the 20th century were forged by events during this period; the after-effects continue into the 21st century.

First, the United States clearly arose as successor to the British Empire, both internationally and in its influence upon Canada. In the words of Innis (1956), Canada had gone from colony to nation to colony. In this context, new notions of English-Canadian nationalism arose with consequences seen 20 years later (Chapter 8).

Second, English Canada's culture changed during this period, largely as a result of mass immigration in the first decade, to be resumed after 1945. Thus was set in motion a further decline of English dominance, the distinctive pattern of ethnicity that marks Canadian provinces, and the enactment of Canada's policy of multiculturalism.

Third, corporate capitalism largely replaced petit bourgeois capitalism. No elements of Canadian society, from family size to social values to urban growth, were left unmarked by this event. By the end of the Second World War, the vast majority of Canadians, including large numbers of women, had become part of the paid labour force.

Fourth, the state gradually came to play a larger role in the lives of Canadians. The crumbling of traditional society and its institutions, accelerated by the wars and the Depression, resulted in a deepening and centralizing of state policies, evidenced particularly in the nascent welfare state. More than ever, state and civil society became inseparable.

Canada, in 1945, seemed a land of promise. On its outskirts, however, lay new perils to Canadian identity, harmony, sovereignty, and peace. The next chapter examines Canada's efforts to wend its way through the postwar world's uncertain waters.

KEY TERMS

Anglo-conformity
import substitution
populist
racism
region
regional alienation
regional differences
regionalism
unemployment rate
xenophobia

CRITICAL THINKING QUESTIONS

1. Why did Canada not adopt the European model of economic development after 1867?

2. In what ways did corporate capitalism benefit from the major wars and other social disasters of the 20th century?

3. Is unemployment a "natural" phenomenon or is it socially produced?

4. In what sense is it possible to think of the First and Second World Wars as one long war?

5. In what ways did the Second World War bring Canada closer into the American economic, social, and political orbit?

RECOMMENDED READINGS

Brodie, Janine. 1990. *The Political Economy of Canadian Regionalism.* Toronto: Harcourt Brace Jovanovich Canada.

Brodie's book explores the different meanings of regionalism while also tying it to political development.

Finkel, Alvin. 1989. *The Social Credit Phenomenon in Alberta.* Toronto: University of Toronto Press.

This book provides a social and historical account of the rise of the Social Credit Party in Alberta in the 1930s.

Krahn, Harvey, Graham Lowe, and Karen Hughes. 2007. *Work, Industry, and Canadian Society,* 5th ed. Toronto: Nelson.

In its 5th edition, this is the definitive text on work and industry in Canada.

Laxer, Gordon. 1989. *Open for Business: The Roots of Foreign Ownership in Canada.* Toronto: Oxford University Press.

Winner of the 1991 John Porter Award for best book published in sociology, this book examines empirically the social and political relationships underlying economic development.

Robin, Martin. 1991. *Shades of Right: Nativist and Fascist Politics in Canada, 1920–1940.* Toronto: University of Toronto Press.

Robin's book details the little known rise of nativist and fascist movements in Canada during the 1930s.

RELATED WEBSITES

Bank of Canada

http://www.bankofcanada.ca/en/about/history. html

Amid the Great Depression, the Bank of Canada was created in 1934 by an act of Parliament as a means of stabilizing Canada's monetary system. This is a history of the bank.

Canadian War Museum

http://www.warmuseum.ca/splash.html

Located in Ottawa, the Canadian War Museum is Canada's national museum of military history.

Status of Women Canada

http://www.swc-cfc.gc.ca/dates/gg/case-affaire-eng.html

This federal government organization promotes the full participation of women in the economic, social, and democratic life of Canada. Its website contains a story on the famous "Persons Case."

CANADIAN SOCIETY ON VIDEO

Between Two Wars. 1987. National Film Board of Canada, 87 minutes, 8 seconds. Three films cover the period from the end of the First World War to the onset of the Second World War. *The Good, Bright Days* (1919–1927), from the Armistice of 1918 to the economic boom of the late 1920s (28 minutes, 55 seconds); *Sunshine and Eclipse* (1927–1934), from the end of the boom to the onset of the Great Depression (28 minutes, 57 seconds); and *Twilight of an Era* (1934–1939), the years leading up to war in Europe (29 minutes, 3 seconds).

On Strike: The Winnipeg General Strike, 1919. 1991. National Film Board of Canada, 19 minutes, 46 seconds. The dramatic story of the Winnipeg General Strike in 1919 as told through the recollections of the men and women who were there.

Reckoning: The Political Economy of Canada, "Part 1: Riding the Tornado." 1986. National Film Board of Canada, 57 minutes, 22 seconds. Explains the phenomenon of boom and bust cycles related to staples-driven economies.

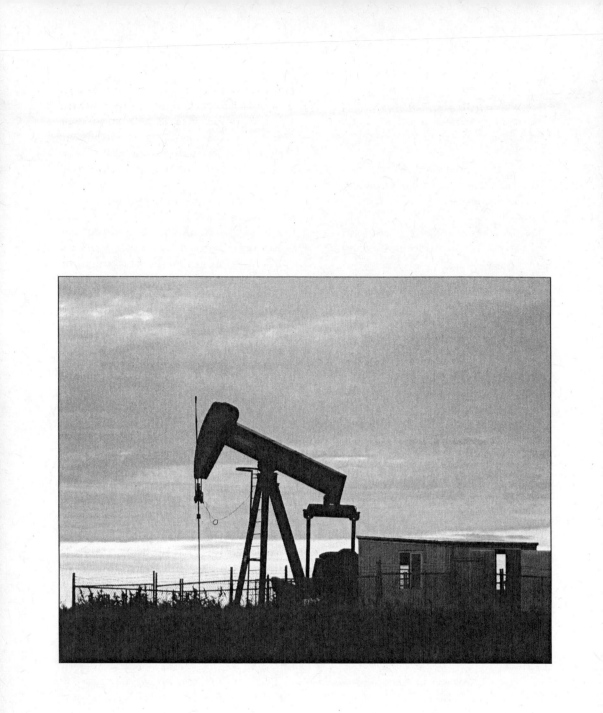

CHAPTER 8
FROM COLONY TO NATION—TO COLONY?

You know, it seems ridiculous. We both speak the same language. We think alike. We behave the same. Don't you think you would be better off as the 49th state?
—U.S. President Dwight D. Eisenhower to Canadian diplomat Lionel Chevrier, 1956

There are two ways to conquer a country—one is by force of arms; the other is by taking control of its economy.
—American Secretary of State John Foster Dulles in the 1950s

Living with you is in some ways like sleeping with an elephant. No matter how friendly or temperate the beast, one is affected by every twitch and grunt.
—Prime Minister Trudeau to the National Press Club in Washington, 1969

INTRODUCTION
The end of the Second World War stimulated in Canada an unprecedented, albeit uneven, period of economic expansion and social and political transformation. Increased demands for skilled labour were ultimately met by immigration and the increased workforce presence of women. Birth rates soared, before resuming in 1956 a longer trend of decline (Li, 1996: 70), and family forms changed. The welfare state evolved, underpinning a compromise between labour and capital. And, on April 1, 1949, Newfoundland joined Confederation, though some Newfoundlanders to this day claim they annexed Canada.

Meanwhile, abroad, the hot menace of fascism was replaced by the Cold War. Anti-communist hysteria gripped the United States and soon found its way across the border. At the Bretton Woods conference held in 1944, Western countries, led by the United States, designed an economic regime meant to rebuild and stabilize the postwar world. Not incidentally, it paved the way for orderly capitalist expansion. Key institutions of this plan included the International Monetary Fund (IMF) and the World Bank (also known as the International Bank for Reconstruction and Development). The General Agreement on Tariffs and Trade (GATT), formed to negotiate tariff reductions and the removal of other trade barriers, joined these institutions in the early 1950s (Lairson and Skidmore, 1997). Politically, the international postwar era also saw the creation of the United Nations, successor to the failed pre-war League of Nations.

Consumption flourished throughout the next decade, underpinned by continued strong economic growth. Suburban Canada was born, aided by the ubiquitous presence of automobiles. Television invaded family living rooms and bedrooms.

The prosperous 1950s gave way in Canada in the early 1960s to renewed concerns of American control. In the context of growing American defeats abroad and social discord at home, and in contraposition to Quebec's demands for sovereignty, a new nationalism arose in English-speaking Canada. In the 1970s, English-Canadian nationalism paved the way for a further expansion of state involvement in the economy and society, referred to as "Canadianization." By the 1980s, however, debt and internal divisions hobbled the Canadian state, setting the stage for adoption of a new developmental paradigm.

This chapter traces the key events and changes that occurred in Canadian society between the end of the Second World War and the Canadian election of 1984, and the state's role in those changes.

CANADA AND THE UNITED STATES IN THE COLD WAR ERA

In 1945, Canada's 12 million people seemed enviably blessed. The country had a large public debt, but also ample resources much in world demand: steel, timber, wheat, and oil, for example. It also had an established industrial and state infrastructure. Abroad, Canada's chief economic competitors lay in ruins. Reconstruction in Europe and the subsequent Korean conflict (1950–1953) fuelled demand for Canadian resources. Meanwhile, at home, a large reservoir of consumer power was ready to be unleashed (Norrie and Owram, 1996). The result was generally high economic growth throughout the 1950s, yet the new prosperity also hid real political, economic, and cultural dangers.

To the north, across the Arctic waters, lay the Soviet Union, which only months before had been a staunch ally. Now it was suddenly the enemy. The period was highlighted by the case of Igor Gouzenko, a Soviet embassy clerk who in September 1945 defected with documents revealing Soviet espionage in Canada (Finkel, 1997). As in the United States, anti-communist hysteria soon became a staple of Canadian political and cultural life.

To the south lay a more subtle threat, however. The United States ended the Second World War as the globe's lone superpower, possessor of the world's strongest economy and a large battle-hardened military. The United States alone also had the atomic bomb, a fact quickly interpreted by several American politicians and religious figures as symbolizing America's divinely chosen status among countries (Ungar, 1991).

More than ever, in 1945 Canada fell under America's sway. Following a secret meeting between Canada's Prime Minister William Lyon Mackenzie King and U.S. President Franklin Delano Roosevelt (1882–1945) at Ogdensburg in 1942, the two countries' militaries became strategically linked. These links became more formal in 1949, when Canada became part of the newly formed North Atlantic Treaty Organization (NATO), an anti-communist self-defence bloc headed by the United States. In the 1960s, Canada also became the United States' northern partner in a continental defence pact, the North American Air Defense Command (NORAD).

Economically, wartime production had stimulated Canada's growth but also increased links with the United States. After the war, American companies began buying up Canada's redundant war factories and retooling them for civilian use. Much the same occurred regarding Canadian resources. In 1952, American President Harry Truman (1884–1972) released the Paley Report (Roberts, 1998). The report, issued as the Cold War heated up, suggested Canada's resource wealth made it a potential economic rival to the United States. The report argued further that the American government should do everything in its power to secure Canadian raw materials, especially uranium, in the service of defending the United States.

America's cultural presence in Canada also grew during and after the war through cinema and radio, and increased again in the 1950s with the rise of television. The fact that a disproportionate number of Canadians found employment in movies and television, both in front of the camera and behind the scenes as writers, technicians, and directors, did not change the impact. The productions were generically American, meant to be sold first to Americans, then resold abroad to foreigners, including Canadians, who were increasingly entranced by that empire's technology, power, and wealth.

But the American presence in Canada was also increasingly demographic and social. Construction of the Alaska Highway during the Second World War (see Chapter 11) was completed almost entirely with American labour and investment, and the development of large-scale oil production in Alberta after 1947 resulted in a further influx of American money, personnel, and expertise (House, 1978; Richards and Pratt, 1979). Calgary quickly became the Houston of the North, and an ethos of rugged individualism slowly replaced the settler traditions of co-operation and community. In the long term, the development of Alberta's oil industry set the stage for interprovincial rivalry and federal-provincial hostility, while furthering a continental approach to development at odds with the tenets of the old National Policy.

Internationally, the immediate postwar period saw the start of the divvying up of the world between state communism, represented by the Soviet Union, and corporate capitalism, represented by the United States. During the early period, the final dismantling of colonialism provided opportunities for both superpowers to expand into new territories, notably the Middle East, Africa, and, especially following the French retreat from Vietnam in the late 1950s, Asia. Both the Soviet Union and the United States took measures to secure their borders and expand their influence throughout this period and after. The Soviet Union invaded Hungary in 1956, Czechoslovakia in 1968, and Afghanistan in 1979. Similarly, the United States, acting on the Monroe Doctrine (Chapter 6), continued a long policy after the 1950s of threatening, destabilizing, and sometimes invading sovereign countries throughout the Americas. Occasionally, as during the Cuban missile crisis in 1963, the boundaries of American and Soviet interests intersected, bringing the world close to nuclear war. For Canada, finding its way in this bipolar world was a task not easily accomplished.

There was one notable similarity, however, between communist and capitalist countries: the continued growth of the state. This was no less true in the case of Canada.

FROM STATE TO "WELFARE STATE"

Far from being a nation-state or even a multinational state, Canada may best be described as a state-nation (see Chapter 1). That is, the state often came first, and then set about constructing the institutions of nationhood. In the course of this construction, Canadian society was also changed in particular ways.

The Hudson's Bay Company was a kind of prototype for early Canadian development, with other corporations following (for example, the Canadian Pacific Railway). From building railways and canals to building defensive fortifications, to the pacification of the West by the North-West Mounted Police to pave the way for immigrants, the Canadian state (including, to a lesser degree, the provinces) acted as chief architect, administrator, and banker. Until the 1930s, much of this involvement was minimalist and remained tied directly or indirectly to furthering private capital accumulation. Slowly, however, the state's involvement in Canadian society entered broader areas of nation-building (such as CBC Radio) and social concern.

To a degree, the state's initially minimalist role in Canadian society in 1867 is understandable given that Canada was a small, still largely pre-capitalist and pre-industrial country. Thereafter, however, the Canadian state and society expanded together. Four periods marked this expansion and transformation (see Rice and Prince, 2000; Johnson and Stritch, 1997). The first period occurred between 1867 and 1914, during Canada's initial industrialization and expansion. The second period occurred between the start of the First World War and the end of the postwar boom, 1914–1929, during which corporate capitalism took hold and Canada urbanized (see Li, 1996). The third period, 1929–1945, began with the Depression and ended with the closing of the Second World War. The fourth period, with which we are primarily concerned here, began in 1945 and continued until the mid-1980s, when changes brought on by neo-liberal globalization (see Chapter 9) further altered the relationship of state and society and the role of government.

Each period saw a gradual shift in government functions in areas of social policy. Rice and Prince (2000) note that responsibility for social welfare changed over time in five important ways. First, responsibility shifted from the private to the state sector. Second, responsibility shifted from lower to higher levels (that is, from municipalities to the provinces or the federal government). Third, the administration and provision of services became more centralized and under the auspices of professional authorities. And fourth, there was a move in policy approaches from remedial to preventive policies.

A fifth related but gradual change saw a shift from particularistic to more universal policies. The Pension Act of 1919 was Canada's first universal program in the sense that it was provided to all returning soldiers without resort to a means test. A further move to standardization and universality occurred with the federal government's introduction of the Old Age Pensions Act in 1927.

In Canada, as elsewhere in the industrialized West, the greatest public expansion into social programs, however, occurred after the Second World War (see Turner, 1981; Rice and Prince, 2000). Influential in this regard were the ideas of British economist John Maynard Keynes (1883–1946), who argued that the state had a role in ensuring economic and, hence, political stability. With full employment as the goal, counter-cyclical measures to ward off market fluctuations became a standard feature of postwar government planning. In the context of the Cold War, such interventions also proved useful in showing that capitalism could be responsive not only to market demands but also to human needs.

As in other countries, the war enlarged,

centralized, and strengthened the Canadian state, increasing its capacity to act. Important models for action were garnered from Roosevelt's New Deal administration in the United States (Chapter 7) and from the Beveridge Report produced in Britain. Within Canada, the Royal Commission on Dominion-Provincial Relations (Rowell-Sirois Commission) in 1940 and the federal government's Advisory Committee on Post-war Reconstruction (the Marsh Report) in 1943 provided similar blueprints for reshaping Canada's system of social security.

Pressures for political change came from a variety of sources, particularly unions, social activists, progressive think tanks (such as the League for Social Reconstruction), and the CCF (see Chapter 7). These pressures resulted in 1940 in King's government bringing in Canada's first Unemployment Insurance Act. This was followed in 1944 with introduction of the Family Allowances Act, a universal program that (at the time) substantially assisted young families in raising their children and, not unintentionally, also encouraged Canada's birth rate.

These tentative steps at reshaping Canada's social security system were nothing compared with what followed, however. Health care provides a specific example of this process of state expansion.

The postwar period saw the Canadian federal government set up a system of national health grants (1948). This was followed in the 1950s by the Old Age Security Act (1951), the expansion of government assistance under the Unemployment Insurance Act (1956), and the passing of the Hospital Insurance and Diagnostic Act (1957), which introduced federal cost-sharing to pay for provincial hospital insurance. In 1965, the compulsory Canada Pension Plan and Quebec Pension Plan were introduced. The following year, the Guaranteed Income Supplement Plan and Canada Assistance Plan were created, and medicare (a system of public health insurance) was introduced with the passage of the Medical Care Act (see Li, 1996: 84–85).

Together, programs such as health care, education, unemployment insurance, social allowance, and others make up what is often referred to as the Canadian "welfare state." What are they and what do welfare states do?

Briefly, the term **welfare state**, sometimes referred to as the Keynesian welfare state (KWS) after John Maynard Keynes, refers to *a system of state provision of people's social needs outside private markets*. Unlike regular commodities that are bought and sold, social needs are de-commodified and provided as a right of citizenship (Esping-Andersen, 1990).

In practical terms, the postwar KWS resulted from a compromise between capital and labour. Labour accepted owners' right to a profit and to make decisions regarding company matters. In return, capital (that is, owners and managers) accepted labour's right to organize and bargain. The state, meanwhile, provided the legal, political, and often financial resources underpinning this compromise. During the Depression and the Second World War, for example, Canada experienced a series of bitter strikes (Roberts, 1998: 7). In 1944, however, the Canadian government passed legislation granting private sector workers the right to organize, to bargain collectively, and to strike (Panitch and Swartz, 1988). This and similar labour legislation and decisions (such as unemployment insurance and the Rand Formula which requires the deduction of union dues from paycheque even if an employee in a unionized workplace does not want to belong to the union) introduced a period of relative harmony to labour relations. In effect, the state set the rules for Canada's postwar form of capital accumulation, but in doing so, the state also shaped more broadly the contours of Canadian society.

The state's greater role in Canadian society after the Second World War was not restricted, however, to areas of health and social security. The late 1960s also saw the state—both federal and provincial—finance a rapid expansion of post-secondary education (Wanner, 1999). Between 1971 and 2001, the percentage of Canadians 15 years of age and older with some post-secondary education rose from 17.1 to 35.6, while the percentage of those with university education climbed from 4.8 to 15.4 (look ahead to Table 13.5). By 2006, 18.9 percent of working-age Canadians had a university degree, while 29.9 percent had a post-secondary certificate or degree (Statistics Canada, 2007a: 154–155).

The state also became more concerned with issues of nation-building and social inequality. Especially worth noting in regard to these are the Royal Commission on Bilingualism and Biculturalism, also known as the Dunton-Laurendeau Commission (Chapter 3); the Hawthorn-Tremblay Report into Canada's Aboriginal peoples (see Chapter 12); and the Royal Commission on the Status of Women in Canada, also known as the Bird Commission. Echoing the call of U.S. President Lyndon Johnson (1908–1973) for the war on poverty, similar efforts were made in Canada, highlighted by a massive government study (1973–1980) into the efficacy of a guaranteed annual income (see Hum, 1983), in which many sociologists (including one of this text's authors) played a small role.

THE CANADIAN WELFARE STATE IN PERSPECTIVE

Beginning in the 1960s, many theorists began arguing that the KWS represented a form of social organization toward which all modern industrial societies, including the Soviet Union, would in time converge (Bell, 1961; Kerr et al., 1964; Galbraith, 1969; Wilensky, 1975). From the beginning, however, no two welfare states were alike. Esping-Andersen (1990) describes three broad types of welfare states: (1) conservative welfare states, such as Austria, France, Germany, and Italy; (2) social democratic welfare states, such as Sweden, Norway, and Denmark; and (3) liberal democratic welfare states, such as the United States and Australia (see also Baker, 1996; Olsen, 2002). Of these, social democratic welfare states have high taxes, but also extensive and universal social programs, while liberal democratic welfare states have low taxes, few social programs, and programs that are means-tested, that is, not available to all. Conservative welfare states fall some-where in between, with moderate to high taxes and fairly extensive programs, but ones that often are designed to maintain traditional class and gender hierarchies.

Canada's form of welfare state is a hybrid of these models. It best fits the liberal demo-cratic model, with its emphasis upon means-testing, modest levels of social transfers, belief in individualism, faith in markets, and protection of private profits (Li, 1996). At the same time, however, Canada's wel-fare state also embraces some conservative elements (for example, an emphasis upon maintaining traditional family and gender roles) and social democratic elements (such as social equality and universality) (see Baker, 1996; Finkel, 1997; Rice and Prince, 2000). Finally, we should note the criticisms of many feminist theorists that none of the existing models adequately deal with the problem of poverty for many women, inso-far as their situation results from barriers to full participation in the labour force. That is, while de-commodification is not unimport-ant to issues of equality, it does not address the real inequalities resulting from a strati-fied labour market (see Olsen, 2002).

By European standards, Canada's wel-fare state programs historically have not been generous or extensive and appear so only when compared with that of the Unit-ed States (see Finkel, 1997; Olsen, 2002). In 2001, for example, Canada spent 20.4 percent of its GDP on social expenditures (including health, education, and social services) compared to the United States,

which spent 15.7 percent. But compare Canada's total also with Germany (30.6 percent), France (33 percent), Sweden (35.1 percent), and Norway (27 percent) (figures in Adema and Ladaique, 2005: 33).

Of course, wherever people live, they still require many of the same services. The difference lies in whether these services are publicly provided, requiring larger tax revenues, or paid for by individuals out of their own pocket, in which case state taxes may be reduced. Comparing the same countries above, for example, the United States in 2004 taxed at a rate of 33.1 percent of GDP (up considerably from previous years), compared with Canada at 33.5 percent, Germany at 34.7 percent, France at 43.4 percent, Sweden at 57.6 percent, and Norway at 59.8 percent (OECD, 2007: 57–58). Note, however, that high taxes do not necessarily mean high social expenditures. Much of the United States' budget goes toward military and policing functions.

It is nice to think that Canadians and their governments would comb the world for policy examples; the reality is that too often Canadian eyes look only southward. So it was that in the late 1980s, Canada faced increased pressure from business lobbyists and their political and media supporters to lower corporate and personal taxes and to accept the minimalist welfare state model of its American counterpart (Li, 1996) in the name of competitiveness (see Chapter 9). Though still distinct in some areas (such as medicare), Canada moved closer throughout the 1990s to the American welfare state model (Olsen, 2002). Closely tied to the rise and fall of Canada's welfare state during the postwar years were also material, cultural, and ideological changes in the role of women.

WOMEN IN THE CHANGING CANADIAN SOCIETY

As the Second World War began, women at last had formal political power, but little actual political, economic, or social power. The war began the process of changing this.

Economically, while many women remained to work the farms deserted by men fighting overseas, many others were pressed into non-traditional occupations, such as welding in wartime factories. Yet others moved out of the clerical ranks to take on higher administrative roles in the growing public service. Fears that the end of war would result in mass unemployment proved unwarranted. Indeed, the demand for skilled labour increased (see below) and women now ably filled it.

Of course, some women did return to the home and to unpaid labour to raise families; the postwar baby boom was about to start. But a large number of women remained in the workplace, though only casually and often shunted to the service end of the labour market, attracted both by the social and economic opportunities. Moreover, the period after 1945 saw an intensification of consumerism that could be met only by families with one-and-a-half (if not two) salaries.

To a degree, women's increasing participation in Canada's labour force mirrored that of other countries. Participation was more intense in Canada, however, and increased even more after 1960. Between 1960 and 1975, female labour force participation rose from 28 percent to 41 percent, increasing again over the next two decades to 62 percent in 2004 (Krahn et al., 2007: 52). In turn, these changes in the female participation rate set off a series of unintended consequences for fertility rates, family structures, gender roles, family and individual finances, and public services, such as the need for daycare. After 1975, for example, dual-income families, rather than single-income families, became the Canadian norm.

Other interrelated factors besides labour economics and increased consumerism were changing the situation of women, however. The idea of greater individual freedom took hold in Canadian society as elsewhere. Likewise, the 1950s saw a loosening of cultural prescriptions for male and female gender roles and behaviours, which were sometimes and sometimes not reflected in Hollywood films. Technological advances in the 1960s—notably, the contraceptive pill— further changed sexual behaviours and gender relationships. In turn, and over time, these things also began changing family structures. Divorce rates rose while, despite the incidence of the baby boom, the average family size declined.

Underlying the changing status of women in Canada (and elsewhere) was also a transformative change in the dominant ideology brought about by feminism. First-wave feminism, beginning in the mid-19th century, sought—largely with success—to gain for women equal property rights and the right to vote. The 1960s brought second-wave feminism, inspired by writers such as Simone de Beauvoir, Kate Millett, and Germaine Greer. Whereas the attention of first-wave feminists had been upon political institutions, second-wave feminists, many of whom had been involved in student protest movements, concentrated on establishing women's organizations from below, in civil society (Brym, 2008: 480). (By the 1990s, some scholars noted the onset of third-wave feminism, launched by women who belonged to ethnic minorities and questioned the dominance of middle-class White women within the feminist movement [Morrow, 1994: 18].)

As in the previous century, those in dominant positions—but also many in Canada at large, including some women— often opposed feminist demands for greater equality. In the mid-1970s, a backlash against the gains made by women began building, finding its political champions in the 1980s and 1990s in a series of New Right political parties and movements. The complaints of these parties and their supporters were not just economic but more often cultural; that is, women's demands (and gains) upset what Hiller (1987) termed the **symbolic order**, that is, *the set of values, beliefs, and behaviours that lend predictability to our everyday surroundings*. More often than not after the 1970s, these fears were focused not only on the feminist movement but also on Canada's changing ethnic and racial profile.

LABOUR MARKETS, IMMIGRATION, AND MULTICULTURALISM

Canada's KWS, like that of other countries, was predicated on a prosperous national economy and full employment, since employed workers could pay taxes and would not draw upon social security. At the macro level, Canada's finances to pay for these expanded programs remained particularly dependent, however, upon the export of raw resources. Meanwhile, Canada's economy after the Second World War also underwent a substantial transformation.

Most especially, Canada experienced continued change in its labour market with jobs in the secondary and service industries coming to dominate. As you will recall (Chapter 7), in 1891, 49 percent of Canada's labour force still worked in primary industry, compared with 20 percent in secondary industry, and 31 percent in the service sector. By 1951, however, 31 percent of Canada's labour force worked in the secondary sector, of which the auto industry was key, while 47 percent were employed in services (Krahn et al., 2007: 60–61).

The following decades saw a further growth in Canada's service industries, while the other sectors declined in relative importance to the economy. At the same time, however, the service sector itself became bifurcated between jobs in an upper tier (employing well-paid and well-educated people, often "symbolic analysts" able to manipulate information) and a lower tier (employing often the young or very old, often marginalized, at low wages in such things as the fast-food, retail, and hostelry industries). By 2004, the service sector employed 74 percent of working Canadians, while the secondary sector employed 21 percent, and primary industries only 5 percent (Krahn et al., 2007: 60), a situation reflected in the increased demand for particular occupations, such as the applied and social sciences and health fields, between 1991 and 2006 (Table 8.1).

Table 8.1
Experienced Labour Force 15 Years and over by Occupation (Censuses 1991 and 2006)

Occupation	1991		2006	
	Number	**%**	**Number**	**%**
All occupations	14,220,235	100.0	16,861,185	100.0
Management	1,383,410	9.7	1,631,730	9.7
Business, finance, and administrative	2,727,160	19.2	3,025,425	17.9
Natural and applied sciences and related occupations	669,970	4.7	1,108,050	6.6
Health	703,930	5.0	950,360	5.6
Social science, education, government service, and religion	917,835	6.5	1,414,325	8.4
Art, culture, recreation, and sport	337,355	2.4	502,195	3.0
Sales and service	3,476,380	24.4	4,037,720	23.9
Trades, transport and equipment operators, and related occupations	2,199,375	15.5	2,550,295	15.1
Occupations unique to primary industry	734,515	5.2	648,310	3.8
Occupations unique to processing, manufacturing, and utilities	1,070,300	7.5	992,765	5.9

Source: Statistics Canada, *2006 Census of Population*, http://www40.statcan.gc.ca/l01/cst01/labor44-eng.htm. Last modified October 3, 2008. Downloaded May 9, 2009. Percentages calculated by authors. Percentages do not add up due to rounding.

At least immediately after the Second World War, however, Canada experienced a heightened demand for labour, especially skilled labour. Some of this demand was met by returning veterans, whom the government retrained under generous financial terms. Women (as noted above) also played a large role in filling demand, especially in the growing service industry (Lowe, 1987; Li, 1996: 149). Canadian industry's demand for labour after the Second World War was inexhaustible, however. Immigration to Canada had virtually ceased during the Depression and subsequent war years (see Table 7.1). Now the Canadian government once more opened the immigration door to let in new workers.

Table 8.2
Immigrant Status and Period of Immigration and Place of Birth, 2001 (total and percent)

Ethnic Origin	Total Immigrant Population[1]	Before 1961	%	1961–2001	%
Americas	837,055	47,835	5.3	789,220	17.3
North America	238,350	34,945	3.9	203,405	4.5
Central America	108,085	1,595	.2	106,490	2.3
Caribbean and Bermuda	294,050	6,985	.8	287,065	6.3
South America	196,560	4,310	.5	192,250	4.2
Europe	2,287,555	809,325	90.5	1,478,230	32.5
Western Europe	423,805	215,135	24.1	208,670	4.6
Eastern Europe	471,365	135,425	15.1	335,940	7.4
Northern Europe	677,015	250,875	28.0	426,140	9.4
Southern Europe	715,370	207,900	23.2	507,470	11.1
Africa	282,600	4,635	.5	277,965	6.1
Western Africa	32,885	75	—	32,810	.7
Eastern Africa	108,035	535	—	107,500	2.4
Northern Africa	93,165	2,595	.3	90,570	2.0
Central Africa	12,920	125	—	12,795	.3
Southern Africa	35,595	1,305	.1	34,290	.8
Asia	1,989,180	28,850	3.2	1,960,330	43.0
West Central Asia and the Middle East	285,585	4,445	.5	281,140	6.2
Eastern Asia	730,595	18,325	2.0	712,270	15.6
Southeast Asia	469,110	2,240	.3	466,870	10.2
Southern Asia	503,895	3,845	.4	500,050	11.0
Oceania and Other[2]	52,095	3,815	.4	48,280	1.1
Total	5,448,480	894,465	100.0	4,554,015	100.0

Notes:
1. Total population does not include non-permanent residents. Discrepancies in percentages are due to rounding.
2. Oceania and Other combined to match regions in Table 8.2.

Source: Adapted from Statistics Canada website at http://www12.statcan.ca/english/census01/products/standard/themes/ RetrieveProductTable.cfm?Temporal=2001&PID=62124&APATH=3&GID=431515&METH=1&PTYPE=55440&THEME=43&FOCUS=0&AID=0&PLACENAME=0&PROVINCE=0&SEARCH=0&GC=0&GK=0&VID=0&VNAMEE=&-VNAMEF=&FL=0&RL=0&FREE=0

At first glance, Canada's postwar immigration policy seems remarkably similar to that during earlier periods of economic expansion (see Chapter 7), especially in favouring immigrants from Britain and western Europe, but there were important differences. While British immigrants at first remained favoured, there were fewer people from that country who wished to come. Also, Canada faced increased competition throughout the 1950s from Australia and the United States for a shrinking pool of labour, especially skilled labour. Thus, Canadian policy gradually stretched to allow more immigrants from non-traditional source countries, first eastern and southern Europeans (especially those escaping communism), and later people from Asia, Africa, and the Caribbean. Changes in the Immigration Act of 1967, which saw the introduction of a point system, furthered this transition. Before this time, race and ethnicity were explicit criteria for entry. After this time, immigration and labour market needs became more closely aligned. The criteria for entry shifted first to educational qualifications, then (by the 1980s) to financial and class (that is, business) qualifications (Harrison, 1996). Table 8.2 compares the birthplaces of immigrants before 1961 with those of later arrivals. Note the dramatic shift away from Europe, especially western and northern Europe, toward immigrants from Asia in particular.

While earlier immigration largely reflected the state's need to populate new territories, immigration after the 1970s was influenced by broader social changes. Cultural changes, including the introduction of the birth control pill in the early 1960s, brought about a rapid decline in Canada's birth rate. By the 1970s, some policy-makers feared Canada's working-age population might one day be insufficient to pay for the expanding services required of an aging population. Immigration thus became tied not only directly to economic needs but also to the growing fiscal requirements of the welfare state (see Li, 1996).

The changes to Canada's immigration policy were particularly noticeable in some major cities (Toronto, Montreal, Vancouver), where sizable ethnic communities arose as the result of **chain migration**: *the tendency of new immigrants to settle in areas already populated by members of their cultural community.* As in the past, however, the settlement of new immigrants was not uniformly spread across Canada. These early settlement patterns continue in the ethnic makeup of Canada's provinces today. As Table 8.3 shows, British ancestry tends to predominate on the East Coast and decline generally as we move westward, while French ancestry dominates in Quebec (see Part 1). By contrast, a large number of people living on the Prairies trace their ancestry to middle and eastern Europe, while the West Coast features a large number of people of Asian ancestry.

Note also, however, the increasingly mixed nature of ethnic identifications in Canada. While a larger proportion of Canadians have either British or French ancestry, these are not exclusive in many instances of other heritages.

In 1969, Canada had adopted the policy of official bilingualism in response to the rise of Quebec nationalism (Chapter 3). Many people accepted (albeit some grudgingly) the need for two official languages to bind the country together and address the demands of Quebec's sizable francophone population. Fewer, especially visible minorities and Canada's Aboriginal peoples, accepted the notion of two official cultures, however. The result was Canada's adoption two years later of a policy of **multiculturalism**, *whereby no culture is officially privileged over another.*

Multiculturalism today is an official mainstay of Canadian identity. Supporters of the policy contend that Canada is leading the way in becoming a postmodern society, and that the country's ability to manage cultural differences adds to its strength, economically, culturally, and politically. The policy also has critics, however. In the eyes of some, multiculturalism merely hides the continuing reality of an ethnic hierarchy in Canada. Others see it as an expensive and destructive policy that encourages people to retain past identities and live in ethnic quarters of Canadian cities rather than forge together a common sense of being Canadian (Bissoondath, 1994).

Table 8.3
Canadian Population, by Place of Birth, and Province/Territory of Residence, 2006 (in percent)[1]

Place of Birth	Canada	Nfld.	PEI	NS	NB	Que.	Ont.	Man.	Sask.	Alta.	BC	Yukon	NWT	Nun.
Born in Canada	79.1	98.0	96.0	94.4	95.7	87.8	70.5	85.7	94.3	82.7	70.9	89.1	92.2	98.2
Born outside Canada	20.9	2.0	4.0	5.6	4.3	12.2	29.5	14.3	5.7	17.3	29.1	10.9	7.8	1.8
Americas	3.3	.5	1.3	1.3	1.6	2.7	4.8	2.8	1.1	2.4	2.7	2.7	1.2	.4
United States	1.0	.3	1.0	1.0	1.4	.4	1.0	.8	.7	1.0	1.6	2.2	.7	.2
Central America	.5	—	.1	.1	.1	.4	.6	.9	.1	.5	.4	.2	.1	—
Caribbean and Bermuda	1.1	—	—	.1	.1	1.1	1.8	.4	.1	.3	.2	.1	.2	.1
South America	.9	—	.1	.1	.1	.7	1.4	.8	.2	.5	.4	.2	.2	.1
Europe	7.6	.9	2.1	2.7	1.7	4.4	11.1	5.7	2.4	6.1	8.9	5.8	2.5	.8
Western Europe	1.5	.2	.8	.8	.6	1.4	1.6	1.4	.6	1.5	2.1	2.8	.8	.2
Eastern Europe[2]	1.7	.1	.1	.2	.1	1.0	2.6	1.7	.6	1.5	1.5	.5	.3	.1
Northern Europe	2.1	.6	1.0	.2	.8	1.7	3.0	1.6	1.0	2.2	4.0	2.2	1.1	.4
Southern Europe[3]	2.3	.1	.3	1.4	.1	.3	4.0	1.1	.3	.9	1.3	.4	.3	.1
Africa	1.3	.2	.1	.3	.2	1.8	1.5	.7	.4	1.2	.8	.3	.8	.1
Western Africa	.2	—	—		.1	.2	.3	.2	.1	.1	.1	—	.3	—
Eastern Africa	.4	—	—	.1	.1	.2	.7	.3	.1	.6	.4	—	.3	.1
Northern Africa	.4	.1	—	.1	.1	1.2	.3	.1	.1	.2	.1	.1	.1	—
Central Africa	.1	—	—		—	.2	.1	—	—	—	—	—	—	—
Southern Africa	.1	.1	—	—		—	.2	.1	.1	.2	.3	.1	.1	—
Asia and the Middle East	8.5	.4	.4	1.3	.7	3.3	12.0	4.9	1.7	7.3	15.8	1.8	3.0	.5
West Central Asia and the Middle East	1.2	.1	.1	.5	.1	1.1	1.9	.4	.2	.9	1.0	—	.3	
Eastern Asia[4]	3.0	.2	.2	.4	.3	.8	3.7	.9	.7	2.4	8.3	.5	.5	.1
Southeast Asia[5]	1.9	—	—	.1	.1	.8	2.3	2.8	.5	2.4	3.1	1.0	2.1	.3
Southern Asia	2.4	.1	—	.3	.2	.6	4.1	.8	.3	1.7	3.3	.3	.2	.1
Oceania and Other	.2	.1	.1	.1	—	—	.1	—	—	.3	.8	.3	.2	

Notes:
1. Total population includes non-permanent residents.
2. For Canada, United Kingdom percentage = 1.9.
3. For Canada, Italy percentage = 1.0.
4. For Canada, People's Republic of China percentage = 1.6.
5. For Canada, Philippines percentage = 1.0.

Source: Calculated from Statistics Canada. 2007a. Citizenship (5), Place of Birth (35), Sex (3), and Immigrant Status and Period of Immigration (12) for the Population of Canada, Provinces, Territories. Census Metropolitan Areas and Census Agglomerations, 2006 Census—20% Sample Data (table); topic-based tabulation, 2006 Census of Population, Statistics Canada Cat. no. 97-557-XCB2006008, Ottawa; released December 4, 2007; http://www12.statscan.ca/english/census06/data/topics. Accessed October 23, 2008. Percentages may not add up due to rounding.

The impact of the "new ethnics" upon Canadian identity was not particularly evident in the 1960s. Nonetheless, a new sense of identity was already emerging in English-speaking Canada.

THE RISE OF ENGLISH-CANADIAN NATIONALISM
After the Second World War, English-speaking Canada remained very British. It was not until the Canadian Citizenship

Act of 1946, for example, that "Canadian citizens" existed. Before that time, Canadians were British subjects, and many—at least those outside Quebec—were quite content to hold British passports.

Into the mid-1960s, Canadian culture outside Quebec also remained decidedly British. At a time when there were only two television channels (CBC and CTV), a large number of British programs competed with American shows to fill the airwaves. Comedy shows such as "Monty Python's Flying Circus" and English adventure shows such as "Danger Man" and "The Avengers" were standard viewing for many English-speaking Canadians growing up.

Canada's British ties were weakening, however. Economically, bilateral trade between Canada and Britain declined sharply after the Second World War, replaced by trade with the United States (see Marchildon, 1995; Norrie and Owram, 1996). Politically, Canada's ties to the throne were also eroding. In 1951, for example, Canada's Supreme Court replaced Britain's Privy Council as Canada's last court of appeal, setting the stage for Canada's later dropping of other British symbols.

Britain's declining role in Canadian life reflected in part a growing pride and confidence among Canadians themselves. Success in the war caused English-Canadians as a whole to become less parochial and to slough off some of their colonial anxieties. Many wanted Canada to take a greater and more independent role among the victorious states. Thus, after 1945 Canada proudly took out membership in the United Nations, NATO, and other international organizations. Likewise, it participated in the Korean conflict (1950–1953) and took a leading role in settling the 1956 Suez conflict, for which Lester Pearson won the Nobel Peace Prize. Unfortunately, each of these paths also led to policy convergence with the United States. Thus, as Canada drew away from Britain's embrace, it also found itself increasingly under America's blanket. The arrival of new immigrants from non-traditional cultures did not immediately remedy the problem; indeed, it added to considerable anxiety.

In short, by the late 1950s, English-speaking Canada was seeking a new vision of itself, an identity. The result was the rise of English-Canadian nationalism, often referred to as Canadianization. English-Canadian nationalism was not supported by all elements. Business generally disliked or feared nationalism in any form. Francophones viewed English-Canadian nationalism as merely a new variation on assimilation. Regional elements often feared Ottawa as much as nationalists feared Americans (Finkel, 1997: 157). Nonetheless, a sizable portion of people in English Canada favoured the heightened nationalism of the time.

The new nationalism was not of one type, however. Some forms expressed nostalgia over the loss of things British (especially the adoption of the Maple Leaf flag over the Union Jack in 1965). Some variations were defensive, a response to the rise of Quebec nationalism or to the increased influence of the United States. Others were frankly imperialist, as when Prime Minister John Diefenbaker (1895–1979) invoked his vision of the Canadian North in the 1958 election (see Chapter 11). The forms came in different political and ideological variations, defying simple description. In general, however, English-Canadian nationalism manifested itself politically, culturally, and economically.

Politically, English-Canadian nationalism can be divided into formal and popular politics. At the formal level, after 1950 Canadian prime ministers found themselves in a series of delicate skirmishes with their American counterparts. Until Roosevelt, most American presidents had ignored Canada. Canada was viewed as an extension of the United States, a place of eccentric country cousins. In the context of the Cold War, however, the United States demanded particular obedience from its allies, beginning with Canada. Thus, the

Diefenbaker administration's (1957–1963) efforts at an independent defence policy, not to mention encouraging trade with Castro's Cuba and Communist China, aroused particular antagonism. President John F. Kennedy (1917–1963) called Diefenbaker an "SOB" and gave encouragement and strategic support to successful Liberal efforts to unseat him in the 1963 Canadian election. Relations between Prime Minister Lester Pearson (1897–1972) and President Lyndon Johnson (following Kennedy's assassination) proved no better, however. Quickly, Canada found itself at odds with the United States over the war in Vietnam and trade policy, especially the 1965 Auto Pact (see Martin, 1982; Norrie and Owram, 1996). Pearson, like Diefenbaker before and Trudeau after, learned the truth of the axiom that states do not have friends, they have interests. Increasingly, the interests of Canada and the United States were diverging.

English-Canadian nationalism manifested itself politically at the popular level. In keeping with the times internationally, many of these expressions were anti-American and directed at American imperialism in Vietnam and elsewhere, themes often picked up on Canadian campuses (see Box 8.1). But there was also widespread revulsion directed at "the American way of life" in general, as reflected nightly on American television. Race riots and the killings of civil rights workers and politicians provided an ample "negative model" for Canadians and for between 70,000 and 125,000 American draft dodgers and deserters (Finkel, 1997: 154) who wanted to build a better society in North America.

Box 8.1
The Canadianization Movement in Sociology

Canadianization at large found its mirror in English Canada's universities and colleges beginning in the late 1960s. The immediate catalyst for a nationalist response was the hiring at Canadian institutions of higher learning of a large number of foreign trained (often American born) academics to meet the demands of a growing student population. Nationalists sought to bring a Canadian perspective to research and teaching in the academy. Among those involved in the Canadianization movement were a number of sociologists, students, and the Canadian Anthropology and Sociology Association.

Canadianization benefited sociology in at least two ways. First, it led to an increase in Canadian curricula and content being taught. A survey of five disciplines (French, history, political science, economics, and sociology and anthropology) at six universities (Dalhousie, Montreal, Carleton, Albert, Simon Fraser, and UBC) shows that the number of undergraduate full-time course equivalents with Canadian content increased by 108 percent between 1970–1971 and 1980–1981, with particularly large increases in sociology and anthropology (Steele and Mathews, 2006: 494–495).

Second, Canadianization also impacted the education of sociologists within Canada. In 1970, only 17.5 percent of full-time sociologists in Canada had received their highest degree in Canada, compared with 63.4 percent who received their degree in the United States. By 1980, these percentages had changed to 29.2 percent and 53.2 percent, respectively. In 2005, 52.3 percent of full-time Canadian sociologists had received their highest degree in Canada, while 31 percent had received their highest degree in the United States (Gingras and Warren, 2006: 513).

The Canadianization movement raises several questions, however. Is a national perspective necessary to understanding sociology? Or are sociological insights inherently universal? Even more intriguing: Is there a need for a revitalized Canadianization movement in sociology today?

What do you think?

Sources: James Steele and Robin Mathews, "Canadianization revisited: A comment on Cormier's 'The Canadianization movement in context,'" *The Canadian Journal of Sociology* 31(4) (2006): 491–508; Yves Gingras and Jean-Philippe Warren, "A British connection: A quantitative analysis of the changing relations between American, British, and Canadian sociologists," *The Canadian Journal of Sociology* 31(4) (2006): 509–522.

English-Canadian nationalism was also cultural. In 1951, the Massey Commission outlined the need for Canada to develop its own cultural institutions and distinctly Canadian voice. The commission's report focused on high culture and drew little initial response, official or otherwise (see Morton, 1997). Eventually, however, such institutions as the Canada Council, the National Film Board, and Telefilm Canada were formed to encourage Canadian culture. Whether these institutions were responsible for the spread of cultural nationalism or not is debatable. Nonetheless, except in the area of television and film, which remained largely overwhelmed by American capital and technology, a distinctively Canadian cultural industry slowly emerged in English Canada. In the area of literature, the 1950s and 1960s saw the rise to prominence of a host of writers, including Pierre Berton, Leonard Cohen, Robertson Davies, Timothy Findley, and Margaret Laurence. (A few intellectuals, notably Marshall McLuhan, even became international cultural icons.) Other writers, often women (such as Margaret Atwood, Alice Munro, and Carol Shields), followed in the 1970s, and were joined later by Michael Ondaatje and Rohinton Mistry, pointing, one might add, to Canada's increasingly multicultural nature.

There had long been a Canadian popular music scene, stretching from jazz to pop to country. Except at the local and regional level, however, much of it was derivative of American music. Canada's climb aboard the rock 'n' roll bandwagon of the 1950s continued this trend. But the late 1960s saw Canadian music also take a nationalistic turn, assisted by the creation of the Canadian Radio and Television Commission, which legislated Canadian content. Groups such as The Band (headed by Robbie Robertson) became internationally known, as did individual artists such as Neil Young and Joni Mitchell. More importantly, each also remained distinctly Canadian, as often evidenced in their lyrics, setting the stage for bands such as The Tragically Hip in the 1990s and Arcade Fire later on. In keeping with the times, the music of this period sometimes took on an overtly anti-American tenor, as in the words to The Guess Who's "American Woman" and Gordon Lightfoot's "Black Day in July" (about the Detroit riots).

ECONOMIC NATIONALISM, OR THE USES OF GOOD THEORY

Among the subgenres of nationalism, however, economic nationalism was arguably the most influential. After years of growth, in the late 1950s the Canadian economy entered a recession (Norrie and Owram, 1996). In this context, a number of influential Canadians—led by political economist Melville Watkins (1963), conservative philosopher George Grant (1965), and Liberal finance minister Walter Gordon (1966)—asked (each in his own way) why Canada continued to be "the world's richest underdeveloped country" (Levitt, 1970: 25). In particular, many noted that Canada's declining economic performance coincided with increased foreign, mainly American, control of the economy. Were the two events related? For economic nationalists, the answer was a definite *yes*.

John Maynard Keynes once remarked that there is nothing so practical as a good theory. But good theory arises out of the need to understand real issues. The economic nationalism of the 1960s arose out of genuine concerns over Canada's future; in turn, it provided impetus for a renaissance of investigation into the roots of Canada's economic, political, and social development (see Laxer, 1991), a renaissance that ultimately had practical impacts upon Canadian policy.

At least initially, these studies took their inspiration from the work of the Canadian economic historian Harold

Innis (1894–1952). Innis's **staples theory** argued that *Canada's founding as a hinterland producer of raw exports for world markets curtailed normal economic and political development*, resulting in it being prone to being caught in a staples trap. The nature of the trap was that, while staple products (such as cod, furs, trees, and wheat) were often seductively profitable in the short term, their prices were inherently unstable and subject to boom and bust. In Innis's view, an economy built upon raw resources alone did not develop the forward and backward linkages and social structure characteristic of a fully developed economy (see Innis, 1995).

Staples theory, based on the historical relationship between the metropolis and the hinterland, bears some relationship to **dependency theory**, which *emphasizes the unequal relationship between the core and periphery in the world capitalist system set in motion by early colonialism* (see Frank, 1975), though the latter also utilizes a Marxian class analysis. Dependency theory did not fit the Canadian situation well, however. After all, by the 1960s, many parts of Canada were heavily industrialized, while residing uneasily with pockets of underdevelopment. Moreover, the benefits of industrialization were—as now—unevenly distributed by gender, race, ethnicity, and region (see Panitch, 1977; Laxer, 1991; Clement, 1997). Hence, the years following the late 1960s saw a "new" tradition of political economy that took analyses of Canadian dependency in different explanatory directions.

Some scholars used **elite theory** to explain Canada's development. Naylor (1975), for example, went back in history to argue that merchants concentrated in export industries, especially the fur trade, had conspired against industrial capitalists to hinder economic development (the merchants against industry thesis). Clement (1975) meanwhile argued that a troika of elites continued to dominate the Canadian economy: a parasite elite (foreign owners and managers), an indigenous elite (Canadian owners and managers), and a comprador elite (Canadians managing companies in Canada for foreign firms).

Others, however, used **class theory** to explain the trajectory of Canadian development. Panitch (1981), for example, argued that, ironically, the relative power of Canada's proletariat during the country's initial stage of industrialization development (1870–1910) hindered capitalism's accumulation of surplus. By contrast, Laxer (1989) argued that Canada had been a successful late industrializing country, but had fallen back into dependency due to the political weakness of its agrarian class during this period, which had prevented Canada from adopting the kind of policies (low taxes, easy credit, the targeted construction of railways, and a robust defence policy) that worked successfully in similar countries, notably Sweden.

Many of these studies focused particularly on the impact of the National Policy in Canada's economic development. You will recall the National Policy's use of tariffs was meant to encourage manufacturing within Canada (Chapter 7). As intended, a number of American branch plants moved to Canada in the early part of the 20th century to feed the Canadian market and also to gain preferential entry at that time into other Commonwealth countries, especially Britain. In the short term, the economy boomed. Employment in new industries soared, out-migration decreased, banks made profits. The long-term impacts, however, were less rosy.

Economic nationalists pointed out several problems that accompanied these branch plants (see Laxer 1991). First, company profits were unavailable for further domestic investment. Finkel (1997: 161) notes that in the 1960s, dividends to American owners exceeded American investment in Canada. Alternatively, the profits were often used to buy up more Canadian companies. Second, branch plants tended to obtain materials and personnel in the home country. Thus, Canada lost the backward and forward linkages, or "multiplier effects," necessary to develop the economy fully. Third, the branch plants were not sources of innovation. Statistics showed Canadian companies invested little in research and development. Instead, Canadian branch plants produced copies of American (or other foreign) products for the local market, a pattern known as the miniature replica effect (Finkel, 1997: 163; Levitt, 1970).

Ultimately, economic nationalists also saw the issue in broader political terms. American Secretary of State John Foster Dulles (1888–1959) had once opined there are two ways to conquer a country: by force of arms or by taking over its economy (Laxer, 1995: 229). The economic nationalists took Dulles at his word, arguing no country could remain politically sovereign for long with an economy controlled by a foreign power. But adopting a national strategy faced a seemingly obdurate problem: the fact that national solutions often gave rise to regional interests and conflicts (see Chapter 7's discussion of regionalism).

THE NEW WEST

No part of Canada changed more than the West after 1945. The changes were particularly apparent in Alberta and British Columbia, which experienced enormous population growth and industrialization. But all the western provinces changed in important ways, and influenced Canada as they did.

In 1941, the populations of the four western provinces were roughly equivalent, ranging from a low of 730,000 in Manitoba to a high of 896,000 in Saskatchewan (see Table 1.1). By 1971, however, a shift westwards was already evident. British Columbia's population had tripled

to 2.2 million and Alberta's population had doubled to 1.6 million, both surpassing Manitoba (under 1 million) and Saskatchewan (932,000). Looking ahead 40 more years, the population changes in the most westerly provinces become even more startling. By 2007, 4.3 million people resided in British Columbia and nearly 3.4 million in Alberta. By contrast, Manitoba's population had stabilized at around 1.2 million, while Saskatchewan's population, even in the midst of growing prosperity, remained at just under 1 million.

These population changes do not tell the whole story. Like the rest of the country, after the war western Canada experienced rapid urbanization (see Driedger, 1991; *Canadian Global Almanac 2000*, 1999: 55; see also Chapter 7). This occurred even in Manitoba and Saskatchewan. Winnipeg, for example, grew from 412,000 people in 1956 to 667,000 in 1996. During the same period, Regina's population went from nearly 90,000 to 193,000, while Saskatoon's population increased from 73,000 to 219,000. The greatest urban growth, however, occurred in British Columbia and Alberta. Between 1956 and 1996, Vancouver's population nearly trebled, from 665,000 to more than 1.8 million people. Victoria's population also increased rapidly from 134,000 to 303,000. In Alberta during this period, Edmonton's population expanded from nearly 255,000 to 862,000, while Calgary's population climbed from 201,000 to nearly 822,000. These figures alone do not tell the tale, however, for many smaller cities and suburbs of larger cities were also spawned during this period. In consequence, the urban centres within areas such as the Vancouver mainland and that between Edmonton and Calgary became largely contiguous.

Today, much of Canada's population (whether east or west) is urbanized, with 33 census metropolitan areas (CMA). (A CMA is an area consisting of one or more adjacent municipalities situated around an urban core of at least 100,000 people.) As shown in Table 8.4, nine of these 33 CMAs are now located west of Ontario; indeed, the west has three of the six largest areas—Vancouver, Calgary, and Edmon-ton—with Calgary having the fastest population growth rate between 1996 and 2006 (31.4 percent), while all four of the CMAs that lost population during this period were east of Manitoba.

Table 8.4
Population of Canada's 33 Census Metropolitan Areas (2006), 1996, 2001, and 2006

	1996	2001	2006	% Increase (1996–2006)
Toronto[1]	4,263,759	4,682,897	5,113,149	19.9
Montreal[1,2,3]	3,326,447	3,451,027	3,635,571	9.3
Vancouver	1,831,665	1,986,965	2,116,581	15.5
Ottawa–Gatineau[1,2]	998,718	1,067,800	1,130,761	13.2
Calgary[2,3]	821,628	951,494	1,079,310	31.4
Edmonton	862,597	937,845	1,034,945	20.0
Quebec[2,3]	671,889	686,569	715,515	6.5
Winnipeg[1,2]	667,093	676,594	694,668	4.1
Hamilton[1]	624,360	662,401	692,911	11.0
London[1,2]	416,546	435,600	457,720	10.0
Kitchener	382,940	414,284	451,235	17.8
St. Catharines–Niagara	372,406	377,009	390,317	4.8
Halifax	342,966	359,183	372,858	8.7
Oshawa	268,773	296,298	330,594	23
Victoria[3]	304,287	311,902	330,088	8.5
Windsor[1]	286,811	307,877	323,342	12.7
Saskatoon	219,056	225,927	233,923	6.8
Regina	193,652	192,800	194,971	.1
Sherbrooke[1,2]	149,569	175,950	186,952	25
St. John's	174,051	172,918	181,113	4.1
Barrie	—	148,480	177,061	n/a
Kelowna	—	147,739	162,276	n/a
Abbotsford	136,480	147,370	159,020	16.5
Greater Sudbury/ Grand Sudbury[1]	165,618	155,601	158,258	-4.4
Kingston[1]	144,528	146,838	152,358	5.4
Saguenay	160,454	154,938	151,643	-5.5
Trois-Rivières	139,956	137,507	141,529	1.1
Guelph	—	117,344	127,009	n.a.
Moncton[2]	—	118,678	126,424	n.a.
Brantford[1,2]		118,086	124,607	n.a.
Thunder Bay[1]	126,643	121,986	122,907	-3.0
Saint John	125,705	122,678	122,389	-2.6
Peterborough[2]	—	110,876	116,570	n.a.

Notes:
1. Figures for 1996 adjusted because of boundary change.
2. Figures for 2001 adjusted because of boundary change.
3. Excludes census data for one or more incompletely enumerated Indian reserves or Indian settlements.
Source: Statistics Canada. 2007b. *Canada Year Book 2007* (Ottawa: Statistics Canada), 386. Percentage change calculated by authors.

Western Canada's population changed in other ways. Settled by massive immigration in the early 20th century, the West had always been culturally, religiously, and ethnically diverse, but this diversity was often suppressed in the name of Anglo-conformity (Chapter 7). After the 1970s, however, as multiculturalism became Canadian government policy, the West allowed its diversity to emerge more fully (see above).

Underlying these population shifts

were fundamental economic changes. The Prairie provinces were originally opened up for agricultural development (Chapter 7). As noted above, changes in the farm economy throughout the 20th century resulted in a reduction in Canada's agricultural labour force overall. In 1951, 15.6 percent of Canada's workforce as a whole were employed in agriculture. By 1971, this had fallen to 5.6 percent. By 1991, the proportion of the Canadian workforce employed in agriculture had dropped to 3.6 percent (Li, 1996: 45), dropping to 2.5 percent in 1996 and is only 2 percent today (Statistics Canada, 2007a: 19). This drop has been less pronounced on the Prairies, however, where even today roughly 7.2 percent of the labour force in Manitoba and Saskatchewan and 3.7 percent in Alberta hold jobs in agriculture (Krahn et al., 2007: 72).

The continuing importance of agriculture to the Saskatchewan economy underpins much of the cultural life of that province, but it also reflects a problem of economic diversity that, until very recently, resulted in a steady out-migration of young workers throughout the 20th century. By contrast, Manitoba experienced a less drastic fate. The province's—in particular Winnipeg's—heyday came just after the First World War. The Winnipeg General Strike of 1919 (Chapter 7) was a seminal event in many ways. Thereafter, declines in agriculture resulted in a similar decline in the fortunes of the Winnipeg grain exchange and the city in general. Still, Manitoba's economy is stable and, compared with that of Saskatchewan, relatively diverse, involving agriculture, mixed farming, mining, hydroelectricity, manufacturing, and services.

Meanwhile, Alberta experienced a post-Second World War boom, beginning with the discovery of oil at Leduc in 1947. Alberta's fortunes did not change all at once, or for everyone. Indeed, Alberta technically remained a "have-not" province within Confederation until the late 1960s. Meanwhile, British Columbia also experienced rapid growth, based on a similar exploitation of its raw resources and that province's geographic location on the Pacific Rim.

Economic growth, large or small, in all the western provinces shared certain characteristics. First, it was invariably government-led. Local capital was often scarce, while private, exogenous capital was reluctant to invest in what often seemed tenuous opportunities for profit. Thus, eastern and (more often) foreign capital and expertise were welcomed in under favourable conditions set by the provincial governments. The 1970s, in particular, saw every western government, of every political stripe, engage in what was termed **province-building**: *an activist approach to economic development on the part of provincial governments.*

Second, economic growth in all the western provinces focused on megaprojects, especially in the North (see Chapter 11). Hydroelectricity in Manitoba, potash and uranium in Saskatchewan, tar sands in Alberta, hydroelectricity and forestry in British Columbia became the hallmarks of economic development in the West. In classically liberal and typically Canadian fashion, the belief was that these projects would create the capital necessary to diversify the economy and break the cycle of boom and bust so common in the West. Often, however, it meant putting the provinces' eggs in one or two baskets. Too frequently, when the world price of the particular commodity collapsed, individuals and governments, who had backstopped the projects with huge amounts of public capital, were left holding the empty bag. People either sat out the downturn or moved on. No region in Canada fit better Harold Innis's description of a "staples trap" than did the West (Watkins, 1963; Drache, 1995).

Third, and finally, economic development in the West invariably involved the exploitation of each province's northern region. Flin Flon in Manitoba, Uranium City in Saskatchewan, and Fort McMurray in Alberta are but a few examples. The result sometimes was the building of temporary resource towns that disappeared in time (such as, again, Uranium City). But the impacts of the changes were always permanent, especially for the Aboriginal peoples living in those areas. In Canada, as elsewhere around the world, the forces of modernity and capitalism displaced the old ways of living (see Chapter 11).

Population shifts and economic growth brought other political and social changes. In the mid-1960s, Porter (1965) noted that Canada's elite were largely British, represented "old money," were highly interrelated through business, political, school, and even marital ties, and were located primarily in central Canada. His findings were generally validated a few years later by Clement (1975), who traced the corporate interlocks underlying the power of this insular elite.

The emergent power of the new West challenged this elite structure (Richards and Pratt, 1979). Throughout the West, but particularly in Alberta, a new regional elite arose, demanding its say in how Confederation should be run. The shift of Sun Life from Montreal to Calgary in the 1970s, followed by the establishment of other financial institutions and corporate head offices in that city, was not merely symbolic. It represented a genuine shift in power within Canada, a change increasingly evident by the early 2000s (see Chapter 9).

The changes in Canada's West did not come without problems. The increased power of provinces led to provincial identification replacing regional identification (Gibbins, 1979; see also Chapter 9). In some communities, cultural and ethnic diversity created tensions. Expansion into the North disrupted Aboriginal communities in particular, and created social problems (see Chapter 11). At the same time, economic development did not always lead to security. From the 1970s on, the West's economy continued to experience waves of boom and bust.

Finally, the changes also heightened traditional tensions between western Canada and the other provinces and the federal government over the structure of Confederation. By the 1970s, many in the West, like others in the past, were coming to view the Canadian government as alien and unsympathetic to their views. They resented the "imposition," as they saw it, of policies such as bilingualism and metrification. They believed Canadian institutions had an eastern bias, and "national" policies, in general, meant central Canadian policies. Thus, the late 1970s and early 1980s saw the rise throughout western Canada, but especially in Alberta, of a number of western separatist movements (Pratt and Stevenson, 1981). Later, in 1987, regional alienation combined with right-wing populism to underpin the founding of the Reform Party (Harrison, 1995) and then, at the cusp of the new millennium, its offspring, the Canadian Alliance Party (Harrison, 2002). In short, the re-emergence of regional alienation, as much a staple of western Canada as wheat, became a central feature of Canadian society in the years following the 1970s.

THE ECONOMIC CRISIS OF THE CANADIAN STATE

Taken as a whole, the period from 1945 until the 1990s was a time of spectacular economic growth for Canada. Canada's gross domestic product (GDP) in 1947, for example, was $91.7 billion (constant dollars). By 1992, GDP had grown to $560 billion. Even accounting for the impact of population growth on GDP, the average Canadian in 1992 was three times better off economically than in 1947 (Norrie and Owram, 1996: 398).

These figures are misleading, however. For Canada, the period can be broken into two halves, the first signalling the prosperous times of an economic "long wave," the second a period of economic decline (Watkins, 1997). But the recession of the early 1970s was not Canada's alone. Every country in the Western industrial world experienced rising unemployment and increased government debt during this period. In Canada after the early 1970s, personal and corporate bankruptcies skyrocketed, while the annual unemployment rate (see Chapter 7) rose steadily, changing also from a temporary or occasional situation to one more long-term and chronic. In this context of rising demands but falling revenues, federal and provincial government deficits and debt also spiked. Canada's massive federal debt per gross domestic product following the Second World War had declined steadily during the prosperous years. Thereafter, however, it began rising alarmingly during the 1980s and early 1990s, with interest payments on the debt eating up a growing proportion of revenues (Li, 1996: 89). Canada's federal debt peaked in 1997 at $588.4 billion (Statistics Canada, 2007a: 246–247), then steadily declined as a result of severe budget cuts and renewed prosperity throughout the 1990s and early 2000s.

What led during this period to the fiscal crisis faced by Western governments and the Canadian government in particular? First, new technologies were beginning to displace workers, hence the rising unemployment that lowered demand for goods and services, while also reducing tax revenues just as state expenditures increased for unemployment insurance and welfare. For Canada, these new technologies cut into jobs in both the primary and secondary sectors. Second, in a preview of globalization (Chapter 9), transnational corporations began shifting finance capital and production to low-wage countries, at the same time avoiding taxation or pressuring governments to lower corporate taxes (Li, 1996: 156–157).

In all countries, these factors combined to weaken the full employment policies upon which the welfare state relied.

Also exacerbating the economic recession of the early 1970s, however, were the economic circumstances surrounding a single commodity, oil. Since the beginning of the second industrial revolution, and particularly with the advent of the automobile, oil and natural gas had increased in prominence and power as commodities. Their worldwide importance became quite apparent in 1973 when, following the Yom Kippur War, the Organization of Petroleum Exporting Countries (OPEC) announced it was limiting supply and increasing the price of oil. The OPEC crisis, as it became known, awakened Americans to the fact their country was no longer capable of ensuring a stable and low-priced oil supply. Hence, discussions began on exploration of previously untapped areas under American control, such as Alaska, and means of securing stable supplies from reliable sources, such as Canada.

On the surface, the crisis should have provided a unique opportunity for Canadian development. With large untapped reserves of oil and natural gas, Canada would seem to have been in an ideal position to take advantage of the escalating market price, but Canada was not.

First, 75 percent of Canada's petroleum and natural gas in 1973 were under foreign control, 58 percent under American control (Li, 1996: 24–25; also, Fossum, 1997). Canada might be the home of large oil and gas reserves, but Canadians had no right of first call on them. Second, while the governments of producing provinces could do quite well from rising prices that translated into increased royalties, non-producing provinces faced only rising costs. The crisis thus pitted the oil-producing provinces, especially Alberta, against the manufacturing provinces of central Canada, with the federal government caught in the middle. But the problem was not merely political. In Canada, as elsewhere, rising oil prices provoked a worldwide phenomenon known as **stag-flation**: *the simultaneous occurrence of a declining economy and increasing unemployment with rising inflation.*

Finally, Canada's fiscal crisis beginning in the 1970s was particularized by its relationship to the United States. In the late 1960s, facing increased competition from the rebuilt economies of Japan and Germany, and in the midst of the widely unpopular Vietnam War, the United States found itself suffering a negative balance of trade with most countries, including Canada. As economic times worsened, the United States government resorted to a time-worn measure: It adopted a series of protectionist measures to buffer American workers, consumers, and companies against the outside world. In 1972, President Nixon came to Canada bearing news that while the two countries might be good friends, there was no special relationship between them. The United States was going to pursue its own agenda, and Canada should feel free to do the same (Martin, 1982).

As an exporting country, with the United States as its major market, Canada was rightly concerned about American protectionism. In 1968, 24 percent of Canada's GDP resulted from exports, a figure six times larger than in the United States. Moreover, 60 percent of Canada's trade was with its southern neighbour (Finkel, 1997: 159–160). Given the American actions and the country's own declining economic prospects, what was the Canadian government to do?

THE RISE AND FALL OF CANADIANIZATION, 1972–1982

In the early 1970s, in the context of Quebec separatism, the federal Liberal government of Pierre Trudeau began taking steps to increase the role of central government, politically and symbolically,

in the lives of Canadians (Chapter 4). The economic crisis of the same period, in conjunction with the federal election of 1972, which saw the Liberals reduced to a minority government propped up by the left-wing New Democratic Party (Appendix 1), likewise gave the federal government impetus to strengthen its role in the economy. For the Liberal Party, it was a remarkable turnaround. Over many years, the Liberals had developed a solid reputation as pro-business, pro-free trade, and pro-continentalist. Yet, during the next decade (1972–1982), the Trudeau government instituted a series of measures designed both to increase the role of government in the economy and to patriate the economy in much the same way that the Constitution was brought home from Britain in 1982. Later than in some parts of society, the government began efforts to Canadianize the economy.

These efforts manifested themselves in several ways, including creation of the Foreign Investment Review Agency (FIRA), designed to oversee foreign takeovers of Canadian companies. Given the specific nature of the economic crisis, however, the heart of Canadianization was a series of measures dealing with oil and gas.

One of these measures was the creation of Petro-Canada in 1975. Today, Petro-Canada is a large private company with retail outlets spread across the country. (In March 2009, the company merged with Suncor.) Petro-Canada's original mandate was very different, however. The federal government originally created it as a Crown corporation for the purpose of exploring and developing oil reserves, mapping out the number of existing reserves in Canada, and generally providing the government with a window on the oil industry.

Canadianization of the economy was a logical extension of the wave of English-Canadian nationalism that swept the country in the 1960s. Certainly, many of the actions taken by the federal Liberals had considerable public support, though this varied from region to region. People in Ontario were the most supportive, while most opposed were people in Quebec and the western provinces, especially Alberta. Many Quebecers, separatist or not, viewed the strengthening of the federal government as threatening their "national" interests. Equally, many in western Canada viewed with suspicion the efforts of the federal Liberals, who had little parliamentary representation in their region. More broadly, many westerners saw this Canadian nationalism as a veil disguising central Canadian interests opposed to their own.

The return of the federal Liberals to power in 1980, following the brief interregnum of Joe Clark's Progressive Conservative government (see Chapter 4), saw the Liberals resurrect efforts to rebuild the central powers of the Canadian state. Thus, a new Constitution was enacted in 1982. Meanwhile, on the economic front, and in the wake of the Iranian Revolution in 1979, which sparked a second major world oil crisis, the Liberals introduced the National Energy Program (NEP) (Fossum, 1997).

The NEP had five purposes. First, it was intended, through a series of taxes on the oil industry, to increase federal revenues with which to deal with the growing debt. Second, the NEP was meant to keep Canadian energy prices below world levels, smoothing out the impact of rising prices between producing and consuming provinces. (At the same time, it also placed a floor on prices should they suddenly drop, thereby protecting producing provinces.) Third, the NEP was designed to foster Canadian ownership of oil and gas through a series of monetary incentives. Fourth, the program was meant to encourage exploration in the Canada lands (such as in the North, particularly the Beaufort Sea), therefore increasing energy self-sufficiency. Finally, the NEP also was explicitly meant to promote energy conservation (Finkel, 1997: 306; Fossum, 1997).

The National Energy Program was the pinnacle of Canadianization. In retrospect, many of its goals (such as its restrictions on foreign ownership and efforts at self-sufficiency) seem modest, the measures it proposed standard elsewhere. But its implementation and timing were poor, and it ran up against powerful enemies. By 1982, the NEP was dead, though not formally buried until 1986 by the subsequent Progressive Conservative government of Brian Mulroney (see Chapter 9). Why did the NEP fail?

First, the NEP was based on pricing projections that failed to materialize (Fossum, 1997). As members of the OPEC cartel began cheating on oil production, the price rapidly declined, throwing economies once more into turmoil and ruining the revenue hopes of both the federal government and the oil-producing provinces.

Second, the NEP and Canadianization in general ran afoul of the newly elected Reagan administration in the United States. Reagan's electoral campaign was based on a promise to the American people to make that country "strong" again. Politically, Reagan promised to confront the threat of the "Evil Empire" (the Soviet Union). Economically, he promised to make the United States self-sufficient and, further, to use the power of the state to open doors for American free enterprise and business. Implementation of the NEP resulted in a series of hostile letters to the Canadian government written by high-level individuals in the Reagan administration, warning of retaliation for Canadian actions that harmed American business interests (Clarkson, 1985).

Third, competing interests and internal fractures within Canada itself undermined Canadianization. These conflicts were not limited to the federal-provincial or interprovincial level, although these were important. For obvious reasons, American-owned businesses in Canada, including many in western Canada's oil and gas industry, opposed Canadianization. But large private corporations in general opposed Canadianization both on theoretical grounds (they did not like government regulation in general) and because they increasingly favoured open borders for capital. These interests lobbied hard to forestall state intervention in the economy, including encouraging the newly elected Reagan administration in its threats toward the Canadian government.

Today, the NEP remains controversial; in Alberta, it is mythic. From the point of view of its detractors, the NEP was an unconstitutional intrusion on provincial jurisdiction that stole millions of dollars from the Alberta treasury and led to a subsequent recession (1981–1982). NEP supporters, however, argue that the program was a legitimate effort by the Canadian government to carve out an economic policy independent of the United States, and they suggest that the policy is unfairly blamed for a downturn that hit all oil-producing regions, including Texas and Oklahoma.

Regardless of the relative merits of these arguments, the fact is that the political and economic failure of Canadianization left the Liberal government and the Canadian state more broadly without an economic blueprint for managing the country Sir John A. Macdonald's National Policy (Chapter 7) of 100 years earlier had led to Canada's industrialization. Its modern equivalent, Canadianization, had attempted to resurrect the role of activist government in shaping the country for the late 20th century. The policy was now in tatters. What path should Canada now take?

ADOPTING FREE TRADE

The Conservative government of Brian Mulroney was elected in 1984, replacing the tired and discredited Liberals, now led by John Turner (see appendices 1 and 2). Two items headed the Tories' policy agenda: a new constitutional arrangement with Quebec that eventually led to the Meech Lake Accord (Chapter 4) and a new economic policy for Canada. In seeking the latter, Mulroney had to look no further than a study recently commissioned by the departing Liberals.

The failure of Canadianization led the Liberal Party to set up the Royal Commission on the Economic Union and Development Prospects for Canada in late 1982. The commission's final report, published in 1985, concluded that the Canadian economy needed less government involvement, that businesses and workers in Canada were insufficiently competitive, and that the only solution was greater reliance upon market forces. The report advocated a policy of free trade with the United States to achieve these changes.

To understand fully the significance of this recommendation, one has to go back into Canadian history. The option of free trade with the United States had always been there; indeed, the Reciprocity Agreement of 1854–1866 (see Chapter 7) was a form of managed free trade (Norrie and Owram, 1996). After 1867 and particularly after the formulation of the National Policy in 1879, however, Canadian economic, political, and social development had been nurtured along an east-west grid. The idea of free trade with the United States persisted, pursued by the Liberal Party and certain supporters, especially western farmers, but it was a minority position. In the elections of both 1891 and 1911, Sir Wilfrid Laurier's Liberals campaigned on a platform of unrestricted trade with the United States, losing on both occasions to the Tories, the first time to Sir John A. Macdonald, the second time to Sir Robert Borden (Appendix 1). Thereafter, the topic of free trade largely disappeared from sight.

Free trade was the ideological plaything of a few academics and "continentalists," those who saw Canada's future within a greater North American whole.

In 1988, the vast majority of Canadians still viewed free trade as a threat to Canadian sovereignty, but two important elements within Canadian society supported the initiative (see Doern and Tomlin, 1991). First, Canadian business, represented by the Business Council on National Issues (since renamed the Canadian Council of Chief Executives) lobbied hard for free trade, in part because much of Canada's business class was already heavily integrated with its American counterparts, in part because it believed such a deal would ensure Canadian access to American markets for export goods and investment capital. Second, several provinces, notably Quebec and Alberta, also supported free trade, the former because its then separatist government believed free trade would loosen that province's dependence upon the rest of Canada and pave the way for sovereignty (see Chapter 4), the latter because it saw free trade as preventing future federal initiatives such as the National Energy Program.

Additionally, Canada faced enormous political and ideological pressures from outside its borders, especially from the United States. The election of Ronald Reagan as American president in 1980, and of Margaret Thatcher as British prime minister the year before, gave political heft to policies favouring minimal government intervention and the pursuit of free trade.

The 1988 election was highly polarized, comparable only to the conscription election of 1917 (Chapter 3). In the end, though, by a narrow margin (only 43 percent of Canadians voted for the PCs), Mulroney's Tories won a majority of seats (see Appendix 1). The free trade agreement was ratified. Almost immediately, the newly elected administration of George H.W. Bush in Washington began pushing for a broader continental agreement that would include Mexico. The United States—militarily, politically, and economically powerful, but resource poor—was poised to access the resources of its two closest neighbours. In the late 20th century, North America quickly emerged as one large trading bloc, with its headquarters in the United States, to compete against other trading blocs that began emerging in Europe and Asia.

Nor was the move to closer ties reversed with the election in 1993 of a new Canadian government. The victorious Liberal Party, which only five years earlier had denounced free trade, under new leader Jean Chrétien in 1993 signed the North American Free Trade Agreement (NAFTA) Accord, bringing together the economies of Canada, the United States, and Mexico. The years that followed saw Canada pursue further economic ties with the United States, while that country spearheaded efforts for global free trade through agreements such as the Multilateral Agreement on Investments. For Canadians, the tepid nationalism of the Trudeau era was quickly swept away.

CONCLUSION

Postwar Canada was built upon an expanding and prosperous economy and a set of welfare state programs to assist the social adjustments necessary to such an economy. These changes in turn resulted in different social arrangements and the emergence of a distinctive English-Canadian identity. Nationalism was the result.

The fiscal crisis beginning in the mid-1970s challenged this vision of Canada. Canadianization was a response to this crisis. In many ways, it was an attempt to create a modern-day National Policy. These efforts crashed, however, against internal, regional divisions and pressures exerted by the United States and its business allies. The failure of Canadianization left Canadian politicians and policy-makers without a clear direction for the country. Much of Canada's political and economic elite sought refuge in closer ties to the United States. The Free Trade Agreement of 1989 was emblematic of this pursuit.

Canada's adoption of free trade closed one of the longest debates in Canadian history. Canada had "joined" the continent, a continent dominated by the most powerful empire in history. For Canadian nationalists, it was a severe blow; for many others, it was merely the unfolding of the natural order.

The future does not unfold as a straight or predictable line, however. Few in 1988 could have guessed that the Cold War was about to end, replaced by a new era marked by American dominance and the spread of neo-liberal globalization, an era with particular consequences for Canada that would end with both renewed pressures for even further integration with the United States and questions about the particular path that Canada had followed.

KEY TERMS
chain migration
class theory
dependency theory
elite theory
multiculturalism
province-building
stagflation
staples theory
symbolic order
welfare state (a.k.a. Keynesian welfare state)

CRITICAL THINKING QUESTIONS

1. Why do you think Canada's welfare state developed in the way that it did during the 20th century?

2. In what ways do changes in family structure and the economy impact upon each other?

3. To what extent is Canada still influenced by British culture?

4. Does Canada have a national economy or a regional economy?

5. Is the notion of government getting out of the way of business, as espoused by free market advocates, a realistic argument?

RECOMMENDED READINGS

Clarkson, Stephen. 1985. *Canada and the Reagan Challenge*. Toronto: Lorimer.
Using official documents, Clarkson details the coercive actions of the American government of President Ronald Reagan in attempting to alter the Canadian government's economic policy in the early 1980s.

Doern, B., and B. Tomlin. 1991. *Faith and Fear: The Free Trade Story*. Toronto: Stoddart.
This book is an essential primer for understanding Canada's adoption of free trade after 1988.

Li, Peter. 1996. *The Making of Post-war Canada*. Toronto: Oxford University Press.
Li's book links social and economic changes as tied together by government social policies.

Olsen, Gregg. 2002. *The Politics of the Wefare State: Canada, Sweden, and the United States*. Oxford: Oxford University Press.
This book compares the different welfare states of Canada, Sweden, and the United States, explaining the variations according to theories in political sociology.

Rice, James, and Michael Prince. 2000. *Changing Politics of Canadian Social Policy*. Toronto: University of Toronto Press.
This book examines changes in Canada's social policies over the 20th century, with an emphasis on the types of programs delivered, who delivered them, and what level of government was involved.

RELATED WEBSITES

Canadian Department of Finance
www.fin.gc.ca/
This ministry develops policies and provides advice to the government regarding the economy.

Canadian Radio-television and Telecommunications Commission
http://www.crtc.gc.ca/
This commission was established by Parliament in 1968 with the role of supervising and regulating Canadian broadcasting and telecommunication.

CBC Digital Archives
http://archives.cbc.ca/economy_business/trade_agreements/topics/536/
This site contains 12 video and two radio clips dealing with the Canada–U.S. Free Trade Agreement.

CANADIAN SOCIETY ON VIDEO

America, Love It or Leave It. 1991. Alioli Associates Ltd., 50 minutes. Examines the exodus of 125,000 American political refugees to Canada during the Vietnam War and their impact upon Canada.

Reckoning: The Political Economy of Canada, "Part 4: In Bed with an Elephant." 1986. National Film Board of Canada, 59 minutes, 48 seconds. Describes the often difficult relationship between Canadian prime ministers and American presidents.

CHAPTER 9

CANADA, GLOBALIZATION, AND THE AMERICAN EMPIRE

New World Order.
  —term used by U.S. president George H.W. Bush on the occasion of the signing of the North American Free Trade Agreement, 1993

For better or worse, by the autumn of [2008], if North America existed it was still more as geography than as governance.
  —Stephen Clarkson, 2008

I take tips from Canada on a lot of things.
  —President Barack Obama, April 2009

INTRODUCTION

The global economic order after 1945 can be divided into two major eras. The Keynesian era, stretching from the end of the Second World War until the OPEC crisis of 1973, comprised the first period. The neo-liberal era, of which Canada's signing of the Free Trade Agreement in 1989 played a major part, comprises the second period.

Situated within the rise of neo-liberal globalization, this chapter examines the political, economic, social, and ideological changes in Canada since the adoption of free trade. Among issues specifically examined are questions of employment, social stratification, and Canadian values. More broadly, however, the chapter examines pressures for further political, economic, social, and military integration into the American Empire. The chapter begins with a discussion of neo-liberal globalization.

NEO-LIBERAL GLOBALIZATION
THESIS AND ANTITHESIS

The Canada–U.S. Free Trade Agreement (FTA) was only part of broader efforts begun in the late 1970s by Western governments (led by the United States), academics, and business leaders to remake the world according to liberal political and economic principles. Based on the ideas of Adam Smith and David Ricardo—hence, often described as "neo-liberal"—proponents of globalization make several assertions.

First, they claim that everyone, consumers and producers alike, benefit in time from free (unregulated) and open trade. Consumers have access to a wider variety of goods and services at lower prices, and resources are used in a more efficient manner than would otherwise occur under protectionist policies. And while those at the top of the economic ladder become wealthier, everyone below also benefits from a larger economic pie and the gradual trickling down of wealth to the bottom. Second, proponents argue that economic freedom is necessary for political freedom and an expansion of human rights. Third, they also argue that global economic integration is inevitable, part of the natural history of progress. The phrase of Britain's then Prime Minister Margaret Thatcher, "There is no alternative" (TINA), quickly became, as post-structuralists might observe, a discursive means of eliminating debate. Finally, at a philosophical level, neo-liberal proponents assert the primacy of the individual over the group or society; as Thatcher also famously remarked, "There is no such thing as society," a statement one prominent sociologist argues is antagonistic of sociology (see Box 9.1).

Opponents of economic globalization dispute these arguments. They note that the world's wealthiest countries got that way not through free trade but through protectionist policies (see Chapter 7). They further argue that, as **neo-liberalism**, defined as *an ideological belief in the efficacy of free markets, limited government, and private property*, has proceeded, the economic situation of many countries and individuals within countries has declined while that of the wealthiest has more than prospered (see Weller et al., 2001). Opponents further argue that rising inequality has resulted in increased social conflict, whether in the Middle East, Africa, South America, or even within the boundaries of the core capitalist countries themselves.

Box 9.1
Neo-liberalism's Challenge to Sociology

Frances Fox Piven is one of the world's best-known and most influential sociologists. As president of the American Sociological Association, in 2007 Piven noted the rise of neo-liberalism and some of its consequences, including inequality, insecurity, environmental destruction, and conflict. But she also argued that neo-liberalism's basic tenets are fundamentally at odds with sociology:

> Although we were slow to recognize it, Thatcher and the neoliberal project she championed declared war on the basic tenets of the sociological enterprise. To be sure, we also study individuals and families, but the sociological enterprise rejects the radical individualism of Thatcher and the personal responsibility [of neo-liberalism]. Our distinctive preoccupation is with the social environments that shape individual and family life.

Piven's call is for sociologists to take a critical stance regarding political and economic trends, adding that "The early 21st century is reproducing the turmoil of the 19th century, and it is also reviving the moral and political concerns that animated some of the best sociological work in the past."

What do you think? Is it possible to merge radical individualism with sociology? What should be the stance of sociologists in the world? Should sociologists merely "interpret the world" or should they, as Marx famously averred, work to change it?

Source: Frances Fox Piven, "The neoliberal challenge," *Contexts* 6(3) (2007): 13–15.

Indeed, opponents contend that neo-liberal globalization is merely an updated name for a pattern of global exploitation that began with mercantilism (Chapter 2), then morphed into colonialism (see Chapter 10), and now in its neo-colonial variant holds countries hostage through trade agreements and debt (Sassan, 2001; Mann, 2008). From this perspective, the "freedom" lauded by neo-liberals is that of the wealthy to exploit the poor and weak unhindered by concerns for democracy, equality, and justice.

Yet, even its opponents admit that the era of neo-liberal globalization that began in the late 20th century differs in some significant respects from past periods of capitalist expansion. First, in many instances neo-liberal globalization has involved a genuine transfer of productive forces from the industrialized North to the underdeveloped South, with consequences for class structures and life conditions both within underdeveloped and developed countries. Second, where capitalist globalization in the past often resulted in intensified conflict between competing capitalist classes and their patron states (as in the First World War), neo-liberal globalization has been marked by a growing convergence of capitalist interests across borders—indeed, an international capitalist class (Panitch and Gindin, 2003).

THE THREE PERIODS OF NEO-LIBERAL GLOBALIZATION

Heuristically, the neo-liberal era can be divided into three relatively distinct periods by decade: (1) ascendancy (the late 1970s and 1980s), (2) triumph (the 1990s), and (3) crisis (the 2000s).

The ascendancy period began with the crisis of Keynesianism in the 1970s, followed by the elections of British Prime Minister Margaret Thatcher in 1979 and American President Ronald Reagan in 1980. Both Thatcher and Reagan avidly promoted neo-liberal policies such as the privatization of public services, the deregulation of finance capital, attacks on the power of unions, the lowering of personal and corporate taxes, and the shrinking of the postwar Keynesian welfare state. The signing of the Canada–U.S. FTA in 1989 provided a symbolic capstone to the era, launching neo-liberalism's next stage.

Unlike this first period, where neo-liberal policies were contained largely within Britain, the United States, and a few other Anglo-democracies (e.g., New Zealand), neo-liberalism's period of triumph saw these policies actively promoted globally. The period was marked symbolically by the collapse of the Soviet Union in 1991, the historic international importance of this event captured by American President George H.W. Bush's heralding of a "New World Order." Lacking an ideological and military adversary, the United States quickly emerged as the "uni-polar" centre of world power. American politicians, economists, and bureaucrats proclaimed neo-liberalism's victory, a.k.a. the "Washington Consensus."

Faced with soaring debts and struggling economies throughout the 1980s and early 1990s, many governments adopted neo-liberal solutions. In the early 1980s Mexico, for example, turned its back on decades of autonomous development and finally (in 1993) signed the North American Free Trade Agreement with Canada and the United States. Other Latin American countries, such as Argentina, followed suit. Nor was the impact of neo-liberal ideology upon political decision making confined to the underdeveloped world. European countries, including the social democratic welfare states of Scandinavia (see Chapter 8), also felt pressured to shrink the role of the state in favour of the supremacy of markets.

Neo-liberalism's good times soon ended, however. A serious recession in the early 1990s had nearly faded from memory when Thailand's currency (the baht) collapsed in 1997. This event should have been a minor event in the overall scheme of things. Instead, the collapse of the baht set off a chain reaction of economic turmoil that continued through Japan, South Korea, and Indonesia, then (in August 1998) northwards to Russia, and finally across the Pacific to Brazil, decimating as it went the emergent middle class in several countries and causing several governments to threaten to default on their loans. In stark fashion, the events of 1997–1998 pointed out a major peril of globalized capitalism that economic crises could no longer be isolated to a single country or region. The problem was made worse by the fact that the organizations set up at the end of the Second World War to manage orderly capitalism (i.e., the International Monetary Fund, the World Trade Organization, and the World Bank) had failed miserably; indeed, their active role in deregulating capital flows exacerbated the crisis and increased inequities across classes, genders, and ethnicities, both within and between the developed and underdeveloped worlds, resulting in social and political unrest (see Bello, 2002: 4–6). As the crisis unfolded, governments (especially in Central and South America) began defaulting on loans and not co-operating with the IMF, setting the stage for several governments in that region to adopt more state-interventionist policies, breaking away from American control, in the years that followed.

Economic and socio-political instability were not the only problems facing neo-liberalism as the 1990s came to a close, however. Nature itself began asserting the limits of economic globalization through a dramatic shift in weather patterns, the concomitant rise of new diseases and micro-organisms, and the depletion of resources (see Harrison, 2005; Stern, 2007). Again drawing attention to the perils of interconnectedness, evolutionary biogeographer Jared Diamond (2005: 23) remarked, "[g]lobalization makes it impossible for modern societies to collapse in isolation…. For the first time in history, we face the risk of a global decline."

In the late 1990s, an array of counter-movements to neo-liberal globalization arose throughout the world. In 1999, a protest at the World Trade Organization meetings in Seattle brought together a cross-section of global society—workers, students, intellectuals, social activists, Aboriginal peoples, and others—drawn from both the global North and South and representing a host of causes, including peace, the environment, and justice. The next couple of years saw similar protests, occasionally resulting in violence, sometimes instigated by state police, in Washington, D.C., Quebec City, and Genoa. Ironically, computer technologies (especially the Internet), which had fostered capitalist expansion, became a chief means by which mass opposition also was mobilized.

In short, as the new millennium began, neo-liberal globalization was under attack from several quarters. Nothing could quite prepare the world for the events to come, however.

THE AMERICAN WAR ON TERRORISM

For years, theorists had suggested that globalization not only connects people in positive ways but also increases tensions in ways that might heighten conflict, especially along cultural and religious lines (Barber, 1996; Huntington, 1996; Sassan, 2001). On September 11, 2001, 19 terrorists, aligned with an extreme Islamic fundamentalist group known as Al-Qaeda, rammed two passenger planes into New York's World Trade Center, killing roughly 2,800 people. Another plane was flown into the Pentagon in Washington, with the loss of nearly 200 more lives. The numbers killed were by some measures relatively small; that same year, for example, the number of people murdered in the United States was 16,037 (*Time*, 2009: 692).

Quickly, however, the attacks entered into American history and mythology alongside Pearl Harbor. As the perpetrators planned, the attacks pierced the American myth of invincibility. They shocked the American psyche and brought home to some the fact that in the 21st century terrorism also had gone global (Keohane, 2002), though others argued it had long been so (Parenti, 1995).

There was understandable sorrow, bewilderment, and anger throughout the United States (Gitlin, 2001). A wave of flag-waving patriotism, mixed with jingoist rhetoric from President George W. Bush, suggested that the United States was prepared to launch a war in perpetuity and without limits or borders against suspected terrorists. American military spending again increased to fight what was dubbed the "War on Terrorism," though the term "war" was clearly inappropriate to describe the situation. (Wars occur between states. In this case, there was no clearly identified enemy and no certainty of what victory might mean.) Dissent and critical discussion of the causes underlying the attacks all but disappeared in America (see Chomsky, 2001). Incidents of students, professors, and media being silenced took on McCarthyite tones (see Gonzalez, 2001).

A few weeks after the attacks, the United States and its allies invaded Afghanistan, where many members of the terrorist group and its leadership resided, and toppled the Taliban regime governing that country. That conflict quickly ended with the Taliban defeated and the Al-Qaeda terrorists dead, imprisoned, or on the run. Afghanistan, an underdeveloped country already ruined by over 20 years of war, began a slow fade from the world's—but not Canada's—television screens and was soon supplanted by Iraq.

In September 2002, the Bush administration released its new National Security

Strategy (Government of the United States, 2002). The document, popularly called the Bush Doctrine, argues that the terrorist attacks made the principle of launching war purely in retaliation (that is, for defensive purposes) inoperative. Instead, the document states that the United States will in future attack in pre-emptive fashion any country it believes may possess, or may seek to possess, weapons dangerous to the U.S. The Bush Doctrine further argues that, because the threat to American interests is now worldwide, the United States is justified in taking military actions anywhere. (Documents later released make clear that the Bush administration also viewed as justified the state's suspension of civil rights, including the use of unlawful confinement, rendition to foreign countries, and torture.) For this reason, some see the Bush Doctrine as an extension of the Monroe Doctrine (Chapter 6). Finally, the Bush Doctrine argues that no country in future will be allowed to compete militarily with the United States.

After months of debate at the United Nations, which attempted collectively to implement a peaceful way of disarming Iraq, the United States, Britain, and a handful of smaller countries (most of them financially indentured to the U.S.) broke with the UN and invaded Iraq in March 2003. The formal war was quickly over, but peace did not come; instead, the next few years witnessed the outbreak of sectarian violence and the deaths of tens of thousands of Iraqi civilians and occupying troops. The war's primary justification—that Iraq had "weapons of mass destruction"—soon proved a fabrication. (No rational person believed the other argument: that Iraq had been involved in the 9/11 attacks.)

Even more profound, however, was the War on Terrorism's long-term impact upon neo-liberal globalization, for even as the spreading conflict diverted financial resources and damaged the reputation of the U.S., upon which neo-liberalism relied, it also re-established the importance of national borders (see Laxer, 2004). Neo-liberal globalization depended upon a borderless world, at least for goods, services, and capital. (The mobility of people is another matter, as the enormous fence the United States erected across the U.S.–Mexico border, even after NAFTA, attests.) The terrorist attacks and events shortly thereafter meant the resurrection of both real and symbolic walls. In the words of then American ambassador to Canada, Paul Cellucci, "Security trumps trade." Thus, the era of neo-liberal globalization gave way, at least partially and in some ways significantly, to heightened fears, the growth of state security, war, and, as soon became apparent, a reassertion of American Empire.

REFLECTIONS ON STATE AND EMPIRE: THE CASE OF THE UNITED STATES

This text began its exploration of Canadian society with a discussion of the concept of the state (Chapter 1). To refresh your memory, and save your returning to earlier pages, we defined the state as *a set of institutions successfully claiming a monopoly over political rule-making and the legitimate use of violence and coercion within a given territory, i.e., a country.* Note that this definition is entirely neutral. States are neither good nor bad. They are merely instruments for achieving certain ends. The specific character of each state arises out of the class, gender, ethnic, ideological, etc., configuration of those who are in control, and the historical period and circumstances of its formation. States come in many forms: feudal, capitalist, fascist, social democratic, communist— even welfare states and warfare states. Every modern society has some form of state because, as you will also recall, states and societies have arisen together; they are inseparable.

Americans traditionally do not like to think of themselves as citizens of an imperial state. For obvious political reasons, American politicians also shy away from describing their country in terms of empire. Increasingly, however, scholars describe the United States as an empire with many of the attributes common to all empires (see Ferguson, 2004; Mann, 2008).

First, empires possess either direct or indirect colonies or exert significant informal control over semi-independent states (Mann, 2008). Puerto Rico remains a U.S. colony, for example, but American control elsewhere is exercised primarily through U.S.-controlled financial institutions such as the IMF and World Bank. As noted, nearly all the small countries that sent troops as part of the U.S.-led coalition that invaded in Iraq were financial dependencies.

Second, empires employ large militaries to police and enforce their will on other countries. According to Johnson (2006: 139–140), the number of American bases around the world in 2005, including those within the United States, totalled 737, with an estimated value of U.S. $658.1 billion, covering nearly 30 million acres worldwide, and employing a total of roughly 2.5 million personnel, both military and civilian, such bases amounting to (in Johnson's words) "small colonies" in themselves.

Third, because they can, empires act alone; that is, they resort to unilateralism in international affairs (in contrast to multilateralism). Alliances are only strategic and often temporary. Under the former presidency of George W. Bush, the U.S. refused to sign a treaty banning land mines and the Kyoto Treaty curtailing the worldwide emission of greenhouse gases, and just before September 2001, ended its 1972 Anti-ballistic Missile Treaty with Russia. It also refused to recognize the jurisdiction of the world criminal court, set up to try war criminals, and an international convention on torture, in both cases because it did not want to subject American citizens, laws, or practices to international judgment.

Fourth, however, empires *do* attempt to impose their laws on others, what is referred to as extraterritoriality. The United States' decades-old embargo on trade and commerce with Cuba provides a good example. American-owned firms based in Canada that trade with Cuba are subject under American law to prosecution. (President Barack Obama has lessened restrictions on American tourism and remittances to that island, however.) Recent American efforts, through trade agreements, to impose American patent law on other countries are also typical imperial acts.

Fifth, empires typically possess a quasi-religious sense of mission that provides a moral, and thus social-psychological, justification for their imperial actions. America's sense of imperial mission is in **civil religion**: *an institutionalized set of beliefs comprising four elements: (1) that America is exceptional; (2) that American values are universal; (3) that American motives are pure and not self-interested; and (4) that God is always with the American nation* (Sicherman, 2007). Former President George W. Bush's repeated use of religious imagery to describe the War on Terrorism as one between "Good" and "Evil" (and his justifications for the invasion of Iraq in 2003) are consonant with both the idea of civil religion and an imperial sense of mission.

Sixth, while—from a structural-functional perspective—all elements work together in any society, those of an empire function specifically to protect and enhance imperial rule. In the mid-1950s, C.W. Mills (1956) described mutually reinforcing relationships among the United States' political, business, and military establishments— what President Dwight D. Eisenhower later famously termed the "military-industrial complex" (Kurth, 1993). That military suppliers, such as Halliburton, made billions of dollars during the Iraq War would not have surprised Mills or, for that matter, Eisenhower. Finally, one might note a fourth leg to America's imperial/corporate state, the media, which in the eyes of some critics acted not as an independent critic of U.S. policy leading up the Iraq War but instead as a complicit propagandist and cheerleader for American actions.

Given its geographical proximity and historical relationship to the United States, the 9/11 attacks and its aftermath necessarily had a huge impact upon Canada. But the full impact of these attacks was further conditioned by nearly two decades of neo-liberal policies that had altered Canada's economic, political, and social fabric, and, in the eyes of some,

integrated the country further within the U.S. orbit.

CANADA'S ECONOMY TODAY

While neo-liberal ideas were already entering Canada before 1988, free trade provided a direct impetus to changes in Canada's economy and society, and some would argue also to its politics. One measure, therefore, of how neo-liberalism changed Canada is to examine Canada today relative to the period before 1988; that is, to compare the economy pre- and post-free trade.

Table 9.1

Canadian Imports, Exports, and Balance of Trade, by Country or Country Grouping,
$ Billions, Percent, and Percent Change, 2003–2008

	2003	2004	2005	2006	2007	2008	% 2008	% Change 2003–2008
Exports	**399.1**	**429.0**	**450.1**	**453.7**	**463.0**	**489.5**	**100**	**22.6**
United States[1]	329.0	350.6	368.4	361.4	356.1	370.0	75.5	12.4
Japan	9.8	9.8	10.2	10.3	10.0	11.9	2.4	21.4
United Kingdom	7.7	9.4	9.4	11.3	14.2	14.2	2.9	84.4
Other European Economic Community Countries	16.4	17.5	18.6	20.9	24.2	25.4	5.2	54.8
Other OECD[2]	12.7	14.2	14.5	16.8	19.7	21.1	4.3	66.1
Other countries[3]	23.5	27.5	29.1	33.1	39.0	47.3	9.7	101.2
Imports	**342.7**	**363.2**	**387.8**	**404.3**	**415.0**	**442.8**	**100**	**29.2**
United States[1]	240.4	250.0	259.3	265.0	269.8	280.7	63.3	16.8
Japan	10.6	10.1	11.2	11.9	12.0	11.7	2.6	10.4
United Kingdom	9.2	9.5	9.1	9.5	9.9	11.2	2.5	21.7
Other European Economic Community Countries	26.0	27.0	29.5	32.5	32.4	35.4	8.0	36.2
Other OECD[2]	19.7	22.3	24.3	23.7	25.0	27.4	6.2	39.1
Other countries[3]	36.8	44.3	54.4	61.6	65.9	76.4	17.3	207.6
Balance (Exports/Imports)	**56.4**	**65.8**	**62.3**	**49.5**	**48.0**	**46.7**	**—**	**-17.2**
United States[1]	88.6	100.5	109.1	96.4	86.3	89.0	91.5	0
Japan	-.1	0	-1.0	-1.5	-2.0	.2	.4	67.0
United Kingdom	-1.5	0	.3	1.7	4.2	3.0	6.4	67.0
Other European Economic Community Countries	-9.6	-9.5	-10.8	-11.6	-8.2	-10.0	-21.4	-4.2
Other OECD[2]	-6.9	-8.1	-10.0	-6.9	-5.3	-6.3	-13.5	8.7
Other countries[3]	-13.3	-16.8	-25.4	-28.6	-27.0	-29.1	-62.3	-118.7

Notes:
1. Includes also Puerto Rico and Virgin Islands.
2. Organisation for Economic Co-operation and Development excluding the United States, Japan, United Kingdom, and the other European Economic Community.
3. Countries not included in the European Economic Community or the OECD.

Source: Statistics Canada, *Imports, Exports, and Trade Balance of Goods on a Balance-of-Payments Basis, by Country or Country Grouping*. Date modified: April 9, 2009. Date downloaded: April 24, 2009. http://www40.statcan.gc.ca/l01/cst01/gblec02a-eng. htm. The percentages are calculated by the authors.

In 1988, free trade supporters argued the agreement would increase Canadian exports (and cross-border trade in general); result in more and better-paying Canadian jobs; secure access to American markets; and encourage efficiency, making the Canadian economy better able to compete in world markets. Have these things occurred?

EXPORTS AND IMPORTS

Even before the adoption of free trade, North-South trade with the United States was increasing in every region of Canada. Free trade only hastened this trend, such that during the first decade after 1988, exports to the United States jumped by 169 percent, while imports, mainly from the United States, also rose by 149 percent (*Edmonton Journal*, 1999c: A3). By the early 2000s, 87 percent of Canada's exports were going to the United States (Grunwald, 2002). As Table 9.1 shows, however, while total trade has continued to grow between the two countries, the percentage of exports going from Canada to the U.S. has recently declined, in part due to demands from other countries for Canada's resources. Still, Canada has a very positive balance of trade with the United States.

At the same time, while U.S. trade is very important to Canada, the reverse is not quite the case. Canada–U.S. trade made up only 16.6 percent of all American foreign trade in 2008, with exports to Canada making up 19.1 percent of all U.S. exports, and imports making up only 15 percent of all goods coming into that country (United States Census Bureau, 2009). In short, the U.S. appears to be more important to the Canadian economy than Canada is to the American economy with, at least on the surface, one notable exception: petroleum.

Petroleum, you will have observed, is not just like any other resource; next to water, it is arguably the world's

most important resource, one, you will also recall (Chapter 8), that led to the controversial introduction of the National Energy Policy in the early 1980s, arousing passionate anger among many western Canadians and from those in the petroleum industry until finally abandoned by Canada. Since 1988, Canada's petroleum industry has boomed, not only in Alberta, but also in Saskatchewan and, with the discovery of offshore reserves, Newfoundland and Nova Scotia, not to mention the North (see Chapter 11). Much of this production is exported to the United States: In 2005, 67 percent of oil was shipped to U.S. markets, most of it from Alberta, even as Canada imported 55 percent of its oil needs that same year (Statistics Canada, 2007a: 311). Today there are a series of pipelines connecting Canada's North (well beyond the Athabasca tar sands) to refineries in California, Texas, and the American East Coast, with more planned by 2030 (Laxer and Dillon, 2008: 25; see also Laxer, 2010).

Canada's supply of oil and gas resources and the United States' demand for them would appear to put Canada in the driver's seat, making it, as Prime Minister Stephen Harper once declared, a rising "energy superpower." Instead, Laxer and Dillon (2008: 9) term Canada an "energy colony." Why is this the case? The answer, they suggest, is a section of NAFTA called the "proportionality clause."

This clause prohibits Canada from decreasing the proportion of oil and gas exports relative to its total supply for the most recent three-year period, even if Canadians experience shortages, a situation that new pipelines to the U.S. will only potentially worsen as its proportion continues to increase (Laxer and Dillon, 2008). Proportionality also works against Canadian efforts at energy conservation and efforts to protect the environment by slowing the pace of development. In

Laxer's (2010) words, "proportionality effectively guarantees the U.S. first call on the majority of Canada's oil and natural gas in perpetuity, or until NAFTA and the Canada–U.S. Free Trade Agreement (FTA), are renegotiated, or ended. Or, until the resources run out."

The charge that Canada has become an energy colony to the United States goes beyond economics, however. Other critics contend, for example, that Canada is absorbing the severe health and environmental costs of development, particularly in the Alberta oil sands, costs disproportionately shouldered by the people of the area, many of them Aboriginals (see Marsden, 2007; Nikiforuk, 2008; see also Chapter 11).

In summary, Canada appears highly dependent upon exports to the U.S., even in such areas as oil and gas production where, according to neo-liberal theory, it should hold a dominant position.

JOB GROWTH AND INCOME

Increased integration of North American production after 1988 meant significant restructuring of Canada's labour markets,

expecially regarding traditional manufacturing jobs in Ontario (see Morton; 1997; Jackson, 1999). Free trade supporters, however, argued that, in the long run, more and better paying jobs would be created in Canada (Lipsey, 2000). Indeed, employment in Canada grew at a faster pace than in the United States throughout the period 1997–2000 (Statistics Canada, 2001a: 83) while unemployment levels also steadily declined. Job growth in Canada continued to grow throughout the next decade until the economic downturn began in 2008. Table 9.2 provides labour force statistics for Canada and the Canadian provinces in March 2009.

The downturn that began in 2007 potentially skews the more general impact of neo-liberal policies and free trade, in particular. At the same time, free trade's opponents were leery even before the recession of job creation and unemployment numbers, instead asking questions about what kinds of jobs Canada's neo-liberal turn had produced. They suggest that far too many of these have been part-time, insecure, and low paying, part of a trend toward non-standard employment (Krahn et al., 2007).

Table 9.2
Labour Force Characteristics, Seasonally Adjusted, Canada and the Provinces, March 2009 (in thousands)

Labour Force	Employment	Unemployment	Participation Rate (%)	Unemployment Rate (%)	Employment Rate (%)
18,294	16,893	1,456	67.3	8.0	61.9

Canada
Nfld. and

	Labour Force	Employment	Unemployment	Participation Rate (%)	Unemployment Rate (%)	Employment Rate (%)
Labrador	254	217	37	59.4	14.7	50.7
PEI	78	69	9	67.2	11.5	59.5
NS	498	453	44	64.5	8.9	58.8
NB	403	365	38	****	9.5	58.8
Que.	4,182	3,836	346	65.2	8.3	59.8
Ont.	7,168	6,548	620	67.5	8.7	61.7
Man.	636	604	32	69.3	5.1	65.8
Sask.	545	520	26	70.3	4.7	67.0
Alta.	2,110	1,987	123	74.3	5.8	69.9
BC	2,420	2,240	180	65.7	7.4	60.8

Source: Statistics Canada, *Labour Force Characteristics, Seasonally Adjusted, by Province (Monthly)*, http://www40.statcan.gc.ca/l01/cst01/lfss01a-eng.htm

What of income? As previously shown in Table 5.1 (Chapter 5), the median income of Canadians in constant dollars in 2005 was $41,401, nearly identical to what it was in 1980 ($41,348). Median income is useful in some regards, but also hides the range of incomes. In this regard, Kerstetter's (2002) study for the Canadian Centre for Policy Alternatives, using Statistics Canada data, shows a growing gap in wealth between the rich and poor in Canada, which we will further explore below.

SECURE ACCESS TO AMERICAN MARKETS

Threats of American protectionist policies being launched against Canada were a chief argument for the FTA in 1988. The Mulroney government insisted the FTA's dispute settlement mechanism would protect Canadian businesses from arbitrary barriers being erected by the American state. Economist Richard Lipsey (1999) argues that the dispute resolution mechanism has worked well, and that Canada would have been much worse off during the economically turbulent 1990s without it. Writing for the C.D. Howe Institute, Macrory (2002) argued (at the time) that since NAFTA, Canada and Mexico had been "subject to far fewer AD [anti-dumping] and CVD [countervailing duty] investigations and orders by the United States than ... other countries, proportionate to trade volume."

For critics, however, such a tepid defence of NAFTA's benefits point to the fact the United States did not give up under the FTA (or NAFTA) its right to make laws restricting trade with Canada. (American trade negotiators in 1988 emphasized the same point.) Indeed, critics argue that the United States has continued to invoke trade restrictions on a host of things, including softwood lumber, uranium, beer, magnesium, steel, pigs, sugar, peanut butter, tobacco, milk, and paper (Dyck, 1998: 92–93). At the

same time, the American government, pursuing the interests of agro-food giants and with the support of some Canadian politicians and governments, have sought to end the Canadian Wheat Board's (CWB) ability to be the single market seller for Canadian wheat, arguing that it is an anti-competitive practice, even though the United States heavily subsidizes its own large corporate agricultural producers and the World Trade Organization has repeatedly found the CWB to be in compliance with trade practices.

EFFICIENCY AND GLOBAL COMPETITIVENESS

Free trade supporters argued in 1988 that the agreement would prepare Canadians to compete in the emerging global economy. Canadian businesses would have to become more entrepreneurial and efficient; workers would be forced to become more productive. A Statistics Canada report (Baldwin and Gu, 2004) suggests that Canada's manufacturing sector did become more productive as a consequence of trade liberalization after 1988 through specializing, innovating, and learning how to compete.

Gross domestic product (GDP) provides one measure for assessing Canada's increased productivity. Maynard (2007) argues, for example, that GDP per capita in Canada compared with the United States has risen fairly continuously since 1994 and was 84.3 percent of American GDP in 2005. Stanford's (2006: 168) comparison of Canada, the United States, and Mexico—the three NAFTA amigos—suggests that GDP in Canada and the United States actually dropped in the period of the FTA (1989–1994), but increased for all three countries, even over their pre-FTA levels, during the period 1994–2003.

GDP is a controversial measure, however. Because it is a measurement of the total value of goods and services produced in a country during a given period, GDP typically goes up not only during good times but also during wars or immediately after a disaster, such as an earthquake, as rebuilding starts. In this sense, GDP says nothing about the quality of life being lived.

Opponents also dispute the economic efficiency arguments of free trade supporters. Jackson (1999), for example, argues that free trade has not brought the investments in research and development that might prepare Canada for the new knowledge economy. Perhaps the strongest economic argument of neo-liberalism's opponents, however, is that, far from being a global player, Canada is less "globalized" today than before free trade. First, Canada is even more dependent today than in 1988 upon the U.S. market (see above). Second, increasingly these exports are in the form of raw resources.

As previously noted (Chapter 8), staples can be a source of great wealth when the world economy is booming, as it did during the recent heyday of globalization (the 1990s and early 2000s). Then, the newly emerging economies in Asia particularly came calling for Canadian minerals, forestry products, agricultural products, and petroleum. A report by Statistics Canada (2007c) in late 2007 noted that Canada's economy, as in the past, was being driven by commodity prices, though Canadians had become less "hewers of wood and drawers of water" than "conveyers of crude and moilers of metals." But, as before, the boom also came at a cost. While the demand for commodities raised the economies of western Canada and the Atlantic region, the manufacturing sector in central Canada suffered (Statistics Canada, 2007b: 130), and when the economic downturn took hold in 2008, all of Canada declined.

Neo-liberalism's proponents concentrate upon the economic benefits of such policies. In a real sense, they "hive off" the economy from wider social or political implications. By contrast, while oppo-

nents of neo-liberalism do not ignore economic questions, some of their strongest arguments centre on the wider social and political consequences of free and unregulated markets. Among Canadian opponents, these arguments included a series of interrelated threats posed by neo-liberalism to Canada's sovereignty, national unity, values, cultural identity, and social cohesion. Have these concerns proven correct?

FOREIGN OWNERSHIP, POLITICAL SOVEREIGNTY, AND "DEEP INTEGRATION"

Free trade supporters view questions of ownership and fears of a loss of political sovereignty as red herrings. They argue that markets are neutral and that companies respond solely to consumer demand. By contrast, free trade opponents in 1988 and today argue that it deliberately removes democratic control of the economy from citizens, placing important decisions in the hands of companies, investment dealers, and shareholders who may have little concern for Canada.

Concern about foreign ownership increased steadily during the 1990s as a host of Canadian companies—Seagram's, Nortel, Nova Corps, Canadian National Railways—were taken over by American corporations, leaving journalist Peter C. Newman (1999: 51) to say that Canadians were quickly becoming "squatters on our own land." The trend continued throughout the new millennium with the demise of such historic companies as The Hudson's Bay Company, Bell Canada, and Alcan. A Canadian Press-Harris-Decima poll conducted in 2007 found that 72 percent of Canadians were worried about the "hollowing out" of corporate Canada and wanted the federal government to do something about it (*Lethbridge Herald*, 2007: B6).

Beyond anecdotal evidence or subjective concerns, what is the level of foreign ownership in Canada today? Has this level changed since 1988? And, if so, how? A Statistics Canada study conducted by Baldwin and Gallatly (2005) argues that foreign ownership or control of key sectors of the economy peaked in the 1960s, declined in the 1970s during the period of Canadianization (especially the Foreign Investment Review Agency), but today has returned to mid-1960 levels. Foreign control is especially noticeable, the report concludes, in the manufacturing sector where, in 1999, foreign firms controlled 52.7 percent of all exports and employed 31.7 percent of all workers in manufacturing.

The push to further "marketize" Canada's resources has been led by the corporate community. Led by the Canadian Council of Chief Executives (formerly the Business Council on National Issues), made up of Canada's largest 150 companies, and pro-business think tanks like the C.D. Howe Institute, the Fraser Institute, and the Conference Board of Canada, corporate Canada has repeatedly called for Canada's "deep integration" into the North American economy. An ongoing series of papers (termed *The Border Papers*) put out by the C.D. Howe Institute, for example, called for such things as a common North American tariff and integrated energy, environmental, and regulatory policies (see Dymond and Hart, 2003; Bradley and Watkins, 2003; Hufbauer and Schott, 2004). In the words of Dymond and Hart (2003: 1), "The time has come to achieve a seamless border with our neighbour, embraced within a new agreement implementing rules, procedures, and institutions consonant with the reality of ever-deepening, mutually beneficial crossborder integration."

Corporate Canada's drive for a "seamless border" was furthered with the formal initiation in March 2005 of the Security and Prosperity Partnership (SPP). Emerging in the aftermath of the 9/11 attacks, the SPP focused on military and energy security, making clear that Canadian and Mexican energy was eyed as the means of ensuring American energy into the future, with Alberta's tar sands a central focus (Laxer and Dillon, 2008). In a similar vein, Ibbitson (2009) has recently called for a bilateral, continental security perimeter around North America and a customs union between Canada and the United States.

As in the past, corporate leaders and their supporters argue the economic merits of "getting inside the American tent," but who would primarily benefit? Might there be other costs? Campbell and Finn (2006: 11) place the push for deep integration within a deeper political and social context:

> The big business push for deeper integration policies has been driven by fear, in the 1980s by the fear of increased U.S. protectionism, and since 9/11 by the fear of security-related border disruptions. But it has also been driven by the goal of harmonizing Canadian policies, regulations, and institutions with those of a more "business-friendly" America, reducing the significance of the border, and foreclosing the ability of any future Canadian government to return to the interventionist policies of the 1960s and 1970s. It is a way to smuggle a corporate agenda, unpopular with most Canadians, through the back door.

Specifically, critics argue that, since the signing of the trade agreements in 1989 and 1993, Canada's social programs have faced cuts (Rice and Prince, 2000; Olsen, 2002). For example, Canada's Family Allowance Program, begun in 1945, was eliminated in 1992, the eligibility qualifications and benefits for Unemployment Insurance (renamed Employment Insurance) were made more stringent, and medicare, arguably the capstone of Canada's welfare state, has come under increased pressure to move away from public administration and universality toward the privatized American model. What further changes might deep integration bring? In rebuttal, however, advocates of neo-liberal restructuring argue that the changes to Canada's welfare state programs were made necessary not by free trade but by the country's rising debt load in the 1990s.

Is Canada becoming more tightly integrated into the United States? Is Canada losing control of its destiny? Clarkson (2008) argues that, nearly two decades after NAFTA, Canada, the United States, and Mexico still operate separately, but that there have been significant changes. Notably, he argues (2008, 461–470), there is a deepened asymmetry between the three countries, with the United States dominant; that the latter also exercises growing hegemony over its other partners, but that both Canada and Mexico also retain "substantial residual autonomy" over their affairs—if they choose to use it. NAFTA, says Clarkson, was meant by its negotiators "to bring down political barriers to trade and investment," but not to fashion the institutions that would further social integration (2008: 459), i.e., to create a *society*.

Canadian nationalists may take some solace from Clarkson's conclusion that formal social and political integration into the American empire is not yet on the horizon. Nonetheless, might tighter economic integration still pose problems for a united, coherent Canada?

Canada is not an easy place to govern. As the economic historian Harold Innis argued years ago, Canada does not have a single, national economy, but rather several regional economies that trade with the United States; Courchene (1998) notes that free trade resulted in a shift from east-west to north-south trade, though interprovincial trade is still the norm. Politically, also, Canada's system of federal-provincial powers is designed to be fractious and often follow the regional

splits found in the various economies; the last several federal elections have pointed out the regional nature of Canadian politics (see Appendix 2), though these results may also reflect problems in the country's first-passed-the-post electoral system.

What finally tied these regional economies together as a nation, a society, was a network of transport systems, communication systems, and social programs (such as medicare), many of them arising after 1945, that facilitated positive and ongoing interactions between people within and across the provinces and territories. In short, becoming and remaining a country meant that Canada also had to become a unified *society*. But this did not just happen. Might tighter integration with the U.S., even short of a formal merger, lead to Canada's internal fragmentation?

Some view such concerns as overstated (see Ibbitson, 2009), that Canadians possess distinct beliefs and values, and a strong identity that will not only fend off American influence but continue also to bind the country together.

POLITICAL IDEOLOGY AND VALUES

We previously examined the notion of ideology in relation to the development of modern Quebec (Chapter 3). Here we want to ask: What are Canada's dominant ideological strains? How do these strains differ from those of the United States? How have they shaped Canadian values and beliefs? And have Canadian values and beliefs changed during the time of neo-liberal dominance?

The American political sociologist, Seymour Martin Lipset (1968b, 1986, 1990, 1996), argued that Canadian political values fall between those of the United States and Great Britain, such that, by contrast with the United States, Canadians are more elitist (hierarchical), conformist, statist, collectivist, and particularist (group-oriented) (Lipset, 1996).

Lipset's thesis is contentious. First, recent scholarship suggests that the American revolutionary leaders were republican individualists, not liberal individualists; the colonial masses believed in "local communalism," not rugged nonconformity; and, in many ways, there was little to distinguish the revolutionaries from the Loyalists (Grabb et al., 1999, 2000). Second, Lipset's emphasis upon the revolution as a founding moment ignores perhaps more important events in American history, notably the Civil War (Chapter 6), while his discussion of Canada often ignores the influence of French culture. Third, Lipset's thesis lacks a dynamic element, thus freezing both countries in time.

Nonetheless, Lipset's depiction of Canada's dominant ideological strain may be accurate for a certain period of time. Research suggests that the War of 1812 and the failed rebellions of 1837–1838 reinforced conservative elements in English-speaking Canada. (Quebec, as we have seen, had its own particular forces shaping a similar conservatism there.) The 19th-century form of English-Canadian conservatism was of a particular type, referred to as Toryism.

In *Lament for a Nation*, Canadian philosopher George Grant (1965) chronicled the importance of Toryism to Canada, arguing that it had been an ideological bulwark against Canada's absorption into the American Empire. Like its British counterpart, English-Canadian Toryism was monarchist, lauded tradition and order, and believed in a natural order of things that extended across class, race, religion, and gender. In its better moments, this latter belief in a natural social hierarchy was balanced by a deep sense of *noblesse oblige* toward those less fortunate, something that, when forged with socialism, gave support to the development of a more extensive welfare state in Canada than found in the United States (Horowitz, 1966).

In Grant's view (1965), however, certain characteristics also distinguished Canadian Toryism from its British forebear. First, Canadian Toryism was staunchly anti-American, thus the Tory party's opposition to free trade in both 1891 and 1911. Second, the Canadian Tory tradition also espoused a particularly strong belief in a positive role for the state both in the economy and in society at large, hence Macdonald's formulation of the National Policy (Chapter 7) and R.B. Bennett's creation of the Canadian Radio Broadcasting Commission in 1932, which led to the founding of the Canadian Broadcasting Corporation four years later.

By the 1960s, however, Grant viewed the Tory tradition in eclipse due to Britain's fading presence in Canadian life and the growing dominance of liberal ideals in Canada and much of the world as promoted by the United States through the economy and new media technologies. For Grant, the end of Toryism meant the end of economic nationalism in Canada, with Canada's ultimate demise as the result. Both the Liberal and Progressive Conservative parties would henceforth become "liberal" parties supporting continental integration into the larger United States.

Lament for a Nation is a seminal book in Canadian thought, but it is not without problems. Notably, in lauding Canada's British traditions, Grant largely ignores the significant contributions of other peoples to the construction of Canada and Canadian identity, a point emphasized by recent scholars.

Resnick (2005: 89), for example, argues that Canada is essentially a European country, comprised of its "European historical connections, a North American geographical setting, multiple national identities, robust social programs, multicultural practices, increasingly secular values, and a multilateral outlook on international affairs," to which he adds one last element setting Canadian political culture off from that of the United States: self-doubt.

Saul (2008), however, refutes Resnick's European depiction of Canada, instead arguing that Canada is in fact an Aboriginal nation (see Chapter 13) that thrives on complexity and nuance. In fact, Saul contends the United States is the far more European country, with its relatively fixed notions of nation and state.

Finally, Michael Ignatieff (2009)— Harvard scholar, current leader of the federal Liberal Party, and George Grant's nephew—contends that his uncle had it all wrong! Ignatieff argues that Grant misunderstood the importance and endurance of differences between Canadians and Americans regarding such issues as freedom and collective rights, and that he ignored the role of Aboriginal and Métis peoples and Quebec. Ignatieff further chides Grant for having given up on Canada at the very moment (1965) when Canada was engaged in a major transformation of itself—strengthening the welfare state, adopting a new flag, embracing bilingualism, becoming multicultural, and patriating the Canadian Constitution with a Charter of Rights and Freedoms. Finally, he notes that the period of neo-liberal globalization—of capitalism on the march—has also witnessed the rebirth of nationalism everywhere, including Canada.

In short, Ignatieff and others argue that Canada is not only itself a distinct society, but one shown to be capable of weathering American and global political, economic, and cultural influence. Are these contentions correct?

Recent scholarship suggests the answer, in general, is *yes*. Important differences in value orientations continue to exist between the two countries, though also mitigated by such sociological factors as class, gender, ethnicity, religion, and region; recent scholarship, for example, has described North America as comprised of four value regions (a liberal Quebec that is drawing the rest of Canada toward it, and a very conservative American South that is drawing the rest of the United States, especially middle America, toward it and away from English-speaking Canada) (Grabb and Curtis, 2005). More importantly, such studies suggest that while some Canadian and American values have converged over time, others have diverged, but, even more startlingly, that Canadians today are more likely than Americans to believe in and experience the American Dream of individual opportunity (Adams, 1998; Hood, 2008).

Box 9.2
Canadian and American Values Compared

Surveys conducted since 1988 conclude that value differences remain between Canadians and Americans. Compared with their American counterparts, these surveys show that Canadians in general are:

- less deferential to authority
- less conformist
- less formally religious
- less characterized by a traditional work ethic
- less accepting of violence
- more desirous of personal autonomy
- more individualistic
- more hedonistic
- more relaxed
- more suspicious of big business

Sources: Neil Nevitte, *The Decline of Difference* (Peterborough: Broadview Press, 1996), 10–18; Michael Adams, *Sex in the Snow* (Toronto: Penguin, 1998).

CULTURE AND CANADIAN IDENTITY

For critics of free trade, culture was a specific concern in 1988. Free trade proponents said at the time that culture was not open to negotiation. Nonetheless, the United States, home to Hollywood production and many of the world's largest music and magazine industries, has since repeatedly pressured Canada to drop "protectionist" policies toward its cultural industries. For the American government, culture is just another commodity, though some argue it is also a vehicle for American imperialism and, in the specific case of some Hollywood movies, even state propaganda (Gardner, 2002). For many Canadians, however, culture is an essential element of identity that must be nurtured and protected or it will be lost, not to mention a major industry worth billions of dollars and employing nearly 350,000 people in 2006 (Statistics Canada, 2007b: 300–301).

Neo-liberal supporters of markets charge that Canadian government regulations, such as those enforced by the Canadian Radio and Television Commission, restrict choice and protect mediocrity. They also argue that public radio and television force people to pay for things for which there is no market demand and otherwise compete unfairly with private business. The counter-argument is that organizations such as the CBC and the National Film Board and cultural subsidies actually provide the means for a greater variety of "voices" that otherwise would be suppressed by a cacophony of mass-market sound coming from the United States (see Gordon, 2002).

Does Canada have a national culture? Pevere and Dymond (1996) argue persuasively that Canada does not or that, rather, the essence of "Canadian" culture arises from its regions. Canada's proximity to the United States allows many of its artists to mirror American culture and therefore to do very well in that marketplace. Shania Twain and Nickelback provide only two examples. They can "pass" as generically American. By contrast, regional artists (Great Big Sea) and films (*My Winnipeg* or *The Necessities of Life*) or those artists whose content remain too resolutely Canadian (The Tragically Hip) are not

as easily sold in the United States. They are "too Canadian." Likewise, one may note the region-specific nature of such acclaimed television shows as "Corner Gas" and "Little Mosque on the Prairie."

What role such cultural artifacts play in Canadian identity is not entirely certain, yet many Canadians do appear to acknowledge and value the distinctive products of Canadian culture and to include them in their identity kits.

SOCIAL COHESION: SOCIAL STRATIFICATION AND INEQUALITY

In recent decades, as several societies have witnessed increased conflict, many sociologists have returned to the age-old question asked by structural-functionalists (Chapter 1): What holds societies together? One of these sociologists, Robert Putnam, coined the term **social capital**, defined as *a positive combination of interaction, reciprocity, and trust* that bonds people to their communities (see Krahn et al., 2009). In turn, social capital is facilitated by a high degree of **social cohesion**, defined as *the bonding effect of society that arises spontaneously out of individuals willingly interacting together toward collective goals*. Social cohesion is enhanced when there is a relative equality of income and life chances while, in turn, high social and economic equality also leads to a better economy (see Osberg, 2003).

We have previously examined social stratification in early Canada (Chapter 2). The question of social stratification is important to again examine here given neo-liberalism's belief in "trickle-down" economics and a minimalist role for the state in reducing social inequalities. What is the nature of Canada's social stratification system today after nearly 30 years of neo-liberal policies? To what extent are the life chances of Canadian citizens more or less equal?

There are two major paradigms for thinking about social stratification and inequality in society. The first employs the neo-Marxist notion of class, updated to reflect the complexity of modern labour markets and especially the rise of managers and technical experts since Marx's time. The second method, termed a measure of **socio-economic status** or SES, combines education, occupation, and income in a composite index (see Box 9.3).

Box 9.3
Neo-Marxist and Socio-economic (SES) Models of Class

Neo-Marxist[1]	SES Model
Capitalist classes	Upper upper
Grand bourgeoisie	Lower upper
Small employers	Upper middle
Petite bourgeoisie	Lower middle
New middle classes	Upper lower
Managers and supervisors	Lower lower
Expert and semi-credentialed workers	
Proletarians	Underclass

Note:
1. Capitalists own the means of production in varying degrees, but may or may not purchase labour. The managerial and supervisory members of the new middle class may have discretionary control over capital and command labour. All members of this class exercise some degree of job autonomy. The proletarians neither own nor control the means of production, do not command labour, and have no assets in the labour market but their labour.

Sources: Adapted from Eric Olin Wright, *Classes* (London: Verso, 1985); Murray Knuttila, *Introducing Sociology: A Critical Perspective* (Toronto: Oxford University Press, 2002).

There are similarities between Marxian class and SES measures of class. Occupation as measured in the SES model, for example, is a reasonable proxy for class in the Marxian sense, but there are also clear theoretical and ideological differences in the manner in which each describes systems of social stratification in modern, capitalist societies. First,

there is a structural relationship among Marxist classes, especially between (as Marx saw it) the two chief antagonists, the capitalist class (or bourgeoisie) and the workers (or proletariat). There is no such relationship between any of the strata described in the SES model. These are merely continuous statistical categories. Second, and related to the first point, people move through life in the Marxist model as members of a group, with the potential of becoming conscious of this affiliation (that is, a **social class**), and acting politically upon this knowledge. By contrast, the people in the SES model are individuals placed in a category on the basis of their individual credentials, a fact that suggests the essentially liberal basis of this model and its further congruence with functionalist explanations of social inequality (see Chapter 1). Third, whereas the Marxian model implies a relatively closed and static society based on the class position to which one is born, the SES model implies a far more open and fluid social structure in which individuals either rise on the basis of merit or fall for lack thereof.

On this latter point of **social mobility**—*the upward or downward movement of individuals or groups from one position in the social stratification system to another position*—both models are probably in error with regard to Canadian society. At least at the top end, and also at the very bottom, social mobility in Canada is relatively low, contrary to the implications of the SES model. At the same time, opportunities for members of the working class and new middle class to rise higher in their individual lifetimes (intra-generational social mobility) or for children to rise higher than their parents (intergenerational social mobility) are greater than envisioned by the Marxist model.

Fourth, the SES model explicitly ignores **wealth** (*the total amount of money and other financial assets owned by individuals or families*) in favour of **income** (*money* *earned through the sale of labour or through investments*). By contrast, the Marxist model concerns all sources of wealth, particularly those that arise out of the ownership of the means of production, for this is also a source of major political power.

With these considerations in mind, what does Canada's social stratification system look like today? How large are social inequalities in Canada today? Table 9.3 provides some answers. Table 9.3 divides the Canadian population into five groups of 20 percent each (quintiles), from the poorest 20 percent of families to the richest 20 percent of families. Note that both the median and the average net worth (in constant dollars) of families in the poorest quintile actually declined from

1999 to 2005, and that this group's average net worth was in fact negative (–$2,400) in 2005. Note also that the objective situation of the next three quintiles improved marginally over this same period, but that the net worth of the second and third groups declined in relative terms. Finally, note that the net worth of families in the richest quintile increased the most, both in objective and relative terms, over this period.

Consider, however, that the top quintile is not itself a single bloc. In 1999, for example, the top 10 percent of families in Canada owned 56 percent of all the country's wealth (Kerstetter, 2002). If this decile is further broken down, it becomes clear that the top 5 (or even 1) percent of Canadians own much of Canada's wealth.

Table 9.3
Distribution of Net Worth in Canada, All Family Units, 1999 and 2005
(2005 constant dollars)

Quintiles	1999				2005			
	% Net Worth	Total Net Worth	Median Net Worth	Average Net Worth	% Net Worth	Total Net Worth	Median Net Worth	Average Net Worth
	%	Millions $	$	$	%	Millions $	$	$
All family units	**100.0**	**3,432,000**	**120,500**	**281,000**	**100**	**4,862,000**	**148,400**	**364,300**
Lowest 20%	0.1	–3,700	1,100	–1,500	0.1	–6,300	1,000	–2,400
Second 20%	2.6	89,700	34,800	36,700	2.3	110,000	37,300	41,400
Third 20%	8.8	302,000	120,500	123,600	8.4	409,000	148,400	153,200
Fourth 20%	20.1	691,000	275,600	282,700	20.2	983,000	361,200	367,600
Highest 20%	68.5	2,353,000	671,600	963,300	69.2	3,367,000	862,900	1,264,200

Source: Adapted from Statistics Canada, *The Wealth of Canadians: An Overview of the Results of the Survey of Financial Security,* Cat. no. 13F0026MIE – No. 001.

Who are the people in this elite? The very wealthiest of Canadians are fairly easy to identify. Many are household names. Table 9.4 lists the names of Canada's 20 billionaires in 2009—up from nine in 1999 (Kerstetter, 2002: 65)—as identified by *Forbes Magazine*. (As a result of the recent economic crisis, the total number of billionaires in the world declined in 2009 to 793 from 1,125 the year previous.)

Of course, billionaires are a rather

select group. Nonetheless, the neo-liberal period did see the salaries and benefits of CEOs rise markedly. Hugh Mackenzie (2009) shows that CEO compensation in Canada soared between 1995 and 2007, from 85 times the average salary of workers to 398 times. In 2007, the top 100 CEOs in Canada received an average compensation of $10,408,054 compared to an average salary of $40,237 for Canadian workers.

In turn, as the average salary of workers has steadily declined in relative terms (and remained largely static in real terms), the circumstances of those outside of the labour market has declined even further. (Note again the bottom quintile in Table 9.3.) Changes and cuts made to Canada's social safety net during the 1990s have had a particularly strong impact on individuals who rely upon non-market sources of income. The result has been a steady increase in the use of food banks throughout Canada. Reports show the number of people using food banks in Canada has risen steadily since the 1980s. In March 2008 (an average month), Canadian food banks assisted 704,414 individuals, 37 percent of them children (Food Banks Canada, 2009). Tied partly to food bank usage, homelessness has also become a feature of Canadian urban life, even in very small towns. It is hard to count people who lack stable accommodations, but recent estimates place the number of homeless people in Canada at between 150,000 and 300,000 (Echenberg and Jensen, 2008).

Table 9.4
Primary Source of Wealth, Estimated Wealth, and 2009 World Ranking of Canada's 20 Billionaires (2003 and 2009)

Name	Primary Source of Wealth	Estimated Wealth in Billions) (U.S.) (2003)	Estimated Wealth in Billions (U.S.) (2009)	World Ranking (2009)
Thomson, David and family[1]	inheritance	14.0	13.0	24
Weston Sr., Galen and family	retail	6.2	5.0	98
Irving, James, Arthur, and John	oil	3.5	3.9	146
Desmarais, Paul and family	financial investments	1.7	2.6	246
Laliberte, Guy	media	n.a.	2.5	261
Sherman, Bernard (Barry)	drugs	2.2	2.5	261
Azrieli, David and family	shopping malls	n.a.	2.1	318
Pattison, Jim	diversified	2.2	2.1	318
Miller, Robert	electronics	n.a.	2.1	318
McCain, Wallace	frozen foods	1.8	2.0	334
Bronfman, Charles	liquor	n.a.	1.8	397
Skoll, Jeffrey S.	eBay	2.8	1.8	397
Lazaridis, Mike	technology	n.a.	1.8	397
Balsillie, James	technology	n.a.	1.7	430
Katz, Darryl	drugs	n.a.	1.5	468
Saputo, Emanuele (Lino)	dairy/food	n.a.	1.3	559
Schnaider, Alexander	financial investments	n.a.	1.3	559
Jarislowsky, Stephen	financial investments	n.a.	1.2	601
Cheriton, David	Google	n.a.	1.1	647
Lee Chin, Michael	mutual funds	n.a.	1.0	701

Notes: Ken Thompson, head in 2003, since deceased; David Thompson now head. Likewise, Edward (Ted) Rogers (Rogers Communications) died in 2008. His estimated wealth at the time was U.S. $5.7 billion, placing him 173 in the world.

Sources: Forbes, "Special report: The world's richest people," 2003, www.forbes.com; *Forbes,* "Special report: The world's billionaires," 2008, www.forbes.com

It must be noted that when it comes to great poverty, great wealth, and positions in between, not all people are treated equally (Grabb et al., 1999). While the average income of women in the labour market is nearing that of men in similar occupations, women in 2003 still earned overall 71 cents for every dollar earned by men (Krahn et al., 2007: 194), though for women aged 25–29, working full-year, full-time, this amount is 81 cents (Statistics Canada, 2003: 9–10). The gap has closed since the 1980s for several reasons. More women are working and working longer. Many are more highly educated and better trained than in the past, resulting in their qualifying for better jobs. Finally, during the 1990s, the gap closed as men's wages actually declined due to job restructuring.

Still, the highest-paid professions remain dominated by men, while women often remain located in fairly specific job ghettos (Krahn et al., 2007). Additionally, women do not often control large corporate enterprises—the source of wealth (note the gender of Canada's billionaires in Table 9.4)—but do disproportionately count among Canada's poor, especially those on some form of welfare. The fact that women are disproportionately represented among the poor has led some policy-makers to speak of the **feminization of poverty**.

Likewise, Canada's system of social stratification continues to reflect differences based on ethnicity and race. The influence of ethnicity and race is not as stark as when John Porter published his seminal tome, *The Vertical Mosaic*, in 1965 (see Nakhaie, 1997; Lian and Matthews, 1998), but ethnicity and race still play a part, most particularly in the case of Aboriginal peoples (Part 3).

Other factors also continue to shape Canada's stratification system. These include regional disparities, physical and mental disabilities, and, increasingly, the impact of age, often involving elderly widows (Curtis et al., 1999). A study produced for Statistics Canada is instructive (Morissette and Zhang, 2001). It shows that people in lower-income circumstances over long periods tend disproportionately to be women, unattached, or lone parents.

In summary, the gap has generally increased between the rich and poor in Canada, a situation replicated in many other Western countries, though none more strongly than the United States. The causes of this appear to be twofold. First, labour markets changes (e.g., declines in manufacturing, increased educational requirements, etc.) have resulted in some individuals increasing their incomes while others' incomes have decreased. Second, tax changes during the past 20 years have allowed the wealthy to keep more of their earnings, while reductions in social programs have meant that those with low-paying and insecure jobs are less protected from market forces.

This poses a question. We noted earlier scholarship suggesting that Canadian values and beliefs have a strong collectivist bent (in contrast to the mythic "dog-eat-dog" individualism of the U.S.). Does growing inequality, including perhaps a tolerance for it, suggest an undercurrent of changes in Canadian values that studies have overlooked? Or are we witnessing merely a temporary phenomenon?

CANADA, THE WAR ON TERRORISM, AND AFGHANISTAN

Soon after the 9/11 attacks, the United States made a series of specific demands upon Canada (see Clarkson, 2002a, 2002b). Militarily, these demands included the creation of a military zone around North America under American command and control. Politically, American demands included Canada's adoption of American immigration policies and common security practices. (Within months of September 11, American and Canadian immigration officials began working side by side at the border. The U.S. has also since changed the entry requirements for everyone, including Canadians, entering the country.)

A few months later, the United States and its NATO allies—Canada among them—invaded Afghanistan, where Al-Qaeda and its leader, Osama bin-Laden, resided and whose Taliban government had provided a safe haven for the organization. Canada was obliged to join the mission under Article 5 of the Treaty of Washington, which states that an attack upon any NATO country is an attack upon all (Stein and Lang, 2007: 10–11).

Article 5 aside, why and how did Canada get involved in the Afghanistan mission? Certainly, Canada and Canadians wanted to show support for the United States after 9/11. But how? And why Afghanistan? Three reasons were paramount.

First, the federal Liberal government in 2001 believed Canada should have a larger presence on the world stage, and saw the Afghan mission as fitting within Canada's post-1960s efforts in international peacekeeping and reconstruction. Second, the mission also had widespread support among much of Canada's military establishment that wanted Canada to pursue a larger and more "muscular" role in the world. Third, Afghanistan was also a trade-off for not participating in the then looming Iraq War, which the United States formally launched in spring 2003. The Afghan mission appeared at the time the "safer" engagement.

Canada's decision not to join the subsequent American-led invasion of Iraq proved a good one, but at the time also posed real problems. The Canadian government viewed the mission as foolhardy and unjustified; it was also unpopular at home, especially opposed by Quebecers. Powerful forces opposed Canada's decision, however, including the U.S. administration of George W. Bush, many political leaders in Canada (such as Alberta's Premier Ralph Klein and then federal Conservative Opposition leader Stephen Harper), and most of the country's big business community, who argued that Canada must join in the war both to support a traditional ally and because not doing so might result in American economic reprisal. No reprisals ever came, but Canada did experience an onslaught of anti-Canadianism from right-wing talk radio and television programs (Harrison, 2007).

The Iraq War was costly in terms of American and Iraqi lives and money and American prestige. Meanwhile, the Afghan conflict continued to simmer, with far greater consequences for Canada; indeed, its short-term military engagement soon morphed into what Stein and Lang (2007) have termed the "unexpected war."

Citizens will support a war as long as it appears just, its purposes clear, the costs minimal, and the conflict winnable. Today, few of these conditions adhere. Many Canadians still support the conflict's humanitarian aims of liberating the Afghan people from the harsh fundamentalist dictates of the Taliban. They also believe, however, that the Afghan government of Hamid Karsai, installed and supported by the Western powers, is corrupt and incompetent, and does not have widespread support among its own people. Some also believe, as in Iraq, that the war's real purpose is to secure an oil and gas pipeline from the Caspian Sea through Afghanistan and on to Pakistan for Western markets (see Dobbin, 2008).

Meanwhile, the costs have mounted. By the end of 2009, 138 Canadian soldiers (and one diplomat) had been killed in action and several hundred more seriously injured. A report written for the Rideau Institute estimates that 193 Canadian soldiers will have been killed and 1,900 more injured by the time the military mission is scheduled to end in 2011 (Macdonald and Staples, 2008). Added to the number of Canadian casualties are those of Afghan civilians who have lost their lives in the war, an estimated 9,270 killed directly between 2006 and 2008 by air strikes by U.S. and other NATO forces (Milne, 2008).

Along with the human toll, the financial costs of war have also risen. Canada's parliamentary budget officer estimates the Afghan mission will cost between $14 billion and $18 billion by the time the troops leave the country in 2011, or about $1,500 for every household in the country (Clark, 2008). Macdonald and Staples (2008) dispute this figure, however, instead estimating the war's financial costs at $28.4 billion by the end of 2011. Beyond the costs, many analysts today, including much of the West's political and military elite, believe the Afghan War is unwinnable by military means and that a negotiated settlement with the Taliban is inevitable (Margolis, 2008; Milne, 2008).

Under all of these conditions, Canadian support for the war effort all but collapsed. On the advice of an independent panel of observers (Government of Canada, 2008), Canada's two major political parties, the Liberals and Conservatives, have agreed that Canada's military role in Afghanistan will end in 2011 (though there are hints that Canada's military involvement may continue in another form, perhaps using military fighter jets for bombing raids), replaced by efforts at reconstruction and development.

Wars change societies, and Canada is no exception (see Chapter 7). Many critics believe the Afghan conflict and the War on Terrorism generally are fundamentally changing Canada. Author and political activist Murray Dobbin (2008) argues the war is not only integrating Canada tighter into the American Empire through defence and security policies, but is also militarizing Canada's values and culture. He further argues the conflict is being "used to justify massive increases in military spending, distorting the role of government and the spending priorities of Canadians," a point supported by Staples and Robinson (2008). They note that Canadian military spending in 2007–2008 was 27 percent higher than before September 11, 2001; that Canada in 2007 was the 13th highest military spender in the world; and that Canadian military spending is today at its highest level since the Second World War and 2.3 percent higher than it was at the peak of the Cold War (1952–1953). Continued military spending at these levels is almost certain to have social consequences, including less money for education, public health care, and a variety of other social

programs that historically have made Canada a "more caring, sharing" society than the United States.

It is important to note that many of the changes occurring in Canadian society since September 2001 have been the result of government and state actions. These include not only heightened security, but, some would argue, also restrictions on free speech, even at the universities (Turk and Manson, 2007), and the use of "rendition" and other questionable practices, as in the case of Maher Arar, to deal with suspected terrorists.

THE GLOBAL ECONOMIC CRISIS: THE END OF NEO-LIBERALISM?

After nearly three decades of global expansion under neo-liberalism, the world economy suddenly went into turmoil beginning in late 2007. The immediate cause was a mortgage crisis in the United States as large numbers of buyers defaulted on their house payments. Quickly, however, the crisis reverberated around the world, bringing down banks and other financial institutions that had given the buyers easy credit. In turn, credit markets seized up, making it harder for businesses to borrow money, resulting in businesses laying off workers. Unemployed workers and consumers already in substantial debt began buying fewer goods and services, leading to even more business layoffs. In short, Depression-era economics (see Galbraith, 1997) returned with a vengeance.

In the weeks and months that followed, some of the oldest and biggest names in American and global finance disappeared—Bears Stearns, Lehman Brothers, Merrill Lynch—while others experienced major changes. Around the world, many banks were effectively nationalized while the collapse of consumer buying also brought low several large manufacturing firms, notably those in the car industry. Under the new

American administration of President Barack Obama, the spring of 2009 saw two of America's big three auto manufacturers, General Motors and Chrysler, go into bankruptcy, with many product lines being shut down and others sold off to foreign manufacturers.

The causes of the 2007–2010 economic crisis will likely be debated for some time, but excessive financial deregulation, growing inequality (making necessary the advent of easy credit), and the sudden rise of oil prices (nearly U.S. $150 in the spring of 2008) were significant contributors. What might be some of the consequences of the crisis?

Government and business leaders have warned against a return to protectionism rather than free trade. Certainly, some amount of protectionism is likely to occur, but it will likely be the result of other problems that the economic crisis has brought to a head, such as the rising price of oil. Given these factors, local, national, and regional markets will likely replace global markets for many goods and services (see Rubin, 2009). Indeed, resource depletion in general, environmental damage, and the continued onslaught of global warming further suggest that the world may be on the cusp of both "re-nationalization" and "deglobalization" (Bello, 2004).

What do these events mean for Canada? Certainly, Canada has also been hit by the global economic crisis. Given Canada's significant trade balance with the United States, it could not be otherwise. The Canadian government of Conservative Prime Minister Stephen Harper, a long-time advocate of small government and unregulated markets, at first denied there was a crisis. Eventually, however, the government committed to running a deficit of $50 billion (for 2009 alone), raising Canada's accumulated federal debt to $1.5 trillion, to deal with the recession's effects. How the economic crisis will play out remains uncertain.

CONCLUSION

Every crisis is an opportunity. If the world is shrinking, might Canadians use the current crises to rebuild their own home in the world; to reconnect the bonds between peoples from coast to coast; to develop the economy for all Canadians and not only foreign corporations?

Nonetheless, as a country heavily dependent upon exports, especially to the United States, the crisis could also hold dire consequences for Canada. This is not a new phenomenon for Canadians, however. Canadians have always faced the task of carving out an existence and an identity as a northern people on the margins of the world economy and under the aegis of empire.

Canada's fate lies not in the stars or in the inexorable workings of some imaginary manifest destiny imposed by others; rather, it lies in the will of its people to find or create new reasons to continue as a society, a country, and a different kind of nation. In this quest, they might look no further for answers than among Canada's Aboriginal peoples who, earlier than most, faced the onslaught of global imperial forces.

KEY TERMS
civil religion
feminization of poverty
income
neo-liberalism
social capital
social class
social cohesion
social mobility
socio-economic status
wealth

CRITICAL THINKING QUESTIONS

1. Why did neo-liberalism become the dominant ideology of the late 20th century?

2. In what sense can the American Empire be said to be a successor to the British Empire?

3. Do values and beliefs either create or arise out of material conditions?

4. Which model of stratification fits Canada best?

5. Is one state's invasion of another country for humanitarian purposes ever justified?

RECOMMENDED READINGS

Adams, Michael. 1998. *Sex in the Snow.* Toronto: Penguin.

Adams' book includes numerous survey results pointing to some startling and unexpected value differences between Canadians and Americans.

Clarkson, Stephen. 2008. *Does North America Exist?* Toronto: University of Toronto Press.

In this book, Clarkson examines the results of the NAFTA agreement, with specific focus on institutions of governance in the three signing countries.

Diamond, Jared. 2005. *Collapse: How Societies Choose to Fail or Succeed.* New York: Viking.

This very readable book presents a wealth of case studies on how human behaviour can result in ecological disasters that impact the survival of societies.

Grant, George. 1965. *Lament for a Nation.* Toronto: McClelland & Stewart.

Though often disputed, Grant's lament for Canada remains nearly a half-century on a keystone of philosophical discourse on Canada's relationship to the United States.

Stein, Janice Gross, and Eugene Lang. 2007. *The Unexpected War: Canada in Kandahar.* Toronto: Viking.

To date, this remains the best book detailing the process by which Canada became involved in the Afghanistan mission.

RELATED WEBSITES

Canadian Council of Chief Executives
http://www.ceocouncil.ca/
This organization is composed of the chief executive officers of roughly 150 major Canadian corporations. Founded in 1976 as the Business Council on National Issues, it was a chief proponent of free trade in 1988.

World Social Forum
http://www.wsfprocess.net/
This loose organization of non-governmental, non-partisan social movements from around the world meets every year in Brazil to discuss alternatives to neo-liberalism.

World Trade Organization
http://www.wto.org/
Founded in 1995, the WTO replaced the General Agreement on Tariffs and Trade, begun in 1947. Its mandate is to seek trade liberalization and regulation.

CANADIAN SOCIETY ON VIDEO

Tar Sands: The Selling of Alberta. 2008. Canadian Broadcasting Corporation, 60 minutes. A critical look at the social and environmental costs associated with the development of the Alberta tar sands.

View from the Summit. 2001. National Film Board of Canada, 75 minutes, 15 seconds. Examines the events surrounding the meeting of world leaders in Quebec City in April 2001 to discuss an agreement for a free trade area of the Americas and the popular groups that assembled to oppose to such an agreement.

PART THREE
CANADA AND THE ABORIGINAL NATIONS

It may seem a bit unorthodox to discuss Canada's First Nations at the end of this volume rather than at the beginning, particularly when historical development is usually perceived as chronological. Our argument, however, is that Aboriginal peoples not only should not be historicized, but that they constitute, if Canadians play fairly, the sector with the most promising future; indeed, Aboriginal peoples are a young and thriving cultural, political, and economic force.

In Part One, we examined Canada's French and English "solitudes." But Aboriginal and non-Aboriginal peoples in Canada constitute another pair of solitudes, separated by history, culture, class, and experience. This separation continues even though Aboriginals, especially in western Canada, are increasingly part of the urban landscape. Instead, state institutions such as the federal Department of Indian Affairs, children's service agencies, welfare agencies, and the courts often mediate this relationship, with the result that the knowledge that non-Aboriginals possess of Aboriginals is largely abstract or anecdotal, indeed stereotypical.

Part Three of this book explores relations between Aboriginal and non-Aboriginal peoples in Canada. As in the previous two sections, the first chapter of Part Three provides a historical overview. Chapter 11 then examines a part of Canada not yet discussed here in detail: the North, a place where Aboriginal peoples still predominate and yet one that is a prime source of Canadian identity. Chapter 12 examines the genesis of recent Aboriginal demands and growing militancy. Finally, Chapter 13 concludes with a portrait of Aboriginal peoples today in Canada, an examination of the major issues still to be resolved in this area, and a discussion of the profound impact that Aboriginals may have in shaping Canadian society in future.

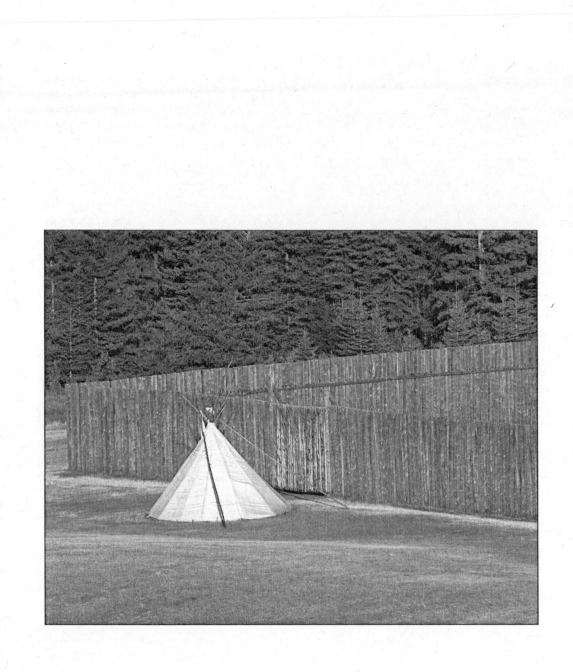

CHAPTER 10

WHEN CULTURAL WORLDS COLLIDE

We had a cross made thirty feet high, which was put together in the presence of a number of the Indians on the point at the entrance to this harbour, under the cross-bar of which we fixed a shield with three *fleurs-de-lys* in relief, and above it a wooden board, engraved in large Gothic characters, where was written, LONG LIVE THE KING OF FRANCE. We erected this cross on the point in their presence and they watched it being put together and set up.

—Jacques Cartier, *Diary*, 1534

But the face of the red man is now no longer seen. All traces of his footsteps are fast being obliterated from his once favourite haunts, and those who would see the aborigines of this country in their original state, or seek to study their native manners and customs, must travel far through the pathless forest to find them.

—artist Paul Kane, 1859

All men were made by the same Great Spirit Chief. They are all brothers. The earth is the mother of all people, and all people should have equal rights upon it.

—Chief Joseph, Nez Perce Nation, 1877

INTRODUCTION

On June 11, 2008, Prime Minister Stephen Harper issued a formal apology to the First Nations of Canada for the government's treatment of Aboriginal children in residential schools. Among other things Harper said, "The treatment of children in Indian residential schools is a sad chapter of our history. Some sought, as was infamously said, to 'kill the Indian in the child.' This policy was wrong, caused great harm, and has no place in our country."

Reactions to the prime minister's announcement varied greatly. Some Aboriginal leaders and interested observers demanded immediate concrete action—fearing more empty promises—to ameliorate social problems emanating from residential school experiences. Others were more positive, believing the apology was a good start toward creating better relations between Canada's Aboriginal peoples and other citizens.

Improving relations between Aboriginal and non-Aboriginal peoples is a huge task, however. The vast majority of non-Aboriginals have little knowledge of past history or of Aboriginal ways. As former Aboriginal leader, the late Harold Cardinal (1945–2005) put it, "We have been fighting for so long now that the original misunderstandings and differences [that] have created this conflict have been forgotten" (Cardinal, 1977: 7). Moreover, unlike other minority groups, of whom Canada's dominant cultures also have little understanding, Canada's First Nations face a range of challenges, including economic underdevelopment, substandard education, often deplorable social conditions, and public misunderstanding, prejudice, and racism.

How did we, Aboriginal and non-Aboriginal peoples alike, get to where we are? And how will we get to the future? In order to understand, we have to retrace our steps. This chapter examines the cultural world of Canada's Aboriginal peoples before and after the arrival of Europeans, including the political economy of the two peoples' early relations. The discussion examines how the dominant-subordinate relationship between the non-Aboriginal and Aboriginal peoples became institutionalized, with consequences for both parties and for Canadian society as a whole.

PRE-CONTACT ABORIGINAL SOCIETIES

Archaeologists inform us that the Aboriginal peoples of North America have been on this continent for 10,000–12,000 years, but the truth is that no one really knows when the first Aboriginal peoples arrived. Some evidence points to an arrival as long as 30,000–50,000 years ago (Dickason, 2002: 6).

For decades, the prevailing theory was that they arrived in North America thousands of years ago via an ice bridge that temporarily linked Asia to this continent. The Bering Strait theory may explain some migrations, but this theory is now seriously questioned. Today, evidence suggests the first immigrants may have arrived by various routes, by boat or raft, across both major oceans.

Initial encounters between the Europeans and indigenous North Americans were limited to the south and central regions of the continent. Northern contact occurred much later. The first Europeans who arrived often failed to make distinctions between resident tribes, but in fact the people they encountered represented a variety of different civilizations and cultures.

In what is today Canada, six distinct cultural areas may be identified among the Aboriginal peoples. These include the Northwest Coast, the North, the Plateau, the Plains, the Mackenzie District, and the Eastern Woodlands. Authorities differ regarding the linguistic varieties, but today three language groups comprise most Aboriginal language families (Wilson and Urion, 1995: 32). The first of the three major linguistic groups is Algonquian, which includes most Canadian Aboriginals and the vast majority in southern Canada east of the Rockies. Two Algonquian groups, Cree and Ojibway, are closely related, implying recent separation. The Blackfoot also appear to be distantly related.

The second major language family in Canada is Athapaskan, with the majority of speakers occupying much of northwestern Canada and Alaska. Because of the limited diversity among this language group, linguists believe this area was more recently occupied.

The third language family is Eskimo-Aleut, represented in Canada by Inupik (Inuktitut), which is identified only in the northern regions from northern Alaska across to eastern Greenland. Apart from any archaeological evidence, this seems to imply that the region has only recently been occupied (see Chapter 11).

Addicted as we are to the magic of the technological age, it is sometimes hard to realize the dramatic cultural changes that have occurred these last several centuries in Canada. The impact on Aboriginal cultures has been considerable, and while many First Nations have successfully adjusted to elements of the technological revolution, others are still determining how they can best participate in this transition.

Cultures may differ materially and non-materially (through their particular languages, values, beliefs, norms, and behaviours) in ways passed on from one generation to the next. From a functionalist perspective, however, all cultures, Aboriginal or other, possess certain elements (Durkheim, 1978; Wissler, 1923). These elements include: (1) language; (2) artifacts (that is, physical objects) that serve functional purposes; (3) social organization; (4) authority and decision-making arrangements; (5) underlying spiritual or religious beliefs and structures; (6) forms of welfare arrangements whereby the aged, the sick, and the young are taken care of; (7) arts and music; (8) forms of property ownership or usage; and (9) a means of educating the young to assure perpetuation of the system.

Pre-contact Aboriginal lifestyles represented a very present-oriented way of life. They enjoyed day-to-day living and took time for leisure activities. Unlike their 21st-century counterparts, Canada's First Nations were never in a hurry to get somewhere else; they were already where they needed to be. They did not have the luxury of placing things in a freezer to save for another day, though they had ways of preserving some foods. Nor did they make use of such future-oriented facilities as savings accounts, pension plans, or registered retirement savings plans; they relied instead on each other and the environment around them. Primary to all considerations was their relationship to nature, the elements— sun, earth, water, wind, fire—and the cycle of natural growth and change.

The Aboriginals' awe of nature did not hinder them from developing elaborate metaphysical belief systems or developing complex forms of food gathering, food preparation, art, and weaponry. Often these cultural elements were related. Food gathering and religion, for example, were highly related activities in nearly all pre-technological societies, but they were still able to live a satisfying way of life. As the late Chief Walking Buffalo (Tatanga Mani) of the Stoney (Nakoda Sioux) Nation put it:

> We were on pretty good terms with the Great Spirit and Ruler of all.... We saw the Great Spirit's work in almost everything: sun, moon, trees, wind and mountains. Sometimes we approached Him through these things. Was that so bad? Indians living close to nature and nature's Ruler are not living in darkness. (Friesen, 1998: 30)

The primary unit of traditional social structure among Aboriginal peoples was the band, often considered a subunit of a tribe (now called a "First Nation"). The chiefs who headed the bands often possessed valuable talents, with varying gifts for leadership in hunting or war, or in other contexts. Chiefs were mentors or servants of the people rather than managers or rulers (Snow, 1977). Real authority within the bands or tribe, however, might reside with the elders, individuals perceived as having wisdom or medicinal knowledge gathered through years of living (Meili, 1991). This diffuse power structure confused the Europeans, who were used to rigid and hierarchical authority structures.

Bands were often formed on the basis of numbers; if a band got too large to set up or shut down camp easily, the people might divide into two subunits. Hunting and gathering bands tended to be small. By contrast, bands engaging in horticulture could accommodate larger populations. Other factors—disagreements or the emergence of a charismatic leader with a following—could also lead to the division of a band. The nomadic bands of western Canada would sometimes meet during the summer months to renew acquaintances, socialize, or celebrate the sun dance.

The Aboriginal peoples of the West Coast and Eastern Woodlands developed elaborate clan systems of social organization. The clans were exogamous and bore animal names such as "Bear" or "Turtle." They were subdivided on a matrilineal basis, and clan mothers were guardians of clan traditions and sacred practices. Clan mothers alone had the right to select and depose chiefs and councils, and had primary authority in such matters as land allotment, supervision of field labour, care of the treasury, the ordering of feasts, and dispute settlement (Johnston, 1964). Chieftainships were not primarily hereditary along patrilineal lines, so a man might pass on his office to his sister's son, the latter not being a member of his clan (Trigger, 1969).

FIRST CONTACT

Beginning in the 15th century, a series of European visitors reached North America. They represented a host of states and nationalities, including Spain, Portugal, England, and France. They arrived not prepared to meet a people whose way of life featured an entirely different view of social organization and government, grounded in an allegiance to high spiritual powers centred in the universe. The Europeans ignored these differences. Armed with a strong sense of **ethnocentrism**, *the tendency of people to see the world only from their own cultural perspective*, they "boldly went where no man [*sic*] had gone before."

Cartier and Champlain were the most important of these Europeans in early Canadian history because of their role in fostering further explorations of the New World. When Cartier returned to France with descriptions of the new land and its inhabitants, the whole of France attended him with extraordinary interest. As proof of his feats, Cartier even kidnapped two young Aboriginals, the sons of Iroquois Chief Donnacona, and brought them back to France with him. Later he returned and endured a most severe winter, but thanks in large part to assistance from the Iroquois, he managed to survive an onslaught of scurvy. This experience could have dampened the enthusiasm Cartier displayed in his first evaluation of the potential of the new country, but explorations continued. Champlain, following Cartier's lead, made friends with the Iroquois and established colonies in Acadia and New France (Chapter 2).

Nearly a century later, in 1610, the English built their first colony in the New World, in Newfoundland. Further settlements followed along the eastern coast and along the St. Lawrence, heightening contact, competition, and conflict between the French and English and their Aboriginal allies.

In Newfoundland, the Europeans (mainly English, Portuguese, and French) encountered the Beothuk. The Beothuk's practice of colouring everything in red ochre—clothing, belongings, weapons,

burial goods, and so on—resulted in the phrase "Red Indian" (Friesen, 1997: 49). There was intense conflict between the two cultures and in the early 19th century, the last Beothuks disappeared, though there is disagreement whether this resulted from intentional **genocide**, *an organized attempt by one society to eradicate another society or subgroup, often, but not always, violently* (see Dickason, 1984; Cook, 1995).

Yet, not all contacts were negative. By contrast, for example, European contact with the Mi'kmaq (Micmac), a neighbouring tribe of the Beothuk, by all accounts was mutually beneficial. The invaders were quite impressed with the Mi'kmaq way of life, particularly their well-built wigwams, their methods of procuring food from both the land and the sea, and their socio-political structures.

Moreover, it was not immediately obvious that contacts between Aboriginal peoples and the Europeans, beginning in the late 15th century, would prove disastrous to the former (Cook, 1995: 22). Aboriginal peoples were central to the fur trade (see below) and also instrumental politically and militarily during both the European wars for dominance of the fur trade in North America and post-revolutionary America's attempt to take over Canada. However, Cook (1995: 22) remarks, "the long-term advantages ... lay with the Europeans: a growing economy, an increasingly complex technology, an expanding population, and a centralized political system supported by military power." The rise and fall of Aboriginal power in relation to the Europeans centred on the fur trade.

THE FUR TRADE

Early 20th-century writings portrayed Aboriginal peoples as victims of the fur trade, but more recent writings provide a more complex view. Cook (1995: 28) stresses three points concerning the fur trade. First, trade among Aboriginals in North America preceded the coming of the Europeans and was occasionally accompanied by conflict. The arrival of the Europeans only intensified the level of both. Second, insofar as eastern and coastal tribes had more immediate contact with Europeans than did the more western and inland tribes, the latter were able to preserve their cultures and base of power for a longer period. Third, Aboriginal peoples were not passive participants in the fur trade, but willing and motivated, and in the early period frequently did very well in bargaining. Not only did local Aboriginals quickly learn to demand better quality in the goods they were purchasing, but they became quite discriminating about the quantity of goods offered to them. Experience was a good teacher.

The beaver was central to the fur trade. Beaver pelts could be "felted" and used for making what became the treasured beaver pelt hat. The popularity of this unique item persisted in the 17th and 18th centuries, and became a badge of social status (Innis, 1962). Everyone in Europe with pretensions to "respectability" wanted a beaver hat, and when the hats began to age, they were refurbished and shipped to South America to grace less particular heads. As Lower (1977: 99) puts it:

> So close was the relationship between the fur trade and the beaver hat that when early in the eighteenth century fashion in Europe decreed that brims should be a little narrower, a crisis ensued in the backwoods of Canada.

When the first Europeans settled along the eastern coast of North America, the First Nations brought them furs in exchange for European goods. Almost immediately, some Aboriginal peoples became intermediary traders between their counterparts further inland and the newcomers. Very soon, this established pattern had to be altered as the heavy European demand for furs resulted in a scarcity of pelts that drove the fur traders further inland. As Innis (1962) later observed, the search for staples—in this case, furs—led to Canada's economic development.

The Europeans quickly learned the value of Aboriginal peoples and their culture in procuring the desired furs. Aboriginal peoples not only trapped and transported the pelts, but, more importantly, knew how to survive in the New World. They knew the habits of the sought-after animals, which plants were suitable as food and medicine, and the best routes to take (Cook, 1995: 27–28). Aboriginal women, in particular, also proved adept as translators and trade negotiators, not to mention valued companions to the European traders (van Kirk, 1999; Saul, 2008). For these reasons, it was to the advantage of Europeans in Canada, unlike the Spanish invaders to the far south, to develop harmonious relations with the Aboriginal peoples (Conrad et al., 1993).

The fur trade gradually carried dangerous consequences for the Aboriginal peoples. Little did the First Nations realize that the enterprise was soon to heap devastating consequences on their traditional way of life through institutional restructuring, deadly diseases, revisionist philosophies, and severe changes to their economic circumstances.

Intensified conflict, both with Europeans and with each other, was one obvious consequence. The introduction of guns raised conflict to new levels and changed the balance of power between Aboriginal nations. No less lethal were the recurrent epidemics unleashed by the Europeans. In 1634, smallpox or measles killed large numbers of Montagnais and Algonquians. Similarly, between 1636 and 1639, a series of epidemics reduced the Huron population from 25,000 to around 10,000 (Dickinson and Young,

2003: 20). In the main, the devastation experienced by Aboriginal peoples from epidemics was unintentional, with a single, notable exception: During the Seven Years War (1756–1763), General Amherst (1717–1797) appears to have been the first person to utilize germ warfare when he ordered blankets contaminated by smallpox to be distributed among France's Aboriginal allies.

Liquor was another danger. Motivated by economic desires, the fur traders did whatever it took to obtain furs. Various items were traded or even given as gifts, but liquor was easily the most damaging. The English traded rum, while the French relied on brandy. Not familiar with either commodity, the Aboriginals did not differentiate between the liquids, which made the traders quite happy, particularly since the two were equally effective as trade items. The long-term effects of the dispersal of liquor led to alcoholism which eventually destroyed the structure of tribal life.

As the fur trade flourished, European traders used the arrangement to enhance the status of tribal leaders in the eyes of their people and to reward them for their efforts on behalf of the trading companies (Ray, 1974). If a band later failed to obtain a sufficient quantity of furs or provisions to pay off its debts, the leader was denied the symbols of office. If, on the other hand, the crop was ample or abundant, Aboriginal leaders were paid in more generous terms.

In the latter years of the 16th century, France attempted to form a monopoly on trade. The attempt failed. Over the next two centuries, France and England repeatedly went to war, ending with the former's final defeated in 1763 (Chapter 2).

THE ROYAL PROCLAMATION

The end of war saw the British government pass the Royal Proclamation of 1763. Fully one-third of the Royal Proclamation was devoted to matters pertaining to First Nations (Johnston, 1989) and remains the founding document for all written negotiations between First Nations and the federal government of Canada. Some critics argue that the Royal Proclamation was intended to dispossess First Nations of both their sovereignty as well as their lands. According to Boldt (1993: 3), the document was based on the "self-serving, villainous doctrine which held that, by right of 'first discovery' a Christian nation was Divinely mandated to exercise dominion over conquered 'non-Christian primitives.'"

The Royal Proclamation decreed that Aboriginals would be allowed to live unmolested on their traditional lands at the Crown's pleasure, the British government thus being established as protector of those lands that "have not been ceded or purchased by us." Boldt (1993: 4) states the Royal Proclamation set forth five important principles. First, the Crown legally held title to all Aboriginal lands. Second, the Crown allowed Aboriginal peoples **usufructuary rights** (that is, rights of possession) to their traditional lands. Third, possession of these lands could be surrendered only to the Crown; thus, incoming settlers could take over Aboriginal lands and use them for their own purposes only after these legal rights had been surrendered by formal agreements such as treaties with the Crown (and, by later extension, the federal government of Canada). Fourth, the Crown could extinguish Aboriginal rights of possession at its discretion, subject to reasonable compensation. And fifth, selected lands described as reserves would be set aside for Aboriginal domicile (on these points, see also Angus, 1991: 67). None of these conditions included the entrenchment of Aboriginal rights as a principle of justice for First Nations, as we will later note.

Yet, before leaving the Royal Proclamation, it should be noted that Aboriginal peoples do not view the document as entirely negative. Some view the Royal Proclamation as also protecting their legal rights. A document prepared by the

Union of Ontario Indians (UOI) in 1970 reads, in part:

> As Indian people we will always see our special Status and our legal rights as flowing from the original sovereignty of our nations. The colonial legal system to a large extent denied that sovereignty, but they never denied the existence of rights based on the aboriginal possession of tribal territories. It was the unauthorized violation of these rights that led to the unrest which [sic] promoted the Royal Proclamation. (quoted in Plain, 1988)

In short, the UOI views the Royal Proclamation, the first constitutional document for British North America, as recognizing the existence of Aboriginal peoples' rights and establishing legal procedures for the surrender of land (Plain, 1988: 31). Likewise, the Penner Commission, formed in 1983 to study Aboriginal self-government, argued that the subsequent writing of treaties was based on the principles of the Royal Proclamation of 1763 (Russell, 2000: 7), but that the treaties in practice did everything the Royal Proclamation said not to do (Krotz, 1990: 166).

The Royal Proclamation is legal; whether its interpretation and application have always been just is another question. As the UOI document notes further, many lands in Canada were never ceded or purchased by the colonial power. Today, as new treaties are being signed, will the procedures established by the Royal Proclamation be applied for the ceding of Aboriginal lands? In Chapter 13, we will examine the making of new treaties.

DECLINE, RESPONSE, AND THE BIRTH OF THE MÉTIS

The end of war and France's defeat did not immediately change the contours of the fur trade, and so did not immediately impact the economic basis of Aboriginal existence. The French merchants were soon replaced in Montreal by a new organization of American and British merchants and French-Canadian voyageurs. The North West Company, as it was called, challenged the Hudson's Bay Company for supremacy in the fur trade, especially in the West.

Nonetheless, the fur trade was in trouble. By the early 19th century, overharvesting, changes in European fashion, and the impact of settlement upon habitat were taking their toll (Innis, 1962). After a long and sometimes bloody struggle (including the battle of Seven Oaks in 1816) to gain control of the fur trade, the Hudson's Bay Company and the North West Company merged in 1821. The merger ended the bitter rivalry between the two companies, but did not end the fur trade's decline. Thus, the company's new governor, George (later Sir George) Simpson (1792–1860) made several policy changes. To increase profits, he ordered that cheaper goods be traded for furs, reduced the use of alcohol as a trade item, and forbade the use of steel traps. He also tried to dissuade Aboriginals from trapping endangered species and taking furs out of season. This augured poorly with the Aboriginal trappers, whose way of life now revolved around the fur economy, and who reasonably insisted they had no choice but to keep on trapping in areas where food was in short supply.

Unaccustomed to long-range planning, the Cree and Ojibway's attitudes toward conservation, territoriality, and trespassing were particularly negative. Simpson fought back, requesting that the British government place the First Nations on permanent, well-defined territories as a means of better implementing his policies. In time, Simpson took even more extreme measures by closing redundant trading posts. By the middle of the 19th century the fur trade labour force was cut back by as much as two-thirds (Ray, 1974: 205).

The Simpson incident is reminiscent of previous Aboriginal expressions of opposition to European actions. Aboriginal bitterness over land-grabbing had been growing since 1760, when Pontiac (1720–1769), an Ottawa chief, organized a pan-Aboriginal confederacy to oppose British policy ("Pontiac's Rebellion," as White historians named it) (Francis et al., 1988: 166). In 1811, Shawnee Chief Tecumseh (1768–1813) led an Aboriginal confederacy of some 30 nations on a series of raids to challenge the cessions of territory, particularly those in Indiana. The raids helped pave the outbreak of the War of 1812 (Chapter 6).

In western Canada, Aboriginal resistance arose on another front. One of the unexpected results of the cultural clash between European fur traders and First Nations was the birth of the Métis people. Among the Europeans, the French proved the most inclined to merge culturally and biologically with the Aboriginals. Traditionally, intermarriage between French settlers and Aboriginal wives has been attributed to a shortage of women in New France and the value of securing interests in the fur trade. More recently, however, Saul (2008: 3) has argued that "By marrying into the indigenous world, most of the newcomers were marrying up. They were improving their situations socially, politically, and economically." And though Dickason (1984: 147) suggests that "Amerindians and French were still distinct entities at the end of the French Regime in 1760," Saul (2008: 2) contends that "Anyone whose family arrived before the 1760s is probably part Aboriginal."

Children of these unions were commonly called "half-breeds" or Métis, meaning "mixed." Eventually, there were enough Métis people to be identified as a separate cultural group. Morton (1970: 46) has described the Métis as hunters, trappers, fishermen, voyageurs, horsemen, and farmers, but, above all, soldiers. Between 1820 and 1869, the Métis settlement at Red River in what became Manitoba was one of the most populated settlements in the West (Sprague, 1988: ix). The Métis represented the chief labour force of the western fur trade and were hit particularly hard by that trade's demise.

The Métis resented previous British indifference to their fate and worried that Canada's politicians would do no better. To protect themselves, the charismatic Métis leader Louis Riel and his colleagues set up a provisional government and took control of the Red River region. Riel today remains a controversial figure. Was he a traitor or a hero? Was he insane or not (Flanagan, 1977; Braz, 2003)? Was he tried fairly, or was he railroaded (Thomas, 1977)?

In the end, this first act of Aboriginal resistance in western Canada ended more or less peacefully with Manitoba's entry into Confederation (1870), though Riel was forced to flee to the United States. The second act played out 15 years later at Batoche (near Prince Albert), with Riel and his followers—Métis and Aboriginal peoples together—defeated, and Riel tried and hung.

Métis resistance has often been portrayed in derogatory terms such as rebellion, insurrection, or defiance, but a strong argument can be made that the Métis were simply defending their native lands. Moreover, the Métis have a unique place in Canadian history, being the only charter group in the country with a history of national political independence before joining Confederation. Under Riel's leadership, the Métis formulated the charter of the Province of Manitoba (Friesen and Friesen, 2004).

Despite these accomplishments, it was only in 1972 that the Canadian federal government acknowledged the Métis as a separate national entity. Since then they have worked hard to attain additional historical and cultural recognition through political action. This was partially achieved in 2003 when the Supreme Court of Canada announced that the Métis were to be regarded as an Aboriginal people. The implications of this status are yet to be determined.

CONFEDERATION AND THE NUMBERED TREATIES

The conflict in Red River and Manitoba's entry into Confederation were only the beginning of Canadian expansion, an expansion that necessarily involved the signing of treaties in the western provinces. By 1870, treaty making in Canada was already well established, the First Nations of Canada having often engaged in friendship treaties and treaties concerning territorial and hunting rights with neighbouring bands prior to European contact, and even treaties with Europeans on a nation-to-nation basis going back more than two centuries (Warry, 1998: 19).

Still, the form and intent of these treaties had changed over time. The first treaties between Aboriginals and Europeans were conducted on the stated basis of "friendship and peace." After that, the treaties focused primarily on land (Dickason, 2006: 103). The later pre-Confederation treaties carried out in the Maritimes generally dealt with military and political arrangements involving land transfers, annuities, or compensation for rights that were given up (Frideres and Gadacz, 2001: 169). By contrast, the post-Confederation treaties, conducted in the West, dealt explicitly with the transfer of land from Aboriginal peoples to the Canadian government. (The BNA Act of 1867 makes reference to Aboriginal rights as follows: Section 91[24] gives the federal government exclusive jurisdiction to make laws in relation to Aboriginal tenure and rights in lands reserved for Aboriginals. No constitutional authority exists for provincial jurisdictions to make laws concerning lands reserved for Aboriginals.)

The opening up of the West for agricultural settlement meant the displacement of the Aboriginal peoples of the region. In counterpoise to the American experience, where a century of warfare and forced internment cleared the way for settlement, Canada (with the notable exception of 1885) resorted to signing what are known as the "numbered treaties".

Treaty no. 1, signed in 1871, involved the Ojibway (Saulteaux) people on the Peguis Reserve, a tribe of Swampy Cree, and others in southern Manitoba (see Box 10.1). Treaty no. 1 is called the Stone Fort Treaty because negotiations took place at Lower Fort Garry, which was built of stone. This began the process by which the government hoped to justify the formation of the Province of Manitoba as a place for incoming non-Aboriginal settlers to reside (Dickason, 2006: 175–176).

Box 10.1

Provisions of Treaty no. 1, Signed with the Peguis (Ojibway) First Nation in 1871

1. the relinquishment of the Indian right and title to specified lands

2. certain hunting privileges

3. annual payments of $5 as compensation to every Indian person involved in these dealings (head chiefs and councillors each received $25 and $15 respectively, as well as a suit of clothes, a British flag, and silver medals)

4. certain lands allocated as "Indian reserves" amounting to 160 acres per family

5. agricultural implements, oxen, and cattle to form the nuclei of herds were offered on a one time basis to the tribes

6. provision for the establishment of schools for the instruction of Indian children

---

By 1877, six more treaties had been signed; by 1899, three more were signed; an 11th treaty was signed in the Northwest Territories in 1921. These latter treaties were not like earlier ones, however. Whereas previous treaties implied an agreement between equals, the numbered treaties imposed the will of the new colonial government. Thus, Aboriginals were enjoined to divide themselves into bands and elect chiefs and councillors to govern themselves. Likewise, Status Indians who wanted to have a vote in Canada or even leave a reserve and go to a bar would have to disavow their "Indian-ness." It is not an exaggeration to suggest that these treaties determined virtually every aspect of Aboriginal peoples' everyday lives.

Two specific factors appear to have determined the approach of Canadian government officials to treaty making. First, the government wanted to set aside specific areas for European settlement; by contrast, as Chief John Snow (2005: 62–63) points out, the land set aside for Indian reserves was very poor and unsuitable for farming. Second, establishing reserves constituted a convenient way for governments to manage Indian affairs since the nomadic First Nations would be settled on relatively small pieces of land (Melling, 1967: 37).

The terms offered in these numbered treaties were generally similar. These terms included surrender of Aboriginal rights and title to traditional lands, and the creation of reserves not to exceed one square mile (1.6 square kilometres) per family of five. The government also agreed to provide a measure of military protection, a small per capita annuity, instruction in the basics of farming, and some form of education (Buckley, 1993: 34). The location of each reserve was determined after consultation with First Nations by someone sent by the chief superintendent of the Indian Affairs Branch (IAB) of the Department of Indian Affairs and Northern Development. Other terms included a ban on intoxicating beverages, a guarantee of hunting and fishing rights, the provision of a school, and the annual award of a few dollars per individual. In Treaty no. 6, for example, the amount was $12 per year. In addition, the government would make provisions of implements, twine, and farm animals so that the reserve residents could take up agriculture.

Some chiefs objected to the amounts of land prescribed for them and voiced their objections. The chiefs rejected the terms of Treaty no. 6 three times before signing it, and the negotiations ended with a fourfold increase in assigned lands, as well as a "medicine chest."

These treaties remain a point of conflict today. In part, this is because the meanings of words are unstable (as post-structuralists would observe). Many elders did not view signing a treaty as meaning the giving up of land, but rather an agreement to share land for the benefit of both sides. Evidence suggests also that some of the treaties were formulated by government agents and simply presented to Aboriginals who did not know what they were signing, and that hard-won oral promises gained by Aboriginals in many cases during treaty signing were also never recognized or honoured by government (Frideres and Gadacz, 2001: 173). Finally, Aboriginal activist and Métis leader Howard Adams (1921–2001) further suggested the treaties are worthless because they primarily furthered the process of colonization (Adams, 1989).

It should also be noted that this view of the treaties is not universally held. Some academics argue that, far from being weak or passive victims of the process, the Aboriginal leaders made the best of an admittedly difficult situation. Friesen (1986), for example, points out that some Aboriginal leaders discussed the terms of the agreements handed to them and, when necessary, manoeuvred, stalled, appeased, and compared offers to get the best deal. Finally, as flawed in content and application as they might be, the treaties in the eyes of some Aboriginal leaders represent a binding contract, in the words of former president of the Indian Association of Alberta, Harold Cardinal (1969), an Aboriginal "Magna Carta" because they were entered into with faith and hope for a better life with honour. In a speech two months before the First Ministers' meeting held in Ottawa on March 15 and 16, 1983, Chief John Snow (quoted in Snow, 1988: 42) stated:

> The Indian treaties with the Crown are real, and we must see to it that the terms of those treaties and related documents are fully included with the new constitution. Without our treaties we would be in the same unfortunate situation as the non-Status and non-treaty Indians. I remind all treaty and registered Indians that the treaties are sacred covenants; they are binding documents and they must not be altered unilaterally by the Government of Canada.

FROM HUNTING AND GATHERING TO AGRICULTURE

As the conditions brought about by the treaties gradually became reality, the Aboriginal peoples were informed that they would soon become sedentary farmers instead of nomadic hunters. Father Albert Lacombe, missionary to the Blackfoot, urged Chief Crowfoot (1830–1890) to lead his people to a way of life that would eventually provide them with a new kind of prosperity. Chief Starblanket (1816–1896), of Saskatchewan, optimistically stated: " we Indians can learn the ways of living that made the white man strong" (Buckley, 1993: 34).

A decade after the first treaty signing, Aboriginal peoples on the Prairies were increasingly motivated to adopt an agriculture mode of economy with the demise of the "supermarket of the plains," as the buffalo has been called. Many Aboriginal leaders could not fathom what was happening to their way of life. Competition among First Nations for the remaining bison grew. Many former warriors resisted

the idea of digging in the ground with a stick. Others grasped at spiritual straws, some believing their religious leaders when they spoke of the Great Spirit's anger with humankind for replacing hunting with ploughing, while some prophets also predicted the eventual return of the animal, perhaps in some other form. (A few years ago, a spokesman for the Smallboy band of Cree in Alberta declared that the buffalo were now coming back out of the ground in the form of oil and gas.)

These incidents aside, how enthusiastic were Aboriginal farmers in the West toward the idea of taking up an agrarian lifestyle? In 1936 historian G.F.G. Stanley (1975) fostered the view, later promoted by Hanks and Hanks (1950) in their study of the Blackfoot Reserve in Alberta, that Aboriginal warriors and hunters looked upon farming with disdain. According to this view, most Aboriginal peoples shunned the concepts of steady work and acquisitiveness promoted by the dominant Euro-Canadian society, though some chiefs changed their minds about farming when they saw the rewards that could be theirs—axes, blankets, and beads.

Carter (1993: 9–10) argues that the view promoted by Stanley and others is based on a dualism theory that recognizes two distinct and largely independent thinking patterns, modern and traditional. In this view, the modern perspective is characterized by high productivity and a market orientation, and is quite receptive to change. It pursues rational and maximizing aims. By contrast, the more traditional (Aboriginal) perspective is regarded as pre-capitalist, subsistence-oriented, primitive, and small-scale. It is depicted as resistant to change and affected by incentives quite different from the modern model. Instead of saving or building for the future, the traditional perspective emphasizes an orientation to the present rather than the future.

Carter (1993) argues against such an essentialist view of European and

Aboriginal perspectives. Europeans have consistently regarded First Nations as adherents to traditional ways of thinking and thus presumably opposed to taking up farming, but Carter notes that East Coast Aboriginals were long involved in horticulture and agriculture; for example, Woodland First Nations were already solidly entrenched in agriculture (growing corn, beans, and squash) when the first Europeans arrived. Similarly, the Iroquois received acceptable land grants on the Grand River in Upper Canada, and met with success in farming comparable to that of their Euro-Canadian neighbours.

Though intentionally hindered by government actions (Carter, 1993), Aboriginal farmers in western Canada also met with success. Carter cites studies by Tobias (1977) and Carlson (1981) as proof that many Plains First Nations in the West were actually quite anxious to take up farming. The Cree people, for example, adopted farming, and much of the political activity of their leaders was taken up with a concern about the lack of promised assistance rendered to them in that regard. Likewise, the Dakota of Manitoba initially showed great enthusiasm about farming until environmental setbacks and government restrictions brought about a period of stagnation (Laviolette, 1991).

The Dakota have continued to thrive as agriculturalists but, since they are relatively recent arrivals from the United States, some authorities have always considered them outsiders. Today the federal Conservative government is attempting to buy out Dakota treaty rights and terminate federal government provisions for Dakota health, education, and welfare. The government insists that technically, the Dakota are immigrants from the United States. While they are considered Status Indians, they do not have a treaty and are entitled to only half the reserve land that treaty nations get. Naturally, the Dakota are resisting the move (Couture, 2008).

COLONIALISM

With the collapse of the fur trade, its replacement by an agricultural and industrial economy, and the easing of tensions with the Americans, in 1830 the British government transferred management of Aboriginal affairs in Canada from military to civil authority. Canada's Aboriginal peoples, lacking an economic base for continued political control of their lives, experienced an abrupt change as civil authorities now sought to "take care of" (i.e., dominate) them.

Until Confederation, protection of First Nations and their lands was the paramount goal. The notion that Aboriginals needed to become civilized gained in importance, but assimilation was regarded as a gradual and long-term process. In 1869, the goals of civilization and assimilation were officially added to government objectives with the passing of the Act for the Gradual Enfranchisement of Indians (Tobias, 1983: 43). Thereafter, Aboriginal peoples were denied any of the original or residual political power recognized in the Royal Proclamation's treaty process. Colonial interests simply dictated that plenary power would be centralized in the Constitution (Schouls, 2003: 41). What is colonialism?

Colonialism is *a complex national system of racial, cultural, and political domination that produces privileges beyond the surplus value generated by capitalism* (Adams, 1999: 7). As a process, colonialism shapes the culture and life of both the colonizer and the colonized, with the important difference, of course, that the former assumes a superior position and assigns the latter an inferior status. Frideres and Gadacz (2001: 4–7) delineate the process of colonization in terms of seven characteristics.

The first characteristic is a colonizing group's invasion of a geographic territory occupied by an indigenous group. The second characteristic is a campaign of deliberate destruction of the indigenous group's social and cultural structures. In Canada, formal programs to carry out destructive policies were enacted between 1830 and 1875 (Surtees, 1969), particularly involving religious denominations and the provision of education designed to assimilate the Aboriginal peoples to European values and norms (see below).

The third and fourth characteristics of colonialism are the interrelated processes of exerting external control while encouraging economic dependency among the conquered people. Typically, the invading nation sends out tetrarchs to run things in the newly acquired territory, rather than assigning such responsibilities to leaders of the colonized peoples. In Canada the federally appointed "Indian agent" filled this role, often admirably, but frequently became a most despised foreign despot among the Aboriginals whose lives he made miserable (Halliday, 1935). Nearly every activity on a reserve had to be approved by the Indian agent, including requests for seed, farm implements or livestock, or even to ask permission to leave the reserve on a temporary basis.

The fifth characteristic of colonialism is the provision of low-quality social services, including health, education, and welfare. This characteristic continues to be manifested in First Nations communities in a host of statistics showing reduced life expectancy, high mortality rates, poverty, inadequate education, high incidence of infectious diseases such as tuberculosis, poor housing, and heavy reliance on social assistance, not to mention alcohol and substance abuse, suicide, physical assaults, child abuse, and family breakup.

The last two characteristics of colonialism are the practice of racism (see Chapter 7) and the establishment of a "colour line." Analytically, racism may be defined as the perspective that tends to stress the real or alleged features of race and supports the use of them as grounds for group and intergroup action (Fairchild,

1967: 246). In practice, this means that some people simply believe one racial category is innately superior or inferior to another. If the practice of **endogamy** (*marriage within one's own group*) is any indication, the enforcement of a colour line has certainly worked in Canada; Aboriginal peoples have the highest rate of marriage within their own ranks— almost 94 percent (Frideres and Gadacz, 2001: 7).

Colonialism continues today, though it is more subtle—what some observers suggest is a form of **internal colonialism**, *the process of continuing settler control and domination of Aboriginal peoples*. Ponting (1986: 86) points to several indicators of internal colonialism: (1) manipulation of information as a form of social control; (2) excessive secrecy or overburdening band members with information; (3) obstructionism versus facilitation in so far as getting information is concerned; (4) manipulation of discretionary funds; (5) withholding of funds; and (6) other means of socio-fiscal control.

Adams (1999) similarly insists that colonialism is alive and well, but argues it is often fostered by Aboriginal organizations themselves. He alleges that leaders in these organizations often manipulate government grants to benefit themselves and not band members. In turn, this arrangement works well for government: By using reactionary Aboriginal regimes, governments can hide their own colonial policies, while crushing Aboriginal efforts toward self-sufficiency by dispersing and disorganizing the population.

Echoing Adams's concerns, Boldt (1993) cautions Aboriginal peoples to carefully monitor their own leaders if they are to attain justice, arguing that their leaders "often manifest the same degree of paternalism, authoritarianism, self-interest and self-aggrandizement in their leadership as their non-Native counterparts" (Boldt, 1993: 141). A corollary to this concern is the matter of accountability. Flanagan

(2000: 197) argues that Aboriginal leaders will never be held accountable by their people as long as the money they spend comes from the public treasury. Therefore, a new definition of Indian self-government is needed. Self-government, however, requires some degree of economic self-sufficiency, something that reserves, where many Aboriginals still reside, were not set up to provide.

THE RESERVE SYSTEM

Indian reserves in Canada were first established following negotiation of the treaties in the late 19th century between representatives of Queen Victoria and the various Aboriginal chiefs. Wuttunee (1971: 111) argues that reserves were designed to take Aboriginal peoples away from their natural habitat and segregate them on small parcels of land so that the surrounding areas would be safe for incoming settlers. Melling (1967: 37f) supports this argument, noting, for example, that no reserves were created in areas where settlers did not migrate, such as the Yukon, Labrador, or the Northwest Territories. It also could be argued that reserves were at least partially designed for the administrative convenience of government. It was a lot easier to deal with Aboriginal "problems" if they were all located on a specific plot of land rather than trying to minister to the needs of a group of nomadic wanderers.

Whatever the underlying reasons, it is clear that much of the land reserved for Aboriginals was unsuitable for farming, the new mode of Prairie economy. Thus, the period after the treaty signings saw Canada prosper under the National Policy (see Chapter 7), while Aboriginal peoples languished. The reserve inhabitants suffered quietly from malnutrition and disease in primeval silence, often far from the hurly-burly of mainstream Canadian life and thus unseen, in semi-permanent havens from the modern world.

Until the 1960s, there was practically no economic development on Aboriginal reserves. Were it not for government transfer payments such as relief family allowance, youth allowances, blind and disabled people's allowances, and old age assistance, few Aboriginal peoples would have survived, though it can be cogently argued that the money provided was insufficient to launch them out of dependency. In 1959, the average income of Aboriginals in Saskatchewan was $200 per year. That same year, the average Saskatchewan citizen was making $1,245. In monetary terms, Aboriginal peoples were making only one-sixth the income of their non-Aboriginal counterparts.

There were exceptions. There are regional differences in the circumstances of Aboriginal peoples. In contrast to their western counterparts, the Algonqian and Iroquois nations did quite well. In farming, as already noted, Aboriginals in eastern Canada, when given the opportunity, did quite well. The same was the case in other areas of economic life. For example, Aboriginal males who had previously been successful voyageurs became river pilots and guided boats and barges loaded with supplies through the rapids to the port in Montreal. When the Grand Trunk Railway began building the Victoria Bridge, some of the same river men learned the skills of the high-beam steel workers, a prestigious occupation that many Iroquois continue to practise today. In short, eastern Aboriginals had built up over time a repertoire of skills usable in the changing economy.

By contrast, when the railway cut through the western plains, Aboriginals were not approached with prospective employment, while their efforts at becoming successful farmers were positively opposed by the Department of Indian Affairs which viewed them as unable to adapt (Carter, 1993). The reserve system, so heavily concentrated in the West, promoted the public's view that Aboriginals constituted at best an alien and dying society, at worst an obstacle to progress (Buckley, 1993: 60).

ABORIGINAL EDUCATION

Colonialism is not merely an economic or political phenomenon. It is also cultural. Where colonial systems have been most successful, they have entered into the psychology of the colonized. The truly colonized individual "apes" the language, beliefs, and behaviours of the colonizer, while denigrating his or her own cultural heritage (Fanon, 1968). Educational institutions have always played a key role in this process.

The campaign to colonize Aboriginal culture via schooling has a long history in Canada. Mission schools were tried in early New France, but soon proved unsuccessful due to low attendance. An alternative plan saw young Aboriginal boys and girls sent directly to France, where they could be "properly educated" and later returned as teachers for their own people, but again, the results were not favourable; more often than not the young Aboriginals returned as marginalized individuals, unable to function in either society. A few died. By 1639, scarcely a dozen had returned to the colony to assist the missionaries. As a result, the practice was ended (Cornish, 1881; Hawthorn, 1966/67; Jaenen, 1986).

The Hudson's Bay Company operated Canada's first schools designed to educate Aboriginal children. The company built and operated them primarily for the children of their employees, but a few Aboriginal children were enrolled. Later, religious orders became the main administrators of schools for Aboriginal students. In 1658, Sister Marguerite Bourgeoys (1620–1700), who later founded the Ursulines, opened a school for French girls in a converted stable, where eventually Aboriginal children were also enrolled (Chalmers, 1974). Around this same period, the Jesuits developed day schools in permanent settlements in New France and tried to lure Aboriginal students with a view to teaching them the Catholic faith and French culture.

The Catholic Oblates, founded in the 1840s, dominated the early stages of missionary schools in Canada. The Grey Nuns (Sisters of Charity), responsible for the education of Aboriginal girls, established their first school, St. Joseph's Academy, in St. Boniface in 1845. Further west, a host of well-known individuals, Catholic and non-Catholic alike, laboured for the same cause. These included James Evans, Robert Rundle, Father Albert Lacombe, Henry Steinhauer (an Aboriginal missionary), and others. Typical of the educational philosophy of the time, Methodist missionaries George McDougall and his son John strove to "Christianize, educate and civilize" the Aboriginals, in their case the Woodland Crees and the Stoneys (McDougall, 1903: 71).

A dramatic shift in policy occurred in 1830 with a scheme to assimilate the Aboriginal peoples. The plan was to establish the First Nations in permanent settlements and commence instruction so that an agricultural form of lifestyle would be possible. Missionaries and schoolmasters were brought in to instruct the children and to teach them to pray, read the Scriptures, and pursue "moral lives" (Friesen, 1991: 14). In 1857, legislation to design education for Aboriginals was passed, entitled An Act for the Gradual Civilization of the Indian. The Civilization and Enfranchisement Act followed in 1858.

This same period saw the start of Canada's experiment in residential schooling for Aboriginal children. Between 1833, when missionary Peter Jones petitioned the Methodist Church to build a residential school among the Ojibway people of Ontario, and 1988, when the last residential school in Canada closed (the McKay Residential School in Dauphin, Manitoba), 80 such schools were in operation.

Among the first of these were industrial schools, begun shortly after 1830 when the civil branch of government took over Aboriginal matters from the military (Titley, 1992). The industrial school experiment in Aboriginal education was short-lived, however.

Late enrolment for many students, short periods of attendance, and lack of funds to support the students in jobs after graduation were some of the problems. More tellingly, Aboriginal parents (with justification) disliked the removal of their children, often to places that were very far away; the industrial schools' deliberate attempts to convert and "civilize" their children at the cost of their heritage; the restrictions on the use of Aboriginal languages; the teaching of "women's chores" to young men (rather than teaching them to read and write); and the work component of the industrial schools, arguing that their children had been sent to school to learn literary skills, not to become unpaid apprentices with full-time jobs (Miller, 1987: 3f)—complaints that echoed through the other types of residential schools that followed.

Confederation in 1867 saw responsibility for educating Aboriginal youth fall to the federal government. The treaties signed shortly thereafter specified that Her Majesty (Queen Victoria) agreed to maintain schools for instruction in such reserves (Brookes, 1991: 168), but the quality and mode were not specifically spelled out. Given governmental assumptions about the demise of Aboriginal culture, why bother providing them with a first-class education? Besides, since the missionaries were already involved in the enterprise, why not continue to finance the residential schools for a few more years until they were no longer required?

Despite Aboriginal protests, the push to have residential schools for Aboriginal children continued, and by the end of the 19th century every region of the nation had boarding schools for them. Promoted by Egerton Ryerson (1803–1882), who in 1844 became the first superintendent of schools in English-speaking Canada, the federal government financed these schools, while churches provided spiritual guidance and management. Ryerson suggested that Aboriginals could not accomplish civilization without a "religious feeling," and thus "the animating and controlling spirit of each residential school should be a religious one" (Brookes, 1991: 20). The Province of Canada endorsed Ryerson's plan, acknowledging "the superiority of the European culture and the need to raise them [the Aboriginals] to the level of the whites" (Haig-Brown, 1993: 29).

A shift in policy was signalled in 1947 in a paper entitled (with admirable honesty), *A Plan to Liquidate Canada's Indian Problem in Twenty-five Years* (Pauls, 1984: 33). The scheme outlined a plan to transfer the authority for the operation of Aboriginal schools from federal to provincial governments, a stance later reiterated in the White Paper of 1969 (see Chapter 12). Integration, rather than assimilation, was to be the basis of the new policy, though given that "integration" was still to be one way, it seemed a distinction without a difference. Aboriginal students would interact with their non-Aboriginal peers, thereby slowly absorbing the values of the dominant European culture (Allison, 1983: 119).

In 1949 the federal government took steps to place administration of residential schools directly into the hands of government bureaucrats instead of religious leaders. That same year, a Special Joint Committee of the Senate and the House of Commons recommended that, wherever possible, Aboriginal children should be educated in association with other children (Friesen, 1983: 48). Despite considerable input from Aboriginal leaders, however, education according to the traditional European format was still perceived as a vehicle for assimilating First Nations (Hawthorn, 1966/67). Likewise, despite mounting criticism, the residential schools continued to operate.

LIFE IN A RESIDENTIAL SCHOOL

Indian residential schools conformed to what the Canadian sociologist Erving Goffman (1961: xiii) terms a **total institution**, defined as *a place of residence and work where a large number of like-situated individuals, cut off from the wider society for an appreciable period of time, together lead an enclosed, formally administered round of life.*

Although only 30–35 percent of Aboriginal children attended residential schools (Steckley and Cummins, 2008: 191), many of them remember with deep pain the experiences they suffered in those institutions (Friesen, 1999: 251f). Life in residential schools meant participating in an entirely different cultural milieu, replete with such alien features as corporal punishment, strict discipline, hard work, loneliness and, worst of all, confinement.

A common feature of total institutions is **identity stripping** (Goffman, 1961), essentially *the removing of articles, personal identification, and other elements that tell individuals who they are.* Children arriving at residential school were often given Christian names to replace their own (though students in a few schools were referred to only by assigned numbers), stiff uniforms in place of their Aboriginal clothing, and a haircut, the latter a sufficient form of insult to a culture that revered long hair. The children also quickly learned that use of their native language was forbidden, and that using it would result in severe punishment, including beatings. The intent of stripping was to make Aboriginal children ashamed of their culture and heritage.

Students quickly found themselves coping with a highly structured, hierarchical institution. Church-employed staff constituted the power structure and the ideological ethos of the school. Many of them were from lower socio-economic backgrounds, were minimally educated, and were often only recent immigrants to Canada, with little understanding of Canada's history or value system, and knew even less about the Aboriginal way of life (King, 1967: 58). They were armed with a strong sense of mission that, when frustrated, found vent in aggression toward the children. Since their identity was derived theologically, they held more authority than parents or students, surpassed in status only by school administrators.

Daily activities in a residential school were quite crude and very public. Initially the huge brick buildings, built on the factory model, had sealed windows. Often, the heavily occupied buildings produced a foul smell and a rank odour, contributing no doubt toward the spread of diseases, notably tuberculosis, which took a fearful toll on Aboriginal youth. At other times, the residences were cold and drafty (Grant, 1996: 123). Bathing was a group activity, with the younger students bathing first. The water was often too hot when they started the ritual, but by the time the older students got their turn, the water was cold and dirty.

The quality of residential food was poor, the quantity scanty, and today former residents frequently recall long periods of hunger. Students sometimes would wolf down their food as fast as possible in hopes of getting an additional helping. Students sometimes stole bread from the kitchen, though punishment was severe if caught; thus, stealing food became a complex operation involving a number of participants in a particular institutional subcultural practice (Haig-Brown, 1993: 99). Once eaten, food was seldom allowed to digest naturally, so the condition of the children's bowels was a major staff concern for which a daily routine was the administration of a laxative to the children, whether they needed it or not.

Even more than in non-Aboriginal schools of the period, the curriculum of the residential schools was primarily based on the three R's—readin', 'ritin', and 'rithmetic—plus a fourth staple—large doses of religion, the latter indubitably the most important of the four components (Perley, 1993: 123). As in the old industrial schools, there was also gender-specific training in some areas: farming and trades for boys, and housekeeping, mending, and knitting for girls. As noted, however, the use of Aboriginal languages was forbidden; likewise, the history or cultures of First Nations was completely ignored. Music and songs reflected only the themes of the new dominant society.

Learning was by rote and academic achievement low. This was partially because teachers had low expectations of their Aboriginal students, but Barman et al. (1986) and Grant (1996: 89) argue that the residential school education was never intended in any case to fully educate Aboriginal youngsters. Had they been properly educated, Aboriginal children may have become so well prepared that they might successfully enter the socio-economic order and become a threat to dominant society. The real purpose of residential schooling was to "kill the Indian in the child"; the real lessons to be learned every day were discipline and obedience. When students later transferred to provincial schools for high school training, they were often ashamed of their poor records; small wonder that less than 3 percent of those children attending residential schools ever graduated from high school.

Residential schools did provide some training in communication arts imported from Europe, and today many Aboriginal leaders can trace their literary beginnings to the years they spent in residential schools. This in no way justifies the existence of that form of teaching and learning, but it offers some measure of consolation. In addition to mastering the basic forms of communication required to negotiate effectively with governments, many students formed lasting friendships with their peers that have endured to this day. (It is interesting, though not necessarily reassuring, to note that the majority of Aboriginal leaders today are products of residential schools.) In some ways these bonds may have partially alleviated painful memories of the cruelties and hardships endured in residential schools.

Perhaps surprisingly, a few residential school survivors have quite positive memories of the experience and today even speak highly of the education they received. For example, interviews conducted with 80 elders from the Kainai (Blood) reserve in southern Alberta, authorized by the Kainai administration in 1995 and 2003, convey several instances of pride and gratitude felt by some former residents (Sikotan and Mikai'sto, 1995; Sikotan, Mikai'sto, and Omahksipootaa, 2003).

These few positive memories aside, the more general long-term impacts of residential schools were negative, however. According to Grant (1996), these impacts include: an inability to express feelings, apathy and unwillingness to work, values confusion and culture shock, anti-religious attitudes, and a long-term negative impact on succeeding generations. Many former residential school dwellers have had to work very hard to overcome the psychological, spiritual, and sexual abuses they suffered. Wax et al. (1964: 46) observed that the overwhelming majority of complaints by Aboriginal children were directed against other Aboriginal children rather than against teachers or school conditions. In turn, those abused in residential schools often became abusers themselves (O'Hara, 2000: 18). The cycle continued with many former inmates' transmitting the abuses they witnessed and experienced at the hands of the staff and teachers onto their own children.

Why did Aboriginal parents enroll their children in such dreadful environments? The answer has many sides. First, residential school conditions were not well known. But, second, parents had no real choice. In many situations members of the Royal Canadian Mounted Police took their children away. Some parents who were having a difficult time supporting their families grudgingly released their children with hopes they would have a better chance in life attending the school and developing their skills (Furniss, 1995). Others followed the recommendation of the local Indian agent, partly in the belief that doing so might gain the agent's approval.

Sadly, when the residential system ended, it was not because the system failed. That should have been the reason, but instead its end came about because of increased government intervention motivated by citizen concern (King, 1967: 87). As a first step toward liquidation, schools run by missionaries were taken over by government bureaucrats in the 1950s, but this stage was brief. Aboriginal parents, some of them educated in residential schools themselves, grew increasingly involved in the education of their children. In 1970, the residential school in St. Paul, Alberta, was turned over to local control after nearly 300 Aboriginal peoples conducted a sit-in at the school (Persson, 1986). Fifteen years later, two-thirds of reserve schools in the nation were either partly or completely managed by Aboriginal school boards.

Over the year, many closed residential schools were simply torn down. Some, however, were converted to other purposes. First Nations bands managed a few; in 1995, for example, Aboriginal management operated six residential schools in Saskatchewan. Several former residential schools became cultural centres, adult learning centres, or private schools. When administration of these schools was transferred to Aboriginal control, the influence of Aboriginal input was quickly evident. It is more than symbolic that, when the final closing exercises of several residential schools transpired in the 1980s (for instance, at Qu'Appelle Indian Residential School in Saskatchewan), Aboriginal dancing and social events often took precedence over denominational activities (Gresko, 1986: 89). Aboriginal culture began its slow rebirth.

CONCLUSION

Contact between Aboriginals and non-Aboriginals in North America occurred in several stages. During the first stage, Aboriginal peoples had a degree of control over the relationship. The outsiders wanted a valuable commodity—furs. They also relied on local know-how in learning how to live in inclement climates. The Aboriginals were pleased to supply furs and expertise in return for various imported products, but the fur trade also carried hidden dangers, such as disease and war, including conflict among Aboriginal tribes. In the long term, the fur trade also eroded Aboriginal culture.

By the time the fur trade collapsed in the early 19th century, the relationship between Aboriginals and non-Aboriginals was no longer that of equals. The Aboriginal peoples were excluded from the agricultural and industrial economies that followed, while Canadian expansion westward exacerbated the decline of Aboriginal culture. Viewed by successive governments as a dying people, Aboriginal peoples gradually vanished from the Canadian landscape into places of physical and psychological retreat and subjugation. For a time, modernity passed them by.

Like the trains that brought western settlement, Canada's economic development proceeded, seemingly unstoppable. On the West Coast in 1896, eyes turned suddenly northward in search of gold. Southern Canada was about to discover its North.

KEY TERMS

colonialism
endogamy
ethnocentrism
genocide
identity stripping
internal colonialism
total institution
usufructuary rights

CRITICAL THINKING QUESTIONS

1. In what ways does the existence of Aboriginal peoples complicate our conventional notions of the nation-state?

2. In what ways does the dominant mode of economic production shape the organizational structure of a society?

3. What lessons does the fur trade hold for Canadian economic development as a whole?

4. What are the similarities and differences between residential schools and other types of total institutions?

5. In what ways are Aboriginal peoples in Canada still subject to colonial rule?

RECOMMENDED READINGS

Braz, Alberta. 2003. *The False Traitor: Louis Riel in Canadian Culture*. Toronto: University of Toronto Press.
Not everyone in Canada perceived Louis Riel as a national villain, certainly not his Métis followers. Braz explores both sides of the question and concludes that Riel's contributions to nationhood have been overlooked.

Cardinal, Harold. 1977. *The Rebirth of Canada's Indians*. Edmonton: Hurtig Publishers.
Considered somewhat of a classic over time, this young Aboriginal leader reached back into history to reveal the many shortcomings of both Canadians and their government in negotiating with Canada's Aboriginal peoples.

Friesen, John W., and Virginia Lyons Friesen. 2005. *First Nations in the Twenty-first Century: Contemporary Educational Frontiers*. Calgary: Detselig.
The authors explore six educational challenges facing Canada's First Nations today: (1) spirituality, (2) leadership, (3) language maintenance, (4) Aboriginal self-identity, (5) school curriculum, and (6) preparation of teachers.

Henlin, Calvin. 2006. *Dances with Dependency: Indigenous Success through Self-Reliance*. Vancouver: Orca Spirit Publications and Communications.
Touted as somewhat of a Bible for Aboriginal economic success, Chief Henlin is a strong proponent of Aboriginal-originated and operated business and economic development.

Steckley, John I., and Bryan Cummins. 2008. *Full Circle: Canada's First Nations*, 2nd ed. Toronto: Pearson Education Canada.
Written in everyday language, this text is a good primer for those not acquainted with Aboriginal affairs in Canada. Topics include prehistory and traditions, culture areas, legal definitions, effects of colonialism, and contemporary issues.

RELATED WEBSITES

Historical Society of St. Boniface
www.shsb.mb.ca/Riel/indexenglish.htm
This is the oldest francophone historical society in western Canada. Among its online offerings is information on Louis Riel.

McGill University's Digital Library
http://digital.library.mcgill.ca/nwc/
This library contains a large number of documents and maps dealing with the fur trade in Canada.

Métis National Council
www.metisnation.ca/
Recognition of the Métis people as one of Canada's three distinct Aboriginal peoples

in the Constitution Act, 1982, paved the way for the creation in 1983 of the Métis National Council. Today, the MNC represents the Métis nation nationally and internationally.

CANADIAN SOCIETY ON VIDEO

More Than Bows and Arrows. 1978. Camera One, 56 minutes. An eye-opening film on Native Americans, the diversity of their cultures, their impact on U.S. culture, and the need for non-Indians to re-examine our ideas about Indians.

The Learning Path. 1993. National Film Board of Canada, 56 minutes, 50 seconds. A moving film that describes the devastating effects of residential/boarding schools on Canadian Indians and the widespread sexual and physical abuse to which they were subjected. One of five videos in the *As Long as the Rivers Flow* series produced by the NFB.

Women in the Shadows. National Film Board of Canada, 55 minutes, 55 seconds. The story of one Métis woman's reconciliation with her past and her people.

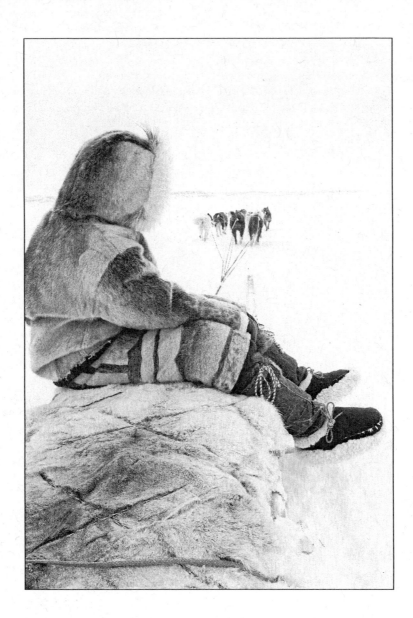

CHAPTER 11

KEEPERS OF THE NORTH

What happens in the North will ... tell us what kind of a country Canada is; it will tell us what kind of people we are.
—Justice Thomas Berger, 1977

Canada has a choice when it comes to defending our sovereignty over the Arctic. We either use it or lose it.
—Prime Minister Stephen Harper, 2007

..., Canadians have never strayed far either physically or spiritually from the Canada–U.S. boundary. We are [a] northern nation in fantasy and imagery only.
—Coates et al., 2008

INTRODUCTION

The vast majority of Canadians live within about 240 kilometres of the American border. Few have ever travelled to any of the territories, yet the North holds a special place in most Canadian hearts. It is a source of national identity.

Unlike elsewhere in Canada, Aboriginal peoples predominate throughout much of the North. They represent a majority in the Northwest Territories and Nunavut. They also make up a sizable proportion of the population in the Yukon and in the northern regions of the four western provinces, as well as in Ontario, Quebec, and Labrador. Canadians at large see the North as part of Canada, but it is overwhelmingly Aboriginal land, and they are its guardians.

The North is also a major source of Canada's present and future, a rich treasure trove of minerals and oil and gas reserves. And it is threatened, first by global warming, and, second, by international challenges to Canada's jurisdiction from other polar countries. For all of these reasons, the North is very much in the news today.

This chapter briefly explores the peoples and history of the North, and the changing relationship of the region with the rest of Canada. Special attention is given to the state's role in the North's gradual integration into Canada and the North's social, economic, political, and environmental challenges.

A PORTRAIT OF THE NORTH

Outsiders to the Far North are amazed that anyone could enjoy life in an environment almost entirely void of trees, and surrounded by great amounts of snow and ice. For about eight months of the year, most of the Arctic is covered with snow and extensive portions of its seas are frozen. The Subarctic seems only slightly more hospitable, a place of pesky blackflies in summer and cold winter twilight. To those raised in the North, however, life in the crowded, fast-paced urban centres of the South seems equally strange and even tantamount to suicide. Besides, the long periods of daylight in Inuit country balance the long, bleak winter.

Canada's North consists of Arctic and Subarctic regions and stretches "north of 60" to the North Pole. The Arctic comprises 3 million square kilometres of ice, water, and tundra, while the Subarctic includes over 4.5 million square kilometres of land. Combined, these regions amount to nearly 80 percent of the land and water mass of Canada, an area populated by nearly 1.5 million people. While these areas together comprise the largest geographic region in Canada, they have by far the smallest economy and population.

Increasingly, the region is a resource frontier for both Canada and the world, with energy and mineral products accounting for most the North's output. But the cold environment of the Arctic and Subarctic also greatly limits economic development and settlement (Bone, 2000: 440).

The Arctic's unique physical environment is primarily a result of the sun's relative absence. The tilt of the earth on its axis keeps the northern area facing away from the sun throughout the winter months and facing toward the sun throughout the summer months. For as long as four consecutive months, from mid-October to mid-February, the Arctic is plunged into darkness. During the summer, it becomes the Land of the Midnight Sun, experiencing constant daylight for a few short months.

During the very short Arctic summers, snow melts, plants grow, and the midnight sun shines over most of the land area. Spring and fall are virtually non-existent in the area. Most Arctic regions experience January temperatures as cold as −40°C or −45.5°C with a mean temperature of only −12°C during the warmest months, though this is rapidly changing (see below). The 200 varieties of vegetation in the Arctic (shrubs, scrub trees, herbs, and lichen) are well suited. They are low to the ground, grow away from the wind, and thrive on a brief and intense growing period.

The Arctic Ocean and surrounding lakes and rivers begin to freeze over in October and remain frozen until May in most areas. The frozen ocean extends the Arctic coastline by hundreds of kilometres, but the ice is not always safe to travel on, and in recent years has been growing thinner. Strong winds often drive vast floating fields of ice across the waterways. Often these islands of ice crash into one another, creating upheavals. A sudden spring breakup can create ice floes that may carry off unsuspecting hunting parties or migrating families (Osborn, 1990: 27–28).

Traditionally, the peoples of the Arctic relied on a variety of game and birds for food. This included the Arctic hare, the Arctic fox, the muskox, and a variety of birds such as rock ptarmigans, sandpipers, plovers, elder ducks, red-throated loons, and ruddy turnstones. Little-appreciated life forms included a variety of obnoxious insects such as small flies, mosquitoes, and bumblebees. Today, many of these species, such as the polar bear, are threatened by climate change.

An obvious treeline separates the Subarctic from the Arctic and consists of four distinct zones: (1) the wooded tundra, (2) the lichen woodland, (3) the closed boreal forest, and (4) the forest parkland. The wooded tundra forms the transition zone. This wooded area contains sporadic patches of spruce and larch trees, and the lichen woodland has a few stands of spruce and pine. The closed boreal forest offers a denser stand of fir, spruce, and pine, while the forest parkland combines elements of forest and grass milieu (Bone, 1992: 21). Subarctic wildlife is more plentiful and includes some 50 species of birds and 600 species of plants.

Over time, climate and geography resulted in the development, by people indigenous to each region, of cultures and technologies suitable for hunters and gatherers. As Bone (1992: 27) points out, the North's fragile physical environment poses unique challenges for modern times. Its cold climate and slow rate of natural growth means it takes longer to recover from modern industrial accidents such as oil spills. Unfortunately, considerations of the environment and the people have not always influenced the North's development.

THE NORTH'S ABORIGINAL PEOPLES

The North's Aboriginal peoples are comprised of three primary groups: (1) the Inuit of the Arctic, (2) the Algonquian-speaking people of the eastern Subarctic (the Cree, the Naskapi, and the Montagnais, with those located in Labrador referred to as Innu), and (3) the Athapascan-speaking people (the Dene), located in the western Subarctic (Brody, 1987: 29). The latter two groups also span the northern portions of several provinces, including

Quebec and Labrador, as well as the western provinces. As Chapter 10 dealt primarily with the Algonquian-speaking people, we will here focus on the Dene and the Inuit.

THE INUIT

Most historians and archaeologists today believe the Inuit are descendants of the Thule Inuit, who spread from the northern coast of Alaska to the Mackenzie Delta in the 11th century, replacing the Dorset people (Crowe, 1974; Wilson, 1976; Purich, 1992). Linguistically, the Inuit language is unique, with no discernible relationship with any New World Aboriginal people. Some scholars believe the Inuit language to be akin to the Uralic languages of Eurasia. The Inuit language probably descended from Aleut, from which it diverged about 6,000 years ago, and thereafter evolved into two distinctive subfamily units, Yupik and Inupik. This includes all dialects between western Alaska and Greenland (Jennings, 1978).

The land of the Inuit is divided into a western portion, which includes the Aleut on the Aleutian Islands as well as the Inuit of Alaska, and a central and eastern region, which embraces all the Inuit from the Mackenzie River Delta east to Greenland. The groups broadly identified as Inuit include: Mackenzie, Copper, Netsilik, Sadliq, Caribou, Iglulik, South Baffin Island, Ungava, and Labrador (Crowe, 1974; Brody, 1987).

At the time of first contact with Europeans, some 22,000 Inuit lived in the North. There is evidence of a fairly widespread exchange of various minerals among the tribes before the arrival of Europeans, including such items as soapstone, iron, and copper, and products made from raw materials like ivory (Crowe, 1974).

Essentially an ocean-oriented culture, the Inuit obtained most of their food supply from the sea. Indeed, water was a major influence on virtually every aspect of Inuit life, from food to technology, domesticity, and the arts. In many ways, the Inuit had a sophisticated culture, fitted to the materials and circumstances of their climate and geography. The Alaskan Inuit and Aleuts, for example, developed the two-holed kayak and, in place of the toggling harpoons that other Inuit used for large sea mammals, a multi-barbed harpoon dart head (Dumond, 1977). Housing construction, from portable summer tents made of sealskin or caribou skin to winter homes of the classic igloo type (Baldwin, 1967) to (in the South) rectangular, semi-subterranean, turf-covered houses of logs, reflected a firm grasp of such things as ventilation and insulation.

The Inuit were probably unique among Canada's First Nations in functioning with a simple social system, unencumbered by elaborate hierarchical forms of governing individuals or bodies. They had no chiefs among them. Contrary to the Western dichotomy of individualism versus collectivism, the Inuit way of life involved a form of **individual egalitarianism**. When food was scarce, supplies were stretched out as far as possible and a spirit of goodwill prevailed. Friendliness was expected; anger was viewed as a form of madness (Coates et al., 2008: 31). Age and gender determined one's status, though the sexes were more equal than in European countries of the day. In hunting, for example, women assisted their husbands in driving animals into an ambush. Still, women had the chief role in raising children and preparing food (Giffen, 1930). Long before it became trendy, Inuit clothing was "unisex," with both sexes wearing loose-fitting fur trousers and shirts, usually made of caribou hide, but sometimes of polar bear or other animal fur (Josephy, 1968).

Polygyny, *the marriage of one man to more than one woman*, was not uncommon. Since the Inuit practised female infanticide, however, there was often a scarcity of women. This being the case, on occasion a man might lend the use of his wife to a friend on a short-term basis. The "wife swap," as Europeans termed it, elicited both sensationalist intrigue and condemnation among outsiders, who understood neither its cultural underpinnings, nor the intricate rules that surrounded the practice, nor the woman's say in the matter (Mowat, 1952; Balikci, 1970; McMillan, 1995). Like the sun dance of the Prairies and the potlatch of the West Coast, the Europeans, especially the missionaries, viewed wife sharing as something to be eradicated.

The Inuit believed in a large host of generally harmless supernatural beings. By European standards they had quite vague concepts of life in the hereafter. Their religious festivities revolved around the seasons and food supply, with celebrations beginning and ending the whale hunt season, and the busy summer months surrendering to slow winters and time for visiting, songfests, games, and storytelling.

Storytelling, along with everyday modelling, were means of transmitting valued Inuit cultural beliefs and values to the young. In some tribes storytellers were designated, while in others both men and women of respect could relate stories. Among the Labrador Inuit, each village had a designated storyteller, while in Alaska certain old men monopolized this art (Giffen, 1930).

Seals and other sea mammals were a chief source of food, though in the summer months fishing and caribou hunting supplemented the Inuit diet. Taylor (1974) describes a typical annual cycle utilized by the Netsilik around the turn of the 20th century. The sea began to freeze around October, the caribou herds departed for the South, and the building of snow houses commenced. Char continued to be taken from the sea until the middle of November, and the women were busy making winter clothes. During December and January the people remained at home,

relying on provisions laid up during the previous summer and fall. The breathing-hole seal hunting began in February when the snow was deep on the ice; other hunting techniques were employed when April and May arrived. These included sneaking up on the seal or catching new pups at the breathing holes. A few stray caribou showed up, and in June when the snow houses caved in from the hot sun, the people moved into tents. Kayaks were prepared for caribou hunting, which continued until the herd disappeared south again.

THE DENE

The Dene (sometimes spelled "Dinneh") speak a dialect of the Athapaskan language (Chapter 10). They share this language family with the Apache and the Navajo of the American Southwest. Abel (1993) suggests these northern people traditionally used the word *Dinneh* to identify the larger population and distinguished separate groups by adding the name of a river or lake associated with their particular hunting grounds. Thus, it is possible to identify a large number of tribes as Dene. Irwin's (1994) comprehensive list of Dene tribes includes the Chipewyan, of the Canadian interior (not to be confused with the Chippewa-Ojibway of Lake Superior); the Dogrib, between Great Slave Lake and Great Bear Lake; the Beaver, along the lower Peace River in northern Alberta; the Slavey, along the southern shore of Great Slave Lake; the Hare, northwest of Great Bear Lake; the Klaska or Nahani, west of the headwaters of the Mackenzie River; the Sekani, in central British Columbia; the Carrier (named for their widows' custom of carrying the charred bones of their dead husbands on their backs); the Chilcotin, south of Carrier lands; the Tahlan, on the upper Stikine River in northwestern British Columbia; and the Tuchone in southern Yukon Territory (see also Crowe, 1974; Ryan, 1995; Massey and Shields, 1995). An official document of the Dene of the Northwest Territories (1975) cites the Chipewyans, Dogribs, Slaveys, and Loucheux as member groups of the larger Dene community.

Like the Inuit, the traditional Dene people were primarily hunters and trappers. Huge herds of caribou and moose were vital components of the Dene diet and culture, supplemented by the fish of lakes and rivers. Predictability of supply was important. Any change could spell disaster for a band. The Chipewyan people, for example, followed the migration patterns of the caribou, and if there was even a slight shift in their migration paths, the band's food supply was affected. In fall these animals were slaughtered by waiting hunters as they passed a certain point, and the meat was cut into strips, dried in the sun, and pounded into pemmican for the winter food supply (McMillan, 1995).

It was customary for the Dene to function as groups of friendly neighbours. Each tribe adapted to its immediate terrain. For example, the Hare, so named for their use of rabbit skins for clothing and shelter, lived in small extended families. divided relatives into two opposing groups. Cross-relatives were in-laws, while parallel relatives were akin to parents, siblings, or one's own children (Ives, 1990). A similar situation prevailed in Slavey country, where the people identified two kinds of relatives—kinsmen and in-laws.

Among the early Beaver and Slavey tribes, marriage patterns represented what Ives (1990) has termed "a polygynous gerontocracy of senior men." Older men often married younger women, leaving a shortage of mates for younger men, as well as a significant number of widows as the husbands died. But family practices were also quite diverse.

The Dene had quite explicit social rules (Ryan, 1995). These rules covered three specific areas: (1) natural resources, (2)

families, and (3) governance or decision making. In turn, these rules were intertwined with the Dene's holistic view of the universe. Rule-breakers were punished in various ways. For minor offences, an elder might deal verbally with the guilty party. Individuals committing more serious offences were often made the subject of a gathering in which they were required to admit guilt and make restitution, followed by a process of reconciliation. If this failed, shunning was possible. Finally, for particularly severe infractions, there was the death penalty, though this seemed to have been rarely used.

A 19th-century visitor to Dene country, Father Petitot, noted that Dene beliefs were reflected in daily practices, but not formalized (Savoie, 1970). A series of lunar beings were worshipped as deities: the midnight sun, for example, was a real national and tutelary god, supremely recognized and worshipped. At the same time, Petitot described the Dene as having a primordial knowledge of a Good Being who was placed above all other beings and possessed a multitude of names, the most usual one being Bettsen-nu-unli ("He by whom the earth exists"). The Hare peoples saw this supreme being as a triad made up of father, mother, and son. Frequently, spirit beings would personify themselves in the form of birds, such as the eagle; the male spirit brought the day and the female spirit brought the night (Savoie, 1970). As in the South, the trickster was recognized, in the form of a raven, as a creator, culture hero, and miracle worker (Merkur, 1991: 215). Finally, the Dene also believed their departed souls could become celestial beings, such as the northern lights (Savoie, 1970).

The Roman Catholic priests who later arrived in Dene territory introduced concepts that blended well with traditional Dene beliefs: love your spouse, be kind to your neighbours, take good care of your children and raise them well, and stay together forever (Ryan, 1995). But the

Dene did not practise the European form of marriage when the missionaries first arrived. Locals often lived together and had several children before they appeared before a priest for a formal European-style marriage. In many instances, priests became viewed as emissaries from God possessing spiritual power and authority, and served also as elders, providing advice and direction, resolving disputes, and meting out disapproval for acts of violation. In effect, priests supplanted traditional shamans, which was understandable enough, given the apparent failure of the latter to ward off the mysterious evils that befell Aboriginal peoples after the Europeans arrived.

There is little doubt that conflict with European society caused some First Nations cultural and spiritual traditions to be altered or even lost. At the same time, Christianity's capacity to fully transform Aboriginal culture was not total; indeed, its influence was in some ways superficial (Brody, 1987: 205). Many sacred practices that the priests frowned upon continued in secret; sometimes, as well, Christianity merged with Aboriginal beliefs—in a process known as **syncretism**—in ways the missionaries did not recognize. In short, Christianity had important effects on Indian culture, but Aboriginal peoples also took what they wanted from the new religion, while retaining many of their old beliefs and values, the shoots of which are seen today in a strong cultural and spiritual renaissance in most Aboriginal communities (Lincoln, 1985; McGaa, 1990).

THE COMING OF THE EUROPEANS

Initial contacts between the northern people and Europeans in the 10th century were not friendly. Erik the Red, a Norwegian who explored Greenland, and whose son, Leif Erikson, later returned to establish a colony in Newfoundland, viewed the locals as quite primitive "little people"

who had no iron and used missiles made of walrus tusks and sharp stones for knives (Osborn, 1990: 77). It was a pattern of contact repeated several centuries later with the arrival of a new band of explorers.

Among these early explorers were John Cabot (in 1497 and 1498), Martin Frobisher (in 1576, 1577, and 1598), John Knight (in 1606), and Henry Hudson (in 1610). Why did they come? In part, they were searching for precious metals, especially copper and gold, but they also had a larger quest: finding a northwest passage to the Orient.

European exploration, beginning in the 15th century with Cabot, was inextricably linked to mercantilism (Chapter 2). In the modern context, we can see this period as an early expression of globalization, with its search for new products and markets and the expansion of trade. While considerable trade occurred overland between Europe and Asia, it also occurred by sea. But a ship sailing to the Orient from Europe, either eastward around the Cape of Africa or westward around South America, might journey more than a year. By contrast, a passage more directly westward would save time and money, hence the search for what Berton (1988) termed "the Arctic Grail."

Ultimately, the Northwest Passage was found. It was not mastered, however, until the Norwegian Roald Amundsen sailed his sloop, the *Gjoa*, through the ice in 1905 (see Berton, 1988). By then, the North had claimed a host of explorers and their ships. Among these was Hudson, who steered a course into a strait that later bore his name and became icebound, whereupon his crew mutinied and set him and a few loyal crewmen adrift in a small boat, never to be seen again. Hudson's lurid fate and that of other disastrous expeditions that followed—from Jens Munk in 1619 to Sir John Franklin in 1845–1849 (see Beattie and Geiger, 1987)—did not dissuade outsiders, however. Far from it; the

North became transformed into a place both mystical and mythical. (Note that Mary Shelley's monster in *Frankenstein*, published in 1819, dies on an Arctic ice floe.) And where mystery's allure failed to attract, Europeans came in search of profit.

And profit there was. In 1665, two disgruntled fur traders from New France, Pierre-Esprit Radisson and Médard Chouart, sieur des Groseilliers, having been turned down by the French government, went to London to meet King Charles II and local merchants to seek their support. The English were more responsive to Radisson and Groseilliers, and shortly thereafter, in 1670, Charles II issued the Hudson's Bay Company charter, granting the company rights to all lands whose waters drained into the Hudson and James Bay's. The Hudson's Bay Company (HBC) thus became the "the vastest empire any private company ever controlled" (Morton, 1997: 75; also Newman, 1998: 54–61).

The company did not immediately thrive. Over the next decades, the French captured HBC forts and burned them to the ground several times, only to see them rebuilt. Gradually, however, the Hudson's Bay Company grew. Defeat of the French in 1763 and amalgamation with the rival North West Company in 1821 left the company unassailable in the North. For roughly the next 50 years, the HBC represented a kind of quasi-government, making rules and regulations, enforcing order, and even providing social services, such as education. Well into the 20th century, the company continued to provide unique services in the North. HBC radio stations, for example, provided—until eclipsed by the CBC—an important means of linking northern communities.

With the advent of the fur trade and the arrival of missionaries, the lifestyle and political economy of the northern Aboriginal peoples changed dramatically. Some initially did quite well with the arrangement. For a hunting people, rifles and ammunition were a real plus. Likewise, certain tribes also initially did well, notably the Cree, who quickly became middlemen and spread westward across Canada. But, as we have noted (Chapter 10), the fur trade also brought negative consequences. In the words of Brody (1987: 199), the "fur trade was built upon the economics of dependency." Trade with the forts became habitual. Hunters became trappers and changed their lifestyles accordingly. The role of women also changed, as they now had to clean and tan additional furs for market. As in the South, disease and alcoholism also took their toll, causing many tribes to break up and eventually perish.

Not all of the North was brought into the world economy all at once. Beginning in the 17th and 18th centuries, some tribes in the Subarctic had initial contact with fur traders pushing north from the St. Lawrence and whalers arriving from the North Atlantic. Others, however, experienced their first contact only in the 19th century. At that time, European ships began regular trips to the Arctic to garner whale oil, baleen (whalebone, used in making corsets), and walrus ivory. In the 1850s, the ships began to winter over, and contact between Europeans and Inuit intensified. The establishment of whaling stations upset the seasonal economic cycle of the settlements, which became handout stations soon known as places where "weekly biscuits were handed out" (Wilson, 1976: 85).

This increased contact brought other material and cultural changes. By the time commercial whaling came to an end (around 1912), "hunters were using rifles, telescopes, sheath knives, jack-knives, hatchets, saws, drills, awls, steels and files. Women cooked in metal pots and kettles, and used steel needles, cotton thread and metal scissors in sewing" (Brody, 1987: 193). Clothing materials and styles also changed, as did music and dancing.

Some changes were decidedly negative, however. Overhunting depleted the whale pods and led to starvation in some instances. Alcoholism, suicide, and disease also took their toll. As early as 1887, Father Emile Petitot quoted a chief of the Chiglit Eskimos on the terrible living conditions among the Inuit: "We are all dying.... [W]e are getting snuffed out day by day and nobody cares about us. No one looks after our sick or pities our misfortunes" (Petitot, 1999: 15). In 1912, Captain Henry Toke Munn described the Inuit of Baffin Island as a "passing race" destined for extinction because of the coming blight of complex European civilization, without whose influence he felt they would be better off. Brody (1987: 193) notes that around this same period the Inuvialuit of the Mackenzie Delta were reduced from a community of 2,000 to about 30. Finnie (1940) later made a similar observation regarding the high death rate of the Copper Inuit in Coronation Gulf.

The Aboriginal peoples further west survived better for a time, outside the thrust of European contact. In 1905, an American sportsman, Charles Sheldon, met some members of the Dene Nahanni tribe who had never made contact with any of the European newcomers, and described them as follows:

> [T]hey were the healthiest and finest looking Indians I have ever seen in the northern country. Most of the men were fine specimens, and also the women, who bore children abundantly and reared them in health and vigour. They were absolutely honest and lived a primitive Indian life. (Finnie, 1948: 40)

The life of northern peoples was about to change, however. As so often in the past history of the Americas (see Wright, 1993), the catalyst for change was gold.

THE YUKON GOLD RUSH

The California gold rush of 1849 begat the British Columbia gold rush of 1858, followed in 1896 by the discovery of gold on a tributary of the Klondike River by George Washington Carmack and his two Aboriginal brothers-in-law, Skookum Jim and Tagish Charley. This was not the first discovery of gold in the North. Robert Campbell, a trader with the Hudson's Bay Company, found gold in the gravel near his trading post at the junction of the Yukon and Pelly rivers in the early 1850s. An Anglican missionary, Robert McDonald, reported traces of gold in Birth Creek near the Yukon–Alaska border in the 1870s (Cruikshank, 1998: 434). This time, however, gold fever became a pandemic.

By the summer of 1897, however, hordes of men were swarming over the Yukon region, some arriving by water, many taking the arduous journey over the White Pass and Chilcoot Pass, then down the Yukon River by a colourful assortment of handmade boats and rafts. By 1898, a total of 30,000 people lived in the Klondike region, of whom about 16,000 resided in Dawson City, which became Yukon's capital. Most of the newcomers knew only three things about the Yukon: it was cold, it was remote, and gold nuggets were available for the picking. The men who arrived were relatively young and well educated, and outnumbered women by a ratio of five to one.

While many of the fortune seekers sought female companionship among the locals, few of these relationships lasted very long. Most of the men soon drifted back to the South, often leaving children behind them. Those who stayed and struck it rich were few. Like other booms, it was the traders, hoteliers, or other providers of goods and services, not to mention the con artists, who made money (Cruikshank, 1998: 451; Berton, 1958). Most of those who remained ended up working for wages, their stay occasioned by either a love of the North or dreams still nursed of becoming wealthy (Fried, 1969).

Sadly for its participants, the 1896 gold rush ended quickly. The boom-and-bust pattern of Canadian development, so familiar to the South, was replicated in the North. Dawson City's fortunes and population experienced a steep decline. For all the wealth generated, little remained to be invested locally. By contrast, between 1902 and 1903 alone, $12 million left the northern territories. Observers blamed an uninterested government and lack of local control for this loss of revenue. Almost overnight, the gold rush ended. Its broader impacts, however, were long term.

First, the gold rush augured the North's full integration into the world capitalist economy. It was a slow process. The fur economy remained strong throughout the 1920s, bringing considerable wealth to the Yukon and the Northwest Territories. Fur towns like Aklavik sprang up, and a few local families got rich, but prosperity was again short-lived. For many people, however, tied only tangentially to the labour market, the downturn was not critical. Meanwhile, companies were increasingly entering the region, searching for exploitable resources. Gold remained in high demand, leading to the foundation of towns at Noranda, Quebec; Kirkland Lake, Ontario; and Flin Flon, Manitoba. Increasingly also, other minerals were mined, such as radium and uranium, in places like Great Bear Lake, high in the Northwest Territories (Careless, 1970: 353). And then there was oil.

It had long been known that the North possessed rich pockets of oil. Writing in his diary in the 18th century, the explorer Peter Pond recounts seeing the thick pitch along the banks of the Athabasca River in what is today northern Alberta. In 1907, Alfred von Hammerstein, known as "the Count," acquired surface and mineral rights to about 48,600 hectares of freehold land downstream of where Fort McMurray stands today, and set about drilling wells. (He was unsuccessful.) A few years later, however, in 1920, the Imperial Oil Company announced the discovery of large amounts of oil at Norman Wells. The announcement temporarily spurred the Canadian government to seek a treaty with the local Dene to pave the way for development. Fortunately perhaps for the Dene, the oil find soon proved significantly smaller than anticipated, and the government dropped its plans to settle the Dene on specified plots of land. Nonetheless, the discovery proved a harbinger of events in the North to come.

Second, while the North's economy as a whole was being transformed, local Aboriginal peoples were frequently left on the margins of these changes. The pattern began with the gold rush, when Aboriginals became bearers for the invading southerners, but rarely staked claims themselves. Similarly, the 1920s and 1930s saw an influx of White southerners seeking their fortunes at a time when jobs "back home" were growing scarce (Brody, 1987). Thus, at a time when the North's Aboriginal peoples found themselves increasingly pressed for work in the old economy, jobs in the new economy (mining, oil, the government bureaucracies) often went to outsiders with the education, skills, and connections to participate.

Third, the gold rush signalled the growing involvement of the Canadian government and state in the lives of northerners. Canada had gained jurisdiction over the West, Rupert's Land, and the North-West Territories in 1870. In 1880, the British government ceded responsibility over the Arctic Islands to Canada, in large part to thwart American and other efforts to claim Baffin Island (Purich, 1992: 31). Canada's failure to enforce jurisdiction, however, subsequently resulted in claims pressed by other countries. Thus, the late 19th century saw a host of countries—particularly Britain, the United States, and Norway—

sending polar expeditions, ostensibly in the name of exploration, but also to "plant their flags" (see Coates et al., 2008).

The Canadian government responded to these threats in various ways. In 1897, the Canadian government sent a reconnaissance mission to Hudson Bay and Baffin Island, where Captain William Wakeham declared Canada's sovereignty over that and surrounding islands. Similar missions followed, leading up the First World War. Between 1913 and 1918, the Canadian government also funded the research of Vilhjalmur Stefansson, whose work quickly popularized for Canadians "their" northern heritage. The government also expanded the number of North-West Mounted Police (NWMP) posts in the Arctic, the first established two years before the Yukon gold rush (Coates et al., 2008: 20), increased to three by 1903, and several more by the 1920s.

In 1922, the Canadian government instituted a yearly patrol of the eastern Arctic to enforce its claims to sovereignty over the North (Purich, 1992: 32–33; also, Brody, 1987). The Royal Canadian Mounted Police, expanded and renamed in 1920 from the NWMP, played an important role in this enforcement, while performing a multitude of other functions and roles, including the North's administrators, social workers, and, perhaps most importantly, explorers. In 1940–1942, the RCMP vessel the *St. Roch*, a kind of floating detachment, travelled the Northwest Passage from west to east, then from east to west in 1944, becoming the first ship to navigate the passage in both directions, while also engaging in unofficial wartime reconnaissance.

Within less than 50 years, Canada's North had been transformed from a peripheral and even exotic appendage to a politically, economically, culturally, and administratively integrated colony of the South. In 1939, the North also began being militarily integrated into the modern world.

THE SECOND WORLD WAR AND THE POSTWAR SOUTH

The Second World War and the subsequent Cold War brought renewed interest in the North, this time not only for its resources, but more immediately for strategic reasons. A major supply route for oil and other military supplies for Alaska moved down the Mackenzie River along a new highway. Local centres like Fort Smith and Whitehorse suddenly burgeoned with population, and Frobisher Bay became a vast military complex. A former ghost town, Churchill, Manitoba, became a military base with a satellite town of skilled and unskilled workers and a large number of unemployed Aboriginal "squatters." War's end saw the economic situation of many of these towns immediately deteriorate, and many people were left financially stranded.

Nonetheless, the Second World War saw a number of large-scale construction projects launched in the North. These included the construction of a series of landing fields, a military base at Goose Bay, the expansion of oil production at Norman Wells, the building of a pipeline from Norman Wells to Whitehorse, and the construction of the Alaska Highway. Both Goose Bay and Gander became strategic links in the North American chain of defence, and between the two of them supplied over 900 warplanes to the United Kingdom (Bone, 1988, 1992).

The Alaska Highway was a particularly monumental task for its time. Originally proposed in the 1930s, construction began finally in the 1940s, partially motivated by Japan's bombing of Pearl Harbor in December 1941. The road was built both to supply Russians with needed materials to fight the Nazi invasion of their country and as a safeguard against a Japanese invasion of North America. The road was over 2,500 kilometres in length, built over muskeg and unstable fields of tundra, and took 11,000 men, including U.S. Army engineers and civilians, to complete the job. Although 80 percent of the highway was built on Canadian soil, the United States government paid the entire cost of $133 million, while Canada absorbed the costs of upkeep. The road had two long-term impacts outlasting the war. First, it stimulated oil and gas exploration in the North. Second, the road's construction had the effect of reinforcing American influence in western Canada, especially Alberta (see Chapter 8).

As important as was the military intrusion into the North, more crucial in bringing about change was the role of the Canadian government (Vallee, 1971). We have seen how the state's presence in the North increased during the gold rush. This presence increased markedly after 1945, with the federal government taking over direct responsibility for economic and social affairs as the Hudson's Bay Company no longer felt obligated to buffer Aboriginals from economic swings in the marketplace.

Soon government facilities existed for services that touched on every aspect of Aboriginal life. To some extent this intervention improved the local way of life. Housing standards were raised, and famine became virtually a thing of the past. Instead of hunting and trapping, new sources of income were generated, including wages, the sale of handicrafts, family allowances, various pensions, and social assistance.

Education was a key area of increased government involvement. As in the South, missionary schools had long existed in the North. Mission schools were opened as early as 1867 at Fort Providence on Great Slave Lake, and in 1874 at Fort Chipewyan on Lake Athabasca (Fisher, 1981). Others followed, with a spate of residential schools set up by missionaries for Arctic and Subarctic children in the 1940s and 1950s (Brody, 1987: 143). As elsewhere, the missionary teachers were armed with an irrelevant curriculum and otherworldly allegiances. The purpose of their "education" was acculturation and assimilation

(see also Chapter 10). Thus, local language training was downplayed, and religious practices related to Aboriginal spirituality were discouraged. Many parents felt attendance at school provided children with less opportunity to observe and participate in traditional Aboriginal life. Boys no longer hunted or trapped with their fathers, and girls were removed from situations where they could take up domestic responsibilities (Cline, 1975: 173).

Prior to the Second World War, direct federal investments in health and educational facilities were virtually non-existent in northern regions (Rea, 1968: 184). After the 1950s, however, government intervention increased in the form of social and educational assistance as a means of integrating Aboriginal peoples into the body of national life.

For government and bureaucrats, the North's increased integration seemed a necessity. In the 1930s and 1940s, the fur economy was still a mainstay of northern families. After 1947, however, the price of furs collapsed and remained low until the 1960s. Many Canadian officials viewed trapping as a dying way of life and were determined to drag the North and its residents into the "modern world." Education and economic development were seen as key elements of this process.

Understandably, the Dene and other peoples of the North viewed government actions, including game laws, with suspicion. Too often, government policies ignored traditional obligations, including land claims. In the eyes of Aboriginals, their traditional hunting lands were being cleared to make way for economic development.

Increasingly, the Dene and Inuit found themselves backed into a corner by the realities of a shrinking resource base, their own geography, and the forces of international markets (Abel, 1993: 268). In the 1950s, settlements based on the fur industry declined. Farther north, some were able to live off the land, living in fishing camps in the summer and organizing hunting parties in the winter (Massey and Shields, 1995), part of what Stabler (1989) has identified as a **dual economy**, *a livelihood earned by both traditional and modern means*. (In 1989, two-thirds of family breadwinners in the Northwest Territories still hunted and trapped.) In the southern Subarctic, however, planned resource towns like Thompson, Manitoba, became major producers of minerals and attracted sizable populations. Sometimes, and by deliberate plan, Aboriginal peoples found employment in these towns. Too often, however, they did not (Bone, 1992: 69).

NORTHERN VISIONS

In the late 1950s, English-speaking Canada was beginning to discover or, rather, make itself. Having broken with Britain over the period of the two world wars, Canada was also in the early stages of trying to separate itself from the United States. In part, these efforts were economic. Thus, in the elections of 1957 and 1958, Conservative leader John Diefenbaker spoke out regarding Canada's need to diversify trade, seek out new markets in Asia, and revive those in Britain. But Diefenbaker also lit a fire in many Canadians' imaginations with visions of opening up the North in much the same way that Sir John A. Macdonald had opened up the West in the 19th century. Concerned about growing dependence on social assistance in the North, and addressing increasing demands for forest products, minerals, and energy, the Diefenbaker government decided to turn things around for northerners. The plan was to transform the fur-trading economy of the North into a resource-based, urban-like economy.

Under Diefenbaker's leadership, Canadian Aboriginals garnered unconditional federal voting rights. Before 1960, they had had to surrender their Indian status, a process known as **enfranchisement**, if they wanted to vote as Canadian citizens.

During the Diefenbaker years, assimilation as an official government policy toward First Nations was also downplayed. For these and other liberating manoeuvres, some observers have jokingly referred to Diefenbaker as "the Lincoln of the North" (McMillan, 1995: 314).

By the late 1950s, Diefenbaker's "northern vision" had growing cultural support. Years before, Vilhjalmur Stefansson's book *The Friendly Arctic* (1921) and subsequent speeches, and Robert Flaherty's film *Nanook of the North* (1922), the world's first full-length documentary, had popularized the North among Canadians and non-Canadians alike (Brody, 1987; Srebrnik, 1998). The harrowing tales of bush pilots in the years after, followed by the popular writings of people like Farley Mowat and Pierre Berton in the 1950s, added further lustre to the North's reputation and its role in Canadian identity.

From the beginning, however, development of the North has faced economic challenges unlike those of any other area of the country. First, the terrain (largely muskeg or rock) is unwieldy. Second, the North's summer season, when outside work is most feasible, is very short. Third, a lack of skilled labour means bringing in people from the outside. (Even today, many indigenous northerners over the age of 40 have little or no formal schooling and are functionally illiterate.) Fourth, the North is far from markets and supplies, resulting in high transportation costs in both directions. Fifth, economic development in the North requires a lot of capital investment. In the past, this has often been supplied by the state, either directly or through loans, or by private, often foreign investors. But private investors often demand generous terms or conditions that relegate the environment and local job creation and training to a distant second place, while the Canadian federal and provincial governments often seemed remote.

Beyond these purely economic factors, there are also significant political, social, and environmental considerations. Many of these began coming to the fore in the 1970s. On the one hand, Aboriginal peoples increasingly developed the political organizations and skills to press their demands for a greater role in economic development and the use of their lands (see Chapter 12). On the other hand, the period 1965–1975 also witnessed a renewed interest in the North on the part of many provincial governments driven by beliefs in activist government and a spirit of province building (Chapter 8). Mega-projects became a feature of the northern part of nearly every province: forestry in British Columbia, the oil sands in Alberta, potash and uranium in Saskatchewan, hydroelectricity and mining in Manitoba and Quebec, and mining in Ontario. These projects introduced modern kinds of employment, a case in point being the hydroelectric project at James Bay.

In the early 1960s, the Quebec government began searching for a northern supply of power (see Chapter 3). These ideas were finally realized in 1971 with Premier Robert Bourassa's announcement of a land agreement between the Cree First Nation at James Bay and the Quebec government that would allow construction of a dam (see Chapter 12). A key part of the agreement was Aboriginal employment in the project. And by 1981, service industries employed 35 percent of the local Aboriginal population. There followed an announcement in 1991 of another stage of the project. In the beginning, many viewed the agreement as a model, and there was considerable praise for its impact on the Aboriginal community. More recently, however, there have been criticisms that the project involved massive unforeseen social and environmental costs borne largely by the Cree people (Clerici, 1999; also Frideres and Gadacz, 2001).

Similar stories arise from other projects, such as the Churchill Nelson River Hydro-electric Project at Pike Lake, Manitoba, the Dryden Chemicals Plant at Dryden, Ontario, and the oil sands developments in Fort McMurray. When the Pike Lake project began, local Aboriginal peoples were told that tremendous benefits would accrue from the project. The end result, however, was that little job training took place and instead outside labour was brought in. At Dryden, the plant flushed its waste of chlorine and other chemicals directly into the Wabigoon River, creating a relatively high level of mercury. Eventually, the mercury worked its way up the local food chain, severely damaging the mental and physical health of people in the local Aboriginal communities who ate the contaminated fish (Bone, 1992: 167). The Aboriginal peoples of Fort Chipewyan in northern Alberta, meanwhile, have been experiencing high rates of unusual cancers that many attribute to contaminated water runoff from the Fort McMurray oil sands seeping into the Athabasca River (see Marsden, 2007; Nikiforuk, 2008).

These instances highlight a further aspect of changes in Canadian society with implications for northern development: increased recognition of environmental considerations. The pressures for economic development upon a poor region with rising unemployment and a diminishing "old industry," such as furs, are enormous. It becomes difficult to imagine why people in such a region might turn down the chance, at any price, to jump aboard the development train.

In the 1970s, however, the people of the North did just that. The oil crises of that decade suddenly made financially feasible the possibility of shipping northern oil and gas to southern markets via an overland pipeline crossing Yukon and the Northwest Territories. Large companies were eager to exploit the moment. Federal government approval was required, however, and though technically able to make decisions for the northern territories, which lack the status of provinces, the federal government was increasingly sensitive to northern residents' concerns. The government struck a commission of inquiry.

The Mackenzie Valley Pipeline Inquiry (better known as the Berger Inquiry, after its chair, Justice Thomas Berger) went on for three years (1974–1977) and may properly be described as the first significant public study of the environmental and social effects of economic development ever conducted in Canada. Altogether, 1,000 people, including 300 experts in 35 communities, testified at the hearings, resulting in 204 volumes of relevant data. Berger's final recommendation was blunt. He outright rejected the pipeline proposal, based on the threat of damage to the local ecosystem, and recommended an alternative route through the Mackenzie Valley after a delay of 10 years.

Today, the North is nearly fully integrated into the rest of Canada and the world economy. The number of Aboriginal peoples working in the old economy and living in the old ways has decreased, replaced—if often tenuously—by work in the new economy: the hydrocarbon industries (including diamonds), government bureaucracies, tourism, and the manufacture of cultural products (such as narwhal carvings and beadwork). Unemployment remains stubbornly high.

To an extent cultural integration is also happening. Most northern peoples today live in permanent settlements. The pickup truck and the snowmobile have long replaced the dog team, and the same assortment of large stores, schools, churches, hospitals, sports arenas, and other institutions found in many small Canadian towns in the South can be seen in the North (Condon, 1987).

Moreover, Aboriginal languages and cultures are no longer being explicitly attacked, though they continue to face enormous cultural pressures, but instead are encouraged (Brody, 1987: 163). The training of Aboriginal teachers has been undertaken and curricula have been amended to reflect local themes.

To be sure, old problems remain to which new ones have been added. High rates of school absenteeism and dropout are still a concern (Tompkins, 1998: 47). Alcoholism, solvent abuse (especially among the young), and murder and suicide rates have increased. The North has also experienced a high incidence of new diseases, such as diabetes and, since the 1990s, AIDS, as well as the return of an old nemesis, tuberculosis.

Amid these changes, and in the context of renewed fears about world energy shortages, the idea of a northern pipeline is being revisited. The newly proposed $18.2 billion Mackenzie Gas Project has the potential to deliver 30 trillion cubic feet of natural gas in the delta and further south to meet the needs in the southern (especially American) market. As in 1977, a joint Review Panel has been holding public meetings to consider social, economic, and environmental implications of such a development (Gregoire, 2007: 58). This time around, however, the project has garnered support from northern people, including Aboriginals; former Justice Berger has even come out in support of a pipeline, saying the North is now ready to handle the associated difficulties while taking advantage of the opportunity.

Ironically, just as the North seems prepared to embrace the pipeline, it may lose out to a competing bid, the construction of a gas pipeline from Alaska to Alberta. However it turns out, the original Berger Inquiry will stand as a landmark in Canada's relations with the North and its peoples. The Berger Inquiry was the first time the wishes of local northerners themselves became central to decision making. The North gained a voice, but the inquiry also had the effect of informing many Canadians elsewhere about the North and about environmental issues generally. In this sense, the North also played a role in shaping Canadians' growing concern, reflected in subsequent years, over environmental matters, a concern, one might add, that is also slowly working its way into sociology (see Box 11.1).

Box 11.1
The Ecological Challenge to Sociology

Catton and Dunlap (1980) argue that traditional sociology is premised on a set of assumptions that human society is exempt from ecological considerations, a broader rubric they term the "Human Exemptionalist Paradigm," which comprises four central beliefs:

1. Humans have a cultural heritage in addition to (and distinct from) their genetic inheritance, and thus are quite unlike all other animal species.

2. Social and cultural factors, including technology, are the major determinants of human affairs.

3. Social and cultural environments are the crucial contexts for human affairs, and the biophysical environment is largely irrelevant.

4. Culture is cumulative, thus technological and social progress can continue indefinitely, making all social problems ultimately soluble.

By contrast, they argue for a "New Ecological Paradigm" based on four very different assumptions:

1. While humans have exceptional characteristics (culture, technology, etc.), they remain one among species that are interdependently involved in the global ecosystem.

2. Human affairs are influenced not only by social and cultural factors, but also by intricate linkages of cause, effect, and feedback in a web of nature, thus purposive human actions have many unintended consequences.

3. Humans live in and are dependent upon a finite biophysical environment that imposes physical and biological restraints on human affairs.

4. Although the inventiveness of humans and the powers derived from that may seem for a while to extend carrying capacity limits, ecological laws cannot be repealed.

Source: William R. Catton and Riley E. Dunlap, "A new ecological paradigm for post-exuberant sociology," *American Behavioral Scientist* 24(1) (1980): 34.

GLOBAL WARMING, THE NORTH, AND CANADIAN SOVEREIGNTY

There is widespread recognition that the world's climate is rapidly changing. There is nearly equal consensus in favour of the global warming thesis that, first, the worldwide temperatures are increasing and, second, that human activity is a major contributor to this temperature rise. Sir Nicholas Stern (2007), former chief economist of the World Bank and adviser to the U.K. government on the economics of climate change, has argued that human-induced climate change is caused by emissions of carbon dioxide and other greenhouse gases, and that if world governments do not take action, the earth's mean temperature will rise by 2°C by 2035, causing millions of people to "suffer hunger, water shortages and coastal flooding...." His report called for a stabilization of world temperatures at levels 25 percent below current levels by 2050 and ultimately 80 percent below current levels.

The Report of the United Nations Intergovernmental Panel on Climate Change (United Nations, 2007a) similarly argued that fossil fuel use was the primary source of increased carbon dioxide in the atmosphere since the pre-industrial period, and noted that 11 of the 12 hottest years on record since 1850 occurred between 1995 and 2006, with a total temperature increase of 76°C. Modelling the range of temperature change scenarios, the same report projects that average temperatures will rise between 1.1°C and 6.4°C during the period 2090–2099 relative to the period 1980–1999 (Weaver, 2008: 208). According to James Lovelock (2009), originator of the Gaia hypothesis, the Stern report's prediction of a 2°C rise is not achievable and that the earth's temperature will rise well above the predicted average, closer to the Intergovernmental Panel on Climate Change's (IPCC) upper projections of a 4–6°C rise. Such a change would mean a massive loss of human and animal life as rising sea levels inundate much of the planet, while many other areas would be rendered uninhabitable due to heat and drought. In turn, these temperature changes would have massive economic, social, and political impacts, including dramatic population shifts and intensified competition for scarce resources, leading, some predict, to war (Dyer, 2008).

What impact might global warming have on Canada and for the North specifically? The IPCC report (United Nations, 2007a) notes that the average Arctic temperature has increased at twice the global average in the past 100 years. Satellite data show that since 1978, the area of Arctic sea ice has shrunk by 2.7 percent in each decade.

In the long term, the impact of global warming upon Canada will be less negative than elsewhere, but still serious. Lemmen and Warren (2007: 23–24) succinctly describe some of the more serious impacts:

> The magnitude of changes in climate will vary across the country, with northern regions and the south-central Prairies warming the most. Average annual precipitation is also projected to rise, although increases in evaporation and transpiration by plants in some regions are expected to more than offset increases in annual precipitation, resulting in increased aridity. More frequent heavy precipitation events, less precipitation during the growing season and more precipitation during the winter are also projected for Canada.
>
> Gradual shifts in average conditions will be accompanied by changes in climate variability and the frequency of extreme weather and climate events. These changes will result in both positive and negative social, economic and environmental impacts.

In the case of the North, the latter is more certainly the case than the former. Cohen (1997) speculates, for example, that changing weather conditions could cause more frequent landslides due to permafrost thaw, lower minimum annual water levels on rivers and lakes, more forest fires, and lower yields from softwoods, impacts off-setting any potential benefits from a longer growing and ice-free season.

For the people of the Far North, global warming could prove particularly disastrous, bringing about what political scientist Franklyn Griffiths has termed "cultural genocide" as the Inuit hunting way of life melts away with the sea ice. "They won't be able to practice a hunting culture at all" (*Edmonton Journal*, 2007).

It is said the Athapaskan and Tlinget elders have cautioned newcomers to the region to respect the glaciers that tradition suggests are living sentient beings. A retired anthropologist, Julie Cruikshank, has observed: "The glaciers were seen as animate as any animals…. They responded to people. They took offence easily. You had to be very circumspect in the way you behaved around them, or you would be served catastrophic consequences" (Montgomery, 2007: 76).

As serious as are the environmental impacts of global warming, the latter may also hold important geopolitical consequences for Canada. As temperatures rise and the ice sheets melt, the dream of a Northwest Passage open to year-round shipping is quickly becoming a reality. Usually clogged with ice during the summer months, for example, the Northwest Passage was almost completely ice-free in August 2008.

Just as they were hundreds of years ago, the commercial attractions of a northern route are obvious, shortening significantly the time needed to ship goods east and west. Should the waterway become ice-free all year round, foreign fleets would seek to use it freely, posing a real threat to the fragile environment from oil leaks and other forms of contamination.

But it is not only the idea of year-round shipping through the Northwest Passage that is attracting renewed interest on the part of several states, notably Russia, the United States, Norway, and Denmark. Global warming has also unlocked the doors to the Arctic's undersea treasure house, a store that includes northern oil and gas—recent geological surveys suggest the Arctic may hold as much as 25 percent of the world's undiscovered oil and gas—as well as valuable minerals, such as diamonds. The fight is on among northern nation-states to secure subsurface rights in the Arctic.

Few Canadians realize that the country's jurisdiction over the region, especially its waterways, is disputed. The United States, in particular, asserts that the Northwest Passage is not an internal waterway of Canada but an international strait. The Russians, by contrast, do not argue with Canada's claim that the passage is a part of Canada's internal waters. Rather, their claim is to the polar seabed (Coates et al., 2008: 2), hence a Russian submarine's symbolic planting of a Russian flag on the seabed under the North Pole in August 2007.

In response to threats to Canada's jurisdiction, Prime Minister Stephen Harper announced in 2007 plans to "build military ice-breakers, upgrade underwater and aerial surveillance capabilities, build a deep-water port, and expand Canada's military presence in the area" (Coates et al., 2008: 172). Much more needs to be done, however, if the North is to truly become part of Canada, and it needs to be done on a consistent, long-term basis. Canadians and the Canadian state have a long history of short-term interest in the North and a comparatively short history of genuine interest in the people who actually live there.

CONCLUSION

For most Canadians, Canada's North remains a place of fantasy and imagery only, a land rich in symbolism and myth, but largely unknown, yet it is important to all Canada in ways that Canadians have not yet recognized.

Since the 1980s, Canada has started to forge a new relationship with the North and its peoples, but progress has been slow and uneven. The creation of Nunavut in 1999 was an important step; likewise, some land claim issues there have been settled, though many remain. Among the most important issues remaining are calls for self-government. This is a call heard elsewhere in Canada by Aboriginal peoples, one that, unheeded, has often led to conflict in recent decades, the subject of the chapter to follow.

KEY TERMS

dual economy
enfranchisement
individual egalitarianism
polygyny
syncretism

CRITICAL THINKING QUESTIONS

1. Why do places such as the North gain such a hold on the human imagination?

2. What examples of syncretism can you identify from other cultures?

3. In what ways are the kinds of megaprojects in the Canadian North similar to those occurring in many underdeveloped countries?

4. How might Catton and Dunlap's "New Ecological Paradigm," if adopted, alter the way sociologists look at issues?

5. Why is the issue of climate change important to Canada as a whole?

RECOMMENDED READINGS

Abel, Kerry. 1993. *Drum Songs: Glimpses of Dene History.* Montreal and Kingston: McGill-Queen's University Press.
This book surveys the culture of the Dene people, who number 12,000, speak five distinct languages, and live in an area of roughly 1.8 million square kilometres.

Bone, Robert M. 2000. *The Regional Geography of Canada.* Toronto: Oxford University Press.
Considered a watershed work on Canada's North, Bone expertly details the topography of this region and outlines the challenges faced by people living there.

Coates, Ken S., P. Whitney Lackenbauer, William R. Morrison, and Greg Poelzer. 2008. *Arctic Front: Defending Canada in the Far North.* Toronto: Thomas Allen.
This book provides an environmental, historical, political, and economic overview of the issues facing the Canadian North today.

Frideres, James S., and René R. Gadacz. 2001. *Aboriginal Peoples in Canada: Contemporary Conflicts,* 6th ed. Scarborough: Prentice-Hall Canada.
Each new edition of this oft-published book documents various contemporary challenges faced by the First Nations of Canada.

Massey, Don, and Patricia N. Shields. 1995. *Canada: Its Land and People,* 2nd ed. Edmonton: Reidmore Books.
Although somewhat elementary in prose and style, this book provides valuable information about the various cultural facets that make up this nation.

RELATED WEBSITES

CBC Digital Archives
http://archives.cbc.ca/economy_business/transport/topics/2349/
This site contains useful video footage on the North, specifically a piece entitled "Breaking the Ice: Canada and the Northwest Passage."

Intergovernmental Panel of Climate Change
www.ipcc.ch/
The United Nations Environment Programme and the World Meteorological Organization established the Intergovernmental Panel of Climate Change (IPCC) in 1988 to provide scientific information on the current state of climate change and its potential environmental and socio-economic consequences.

Mackenzie Gas Project
www.mackenziegasproject.com/
Since the mid-1970s, discussion has gone on regarding the building of a natural gas pipeline along the Mackenzie Valley. Information on the Mackenzie Gas Project can be found at this site.

CANADIAN SOCIETY ON VIDEO

Kalvak. 1970. The Arctic Institute of North America, 20 minutes. Details the life and career of Inuit artist, Helen Kolvak.

People of the Ice. 2003. National Film Board of Canada, 52 minutes. Examines the Inuit way of life and how it is threatened by global warming today.

Rush for Gold: The Klondike Gold Rush, 1987. 1991. National Film Board of Canada, 20 minutes, 7 seconds. Captures the excitement and tragic events of the Yukon Gold Rush and the early technologies employed in mining the gold.

The Necessities of Life. 2008. 102 minutes. The film traces the removal by boat from Baffin Island in 1952 of an Inuit hunter (played by Natar Ungalaaq) to a Quebec City sanatorium.

CHAPTER 12

THE FIGHT FOR JUSTICE

The day will come when Indians will not be concerned with struggling for their basic rights only, but for the basic rights of all.

—Cree lawyer William Wuttunee, 1971

The governments of the day ... do not want to discuss ways of transforming legal or political institutions to include indigenous peoples in nation-states. They do not want to end their national fantasies and myths about our nations. They do not want to expose the injustices that have informed the construction of state institutions and practices.

—Marie Battiste and James (Sa'ke'j) Youngblood Henderson, 2000

However noble and necessary justice is to our struggles, its gaze will always be backward. By itself, the concept of justice is not capable of encompassing the broader transformations needed to ensure coexistence. Justice is one element of a good relationship; it is concerned with fairness and right and calculating moral balances, but it cannot be the end goal of a struggle....

—author and professor Taiaiake Alfred, 2005

INTRODUCTION

Well into the 20th century, Aboriginal peoples remained hidden from mainstream Canadian society. Occasionally, they escaped the reserves, often as athletes, some, like Tom Longboat, quite famous, others toiling as baseball or hockey players. The two world wars of the 20th century provided another opportunity for escape. During the Second World War, some 3,000 Status Indians and an unknown number of Métis and other Aboriginal peoples enlisted, several of whom were decorated for valour. In general, however, the colonial reserve system fulfilled its function of segregating Aboriginal peoples from Canadian society. But gradually, they have begun reclaiming their voice. This chapter examines this process of reclamation and the search for justice, a process that continues today, sometimes in conflict, sometimes in co-operation. It begins with a discussion of the emergence of Aboriginal organizations capable of fighting for positive change.

ABORIGINAL CAPACITY AND THE HAWTHORN REPORT

Under the Indian Act, enacted in 1876, members of Indian organizations were prevented from meeting by a pass system that forbade individuals to leave their reserves without permission of the Indian agent. Under Section 141 of the same Act, introduced in 1927, it was an offence to raise money for the purpose of advancing Aboriginal claims (Purich, 1986: 185).

Despite these impediments, a few Aboriginal organizations *did* emerge in Canada during the 1930s and 1940s. These included the Native Brotherhood of British Columbia, the Indian Association of Alberta, and, with the encouragement of that province's CCF government, the Union of Saskatchewan Indians. In the 1960s the federal government's decision to fund Aboriginal organizations meant the further growth of other organizations. The National Indian Brotherhood (NIB) was formed in 1968 when the National Indian Council split into two factions, the NIB and the Canadian Métis Society. These and other, newer Aboriginal organizations experienced some success through lobbying, organizing, and protesting. Together, these organizations drew attention to a wider range of concerns that went beyond individual First Nations (Frideres and Gadacz, 2001), and finally convinced governments to also take a hard look at a community within Canada too long ignored. The result was the Hawthorn Report.

In 1963, the federal government asked University of British Columbia anthropologist Harry Hawthorn to study the living conditions of Canada's Aboriginal peoples. This was at a time when Canada was rapidly becoming urbanized, but Aboriginals, rural and confined to reserves, still made little impression upon most Canadians. Hawthorn's subsequent study (1966–1967) stunned everyone, however, including government leaders. Few knew or had taken the time to find out about the devastating conditions under which most Canadian Aboriginals were living. The Hawthorn Report catalogued the plight of Aboriginals from high rates of unemployment and poverty to health problems, including malnutrition, and a resultant life expectancy that was dismally below that of other Canadians. It made clear that Aboriginal housing was substandard and education was inadequate. Finally, the report made an important plea that Aboriginal peoples should be extended the same rights as other citizens *and* be assured that their legal rights as Status Indians also be honoured, a plea captured in the term **citizens plus**.

The Hawthorn Report was delivered in the context of a great deal of discussion of human rights and fundamental freedoms. The American civil rights movement spilled over into Canada and forced the government to focus attention on neglected minorities. The Red Power movement and Vietnam War demonstrations in the U.S. threatened many Canadians who feared that similar protests might occur in their country, fears amplified by the armed occupation of Anicinabe Park in Kenora, Ontario, and a near riot on Parliament Hill (Purich, 1986: 188).

Fear alone does not explain the majority reaction, however. The 1960s in Canada, as elsewhere, reflected a sincere if paternalistic belief in providing opportunities for neglected communities to "join" the rest of society. Unfortunately, these efforts implied that all responsibility for accommodation lay within the minority camp. These efforts further assumed that education and good teaching were the chief vehicles for equalizing opportunity and minimizing differences (Friesen, 1993: 7).

In 1967, Canada celebrated 100 years as a nation. It was also a time of civil unrest, and there were many questions about relationships between people and institutions, including provincial and federal governments. Similarly, the role of the United States in the Vietnam War was under scrutiny, city parks were full of "hippies," universities were sites of "sit-ins," and anti-establishment marches protesting all sorts of things were frequent. Against this background, while clutching the Hawthorn Report, in 1969 Pierre Trudeau's Liberal government made public its new Aboriginal policy in a White Paper.

WHITE PAPER, RED PAPER

The Trudeau administration, which came to power in Ottawa in 1968, was modernist to a fault; that is, it believed firmly in the role of the state in society and, at the same time, the values of liberal individualism and economic progress. In this vein, the Liberal government decided to adopt a new Aboriginal policy, the intent of which was to resolve Aboriginal land claims and to eliminate distinctions between Aboriginal peoples and other Canadians. Aboriginal peoples were to be made individually self-reliant. Indian status was to disappear as a meaningful term in law (Boldt, 1993: 18).

The government's deliberations on Aboriginal policy occurred against the backdrop of one of the most important studies ever conducted in Canada. The White Paper (Government of Canada, 1969) included the following proposed government actions:

1. Abolish the Department of Indian Affairs and Northern Development.

2. Repeal the Indian Act.

3. Transfer all responsibility for Indian programs to provincial administration. Provide economic assistance to those reserves that are furthest behind.

4. Formulate a policy to end treaties.

5. Appoint an Indian claims commissioner.

6. Recognize the contributions that Indian people have made to Canadian society.

Many Aboriginal leaders immediately and vigorously denounced the government's White Paper and were joined in their repudiation by a number of non-Aboriginal social and political organizations. In his book, *The Unjust Society*, a prominent young Aboriginal leader, Harold Cardinal, contrasted the White Paper with Pierre Trudeau's vision of a "Just Society," calling the White Paper "a programme which offers nothing better than cultural genocide" (1969: 1).

The first official reaction to the White Paper came in the form of the Red Paper in 1970 (Indian Chiefs of Alberta, 1970). Authorized by the Aboriginal chiefs of Alberta, the Red Paper heavily criticized the White Paper, claiming that it was a document of despair, not hope. The framers of the Red Paper contended that, if the proposals of the White Paper were implemented, within a generation or two Aboriginals would be left with no land and the threat of complete assimilation. (Indeed, the White Paper made clear that the government did not accept the notion of Aboriginal rights.) The Red Paper itself soon drew strong criticism, however,

notably by Cree lawyer William Wuttunee (1928–) in his book *Ruffled Feathers* (1971), who accused the Red Paper's authors of fostering a treaty mentality and supporting a buckskin-and-feather culture.

A second major paper critical of the White Paper emanated from the Union of British Columbia Indian Chiefs and became known as the Brown Paper. The Brown Paper argued that the special relationship between Aboriginals and the federal government, developed through the years, should not be negated. Indeed, the framers of the Brown Paper insisted that this relationship carried immense moral and legal force and should constitute the foundation for future co-operative policy-making. The Brown Paper also made reference to the principle of self-determination and suggested that bands should take over aspects of reserve administration at local levels. In this, the authors of the Brown Paper joined with other Aboriginal organizations in asking the Indian Affairs Branch to provide the necessary financial resources to develop their plans, programs, and budgets toward that end.

Officials of the Government of Canada were surprised and dismayed by the response of Aboriginals to the White Paper. Government officials' surprise was not related solely to the forcefulness of the response. They were also surprised by the articulate and organized nature of Aboriginal response to the White Paper. Faced with such opposition, in 1970 the federal government decided not to proceed with implementing the White Paper (Purich, 1986: 187).

Nonetheless, the White Paper and the ensuing controversy had several important impacts. First, the White Paper resulted in the renewed growth of Aboriginal organizations on the Canadian scene. Second, it led to an immediate change in government land claims policy with the appointment of an Indian claims commissioner in 1969. (The appointment was one of the few White Paper's recommendations acceptable to most Aboriginals.)

This second impact subsequently led (in August 1973) to the federal government announcing a comprehensive land claims policy recognizing two broad categories of claims: comprehensive claims based on Aboriginal rights, and specific claims based on specific legal commitments. Funding to pursue these claims was made possible through a newly established Office of Native Claims. In 1975, the Dene of the Northwest Territories became one of the first Aboriginal groups to claim First Nation status. The following year the Inuit Tapirisat proposed a land claim settlement that eventually gave birth to the territory of Nunavut on April 1, 1999 (Geddes, 2000) (see Chapter 13).

The White Paper's third impact is harder to measure, but no less important. The debate surrounding the White Paper and Aboriginal response to it educated many in the non-Aboriginal community about the issues facing Aboriginal peoples. It was knowledge reinforced on many occasions over the next 30 years through commission reports, constitutional meetings, and conflict.

ABORIGINALS AND THE 1982 CONSTITUTION

In February 1980, Prime Minister Pierre Trudeau declared his intention to bring home Canada's Constitution (Chapter 4). Immediately, a number of Aboriginal organizations began lobbying both the federal government and the British Parliament to include Aboriginal rights in the process of patriation. The lobbying worked, for in January 1981 Minister of Justice Jean Chrétien introduced an amendment to the proposed Constitution that would "recognize and affirm" the Aboriginal and treaty rights of Canada's Aboriginal peoples. The amendment included in its recognition the existence of Indian, Inuit, and Métis peoples.

Chrétien also proposed that a conference to define Aboriginal rights be held within two years of the date when the patriation process would be complete.

Almost immediately, however, these amendments ran into problems. On November 5, 1981, all provinces except Quebec agreed to repatriation, but this incomplete consensus was achieved by dropping Aboriginal rights from the Constitution. Then the first ministers reversed their position, agreeing to the inclusion of these rights on condition that the word "existing" would be added. This meant that Aboriginals could expect no new rights, and that only the rights they already possessed would be endorsed by the Constitution. Many feared that this condition would hinder the development of Aboriginal self-government, fears that were well justified (see below).

On April 17, 1982, Canadians could finally say that they had their own Constitution. For Aboriginal peoples, the new Constitution remained incomplete, but nonetheless represented an important step. It affirmed existing Aboriginal rights in broad terms and thus opened the door for making land claims. For the first time, the Métis, along with the Inuit, garnered specific mention in Canada's Constitution. Furthermore, the document set out a process of ongoing constitutional conferences aimed at defining Aboriginal rights and giving Aboriginal peoples the opportunity to present their views. Finally, the Canadian Charter of Rights and Freedoms not only recognized and affirmed Aboriginal and treaty rights, it also put a spotlight on what some observers saw as the Indian Act's discriminatory provisions.

WHO IS AN INDIAN?

Since the establishment of the Indian Act in 1876, legislation governing Aboriginals had defined who was an Aboriginal in a way that discriminated against women. To begin with, on "the day that the government counted the Indians," all who "stood in line" became Status Indians by law. This afforded them the privilege of having matters pertaining to health, education, and welfare delivered directly through federal auspices. Children born to Status Indians were added to the Indian Register.

But what happened if a Status Indian woman married a non-Status male (either Aboriginal or non-Aboriginal)? In these cases, she lost her status rights. Likewise, any children born to her also were deprived of status. This was not true for males, however. In fact, if a Status Indian man married a non-Status woman (either Aboriginal or non-Aboriginal), that woman became a Status Indian. This gender discrimination bothered many people, particularly since the 1973 Lavell case, which upheld this discriminatory provision of the Indian Act. The terms of the Charter of Rights and Freedoms may have been influenced by the 1975 case of Sandra Lovelace, who took her complaint of gender discrimination to the Human Rights Committee of the United Nations. In 1981 this committee decided that her case was one of "an unjustifiable denial of her rights under the United Nations' Covenant on Civil and Political Rights" (Miller, 2000: 357–358).

The issue of how Aboriginals traditionally viewed women's rights was complex. Aboriginal women were not unanimous in endorsing the equal-rights amendment that would end Status women's loss of their rights through marriage to non-Status males. Of eight national First Nations organizations, only four endorsed the bill. One group of Indian women launched a demonstration in Ottawa protesting the bill. Some argued that women who married "outside" knew very well what they were doing. Insofar as Aboriginals believe tribal spirituality is mainly transferred through women, who alone have the power to give life, marrying outside was viewed by some Aboriginals, male and female alike, as disregarding the spiritual welfare of the band. Hence, some believed that women doing so deserved to lose their status and should not be permitted to opt back in. There were also bands that refused to return band membership to women who were able to regain status through the auspices of Bill C-31. The result has been a new division in First Nations communities. As one Aboriginal individual remarked to one of the authors when a neighbour regained status, "Oh, so now she is a Bill C-31 Indian!"

The arguments put forward by those who objected to Bill C-31 were decidedly out of step with Canadian society and with many in the Aboriginal community. In 1985, Bill C-31 was passed, eliminating sexual discrimination, abolishing the concept of enfranchisement, and providing for those who had lost their Aboriginal status to gain partial reinstatement. The bill had the almost immediate effect of greatly enlarging Canada's Aboriginal population. By 2001, more than 105,000 people had regained Indian status under Bill C-31 (Frideres and Gadacz, 2001: 35) (see Chapter 13).

The conferences specified in the Constitution began with one held March 15–16, 1983. This first conference was followed by three additional conferences. From the beginning, at least one practical problem beset these conferences: that of representation. Through tradition and the Indian Act, Status Indians had a recognized seat at the gatherings. This was not the case, however, for Métis people and non-Status Indians. In the past, the Native Council of Canada (NCC) had spoken for Métis people, but the Métis disagreed with the NCC's definition of Métis (anyone of mixed blood) and wanted a more explicit definition, including the origins and domicile of the Métis in the Red River area. Similarly, non-Status Indians demanded equal rights with Status Indians. By contrast, the Métis were not requesting status rights; they simply wanted to be recognized as a distinct Aboriginal group.

In the end, Prime Minister Trudeau asked the NCC to represent Métis inter- ests, a move that caused a further split in the Aboriginal community. A new organization, the Métis Nation Council, was then formed by a group of dissidents who launched a court case to demand that their interests also be represented at constitutional conferences. When the first conference was over, it was agreed that no constitutional changes affecting Aboriginal rights would be made without a constitu- tional conference for that explicit purpose, to which Aboriginal representatives would be invited (Schwartz, 1986: 127). It was fur- ther agreed that future land claims would include a definition of "existing rights" and that sexual equality would be guaranteed, hence the later passing of Bill C-31.

FROM MEECH LAKE TO OKA AND BEYOND

The failure of the Meech Lake Accord in 1990 had important consequences for Quebec–Canada relations (Chapter 4). The Meech Lake Accord likewise had important consequences for Aboriginal peoples.

From the beginning, groups of First Nations opposed the Meech Lake Accord. They feared that the Accord's provisions recognizing Quebec's specificity would lead to a similar delegation of powers to the other provinces, including jurisdiction over Aboriginal affairs. Symbolically, the phrase respecting Quebec as a "distinct society" also rankled with Aboriginals, who believed that the Accord completely overlooked their historical traditions; indeed, it identified Quebec as the "fore- most distinct society" in Canada, implicitly building on the notion of "two founding races" (French and English) while ignoring the pre-existence of Aboriginal peoples on the continent. They were further upset that

Canada's first ministers had long rejected the entrenchment of Aboriginal rights on the grounds that the concept was too vague and undefined, yet suddenly they were quite willing to grant similar rights to the province of Quebec (York, 1989: 266).

Technically, the Meech Lake Accord died on the East Coast when the Newfoundland legislature failed to vote on it. In fact, how- ever, the Accord's final defeat can be attrib- uted to the actions of one lone individual, Elijah Harper (1949–), an Aboriginal NDP member of the Opposition in the Manitoba legislature. By the spring of 1990, the House of Commons and most provinces had given the Accord approval. Newfoundland and Manitoba had not, however, and time was running out. The agreed-upon procedure required that for the Manitoba legislature to vote on the Accord, and thus make the dead- line, there had to be unanimous approval by the members. When the proposal to cut debate short was put forward, however, Harper stood alone in refusing approval. Without this approval, the Accord could not be passed in time. Newfoundland's govern- ment knew this outcome already on the day it also refused to vote on the Accord.

The Accord's failure had profound con- sequences for Aboriginal–non-Aboriginal relations not only in Quebec but elsewhere in Canada. The first consequence of this failure was a series of actual confronta- tions between Aboriginal peoples and Canadian governments that escalated in several instances to armed conflict.

The most immediate and famous of these conflicts occurred in Oka, Quebec. Cross and Sevigny (1994: 80) describe the events:

> Everything began on a nice day in March 1990, when the Municipal Council of the Village of Oka [outside Montreal] adopted the proposal to expand the area's golf course. In one stroke, Oka's Pines and Mohawk cemetery at Kanehsatake were threatened. To

protect their land and the graves of their ancestors, the Mohawks erected a barricade to make the Whites understand that they intended to protect their land against all invaders.

As with any conflict, however, the roots of the Oka Crisis (as it quickly became known) were much older. In fact, the conflict dated back to 1717, when King Louis XV of France granted the land in question to the Seminary of St. Sulpice to set up a mission for the resident Aboriginals, mainly Huron, Algonquin, and Iroquois. By French law (which never recognized Aboriginal land title), later confirmed by British and Canadian governments, the lands of Kanesatake (Oka) did not legally belong to the Aboriginal inhabitants, but to the Aboriginals, this was their land (Dickason, 2002: 343–346). Indeed, for many Mohawks and their supporters, such legal decisions merely reinforced the notion that law and justice are often strangers, and that the Canadian legal system is simply another tool for state oppression, an idea with which many conflict theorists would find sympathy.

The crisis escalated into violence when the Quebec police decided to capture and take down the barricades, resulting in the death of a police officer, the exact circumstances being uncertain to this day. The Canadian government quickly sent in 2,500 soldiers to surround the reserve now guarded by khaki-clad Mohawk "warriors," bearing automatic rifles. Sympathy barricades arose on other Mohawk reserves nearly. The crisis lasted 11 weeks, during which many Canadians, Aboriginal and non-Aboriginal alike, feared a horrible bloodbath (Alfred, 1995: 100). Thankfully, this did not occur. On September 26, 1990 the crisis ended with the Mohawk warriors putting down their weapons and walking out from behind the barricade. Only

a few dozen Mohawk warriors were tried in court; a few were convicted on minor offences and sentenced to short periods in jail.

Today, there remains a great deal of mistrust between Mohawks and the Quebec and federal governments, and between Mohawks and the surrounding non-Aboriginal community. But there are also fractures within the Mohawk community between moderate and hardline Mohawk nationalists, worsened since 1990 by the emergence of criminal gangs thriving on gambling and smuggling (primarily of cigarettes, but also guns). As for the disputed land, in June 2000 the Kanesatake Mohawk band signed a deal with Ottawa gaining control (but not legal title) of their affairs, while the Mohawk band council has gained the right to establish bylaws, zoning regulations, and a process for resolving disputes on those lands, a situation akin to self-government (see below).

The Oka Crisis must be viewed in a larger context, however. We have already examined Aboriginal resistance in the 18th and 19th centuries (Chapter 10). Aboriginal peoples have never given up—nor can they give up—the fight (whether militantly or politically expressed) for self-governance. Long before Oka, there had been confrontations. In 1969, for example, Mohawk Indians from the St. Regis Reserve blocked the international bridge between Canada and the United States near Cornwall, Ontario. In September 1989, the Barriere Lake Algonquin of Quebec blockaded six logging roads in an effort to save their traditional hunting grounds and way of life.

After Oka, the number of confrontations increased and were no longer confined to Quebec, among them: Ipperwash in Ontario (where an Aboriginal protester, Dudley George, was killed by the Ontario Provincial Police), the Old Man Dam in Alberta, and Gustafson Lake in British Columbia. Today, such confrontations still occur (see Box 12.1).

Box 12.1
The Caledonia Story

Canada's longest Aboriginal occupation began on February 28, 2006. The dispute, involving the Six Nations of Grand River, Ontario, centres on a 40 hectare parcel of land at Caledonia, Ontario, near Hamilton. Like Oka, the origins of the dispute go back a long way, in this case to 1784 when the British government awarded the Six Nations 385,000 hectares of land in exchange for their allegiance during the American War of Independence. According to the federal government, the land was later bought back in 1841; according to the Six Nations, however, the land was only leased to the government at that time. The dispute has simmered since that time, with the land having been sold (first, in 1848), an action that the Six Nations insist they never agreed to nor for which have they received adequate compensation.

Despite litigation, a developer bought the land in 1992 and in 2005 registered plans to build a housing development. This action sparked protests that began in early 2006, causing work at the site to cease immediately. The Ontario government obtained a court injunction in April 2006 to have the protesters removed, leading the Ontario Provincial Police to raid the site and arrest more than a dozen people. However, as word of the arrests spread, hundreds of Aboriginal peoples quickly descended on the site and set up barricades that remained up for several months. Meanwhile, relations between the Six Nations and the residents of Caledonia deteriorated, with several incidents of violence reported and accusations the police have played less than a neutral role.

In 2007, the federal government made an undisclosed offer to the developer and pledged $1 million in compensation to Caledonia's businesspeople. The Six Nations leaders refused the federal offer of $26 million and in 2008 erected new barricades. The saga of protests, violence, and land claims continues.

Why have Aboriginal protests increased in recent decades? Clearly, the protests reflect a great deal of frustration on their part. Anger and discontent do not alone lead to political action, however. Examining the increase in Aboriginal protests in recent years, the sociologist Ramos (2006) has concluded that the increase in Aboriginal-launched protests is positively related to the number of Aboriginal organizations; that is, successful political action requires organization. By contrast, Ramos argues that the incidence of Aboriginal protest movements appears somewhat unrelated to the rise of either pan-Indian ideology or the availability of resources. Ultimately, Aboriginal mobilization seems characterized by differences among communities, organizations, and status groups.

Oka and these other confrontations alarmed many Canadians, both Aboriginal and non-Aboriginal alike. (Regrettably, in some quarters, racism and prejudice also reared their heads.) The sight of Canadian soldiers and police squaring off against Aboriginal protesters revealed starkly the depth of the divide between Canada's other "two solitudes" and the possible dangers if that gulf was not addressed. For 20 years, Canada–Quebec issues had dominated the political agenda. In the context of the failures of the Meech Lake and Charlottetown accords, and in the aftermath of Oka, Aboriginal–non-Aboriginal issues came to be seen as parallel to Canada–Quebec issues. They became better known to the general public and gained support, albeit sometimes grudging. Within government circles, a heightened sense of urgency over such things as treaties and the Aboriginal right to self-government also emerged (Mercredi and Turpel, 1993: 209–210). The creation of the Royal Commission on Aboriginal Peoples was a tangible result of this changed mood.

THE ROYAL COMMISSION ON ABORIGINAL PEOPLES

In the wake of the failure of the Meech Lake Accord and the Oka Crisis, in 1991 the federal government established the Royal Commission on Aboriginal Peoples (RCAP) (Indian and Northern Affairs Canada, 1996). Chaired by former Assembly of First Nations Chief George Erasmus and Quebec Judge René Dussault, the commission included seven members, four of them Aboriginal and three of them non-Aboriginal. A number of public meetings were held, transcripts were analyzed, and a great deal of research was undertaken, though it is clear both from the structure of the report and from the public hearings that the commissioners regarded their task as an exercise in public education as well as a government investigation (Miller, 2000: 385).

Altogether, the Royal Commission cost $50 million. Its final report in 1996 consisted of five volumes, over 3,500 pages, and 400 recommendations. The report's main findings were contained in five sections.

In essence, the report recommended a major reconstruction of Canadian society so that justice and equality would be better assured for Aboriginal Canadians. Two specific and urgent concerns of the report had to do with the high suicide rates in Aboriginal communities and the high incidence of Aboriginal peoples in jail, especially in the western provinces, which raised issues regarding the fairness of Canada's criminal justice system. The commission recommended swift action in these areas, starting with a meeting of the various bars, law societies, and lawyers' associations. It urged increased government expenditures in preventive programs.

More broadly, the RCAP also recommended rewriting the principles of the Royal Proclamation to reflect the new nation-to-nation concept of negotiation, as well as a new constitutional foundation

by which to perceive the past treaty-making process. In the words of Ponting (1997a: 470), the report recommended at its core "the re-balancing of political and economic power between Aboriginal nations and the Canadian governments." Among its many recommendations was the formation of an Aboriginal parliament with an advisory but no law-making authority. This was seen as a first step toward creating a House of First Peoples as the third chamber of the Parliament of Canada. The commission also recommended the abolition of the Department of Indian Affairs and Northern Development and its replacement by two departments: the Department of Aboriginal Relations and the Department of Indian and Inuit Services.

The RCAP also recommended creating a number of new organizational structures, including an Aboriginal Peoples' International University along with Aboriginal student unions and Aboriginal residential colleges, and an Aboriginal Languages Foundation that would parallel the work of the international university and supplement its efforts to maintain Aboriginal languages and culture.

The Liberal government's response to the report was to set up in 1998 a special healing fund in the amount of $350 million to be used over a four-year period as a token of the government's apology for the treatment of Aboriginals in residential schools, and to approve an increase of $250 million in their next year's budget as a means of supporting the Aboriginal cause. The response of others was often critical, however.

While Phil Fontaine (1944–), grand chief of the AFN, generally approved of the recommendations, suggesting that they were the best one could hope for at the time, most Métis, Inuit, and non-Status Indians were critical of it and subsequent government actions as favouring Status Indians. Others noted the report's lack of emphasis on the situation of urban

Aboriginals, privileging reserve life and cultural persistence over solving socio-economic problems across the board (Allan Cairns cited in Miller, 2000: 385), a particularly important consideration, since more than one-third of Canada's First Nations now live in urban centres (see Chapter 13).

Likewise, the report also met with strong criticism in the non-Aboriginal community. One of the report's harshest critics is University of Calgary political scientist Thomas Flanagan (2000). Flanagan disagrees with the assumption that first habitation gives Aboriginals any particular rights over later arrivals; he argues that because Aboriginal peoples never continuously settled the land, but were nearly always in motion, they have no legitimate territorial claims, and contends that Aboriginal peoples are not nations, but rather subordinate communities within the nation of Canada, and hence lack a legitimate basis for claims to self-government.

While Flanagan acknowledges the current plight of Aboriginal peoples and their communities, he argues the solution does not lie in collective, racially based claims for political status and Aboriginal community property rights. Instead, Flanagan argues for a "realistic" interpretation of the ongoing relationship between Aboriginals and non-Aboriginals, including a full integration of Indian peoples into the modern economy, implying a willingness to leave the reserves, if necessary, and relocate to where there are jobs and investment opportunities (Flanagan, 2000: 7).

What can we make of Flanagan's criticisms? Setting aside counters to his particular arguments, the interesting thing are the "modernist" values upon which they are based. Seen this way, Flanagan's arguments point to the wide cultural gap remaining between Aboriginal and non-Aboriginal understandings of such things as social relationships, individualism, private property, capitalism, and notions of state and nation.

Today, few of the Royal Commission's recommendations (see Indian and Northern Affairs Canada, 1996) have been implemented. Nonetheless, its report set Canadian society on a new path in dealing with several Aboriginal issues. These issues include dealing with residential claims, revising or eliminating the Indian Act, settling existing land claims, signing modern treaties, and defining and implementing self-government, to which we now turn.

RESIDENTIAL CLAIMS

We have seen the role that residential schools played in the colonization of Aboriginal peoples (Chapter 10). Not all Aboriginals are products of Canada's residential schools, the last of which was closed in 1988. In fact, only about 30–35 percent of Aboriginal children ever attended residential schools. While some residents enjoyed life in these schools and report no unfortunate experiences, many more experienced years of physical, sexual, and psychological abuse, the effects of which were often visited upon later generations. The evidence for these claims is not seriously challenged. The ramifications, however, have been enormous.

Seeking legal redress for the abuses they had suffered, former residents of the schools were encouraged to bring forward their demands for justice. (The government defined abuse in narrow terms, excluding damages pertaining to loss of language and culture.) By April 1, 2000, there were 6,324 cases before the courts, many of them naming the Anglican, Presbyterian, Roman Catholic, and United Churches, as well as governments in their litigations (O'Hara, 2000). The Anglican Church was hit hard by legal costs arising from some of the first court cases, with total legal costs for nine dioceses alone exceeding $9 million. In a particularly well-known instance, the Diocese of Caribou declared bankruptcy and officially closed at the end of 2001 (*Edmonton Journal*, 2001).

Ironically, the plaintiffs have often received little of the money won through litigation. In one case, in 2001 the Supreme Court of British Columbia found the United Church of Canada 25 percent responsible and the federal government 75 percent responsible for damages suffered by six Aboriginal plaintiffs, and awarded them $500,000. The group had originally asked for $5 million, but after lawyers deducted 40 percent for their expenses, and after court costs were calculated, there was little money remaining (*Calgary Herald*, 2001).

On April 5, 2007, there was an end of sorts to residential claims. The Canadian courts approved the awarding of financial settlements to Indians who had endured time in residential schools. A fund of $1.9 billion was established to make payments to former residential school students on the basis of their time in the schools: $10,000 for the first year and $3,000 for each year (or part of) thereafter. Applicants had until August 20, 2007 to submit claims. Those not wishing to participate in the program were required to submit an opt-out form and forward it to the federal office in charge. They would still be free to launch individual cases against the government at their own cost (*Eagle Feather News*, 2007: 7).

THE INDIAN ACT

The Indian Act has not been substantially changed since its enactment in 1876. The federal government has on several occasions suggested either revising or even abandoning the Act, most notably in the White Paper of 1969 and again in 1999. Aboriginal responses to the idea of changing the Indian Act have been mixed, with most Aboriginals and their organizations rebuffing these suggestions, a response

that will likely surprise non-Aboriginal readers. Why is this the case? Why are many Aboriginal peoples reluctant to eliminate an Act at the heart of colonial oppression?

While some Aboriginal leaders clearly view the Indian Act as hindering efforts to get ahead, others view it as actually protecting certain of their rights, while still others support changing the Indian Act, but dislike the federal government's process for making changes, especially efforts at speaking over the head of the AFN leadership to the Aboriginal grassroots directly. They want the government to work through the AFN, which represents about half of Canada's Aboriginal peoples.

Three key issues in the Indian Act are viewed by most Aboriginal peoples as needing redress. First, the Indian Act does not make clear the powers of chief and council or the legal standing and capacity for Aboriginal bands and band councils to sue, to contract, to borrow, and so on. Second, the Act does not outline a clear and consistent system of determining band leadership selection and voting rights. Some bands follow procedures outlined in the Indian Act for the election of chiefs and councils, while others continue to follow a hereditary system of appointment with which the government has no power under the Indian Act to interfere. Additionally, while the Indian Act allows off-reserve Aboriginals to vote in band elections, they cannot run for the office of councillor, but can apply for the office of chief; in fact, one does not have to live on a reserve or even be a band member to run for that office. Third, the Indian Act has few rules ensuring that First Nations communities will be run in a fair and equitable manner. While many First Nations bands have in place their own system of accountability, these vary in structure and function, with many Aboriginal band members feeling that they have no control or say in bylaws, annual reports, accounting, and band budgeting. Many Aboriginal peoples likely agree that changes to the Indian Act are required in these three areas.

The push for changes to the Indian Act has gained momentum from recent court rulings in such areas as reserve elections and matrimonial and property rights for Aboriginal women. Today, legislation to replace the Indian Act continues winding its way through Parliament. A few years ago the government set aside a budget of $13 million for the project, though the recent economic downturn may hinder attempts at making progress.

EXISTING LAND CLAIMS AND MODERN TREATIES

We have previously examined the historical development of treaties in Canada (Chapter 10). Two types of claims under the treaty process need differentiation. Aboriginal peoples' claims under negotiation with the federal government involving *promises not fulfilled or interpretations of what was promised by either the treaties or scrip* are referred to as **specific claims**. Aboriginal peoples' claims *involving lands that they have never legally surrendered* are referred to as **comprehensive claims**. The latter include large areas of British Columbia and the North.

The need to deal with both specific and comprehensive claims has intensified in recent decades for two reasons. First, as Canadian economic development has shifted northward, governments and companies have wanted to ensure jurisdiction. Failure to make agreements in the NWT and Yukon, for example, where Aboriginal land claims have been based on the customary principle of Aboriginal rights (see Wittington, 1985), is currently holding up the transfer of Crown lands and the consequent construction of pipelines.

Second, Aboriginal peoples themselves have become more politically aware and adept in pressing their claims. An example of this is a pact signed in 2000 between the Blood, Peigan, and Siksika of Alberta and the Blackfeet of Montana nations, all members of the once mighty Blackfoot Confederacy that, before Treaty no. 7 was signed in 1877, controlled the southern third of Alberta stretching into Saskatchewan and Montana. The pact is meant to draw the government's attention to their concerns, including honouring Aboriginal rights, renewing tribal customs, and restoring lands that they insist were wrongfully appropriated from the Confederacy (*Edmonton Journal*, 2000c).

In some instances, Aboriginal claims have received sympathetic treatment from non-Aboriginals. An example is the decades-long claim of the Lubicon band of northern Alberta for about 10,000 square kilometres of land where oil production is underway and the Daishowa Pulp Mill has been operating. A significant amount of development has been undertaken in the area in the form of new roads and drilling sites, which have had a detrimental effect on wildlife, but the Lubicons have not benefited from the arrangement (Goddard, 1991). In 2008, Nova Gas Transmissions, a Trans-Canada Corporation subsidiary, applied to the Alberta Utilities Commission to construct a major gas pipeline through Lubicon land. Unlike previous projects, the Lubicon band was consulted, but did not give approval, and was denied formal intervener status on hearings into the project. As of today, the project seems to be going ahead.

In some instances, Aboriginal claims have faced strong opposition and sometimes resulted in violence between Aboriginals and non-Aboriginals. In the summer of 2000, for example, riots over lobster fishing broke out in Burnt Church, New Brunswick. A Department of Fisheries and Oceans boat had rammed an Aboriginal boat broadside, demolishing it and overturning several occupants into the water. The dispute was resolved later that fall when the Burnt Church band agreed to stop fishing three weeks earlier than they had planned. By then, the lobsters had already started their seasonal migration to colder waters, making them harder to catch.

It is the settlement of comprehensive claims that has caused the most concern, however. As noted in Chapter 11, the first comprehensive agreements were signed in the late 1970s by the Quebec government with the James Bay Cree of northern Quebec. The Inuvialuit agreement, dealing with lands in Canada's Far North, followed in 1984, extinguishing Aboriginal title to the western Arctic in return for ownership of 96,000 square kilometres of territory and $55 million (combined) in benefits and money for economic development (Dickason, 2002: 405). After 14 years of negotiation, a similar agreement, the Dene/Métis Western Arctic Land Claim agreement, was cancelled by the federal government, which refused to renegotiate the extinguishing of Aboriginal title (Dickason, 2002: 406; see also Geddes, 2000). This was quickly followed, however, by a series of other, smaller agreements signed with bands in Yukon and the Northwest Territories.

Finally, in 1999, the territory of Nunavut was created. Nunavut (meaning "our land") began as a proposal submitted in 1976 by the Inuit Tapirisat of Canada organization. After years of exhausting negotiations, boundary disputes, and meetings with Dene and Métis representatives who had their own agendas, the residents of the NWT passed their own plebiscite on the issue in 1992 (Momatiuk and Eastcott, 1995). The federal government eventually accepted the proposal, and in 1999 Nunavut became the permanent home of the Inuit. About 85 percent the territory's population is of Inuit heritage, and the area they occupy comprises more than 2.2 million square kilometres, more than one-fifth of Canada's land surface. The area represents the largest land claim in Canada's history (Dickason, 2006: 255).

The territory's capital is the town of Iqaluit, formerly known as Frobisher Bay.

As many of these agreements have dealt with sparsely populated northern lands inhabited mostly by Aboriginal peoples, non-Aboriginal Canadians have raised few questions. Not so, however, in the case of treaty claims and land settlements further south, especially in British Columbia.

The situation regarding treaty negotiation in British Columbia is unique. Aside from 14 small treaties signed with Governor James Douglas in the middle of the 19th century, and the overlap of Treaty no. 8 into their territory, British Columbia had never, until recently, negotiated treaties with First Nations. For years, the Province of British Columbia denied having any legal obligations to Aboriginal peoples. In 1992, however, a newly elected New Democratic government opened discussions pertaining to 47 land claims, promising to resolve them (Dickason, 2006: 288).

The total area of British Columbia is 932,000 square kilometres. By October 1999, negotiations were in process for claims amounting to 703,832 square kilometres of the province (Frideres and Gadacz, 2001: 223). The Nisga'a people of northern British Columbia, whose claim was settled in 1999, provide a kind of case study of contemporary land claims.

The Nisga'a were never militarily defeated, nor did they ever sign a treaty with the Government of Canada ceding lands. They first pressed their claims in 1887 when a group of Nisga'a chiefs travelled to Victoria. The government ignored them and took no action until 1976. Even then, it was a token acknowledgement. Twenty years later, in March 1996, government and the Nisga'a leadership signed an agreement in principle. The agreement gave the Nisga'a a cash payment of $190 million (later increased to $500 million) and established a Nisga'a central government with administrative, municipal-like responsibilities for 2,000 square kilometres of land in the Nass River Valley. Additionally, Nisga'a ownership of surface and subsurface resources was safeguarded, as well as rights to salmon stocks and wildlife harvests. In 1999, the 5,000 members of the Nisga'a First Nation ratified the treaty and in April of the same year, the British Columbia government and the federal Parliament passed the agreement into law. The Senate passed the bill on April 13, 2000, completing the treaty process (Steckley and Cummins, 2008: 143).

The agreement has encountered criticism. Interestingly, not all Aboriginals are pleased with the Nisga'a agreement. They dislike the fact that federal and provincial income tax laws, the Charter of Rights and Freedoms, and the Criminal Code now apply to Nisga'a government. (A group of dissidents have launched a court challenge to the agreement.)

By far the strongest criticisms have come from the non-Aboriginal community (Frideres and Gadacz, 2001: 184, 227). Many non-Aboriginal concerns over comprehensive claims are unfounded. There is no likelihood, for example, that Aboriginals will confiscate the lands on which Vancouver sits and have non-Aboriginals evicted, as is sometimes argued. More legitimate concerns about the process and outcomes of land claims negotiations have been expressed, however.

Smith's (1995) argument that there is no legal basis for comprehensive land claims seems today unsupported by the Supreme Court. His other four concerns, however, bear consideration: (1) that such land claims agreements are actually constitutional agreements that are binding upon subsequent generations and therefore do not provide for sufficient flexibility; (2) that such agreements open the way for endless negotiations, ever-escalating demands, the creation of more bureaucracy, and mounting costs;

(3) that the land claims agreements (and concomitant rights and benefits provided to Aboriginal peoples) are race-based and will actually hinder the chances of ordinary Aboriginals from entering fully into Canadian society; and (4) that land claims raise jurisdictional concerns, including whether Aboriginals under the agreements will be subject to Canadian law, including the Constitution's Charter of Rights and Freedoms. Ultimately, many of these concerns speak to a larger issue addressed by the Royal Commission: the issue of self-government.

SELF-GOVERNMENT AND SELF-DETERMINATION

Long before the arrival of the Europeans, Aboriginal peoples in Canada successfully governed themselves. Historical examples of self-government in Aboriginal communities include the Iroquois Confederacy, circa 1570 (from which some elements of the American Constitution were drawn), and the eastern Maritime Mi'kmaq First Nation, which existed prior to European contact and operated a seven-state democratic system presided over by seven chiefs and a grand chief who lived on Cape Breton Island. Subsequent colonialism destroyed many of these organizational structures, but First Nations peoples have never ceased their fight to regain control over their lives.

Aboriginal claims for self-government rest on three planks (Schouls, 2003: 115–116). First, as originally sovereign nations, Aboriginal nations have an inherent right to create and maintain their own identities, cultures, languages, values, and practices, and therefore they should have the right to choose their own form of governance. Second, even though Canada's Aboriginal peoples live under the Crown's protection, this does not in any way reduce or diminish their historic right to self-government. The original agreements between government and First Nations (treaties) were signed as equal partners—nation to nation. Therefore, any model of self-government must constitute more than mere self-administration. Third, because the original treaty-making process was initiated on a principle of reciprocity·and consent, there is no valid reason to ignore or even seek to improve this arrangement, but merely to adhere to the original agreements. Ultimately, the desire for self-government may also be justified as a means of redressing the harm done by a "foreign" government—that of Canada—and ensuring it does not happen again (Buckley, 1993).

Aboriginal peoples have been demanding the right of self-government within Canada for quite some time, but these demands have either been ignored or faltered amid efforts to arrive at a workable application of the term's meaning. In language reminiscent of the Lesage Liberals in Quebec in the early 1960s (Chapter 3), the Union of British Columbia Indian Chiefs, for example, defined its position on self-government in this way:

> We must be masters in our own house, in order to survive as Indian people. There is no basis in the laws of Canada to restrict the recovery of Aboriginal rights because we have never given up our rights to control our own lives and means to live. (Wall, 2000: 144)

Paternalism, an offshoot of colonialism, has continued to infuse government-Aboriginal relations. During the constitutional discussions in the early 1980s, however, real efforts were begun in earnest to define self-government.

In 1983, the federal government released a report prepared by the Special Committee on Indian Self-Government in Canada (also known as the Penner Report). The Penner Report dismissed the terms and intent of the Indian Act as out of date and ineffective for contemporary negotiations and made several recommendations calling for government to establish a new kind of relationship with Aboriginal peoples based on the notion of Aboriginal self-government. Among specific recommendations, the report recommended that Aboriginal governments be made accountable to their own people; that bilateral federal-Aboriginal agreements govern respective jurisdictions, with the federal government ceding all areas of competence required for Indian First Nations to govern themselves effectively and ensuring that provincial laws would not apply to Aboriginal land except with Aboriginal consent; and that complete control be given First Nations over their lands and resources, with financial backing through federal grants and the settlement of land claims. Finally, the report also originated the concept of a third order of government with respect to Aboriginal self-government (Tennant, 1988: 329).

The federal government's response to the Penner Report was to try to entrench Aboriginal self-government for Status Indians at a first ministers' meeting in 1984. At that meeting, Prime Minister Pierre Trudeau pursued the report's initiatives, but found little agreement among the premiers. Brian Mulroney's government made similar proposals in 1985 and 1987, but again consensus was lacking. The governments of Alberta, British Columbia, Newfoundland, and Saskatchewan in particular were reluctant to support federal proposals for Aboriginal self-government without a full definition of costs and terms (Miller, 1988: 304).

But it is likewise true that some Aboriginal organizations also found the self-government proposals inadequate while, for its part, the federal government appears only to tacitly recognize the "inherent right" of Aboriginal peoples to negotiate for self-government (Asch, 2002: 67), a recognition that carries no fundamental meaning.

(Ottawa has left the door open for the negotiation of self-government in the Dene-Métis and Yukon claims, but only on the condition that this kind of right does not receive the same constitutional protection accorded the rest of the settlements, meaning that any constitutional recognition of the Aboriginal right to self-government, gained by the Dene-Métis constituency, cannot be used as a precedent in any other sector of the Aboriginal community.)

Several specifically contentious issues lie at the heart of problems in defining and implementing self-government.

TIMING

There is little doubt about Canada's First Nations communities' desire for self-government. The people are quite weary of being regarded as wards of the government (Kulchyski, 2005: 15–17). Thus far, however, the Department of Indian Affairs and Northern Development has continued to exercise control and to decide which bands are at a sufficiently advanced stage to be ready for self-government (Angus 1991: 33), raising questions about the government's sincerity in pursuing the matter.

TERRITORIALITY

The intent of recent land claims settlements has been to define the idea of Aboriginal self-government. It is less clear how one might implement self-government in urban areas where a significant and growing number of Aboriginal peoples live, some on urban reserves (Barron and Garcea, 1999) (see Chapter 13). Implementing self-government is difficult enough when confined to a single, uncontested geographical space. It is even more problematic when different institutions and rules govern different groups of people within the same space.

LEVEL AND FORM OF GOVERNMENT

The Canadian government has tended to view "self-government" as approximating the level of Canadian municipalities, often transferring certain responsibilities to local Aboriginal bands and councils, which, in turn, act as financial administrators (Asch, 2000: 67). By contrast, Aboriginal organizations want assurances that their actual institutions will be protected in the Constitution, which municipal governments are not, and that such self-governing institutions would be on more or less the level of provincial counterparts. Kulchyski (2005: 15–17) argues, moreover, that for many Aboriginal leaders, achieving a measure of self-government is not simply a matter of transferring powers from government to local bands, but that the matter of form—what kind of governance will be initiated—is of immense importance.

GOVERNANCE STRUCTURE

Whatever form it takes, if Aboriginal self-government is ever realized, there will have to be a recognized structure for exercising that authority (Angus, 1991: 32). Kulchyski (2005: 15–17) notes, however, that federal negotiators have attempted to fit Aboriginal self-government into the existing operations of the Canadian state, and thus failed to recognize that existing governmental structures are not necessarily appropriate or functional in Aboriginal communities.

JURISDICTION

Angus (1991: 32) states that in order for Aboriginal self-government to succeed, the Canadian government must recognize Aboriginal authority in specific areas of jurisdiction. Fleras and Elliott (2007: 192) suggest that Aboriginal jurisdiction will likely include control over: (1) the delivery of social services such as policing, education, and health and welfare; (2) resources and use of land for economic development; (3) the means to protect and promote distinct cultural values and language systems; (4) band membership and entitlements; and (5) local expenditures according to Aboriginal priorities rather than those of government or bureaucracy, with some variation at play with regard to the different Indian bands. On this latter point, Kulchyski (2005: 15–17) similarly argues that Aboriginal self-government must be tailored to meet local needs if it is to succeed. Unfortunately, such a degree of flexibility is often lacking in Canada's national programs.

CITIZENSHIP

Is the notion of Aboriginal citizenship, and all the rights and privileges that entails, commensurate with that of Canadian citizenship? Flanagan (2000) argues that Aboriginal militants tend to define self-government in racial terms and cautions that the idea of Aboriginal self-government, embedded in broader notions of Aboriginal self-determination, contributes to cultural exclusiveness and divisions, which others contend moreover may have unanticipated and negative consequences. Cairns (2000) opines, for example, that the notion "we are not you" (Denis, 1997), if carried too far, may give non-Aboriginals a convenient excuse for withdrawing responsibility, financial or otherwise, for the condition of Aboriginal peoples.

Others view such fears as unwarranted, however. Frideres and Gadacz (2001: 251) suggest that First Nations will never gain the rights of self-determination and status of self-government envisioned by their more radical members. Governments will see to it that any arrangement for Aboriginal self-government will harmonize with existing Canadian laws, including the Charter of Rights and Freedoms. To date, this appears to be the case.

ECONOMIC SELF-SUFFICIENCY

Many of Canada's reserves do not have a strong economic base and cannot support the people who live there. In consequence, large numbers of Aboriginals have moved and are moving to Canadian cities in search of jobs and other opportunities, while many of those remaining on the reserves are supported by government social assistance and welfare. But how can a people be termed self-governing if they are dependent upon financial support from "external" governments? Boldt (1993: 261) argues that:

> Any proposal that Indian political autonomy and culture should be financed by another government makes a mockery of Indian nationhood. It is a manifestation of the "culture of dependence" in the political sphere. Such an arrangement is a design for continued subordination and paternalism.

It has often been said that Canada does not work in theory, but does in practice. This holds particularly true for current efforts at Aboriginal self-government. Despite seemingly interminable debates about how it will work, at the concrete level things are progressing. In 1986, for example, the Sechelt band of British Columbia gained a form of self-government that has since served as a model for other bands. The Sechelt band assumed powers to legislate matters that range from zoning and land use to education on their reserve. Today, both federal and provincial governments respect the application of these rights so long as they are consistent with federal and provincial laws. Moreover, the Sechelt agreement has paved the way for similar recognition of rights for all Indian bands in Canada that previously had to negotiate with the federal government even over peripheral matters (Russell, 2000: 163; Asch, 2000: 67; Bird et al., 2000).

In the meantime, efforts toward the very tedious and complex process of reaching agreement on self-government continue (Ponting and Henderson, 2005). Few observers are optimistic about fast results. Henderson (2000: 167) accuses legal bureaucrats of unreflectively asserting colonial privileges and power when dealing with the issue of self-government, but others are a bit more optimistic. Hylton (1999) observes that some progress toward Aboriginal self-government has been made in terms of both federal attitude and experiences reported by some Aboriginal bands. He notes:

> Aboriginal people in Canada are increasingly engaged in the practice of self-government.... [A] number of Aboriginal nations have already negotiated far-reaching self-government agreements.... [T]he federal government appears more ready than previous administrations to enter into new arrangements with Aboriginal people. (Hylton, 1999: 432)

Finally, others suggest that the debate over self-government actually obscures the more important notion of self-determination. In the words of McDonnell and Depew (1999: 353), "The processes associated with self-government are so powerfully unilateral in their focus that they have all but displaced considerations relating to self-determination." Boldt (1993) similarly argues that beyond self-government, the survival of Aboriginal cultures requires Aboriginal peoples to develop a clear vision and consensus about their future. They must assess the damage that colonialism has inflicted on them in the past and continues to do today, and invent ways to stop the processes of assimilation and acculturation. They must further critically evaluate what must be done and mobilize their people in an effort to make that identity a reality. "Such a process of cultural revitalization will necessitate a purge of corrupting colonial institutions, and of traits derived from the culture of dependence and from Euro-Western acculturation" (Boldt, 1993: 219). Self-government alone will not do these things.

CONCLUSION

The movement of Aboriginal peoples from Canada's backstage to front stage resulted in heightened conflict between Aboriginal and non-Aboriginal peoples after the 1970s, yet, as conflict theorists would argue, such conflict also paved the way for dealing with a host of problems previously ignored. In turn, the start of the 21st century has slowly seen the renewal within Aboriginal society and recognition within non-Aboriginal society of its Aboriginal roots. The following chapter examines Aboriginal society today and what its transformation might hold for Canada.

KEY TERMS

citizens plus
comprehensive claims
specific claims

CRITICAL THINKING QUESTIONS

1. Why did so many studies, such as the Hawthorn Report, arise in Canadian society during the 1960s?

2. Why did Aboriginal peoples respond to the White Paper as they did in 1969?

3. What lessons does the Oka Crisis provide for governments in conflict with minority groups?

4. Why have so few of the Royal Commission's recommendations been enacted?

5. What problems do notions of Aboriginal self-government pose for mainstream ideas of the state and nation?

RECOMMENDED READINGS

Bird, John, Lorraine Land, and Murray McAdam (eds.). 2000. *Self-Government in the New Millennium: Nation to Nation: Aboriginal Sovereignty and the Future of Canada.* Toronto: Irwin Publishing.

This is one of the first books to address the question of Aboriginal self-government, and does so from the perspective of informed authorities.

Dickason, Olive Patricia. 2006. *A Concise History of Canada's First Nations.* Toronto: Oxford University Press.

This is an abridged edition of Dickason's classic work covering the history of Canada's Aboriginal peoples from the time of European contact to the present.

Fleras, Augie, and Jean Elliott Leonard. 2007. *Unequal Relations: An Introduction to Race, Ethnic, and Aboriginal Dynamics in Canada*, 5th ed. Toronto: Pearson Canada.

The authors expertly juxtapose the various socio-economic and cultural challenges faced by both Aboriginal peoples and immigrant communities in Canada.

Snow, Chief John. 2005. *These Mountains Are Our Sacred Places: The Story of the Stoney People.* Calgary: Fifth House.

Although primarily an in-depth case study of the Stoney First Nation in Alberta, the narrative outlines much broader implications for other First Nations as well.

Warry, Wayne. 2007. *Ending Denial: Understanding Aboriginal Issues.* Peterborough: Broadview Press.

This is an in-depth, objective appraisal of a variety of legal and socio-economic frontiers faced by Canada's First Nations.

RELATED WEBSITES

Canadiana.org

www.canadiana.org/citm/index_e.html

This is a national body made up of distinguished scholars and representatives of major research libraries from across Canada. The organization hosts a digital archive, Canada in the Making, containing a collection of narrative text, primary documents, maps, and photos.

Government of Nunavut

http://www.gov.nu.ca/

The official website for the government of Nunavut.

Royal Commission on Aboriginal Peoples

www.ainc-inac.gc.ca/ap/rrc-eng.asp

In the wake of the Oka Crisis, the Canadian government established the Royal Commission on Aboriginal Peoples. The commission's final report can be found at this site.

CANADIAN SOCIETY ON VIDEO

No Turning Back: The Royal Commission on Aboriginal Peoples. 1997. National Film Board of Canada, 48 minutes. Film produced by Aboriginal filmmakers who followed the Royal Commission for two-and a half years on its journey to more than 100 communities.

Oka: Behind the Barricades. 1998. National Film Board of Canada, 311 minutes, 29 seconds. This collection of four videos exams the events of summer 1990, when the Mohawk community and the governments of Quebec and Canada faced off against each other. The four videos are: *Acts of Defiance* (104 minutes, 32 seconds); *Kanehsatake 270 Years of Resistance* (119 minutes, 14 seconds); *Spudwrench-Kahnawake Man* (57 minutes, 46 seconds); and *My Name Is Kahentiiosta* (29 minutes, 49 seconds).

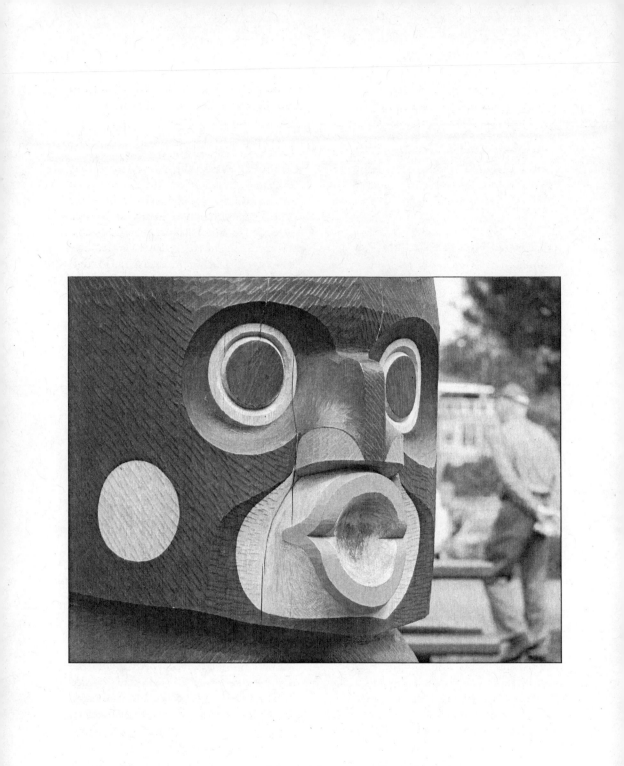

CHAPTER 13
NEW LEARNING PATHS

[T]oday it is popular to be an Indian. Within a decade it may be a necessity. People are not going to want to take the blame for the sorry state of the nation, and claiming allegiance with the most helpless racial minority may well be the only way to escape accusation.

—Oglala Sioux elder and scholar Vine Deloria, Jr., 1995

Our people have come into their own—there's no doubt about it—but now we have to build an audience. We have to do what we can to ensure that the beautiful power of our voices is heard…. Our stories are full of both sorrow and joy and it is important that we share them.

—actor Gary Farmer, 2005

We are a Métis civilization.

—author John Ralston Saul, 2008

INTRODUCTION

There is much unfinished business surrounding Aboriginal and non-Aboriginal relations: land claims, new treaties, the abolishment in time of the Indian Act, and the implementation of genuine self-government, not to mention real economic and social equality. Above all, there is the need for healing. But that is to be expected. Every society has unfinished business. As we noted in Chapter 1, societies are not a static thing; they are a process.

This concluding chapter of Part 3 examines Aboriginal society in all its complexity as it exists today, including some of the current experiments going on in Aboriginal communities and its new group of leaders. Along the way, the chapter also examines how Aboriginal values embedded within a traditional world view might fit into a modern Canada. Finally, the chapter looks at how Canadian society could benefit—if it chooses—from rediscovering its Aboriginal roots.

POPULATION DYNAMICS

When Columbus first arrived from Europe, the total population of North and South America was about 57 million people, 4.5 million of whom lived north of Mexico (Cook, 1995: 33). Of these, about 500,000 lived in what is today Canada. Shortly after Confederation, however, Canada's Aboriginal population had sunk to 102,000 (Ponting, 1997b: 68) and did not rise again until the 1940s. Since then, however, the population of Status Indians in Canada has steadily risen. Today, the number of Status Indians in Canada totals roughly 700,000, while nearly 1.2 million people report Aboriginal ancestry. Overall, the proportion of Aboriginals in Canada has also increased. According to the 2006 census, today they comprise 3.8 percent of the Canadian population, up from 3.3 percent in 2001, the largest increase being among the Métis segment of the Aboriginal population (see Table 13.1).

The increase in Aboriginal population is especially impressive given that infant mortality rates for First Nations communities continues to be higher than the Canadian rate, 6.4 per 1,000 live births versus 5.2 per 1,000 live births, respectively (Treasury Board of Canada Secretariat, 2005).

At the same time, while the life expectancy of First Nations and Inuit people, both male and female, has increased, it also continues to lag behind that of people in the general Canadian population. Life expectancy for First Nations men in 2001 was 70.4 years in 2001, compared to 77.1 for men in the Canadian population; while for First Nations women, life expectancy was 75.5 years in 2001, compared to 82.2 years for women in the Canadian population. In 1999, the life expectancy for Inuit in Nunavut was estimated at 67.7 years for men and 70.2 years for women (Treasury Board of Canada Secretariat, 2005).

Table 13.1
Aboriginal Identity Population, Percentage Changes 1996–2006

Aboriginal Identity Population	2006 Counts	Distribution (2006)	% Change (2001–2006)	% Change (1996–2006)
Total population	31,241,030	100.0	5.4	9.5
Aboriginal identity population	1,172,790	3.8	20.1	44.9
Non-Aboriginal identity population	30,068,240	96.2	4.9	8.4
Total Aboriginal identity population	1,172,790	100.0	20.1	44.9
North American Indian	698,025	59.5	14.6	29.1
Métis	389,780	33.2	33.3	90.9
Inuit	50,480	4.3	12.0	25.5

Source: Statistics Canada, "Aboriginal identity population, 2006 counts, percentage distribution, percentage change for both sexes, for Canada, provinces and territories—20% sample data," 2006 Census, http://www12.statcan.ca/english/census06/ data/highlights/Aboriginal/pages/Page.cfm?Lang=E&Geo=PR&Code=01&Table=3&Data=Count&Sex=1&StartRec=1&Sort =2&Display=Page. Date modified: January 15, 2008. Downloaded May 12, 2009.

Why has Canada's Aboriginal population increased so rapidly in recent years? First, the passage of Bill C-31 in 1985 (see Chapter 12) allowed many Aboriginal women to regain their status. A little more than a decade later, more than 105,000 individuals had regained their status (Frideres and Gadacz, 2001: 35). Second, Aboriginal birth rates, though declining, remain high above the Canadian average. One consequence of this continued explosion of Aboriginal births is that Canada's Aboriginal population, compared with the general population, is very young. While the median age for Canadians as a whole was 39.2 in 2006, it was 39.7 for members of the non-Aboriginal identity population versus 26.5 for those in the Aboriginal identity population. Especially of note, the median age of Aboriginal females in 2006 was 27.7, still well within normal child-bearing years (see Table 13.2).

This raises a point worth noting. One of Canada's fast-emerging problems is its aging population, with consequences, among other things, for the country's labour force needs. Might Aboriginal peoples be the solution? Might Aboriginal births rescue Canada from demographic decline?

Where do Aboriginal peoples primarily live? We have seen previously that a population shift is occurring throughout Canada (Chapter 8) as people migrate to the economically vibrant and relatively younger West. A similar shift is occurring within Canada's Aboriginal population,

Table 13.2
Canadian Aboriginal and Non-Aboriginal Population by Gender and Age, 2006 (in thousands)

	Total	0–14	15–24	25–34	35–44	45–54	55–64	65+	Median Age
All Canadians	31,241	5,577	4,208	3,987	4,794	4,951	3,650	4,074	39.2
Males	15,326	2,855	2,146	1,947	2,347	2,425	1,791	1,814	38.3
Females	15,915	2,721	2,062	2,040	2,447	2,526	1,858	2,261	40.0
Non-Aboriginal identity population	30,068	5,228	3,996	3,826	4,625	4,808	3,568	4,018	39.7
Males	14,754	2,677	2,040	1,871	2,268	2,357	1,752	1,788	38.8
Females	15,314	2,551	1,956	1,954	2,356	2,451	1,816	2,230	40.5
Aboriginal identity population	1,173	349	212	162	169	143	81	56	26.5
Males	572	178	106	76	79	68	39	26	25.2
Females	601	170	106	85	90	76	42	31	27.7

Source: Modified from Statistics Canada, "Population by age groups, sex and Aboriginal identity groups, 2006 counts, for Canada, provinces and territories—20% sample," Census of Population, 2006, http://www12.statcan.ca/english/census06/data/ highlights/Aboriginal/data. Modified January 15, 2008. Downloaded June 15, 2009. Any differences due to authors' rounding.

though it is birth rates rather than inter-provincial migration that are the primary factor. Table 13.3 shows that while Ontario has the largest Aboriginal identity population (242,000), the Aboriginal popula- tions of the western provinces are not far behind; indeed, nearly half of Canada's Aboriginal identity population today reside in western Canada, where birth rates are among the highest in Canada.

Table 13.3
Aboriginal Identity Population for Canada, Provinces, and Territories, 2006

Non-Aboriginal	Total Population	Aboriginal Identity Population	North American Indian	Métis	Inuit Identity Population
Canada 30,068,240	31,241,030	1,172,785	698,025	389,780	50,480
Newfoundland/Labrador 477,160	500,610	23,455	7,765	6,470	4,715
Prince Edward Island 132,475	134,205	1,730	1,225	385	30
Nova Scotia 878,920	903,090	24,175	15,240	7,680	325
New Brunswick 701,995	719,650	17,650	12,385	4,270	185
Quebec 7,327,475	7,435,905	108,425	65,085	27,980	10,950
Ontario 11,786,405	12,028,895	242,495	158,395	73,605	2,035
Manitoba 958,115	1,133,515	175,395	100,640	71,805	565
Saskatchewan 811,960	953,850	141,890	91,400	48,120	215
Alberta 3,067,990	3,256,355	188,365	97,275	85,495	1,610
British Columbia 3,878,310	4,074,385	196,075	129,580	59,445	795
Yukon Territory 22,615	30,190	7,580	6,280	800	255
Northwest Territories 20,420	41,060	20,635	12,640	3,580	4,160
Nunavut 4,405	29,325	24,915	100	130	24,635

Source: Statistics Canada, "Aboriginal identity population by age groups, median age, and sex, 2006 counts, for Canada, provinces, and territories—20% sample data," *2006 Census Data,* http://www12.statcan.ca/english/census06/data/highlights/ Aboriginal/pages/Page.cfm?Lang=E&Geo=PR&Code=01&Table=1&Data=Count&Sex=1&Age=1&StartRec=1&Sort=2&Dis play=Page. Modified January 15, 2008. Downloaded May 12, 2009.

RURAL AND URBAN RESERVES

A significant issue in population shifts within the Aboriginal community is the movement of Aboriginal peoples from rural areas to urban centres and the emergence of urban reserves. According to the 2001 Canadian census, the on-reserve population of Registered (Status Indians) Indians in Canada was 286,080, compared to 690,225 who lived off-reserve. Of the latter, 196,130 Registered Indians lived in rural areas, while 494,095 lived in urban areas.

Administratively, First Nations communities are described as tribes with subdivisions known as bands. There are more than 600 Indian bands in Canada. The term **band** referred originally to *small cultural and linguistic groups living together, or coming together at various seasons and times, as part of a larger Aboriginal society,* such as the Cree or Inuit. Today, the term describes *a local unit of adminis-tration, operating under the Indian Act* (see Chapter 12). Most bands consist of about 500 members. A few bands, however, such as the Six Nations band in Ontario with nearly 20,000 members (*Canadian Global Almanac 2000*, 1999: 48), are very large.

Many Aboriginal peoples continue to live in rural areas, in the northern parts of Canada's provinces, and in the territories. Increasingly, however, Aboriginal peoples, both Status and non-Status, are also moving to Canada's cities and towns. The urbanization of Canada's Aboriginal peoples has received considerable attention from sociologists over the last three decades. Much of this attention has centred on negative statistics emanating from the great difficulties that many Aboriginals have in adjusting to urban life. Despite these difficulties, exacerbated by discrimination, prejudice, and racism, they continue to migrate to Canada's cities. Education and employment opportunities appear to be the main reasons for this migration, though migration theory suggests that other factors may also be important (Cooke and Bélanger, 2006).

Western Canadian cities have been a prime site of Aboriginal migration (see Statistics Canada, 2008). Winnipeg, for example, is home to the largest urban Aboriginal population—68,380 or 10 percent of its population. Edmonton is second with 52,100 or 5 percent of its population. Vancouver is third with 40,310 or 2 percent of the population. Prince Albert, Saskatchewan, is unique in its population breakdown; Aboriginals comprise 34 percent of that city's population. One related recent phenomenon of the reserve to urban relocation has been the emergence of urban reserves, the creation of reserves within populated urban centres.

Saskatchewan is the birthplace of urban reserves. In 1976, the Saskatchewan and federal governments and Aboriginal leaders signed an agreement, the Saskatchewan Formula, through which land equity would be worked out. A change of provincial government (from NDP to Conservative) saw the deal temporarily abandoned, but the NDP's later return to power saw the Saskatchewan Treaty Land Entitlement Framework Agreement signed in 1992. The agreement set aside $446 million to purchase land on which to develop urban reserves (Barron and Garcea, 1999: 15). That same year, 28 of Saskatchewan's 70 Indian bands signed on, and 28 urban reserves were created, nine of them in larger centres (Steckley and Cummins, 2008: 141).

Barron and Garcea (1999: 24) state three reasons for the creation of urban reserves. The first reason is that they are directly related to treaties and treaty land entitlement. When treaty nos. 4, 6, and 7 were drawn up (see Chapter 10), the conditions were that every family of five would be awarded a full section of land, but the federal government often failed to live up to this arrangement and simply shortchanged Aboriginal peoples. A century after the first 10 numbered treaties were signed, Aboriginal peoples comprised a full 3 percent of Canada's population, but possessed only 0.02 percent of available land. (In Saskatchewan, alone, almost 30 bands were shortchanged when land entitlements for reserves were negotiated.) In effect, the 1992 agreement settled an outstanding claim by offering bands compensatory funds with which to buy private real estate holdings.

A second reason is that urban reserves are closely associated with First Nations' desires to develop and diversify economic opportunities. Federal land was found for development in Saskatoon, for example, and later transferred, after negotiations, to Aboriginal ownership.

A third reason is that for many Aboriginal peoples, urban reserves are a territorial expression of the inherent right of self-government. They want to be full players in the dominant society, not as assimilated members of that society, but as people with their own distinct cultural identity. Urban reserves function as an extension of a band's national land patrimony and authority to make decisions over their own lives.

On this latter point, urban reserves clearly tie into demands for self-government (see Chapter 12). The concept of a bonded community offers not only strong encouragement for economic development but also the opportunity necessary for participants to formulate some kind of self-government to determine rules for living, show respect for others, and set community goals.

Who inhabits urban reserves? Like any community, urban reserves comprise a variety of lifestyles, but three major groups can be identified. The first group are those who live on the urban reserve and work either on the reserve or nearby; their social ties are thus localized. The second group are those who live off-reserve but who work in the particular town or city where an urban reserve is located and have relatives or close friends on the urban reserve; their socializing straddles the urban reserve and its immediate environs. The third group are those who live on a rural reserve and come to the urban centre primarily to work; their social life is almost entirely based outside the urban area.

Urban reserves have faced stiff opposition, particularly from local non-Aboriginal politicians, though politicians at other levels have also expressed concern. Their opposition often stems from concerns that any form of reserve government could establish rules and laws that might contradict those passed by city council; that the establishment of a different kind of neighbourhood might affect federal and provincial grants to cities and towns; and that urban reserves might turn into ethnic ghettos. Without doubt, some of these objections were grounded in prejudice and discrimination. But urban reserves do raise some legitimate jurisdictional questions, reflecting the complexity and newness of such ventures.

By law, the federal government has responsibilities to Aboriginal peoples, but in the case of urban reserves appear to have abdicated these responsibilities, instead turning governance matters over to the provinces. In turn, provincial governments seem determined to hand over control of Aboriginal programs and service funds to Aboriginal peoples. Bobiwash (1997: 91) notes that in Saskatchewan, for example, the provincial government identified up to $550 million a year in the areas of health, education, justice, and social services that could eventually be transferred to band administration. Such a move may have commendable features, but it too easily allows the federal government to shirk its responsibilities toward First Nations communities. Moreover, the legality of whether provinces have authority to negotiate agreements with Aboriginal governments is in question. As Bobiwash (1997: 91) notes:

> Among the arguments used by the federal government in regards to provision of social services for off-reserve Native people has been that if provinces are the main beneficiaries for lands and resources under Lands and Resources Transfer Agreements and Acts (by which the provinces also became parties to later treaties such as the Williams Treaty of 1923), then some of those benefits ought to go to off-reserve Native People.

Finally, on a hopeful note, one may observe that new arrangements sometimes have a way of bringing various parties together, and often the exchange of ideas fosters goodwill. As Makela (1999: 89) suggests, "The development of urban reserves presents great opportunities for both Aboriginal and non-Aboriginal people ... with the issues at stake reaching beyond matters of tax-loss compensation or bylaw compatibility." Above all, urban reserves express the hope of sharing wealth and power in the pursuit of providing equal opportunity for education, employment, adequate housing, and other social benefits.

HEALTH, LABOUR FORCE PARTICIPATION, AND INCOME

As already noted, First Nations infant mortality rates are higher than rates in the general Canadian population, and life expectancy among both First Nations and Inuit peoples, for both men and women, is lower than among their non-Aboriginal Canadian counterparts. These results are largely attributable to the poor housing conditions in many First Nations reserves or in the North, conditions comparable to those in the world's least-developed countries. On-reserve housing is generally substandard and often poorly ventilated. The homes are too hot in summer and too cold in winter. Running water is frequently a luxury. (In November 2007, 31 people on the Peigan reserve in southern Alberta were evacuated from five homes that were condemned in part due to serious mould problems.)

Such conditions are a major cause of serious health problems. Tuberculosis is less a threat than in the recent past, but it has been replaced by the scourges of diabetes, AIDS, and drug and alcohol abuse. The fact is that for a substantial number of Aboriginal peoples on and off the reserves, life is fraught with danger and hopelessness. Suicide rates, especially among young Aboriginals (15–34 years), eclipse the Canadian average; suicide rates in Nunavut are especially high. Likewise, interpersonal violence within Aboriginal communities plays a part. Especially in western Canada, each year a disproportionate number of Aboriginal children are taken into care by provincial welfare agencies; not surprisingly perhaps, Aboriginals, many of whom as children were wards of the state, also comprise a disproportionate number of inmates within adult correctional institutions (Statistics Canada, 2001b).

While on-reserve conditions are generally poor, the situation of Aboriginals migrating to urban areas is often not much better. While cities may provide some of them with increased opportunities and more accessible services, many of them also find that they have to contend with a myriad of other challenges not experienced on the reserve, such as cultural alienation and racism (Buckley, 1993; Fox and Long, 2000).

Such social facts are not disconnected from other factors and consequences. Thus, in general, poor health and poor social outcomes tend to correlate highly with low socio-economic status (SES), especially related to an individual's family of origin. Though the situation is improving, many Aboriginal peoples continue to live below the poverty line, and many are also on some form of social assistance (Frideres and Gadacz, 2001: 120).

In recent decades, however, this economic situation has improved. Since 1971, the proportion of First Nations in the labour force has steadily increased, though it still trails that of other Canadians. In 2001, Aboriginal peoples made up about 2.5 percent of Canada's labour force, roughly 652,000 Aboriginal peoples aged 15 and over. Compared with non-Aboriginal counterparts, Aboriginal peoples had both lower participation (60.6 percent versus 66.1 percent) and employment rates (49.7 percent versus 61.8 percent) and a much higher unemployment rate (18.0 percent versus 6.5 percent) (Luffman and Sussman, 2007).

The economic circumstances of Aboriginals are not uniform, however. As in the non-Aboriginal community, one's life chances are influenced by such factors as place of residence, gender, and class, to give three examples. Aboriginal peoples in Quebec, Manitoba, and Saskatchewan tend to have very high unemployment rates compared with their counterparts elsewhere; Aboriginal females tend to earn less than Aboriginal males; while, within Aboriginal bands, class and status differences are often marked.

One obvious factor influencing income is whether Aboriginal peoples remain on reserve or not. On-reserve Aboriginals are less likely than their off-reserve counterparts to enter the labour force for a very good reason: There are fewer jobs to be had. But the situation of off-reserve Aboriginals seeking employment is often not much better, with a rate of 17 percent unemployment at any given time (Frideres and Gadacz, 2001: 95–97).

One may also note marked differences in income among the various categories of Aboriginal peoples. Table 13.4 compares the average income of Aboriginals and non-Aboriginals in 2005.

Table 13.4

Average Income, Aboriginal Identity, Registered Indian Status, and Aboriginal Ancestry for the Population 15 Years and over with Income of Canada, Provinces, Territories, 2005

	Total Population	Non-Aboriginal Identity Population	Total Aboriginal Identity Population	North American Indian[1]	Métis[1]	Inuit
Canada	35,501	35,872	23,935	20,996	28,227	25,461
Newfoundland/ Labrador	27,636	27,856	22,595	20,439	23,850	24,713
Prince Edward Island	27,769	27,830	21,796	22,009	n.a.	n.a.
Nova Scotia	30,187	30,358	22,796	20,119	26,312	23,793
New Brunswick	28,450	28,643	19,549	18,656	21,033	n.a.
Quebec	32,074	32,176	24,187	23,334	25,375	26,074
Ontario	38,106	38,318	26,156	24,285	29,244	28,301
Manitoba	31,323	32,843	20,761	16,470	25,838	19,927
Saskatchewan	31,616	33,108	19,939	16,069	25,876	n.a.
Alberta	42,241	42,998	27,190	22,158	31,980	28,557
British Columbia	34,520	35,002	22,934	20,431	27,871	22,265
Yukon Territory	38,687	41,697	27,926	27,090	34,224	n.a.
Northwest Territories	44,422	55,975	30,353	27,362	44,932	25,337
Nunavut	34,182	65,546	25,561	n.a.	n.a.	25,193

Note:
1. Single responses only

Source: Statistics Canada, "Income statistics (4) in constant (2005) dollars, age groups (5A), Aboriginal identity, Registered Indian status and Aboriginal ancestry (21), highest certificate, diploma or degree (5) and sex (3) for the population 15 years and over with income of Canada, provinces, territories, 2000 and 2005—20% sample data," 2006 Census Data, http://www12.statcan.gc.ca/census-recensement/2006/dp-pd/tbt/Index-eng.cfm. Downloaded June 13, 2009.

Sociologists are trained to look for patterns in data. (The old saying that "the exception proves the rule" proves nothing and is statistical false.) Table 13.4 reveals at least three recurrent patterns. First, the average income of non-Aboriginal identifiers in every province is consistently higher than that of Aboriginal identifiers. Second, there are consistently significant differences within the Aboriginal community, with the members of the Métis community in most provinces and territories having the highest average income earnings, followed by the Inuit, and finally those identified as North American Indians. Third, the table also confirms that a province's or territory's economic circumstances has an important impact on income—note Alberta and the territories—though it does not change the distributional pattern overall.

Taken together, one might view the situation of Canada's Aboriginal peoples as hopeless. In fact, there are many signs of hope. Several Aboriginal bands today, led by a new generation of young, entrepreneurial leaders, are changing the culture of First Nations reserves (see Box 13.1). As in much of the world, however, the hope and the promise for Canada's Aboriginal peoples lies in education.

Box 13.1
Profiles in Aboriginal Leadership

The Osoyoos Indian band of south central British Columbia is a storied economic success. Led by Chief Clarence Louie (1961–), one of several young Aboriginal leaders emerging today, the Osoyoos band boasts nearly a dozen successful local businesses, including a golf course-hotel-residential complex, a vineyard, a campground, a recreational vehicle park, a construction company, a ready-mix concrete company, a gas bar, and a convenience store. Together, these business ventures bring in revenues of more than $15 million annually— seven times the revenue it receives from the federal government.

Similar success stories can be found throughout Canada:

- The Fort McKay First Nation in northern Alberta and Suncor recently launched a joint partnership to establish a business "incubator" to encourage, support, and promote entrepreneurial activities and start-up businesses in the community.

- The Membertou First Nation of Sydney, Nova Scotia, has partnered with the Cape Breton YMCA to deliver entrepreneurial courses to their members. The deal will offer free training in business ventures to 1,100 Mi'kmaq who may be interested in turning their ideas into business ventures.

- In July 2008, the Stoney Nation of Morley, Alberta, opened a $65 million casino complex.

EDUCATION

Education is a known factor in occupational attainment and economic prosperity in Canada. Historically, Aboriginal educational levels have lagged behind those of other Canadians. Today, however, educational achievement among Aboriginal youth is at an all time high.

The 1981 Canadian census revealed that only 2 percent of Aboriginal youth held university degrees compared with 8.1 percent of the non-Aboriginal population. The Report of the Royal Commission on Aboriginal People (RCAP), published in 1996, indicated that 4.2 percent of Aboriginal individuals held university degrees, and that 21 percent of Aboriginal peoples had completed college certificates. In 2001, as Table 13.5 shows, 7.8 percent of Aboriginal identifiers had attained university and 15.1 percent had attained college, up substantially from 1991, with the sharpest increase being among Aboriginal women, though the educational level of Aboriginal men is also increasing. However, it must also be noted that 22.6 percent of all Canadians had also had attained university while 17.9 percent had attained college, and that these percentages have also increased since 1991 (Frideres and Gadacz, 2001: 111).

Table 13.5
Population Aged 25–64, by Level of Educational Attainment and Sex, Canadian Population as a Whole and Individuals Reporting Aboriginal Identity, Canada, 2001

	All Canadians						Aboriginal Identifiers					
	Both	%	Men	%	Women	%	Both	%	Men	%	Women	%
<High School	4,573,120	22.7	1,874,785	23.4	1,823,455	22.0	171,725	38.7	86,495	41.3	85,225	36.4
High School	3,898,400	23.9	1,796,465	22.5	2,101,940	25.4	101,365	22.9	45,770	21.8	55,575	23.8
Trades	2,097,145	12.9	1,323,705	16.5	773,450	9.3	69,265	15.6	41,340	19.7	27,940	11.9
College	2,917,890	17.9	1,201,225	15.0	1,716,670	20.7	66,805	15.1	23,580	11.2	43,225	18.5
University	3,676,620	22.6	1,804,240	22.6	1,872,390	22.6	34,465	7.8	12,440	5.9	22,015	9.4
Total	14,539,600	100.0	8,000,420	100.0	8,287,905	100.0	443,625	100.0	209,625	100.0	233,980	100.0

Source: Adapted from Statistics Canada's website at http://www12.statcan.ca/english/census01/products/standard/themes/RetrieveProductTable.cfm?Temporal=2001&PID=73631&APATH=5&GID=517770&METH=1&PTYPE=55496&THEME=45&FOCUS=0&AID=0&PLACENAME=0&PROVINCE=0&SEARCH=0&GC=905&GK=CMA&VID=0&VNAMEE=&VNAMEF=&FL=0&RL=0&FREE=0.

The increasing success of Aboriginal peoples reflects in part experiments on the educational front. Universities are becoming more responsive to their needs. As of fall 2008, York University, for example, sanctions graduate research in Aboriginal languages, with graduate students now able to defend their research in any of 50 Aboriginal languages. Elsewhere, special pre-medicine courses for Aboriginal students are available, and medical faculties are beginning to accept mature students with community-based experiences in place of university degrees (Warry, 2007). These victories, hard fought for and well deserved, have begun showing positive results.

Similar experiments are also being tried at lower educational levels. For example, some schools in British Columbia are inviting local elders to share their knowledge and celebrate ceremonies with students and teachers. The Qualicum school district even has an Elder-in-Residence program in which an elder will spend one day a week in local schools, demonstrating traditional cultural activities and teaching life lessons.

CONTRASTING WORLD VIEWS

Classical sociologists, such as Émile Durkheim (see Chapter 1), often contrasted the fundamental values and beliefs of traditional society with those of the modern industrial society that was emerging; that is, they contrasted the overarching **world view** by which each society defined reality.

It is simplistic—and sometimes dangerous—to dichotomize world views, yet if we employ them as Weberian "ideal types" and do not reify them, such descriptions can serve a heuristic purpose.

At the macro-level of cultural analysis, one can identify several differences between the world views held by traditional and modern societies, differences that often continue to manifest in day-to-day misunderstandings between Aboriginal and non-Aboriginal peoples in Canada.

THE SACRED AND THE PROFANE

Durkheim (1978) described two exclusive philosophical worlds existing side by side. The first is the **profane world**, *the world of the everyday, the expected, the mundane, the explainable*. The second is the **sacred world**, *the world of mystery, uncertainty, and even danger*. The latter existed before time, and will continue to live after; it is perpetual. According to Durkheim, the sacred cannot and should not be approached with the idea of exploitation or domination, nor should one tamper with the elements or workings of the universe. The sacred is to be treated with awe, even reverence. This contrast between the sacred and the profane well describes a fundamental difference between traditional and modern societies; between the traditional Aboriginal and dominant Canadian societies. However, it yields nothing to the notion of flexibility or transition, a fact that is readily visible in contemporary Aboriginal communities.

The early European invaders underestimated the extent to which spirituality was valued by Aboriginal peoples in their daily lives (Friesen, 1995; Witt, 1998; Hanohano, 1999). This reality remains underestimated and misunderstood by non-Aboriginals today who have long ago abandoned the spiritual roots of their society. For many Aboriginal leaders, their spirituality serves as a foundation for land claims and language revitalization programs. Current negotiations between non-Aboriginal industries and Indian bands have altered this stance in the interests of coping with and even expanding economic development in Aboriginal communities.

Many other differences between traditional Aboriginal and non-Aboriginal culture follow from the former's greater acceptance of this spiritual or sacred realm.

SPIRITUAL HOLISM VERSUS SCIENTIFIC EMPIRICISM

In contrast to modern cultures, traditional cultures experience no unease at the thought of multiple realities, spiritual or phenomenological, simultaneously operating in the universe. Likewise, the world is seen as a single, if complex, phenomenon; its elements cannot be studied and tested in isolation. Dreams, visions, and other spiritual experiences are considered as valid a source of knowledge as scientifically and empirically derived truths. Today's successful Aboriginal entrepreneurs often add to their traditional repertoire of knowledge such things as university research, innovation, and strategic economic planning.

CYCLICAL VERSUS LINEAR NOTIONS OF TIME

For traditional (pre-industrial) peoples around the world, time is cyclical, tied to hunting and growing seasons. The Industrial Revolution and the advent of capitalism resulted in a changed conception of time—"wasting time," "lost time," "time is money"—that sees time as linear, a direct offshoot of this being the notion of "progress," the notion that "Every day, in every way, things are getting better and better." Conflicts over the meaning of time remain a constant and frequent element in relations between Aboriginal and non-Aboriginal peoples, but also within Aboriginal communities today that are attempting to take control of their own economies.

COMPETING NOTIONS OF CAUSE AND EFFECT

Both traditional and modern world views recognize the notion of cause and effect. The modern world view subscribes, however, to the belief that such effects can be controlled; indeed, that by designing the right tools and approaches, people can even improve upon nature and perhaps tailor effects to their own advantage. By contrast, people in traditional societies view themselves as part of a great chain of existence in which all elements of creation are interrelated and interdependent (Ross, 1992). Moreover, as with time, this chain is not linear, but rather a kind of "daisy chain." If any single element is subjected to pressures or is otherwise tampered with, there are sure to be repercussions in the grand scheme of things. The implications of this belief are profound, and bear similarity to what sociologists refer to as **unintended or unanticipated consequences** (Merton, 1968). Aboriginal culture includes an inherent warning not to seek to dominate or exploit the mysterious workings of nature, but to work in harmony with them (Suzuki, 1992). It is a warning against hubris. Given escalating concerns over the environment, Aboriginal peoples may be correct in suspecting both the idea of progress and the further assumption that damages caused by technology can always be rectified by still another scientific discovery or adjustment.

THE COLLECTIVE VERSUS THE INDIVIDUAL

As previously noted (Chapter 5), modernity's greatest invention, and perhaps also its greatest illusion, is that of "individualism," often contrasted with the "group." Non-Aboriginals tend to view Aboriginal culture as collective and conformist in contrast to modern non-Aboriginal society's extolling of individualism. This view is simplistic, to say the least. Family loyalty *does* have a high priority in traditional Aboriginal thinking, and the individual is expected to submit to group and community demands (Dion, 1979; Surtees, 1969). And, in turn, this *does* put limits on one's individuality and may hinder achievements in the contemporary socio-economic culture of the nation. (Plant managers are rarely sympathetic to individuals who take time off to tend to personal family matters, though perhaps they should. Might this change as Aboriginals become industrial managers?)

There is a paradox, however. Beyond these restraints, the community also guarantees the individual emotional security, support, and a particular identity. This identity is assigned and sometimes amended, and, if need be, taken away from the individual. Generally the process also fosters a subtle kind of non-interference, though this too has limitations in a postmodern society. The community, for example, will soon "put in line" individuals who "show off" too much. In extreme cases, individuals who step beyond community limits may find themselves shunned as punishment.

EGALITARIANISM VERSUS HIERARCHY

Modern Western societies frequently parade their democratic political cultures. The foundational element of democracy is equality, however, and on this measure traditional societies, including those of Canada's First Nations societies, were exceedingly democratic. Age and gender (male) were the only certain markers of status; otherwise, authority rules tended to be complex and shifting. This confused the Europeans, whose own traditions were akin to a caste system; Aboriginal decision-making processes still confuse many Euro-Canadians today.

In fact, few followers of *Robert's Rules of Order* could endure a traditional Aboriginal meeting. Aboriginal rules are different from those of non-Aboriginals. Elders, chiefs, and respected spokespeople prescribe the procedures for a meeting simply by their behaviour, and no one takes issue with this. In the most traditional format, every challenge faced by a tribe must be resolved communally. Industrial and government negotiators frequently become quite impatient with such processes, especially when elders decide that a lengthy sweet-grass ceremony should precede the deliberations. If negotiations toward industrial development are to continue, it will require a significant "rewriting of rules and attitudes" (Fleras and Elliott, 2007: 347).

SEEKING A THIRD WAY

We have previously noted (Chapter 10) that the role of the non-Aboriginal educational establishment—both residential schools as well as day schools—was to silence expressions of Aboriginal culture. Over time, the process of educational imperialism had a crushing effect on Aboriginal communities. Several generations lost their languages and transformed their cultures, sometimes resulting in psychological and social upheaval for their members. In recent years, a growing crescendo of Aboriginal voices has emphasized the importance of reviving traditional knowledge and spirituality (Meili, 1991; Cajete, 1994; Couture, 1991; McGaa, 1995; Johnston, 1995; Bear Heart, 1998; Weaver, 1998; Battiste, 2000; Battiste and Henderson, 2000). But there have also been repeated calls from some, in both the Aboriginal (Henlin, 2006) and non-Aboriginal communities (see Flanagan, 2000), for Aboriginals to adopt modern ways, to—as it were—"get with the program." Is it possible to combine traditional Aboriginal world views and values with those of modernity, to adapt them to the dominant socio-economic environment? Is there a third way between traditional and modern values? This is a major challenge facing not only Aboriginal peoples but Canadians as a whole.

Yazzie (2000) argues that if First Nations want to retain elements of their traditional belief systems, they must first throw off the yoke of epistemological colonialism, and commence the truth-finding process within themselves. Political self-determination begins with internal sovereignty, which means taking control of one's personal, family, clan, and community life. Essentially this will require the valuing of tradition while mingling aspects of contemporary Euro-Canadian value systems. This task will not be easy. As Findley (2000) notes:

> The task of opposing the dominant orthodoxies of modernity from a position at their ever-extending margins, or from a strategically primitivist place outside, is crucial and dangerous work.... Significant numbers of Euro-Canadian scholars have become remarkably good at critiquing the pretensions and practices of modernity and defending marginalized groups, but they do so within institutions among whose faculties Aboriginal people are minimally represented.

Maintaining or even retrieving traditional Aboriginal culture is made problematic by the fact that many First Nations today are significantly "modernized," while others are marginalized between their traditional and European cultures. Those who attempt to remain oriented to traditional ways ironically find themselves joined by some elements within the dominant non-Aboriginal community who have themselves rejected modern Western values (materialism, individualism, secularism) and seek in Aboriginal culture a solution to modernity's perceived ills.

How have Aboriginal peoples adapted to the challenges of modern Western and capitalist society? Friesen and Friesen (2005: 156–158) and Schultz and Kroeger (1996) describe five types of responses by groups within the Aboriginal community.

The first group, traditionalists, respond by clinging tenaciously to the old ways and ignoring or denying the changes. Traditionalists have strong ties to the old ways, culturally as well as spiritually, and are therefore able to ignore modern developments while continuing to live with both eyes on the past.

The second group is made up of lost-identity individuals who feel powerless in the current of socio-economic change and often fall prey to social and cultural breakdown. They often develop confused identities and exhibit characteristics of deprivation, grief, and dependency, and often drift into poverty.

The third group are new traditionalists or "born-again" Aboriginals with little knowledge of the old ways, but who like to dress in traditional garb, wearing braids, sporting ribbon shirts, and displaying items of beadwork. Unaware of the impracticality and difficulty of such an existence today, they nonetheless often extol the virtues of hunting, gathering, and fishing societies. Often youthful, articulate, and college-educated, members of this group seek a cultural renaissance of sorts.

The fourth group are those assimilated completely into the modern world, albeit often unconsciously. This requires adopting new norms and forming new social alliances. For this group and its proponents, maintaining an Aboriginal cultural identity is secondary to economic development (Henlin, 2006).

The fifth group is comprised of those who might be called internationally minded human beings of First Nations background. (There are increasing contacts between Aboriginal peoples in Australia, New Zealand, South America, Scandinavia, the United States, and Canada.) These individuals seek to balance and appreciate the contributions of both Aboriginal and non-Aboriginal cultures, placing a great deal of value on their own heritage without belittling that of others. They are often quite open to alternative ways of thinking, such as finding ways to protect the environment while also supporting technological and industrial advancement.

EDUCATION, IDENTITY, AND CULTURAL SURVIVAL

The current resurgence of traditional Aboriginal values is the result of Aboriginal peoples' demands for the right to educate their youth in the ways of their knowledge and heritage (Battiste and Henderson, 2000: 87). These demands are encased in broader understandings that Aboriginal self-esteem and survival of the community depend upon cultural renewal (Antone, 2000). At the same time, these demands are not merely to have Aboriginal components added to the content of non-Aboriginal curricula in schools. Rather, there is an understanding that Aboriginal teachings must have a broad cultural foundation (Witt, 1998: 270; also Marker, 2000). As Verna Kirkness (1998a: 12–13), a Cree professor emeritus at the University of British Columbia, argues, the survival of Aboriginal culture must move beyond mere rhetoric to the actual practice of culture in everyday life beyond the school.

Many view the revival of Aboriginal languages as key to the transmission and survival of Aboriginal knowledge and culture (Kirkness, 1998b). Likewise, many believe the Canadian government must play a greater role in ensuring the vitality of Aboriginal languages. Fettes and Norton (2000), for example, argue that the federal government should establish a program for Aboriginal languages within the Department of Canadian Heritage (see also Battiste, 2000: 199).

Things are improving. Young Aboriginals are becoming aware of their past history, assisted by elders who pass on cultural lessons, often in traditional ways—through storytelling, modelling, and on-the-job training—and by Aboriginal teachers who have been trained to work in their own communities. Likewise, there have also been improvements in educational facilities, local control of schooling, counselling services, and support groups, and school curricula have been revised to include more culturally relevant content. From kindergarten to grade 12 and beyond, Aboriginal peoples are slowly gaining control of their own schools, their own education, and their own lives.

Mainstream Canadian society need not romanticize traditional Aboriginal culture or its values, nor, however, can these things be ignored. The fact is there is still a large gap between the values and beliefs embedded in First Nations' culture and those of modern society. The latter has little understanding, and even less appreciation for a lifestyle focused on living in harmony with nature, respecting the earth, believing in the interconnectedness of all living phenomena, and honouring the Creator in one's daily life (Friesen, 1995; Brascoupé, 2000). In the words of well-known Métis architect Douglas Cardinal, Aboriginal culture amounts to a "different way of being human" (Buckley, 1993: 174). The question for non-Aboriginal Canadians at the start of the 21st century is whether they are open enough to accommodate, learn from, and perhaps even embrace such a divergent world view.

WE ARE YOU: CANADA AS AN ABORIGINAL SOCIETY

In Chapter 9, we looked at how various political philosophers have described the nature of Canadian society. For Lipset (1990), you will recall, Canada is a British Tory country; for Grant (1965), Canada was a Tory country, but is now a modern Liberal (and liberal and, hence, American) country; while for Resnick (2005), Canada is a European country, and on and on.

More recently, John Ralston Saul (2008) has proffered a very different, even radical, thesis: That Canada is a Métis civilization, an Aboriginal country. Saul points out the many practical contributions that Aboriginal peoples have made to Canada, from different kinds of foods to canoes.

But Saul's argument goes beyond an historical homage to a lost culture; rather, he argues that Aboriginal ways of thinking and behaving, of solving problems, continue in the kind of society that Canada has become. He argues that several strategic elements, linked to Canada's Aboriginal nature, shape how Canadians see themselves (Saul, 2008: 54–55):

> Our obsession with egalitarianism. Our desire to maintain a balance between individuals and groups. The delight we take in playing with our non-monolithic idea of society—a delight in complexity. Our tendency to try to run society as an ongoing negotiation, which must be related to our distaste for resolving complexities. Our preference, behind a relatively violent language of public debate, for consensus—again an expression of society as a balance of complexity, a sort of equilibrium. Our intuition that behind the formal written and technical face of our society lies something more important, which we try to get at through the oral and through complex relationships. Our sense that the clear resolution of differences will lead to injustice and even violence. And related to that our preference for something that the law now calls minimal impairment, which means the obligation of those with authority to do as little damage as possible to people and to rights when exercising that authority.

Ultimately, Saul's call is for Canadians to escape colonially imposed ways of thinking, to thereby see—to imagine—ourselves based on the truth of how Canada has been built, without which Canadian society will continue to stumble and fail.

In issuing his call, however, Saul also reverses a centuries-old practice of Euro-Canadian ethnocentrism. There are many, sympathetic or otherwise, who claim that Aboriginal traditions and practices have no relevance in a modern, competitive society (see Flanagan, 2000). Indeed, they argue that Aboriginals have "much to learn" from modern Euro-Canadian society; that the way forward lies in becoming more like the dominant culture. Saul's critique (2008), and that of Davis (2009), takes us in a more interesting and perhaps more fruitful direction, enjoining us to ask such questions as: What have we lost? and What might we yet relearn? (from traditional cultures).

What lessons might non-Aboriginal peoples learn from Aboriginal peoples, their values, and their heritage? We provide one example, dealing with crime and justice.

Despite a general decrease in incidence of crime, many Canadians remain fearful, and because they are afraid, Canadians are often persuaded that more police, stiffer sentences, and bigger jails are a solution. Most criminologists view such policies as ineffective except in dealing with a few select types of crime; the United States is a shining testament to the failure of "getting in touch on crime." Severe punishment seems ineffective in dissuading criminal behaviour, while victims themselves often feel unsatisfied sometimes even re-victimized by a legal system that often seems remote.

Consider the example of Aboriginal justice. In pre-contact days, Aboriginal peoples employed storytelling, ridicule, and shaming as methods of keeping people in line. In more serious cases, they would put an offender in a circle of elders, who would offer advice and mete out punishment to the offender (Warry, 2007: 173–174). This gathering of elders would demand change in the offender's behaviour and determine an appropriate punishment for the misdeed. Sometimes called a **sentencing circle**, this approach has been revived in many Aboriginal communities, although it has been altered slightly. Today, such circles include offenders, victims, community members, and justice professionals who meet face to face to discuss offences and determine ways to ensure that justice is meted out (Chiste, 2005: 224–225). A decade ago, the Yukon had organized about 300 sentencing circles, more than any other community in Canada. Likewise, in Saskatchewan, about 100 sentencing circles had been initiated, with several more in British Columbia, Manitoba, and Quebec (Steckley and Cummins, 2008: 241). The secret element in sentencing circles is making the offender deal directly with the victim and the community at large. Wrongdoing involves a tearing of the social fabric. The intent of the sentencing circle is to repair the wound. Might such an approach work in non-Aboriginal communities?

CONCLUSION

Our world continues to change at an accelerating speed. Ironically, however, many of the biggest changes in Canada today and in the foreseeable future involve Aboriginal peoples— those who were there at the forefront of changes 400 years ago, then forgotten, are now once more prominent for, as former minister of Indian Affairs and Northern Development, Robert Nault, remarked in 2004, "We have the best-educated generation of First Nations peoples ever. They are well-trained and equipped to make their way in the global, knowledge-based economy."

Nor is this situation peculiar to Canada. Throughout many parts of the world long ago colonized, Aboriginal peoples have begun reasserting their political rights and cultural identities. This has particularly been the case in the former British colonies—Canada, the United States, Australia, and New Zealand (see Fleras and Elliott, 1992). But a resurgence of Aboriginal peoples is also apparent in Latin America; the Mexican Zapatista movement provides only one prominent example.

We began our search for Canadian society with a discussion of notions of country, nation, and state. We noted the problematic nature of these terms, and the uniqueness of Canada in trying to fit them into the Canadian experiment. The case of Aboriginal peoples in Canada provides perhaps the most striking example. Canada remains a country. It constitutes also, we would argue, a unique society. Part of Canada's uniqueness, however, resides in the complex manner in which states and markets have been involved in its creation, and the creative manner in which more than one nation has been accommodated to that grand design.

One thing is particularly clear: Canada's Aboriginal nations will play a major and growing role in shaping the kind of society Canada will become in the remaining years of the 21st century. As Phil Fontaine, grand chief of the Assembly of First Nations, recently observed, "The future of First Nations and Canada's future are intricately linked."

KEY TERMS
band
profane world
sacred world
sentencing circle
unintended or unanticipated consequences
urban reserves
world view

CRITICAL THINKING QUESTIONS

1. As Aboriginal communities in Canada change and adapt, what kinds of conflicts might we expect to arise within the communities?

2. What factors might explain differences in educational attainment between males and females in both Aboriginal and non-Aboriginal communities?

3. Are the inequalities between Aboriginal and non-Aboriginal peoples in Canada more similar to a class system or a caste system?

4. Is a "third way" between traditional and modern world views possible? What might it look like?

5. What lessons might non-Aboriginal societies learn from Aboriginal societies in meeting the challenges of the 21st century?

RECOMMENDED READINGS

Davis, Wade. 2009. *The Wayfinders: Why Ancient Wisdom Matters in the Modern World.* Toronto: House of Anansi Press.

Destined to be a classic, Davis's book, the 2009 Massey Lecture, examines traditional cultures around the world and "why ancient wisdom matters."

Friesen, John W., and Virginia Lyons Friesen. 2008. *Western Canadian Native Destiny: Complex Questions on the Cultural Maze.* Calgary: Detselig.

The authors document a series of contemporary Aboriginal issues, including urban adjustment, health, justice, education, cultural identity, land claims, economic development, and self-government.

Ross, Rupert. 1992. *Dancing with a Ghost: Exploring Indian Reality.* Markham: Reed Books.

This is one of the first studies to address the issue of legal justice and cultural maintenance among Canada's Aboriginal communities, specifically targeting Ontario's Ojibway community.

Schouls, Tim. 2003. *Shifting Boundaries: Aboriginal Identity, Pluralist Theory, and the Politics of Self-Government.* Vancouver: UBC Press.

Schouls argues that Aboriginal self-government is not about cultural maintenance, but about equalizing current imbalances in power, and that Canada's First Nations should therefore be given the opportunity to construct their own identities.

Warry, Wayne. 2007. *Ending Denial: Understanding Aboriginal Issues.* Peterborough: Broadview Press.

Warry examines the problems and obstacles that confront Canada's First Nations in their quest to wrest control of their institutions away from the federal government.

RELATED WEBSITES

Aboriginal Canada Portal
http://www.aboriginalcanada.gc.ca/acp/site.nsf/en/ao35225.html
The Government of Canada hosts a site, Aboriginal Canada Portal, containing important statistics and maps.

Assembly of First Nations
www.afn.ca/
The Assembly of First Nations is the national representative organization of the First Nations in Canada.

Turtle Island Native Network
www.turtleisland.org/news/news-justice.htm
This is Canada's Aboriginal news and information network.

CANADIAN SOCIETY ON VIDEO

Circles. 1997. National Film Board of Canada, 57 minutes, 45 seconds. Examines justice and community healing, hope, and transformation, bringing together the traditional Aboriginal justice circle and the Canadian justice system.

Mohawk Girls. 2005. National Film Board of Canada, 62 minutes, 45 seconds. Film examines the lives of three Mohawk teenage girls in Kahnawake reserve and the hope, despair, heartache, and promise of growing up Aboriginal at the beginning of the 21st century.

No Turning back: The Royal Commission on Aboriginal Peoples. 1997. The National Film

Board of Canada, 47 minutes, 20 seconds. The video begins with footage of the Oka standoff and other First Nations' protests of the 1990s, then interviews the commissioners of this inquiry and highlights some of the presentations.

Urban Elder. 1997. National Film Board of Canada, 28 minutes, 54 seconds. Depicts the role of Vern Harper, an Aboriginal ceremonial elder in a large Canadian city.

CHAPTER 14

CANADA IN THE WORLD AND IN THE FUTURE

Much will have to change in Canada if the country is to stay the same.
—Abraham Rotstein, 1964

We peer so suspiciously at each other that we cannot see that we Canadians are standing on the mountaintop of human wealth, freedom, and privilege.
—Prime Minister Pierre Trudeau, New Year's message, 1980

The Global Village is nothing more than Canadian culture writ large.
—author John Gray, 1994

INTRODUCTION

Canada is rapidly approaching its 150th birthday. Some believe it shows little wear and tear, with the promise of its best years yet to come. Others believe it is facing significant strains, with many important challenges on the horizon.

This chapter concludes with a look at some of the most pressing issues facing Canadian society in the years ahead. Before doing so, however, the chapter briefly examines Canada in relation to other countries, based on the most recent United Nations Human Development Report.

COMPARING CANADA: METHODOLOGY

In the recent age of globalization, comparisons between various countries have been commonplace. International organizations, such as the United Nations and World Bank, regularly put out lists of data for every country on the planet.

Comparisons must be meaningful, however. Imagine, for example, comparing a top-level National Hockey League player's slapshot with that of an eight-year-

old player or, likely worse, either of this text's authors. The point is there must be a legitimate basis for comparison. Usually this means that, at least on some factors, the groups compared are the same. The presence of constants on some variables makes any differences meaningful. What countries might provide a sound basis for comparisons with Canada?

Several countries are often grouped together on different bases. For example, the Anglo democracies (Australia, Canada, New Zealand, the United Kingdom, and the United States) share cultural similarities, including legal and political systems. Slightly overlapping the Anglo-democracy group is another group termed the "White" dominions (Argentina, Australia, Canada, New Zealand, and Uruguay), countries in the New World largely settled by Europeans (Laxer, 1989). A third grouping can be derived from Olsen's (2002) typology of different types of welfare states (Chapter 8), and his own specific study of Canada, the United States, and Sweden, Canada's system being a kind of hybrid. Finally, we might construct a group for specific comparison with Canada comprised of its former imperial rules, Britain and France.

Putting together all of these groups, we arrive at the following countries for comparison with Canada: Argentina, Australia, France, New Zealand, Sweden, the United Kingdom, the United States, and Uruguay.

CANADA AND ITS COMPARATORS: THE HUMAN DEVELOPMENT INDEX REPORT

There are a number of organizations, including the International Labour Organization and the U.S. Central Intelligence Agency, that provide reliable national and international data on a host of subjects. One of these is the United Nations' Human Development Report Office (HDRO) (United Nations, 2007b), which publishes an annual report assessing country achievements in different areas of human development based on an index. The countries are classified in four ways: (1) by human development (including education), (2) by income level (high, middle, and low), (3) by major world aggregates, and (4) by region. The **Human Development Index** (HDI) lists countries as high on human development if they score 0.800 or above; medium if they score 0.500–0.799; and low if they score less than 0.500. The HDI lists countries as high in income if gross national income per capita is U.S. $11,116 or above; middle if it is between U.S. $906 and U.S. $11,115; and low if it is U.S. $905 or less. Table 14.1 compares the selected countries chosen on HDI trends since 1980.

For several years in the early 2000s, Canada held first place on the HDI, but in

Table 14.1
Human Development Index Trends for Select Countries, 1980–2006

	1980	1985	1990	1995	2000	2005	2006	Rank (2006)
Argentina	0.790	0.794	0.801	0.822	0.849	0.854	0.860	46
Australia	0.870	0.881	0.900	0.935	0.951	0.963	0.965	4
Canada	**0.892**	**0.915**	**0.935**	**0.941**	**0.950**	**0.965**	**0.967**	**3**
France	0.875	0.886	0.908	0.927	0.940	0.953	0.955	11
New Zealand	0.860	0.872	0.881	0.909	0.927	0.943	0.944	20
Sweden	0.882	0.893	0.904	0.935	0.952	0.957	0.958	7
United Kingdom	0.858	0.868	0.888	0.927	0.929	0.944	0.942	21
United States	0.892	0.906	0.920	0.933	0.944	0.950	0.950	15
Uruguay	0.774	0.781	0.799	0.815	0.836	0.854	0.859	47

Source: United Nations, *Human Development Indices*, Table 1 (New York: United Nations Human Development Report Office, 2007: 25–28).

2006 ranked number three in the world (at 0.967), just behind Iceland and Norway, both with index scores of 0.968. Of the countries chosen for comparison, Canada's ranking was close to another Anglo democracy, Australia, but not particularly close to the other countries in this group, New Zealand, the U.K., or the U.S. Indeed, the next most similar country to Canada on the index was Sweden, another northern country with a small population and established welfare-state traditions. Some of the factors underlying these differences are suggested in Table 14.2.

Table 14.2 shows that male incomes in Canada are on par with the U.S. and ahead of other countries, but that female incomes in Canada trail many of the

Table 14.2
Human Development Indices for Select Countries, 2006

	Life Expectancy at Birth (Years)		GDP Per Capita PPPU.S. $		Life Expectancy Index (F and M)	Education Index (F and M)	GDP Index (F and M)
	F	M	F	M			
Argentina	78.8	71.3	8,595	15,485	0.834	0.946	0.799
Australia	83.4	78.7	27,866	33,035	0.934	0.993	0.968
Canada	**82.7**	**78.0**	**26,055**	**40,000**	**0.924**	**0.991**	**0.986**
France	83.8	76.8	24,529	39,731	0.923	0.978	0.963
New Zealand	82.0	77.9	21,181	29,391	0.916	0.993	0.923
Sweden	82.8	78.4	30,976	37,067	0.928	0.974	0.973
United Kingdom	81.3	76.9	26,863	38,596	0.903	0.957	0.966
United States	80.6	75.4	25,613	40,000	0.884	0.968	1.000
Uruguay	79.6	72.4	7,456	13,097	0.851	0.955	0.772

Source: United Nations, *Human Development Indices*, tables 2 and 4 (New York: United Nations Human Development Report Office, 2007: 29–32).

other countries, especially Sweden. It also shows that life expectancy in Canada, for both males and females, is high, surpassed only by Australia and France for females and only Australia and Sweden for males.

Life expectancy is generally a good proxy measure for other things going on in a society, such as income, education, and welfare-state programs, as well as general environmental conditions. Note, for example, Canada's relatively high index scores on life expectancy, education, and income: 0.924, 0.991, and 0.986 respectively. By contrast, note the high index score for the United States on income—the index is set against the American dollar, hence the 1.000 score—but the relatively poor index scores for life expectancy and education. In short, a good society is more than the sum of its income. It is the distribution of that income and the sum of choices made on how it will be spent. In the years to come, this is just one of many decisions that Canadians will have to make.

ISSUES AND CHALLENGES TO CANADIAN SOCIETY

In Chapter 1, we defined "society" as follows:

> A society is defined as the prod-
> uct of relatively continuous and
> enduring interactions, within a
> political territory, between people
> more or less identifying themselves
> as members of the society, these
> interactions being maintained by
> an ensemble of political, economic,
> cultural, and other institutions,
> the sum of such interactions being
> in excess of interactions occurring
> with similarly defined societies
> external to the given territory.

We have taken as a given throughout this text the notion that something termed "Canadian society" exists as a sociologi-

cal construct amenable to study. For several hundred years, the people inhabiting the political territory of Canada have interacted, sometimes in hostility (but also in amity), more often in tolerance, but perhaps also unconsciousness. The creation of a Canadian society has meant the intensification of these interactions and knowledge (or at least imagined knowledge) of a large assortment of others, from Cape Spear to Vancouver Island to the Arctic Circle. No society remains static, however; even less so in the 21st century. Several issues are likely to bear particularly strongly on the nature, direction, and interconnectedness of Canadian society in future.

THE ISSUE OF STATE, MARKET, AND SOCIETY

A central argument of this book has been that the concepts of state, market, and society are inseparable. What is the proper balance or relationship between the three elements, however?

Historically, in Canada, the three often expanded and thrived together, with the state often taking a lead hand, creating a national economy, encouraging immigration, facilitating the means of transportation and communication, and overseeing the establishment of a host of important institutions.

For a time in the late 20th century, however, the role of the state in general appeared in decline, beset by pressures from below (local communities, regional interests, and sometimes long-suppressed sub-national groups) and from above (free-market entrepreneurs, transnational corporations, and global political organizations) (see Bell, 1993; Robbins, 2008). For Canada, specific pressures have also been exerted by the United States through its enormous economic and cultural influence, not to mention obvious geographic proximity (see Clarkson, 2008).

The worldwide economic crisis that

began in 2007 has witnessed the state's rebirth, perhaps putting an end to the idea (*à la* Lenin) that it would one day "wither away." The state's functions may change, but it seems here to stay. The triumvirate of state, market, and society, we say again, is inseparable, but both states and markets are instruments of power. Who will control them? What is the role of society itself in managing states and markets?

THE ISSUE OF INCLUSION

Noted sociologist Daniel Bell (quoted in Swedberg, 1990: 222) has remarked that "people can only identify with society if the society feels a responsibility to them." Economic and political turmoil in the first half of the 20th century resulted in the creation of the welfare state, at least one function of which was to equalize the life chances of Canadian citizens and, more broadly, enhance social solidarity (chapters 8 and 9).

Canada has made great strides in reducing social inequalities in recent years, but there remain many structural barriers needing redress. Note, as shown in Table 14.2, the discrepancy between male and female incomes. Likewise, ethnicity and race continue to play a large role in deciding life chances and social status for many people in Canada. Unless dealt with, might Canada risk alienation and fragmentation?

THE ISSUE OF DIFFERENCE VERSUS SIMILARITY

Much of our discussion in this text— from the historic demands of francophone Quebecers for cultural protection and recognition to English Canada's long search for itself, to the formulation of a multicultural Canada, to the re-emergence of Aboriginal peoples at the heart of Canadian society—have centred on the notion of identity. Diversity is widely viewed as strengthening Canadian society by making it more adaptable to change.

What is the "right" balance between diversity and uniformity? On what matters is agreement (uniformity) necessary? In what areas is insistence upon uniformity problematic, perhaps even threatening other important societal values, such as respect for individual or minority differences? What programs and policies are required to ensure sufficient positive interactions and tolerance among Canadian citizens of different backgrounds? What should be the role of educational, employment, and cultural institutions in fashioning a coherent Canadian quilt from this country's various threads?

THE ISSUE OF FAUX DEMOCRACY VERSUS DEEP DEMOCRACY

Defined simply, **democracy** means *rule by the people*. Today, many Canadians believe that Canadian democracy is in crisis. Evidence for this is found in declining voter turnout at elections—at just over 59 percent, turnout for the 2008 federal election was the lowest in Canadian history—and surveys showing considerable alienation among Canadians. To address these issues, some people have suggested specific changes to the political system, such as a revamped Senate or the introduction of a proportional representative system of voting.

Others, however, believe the problem is deeper. What does democracy really mean? Who are "the people"? Is democracy just about voting or rule by the majority? Or is it something more—a way of life, a culture? Is political democracy possible without economic democracy?

THE ISSUE OF A WEALTHY VERSUS A HEALTHY (AND SUSTAINABLE) ECONOMY

Despite, or perhaps because of, 400 years of development, Canada remains largely a resource hinterland to the world economy. This has sometimes brought Canada prosperity, though it has not often been sustained or distributed equally. At the beginning of the 21st century, Canada possesses at least two major resources, in particular, that will continue to increase in demand: oil and water. At the same time, however, Canada and the rest of the world face a threat that has been too long ignored: environmental depletion and destruction (Chapter 12). Canada has a major role—some would say a responsibility—to protect and nurture its resources for the good of the planet. But Canadians also want jobs and prosperity, not to mention warmth during cold winter nights, hence Canadians per capita are among the heaviest energy users in the world. How will Canadians "square the circle" of maintaining a prosperous and sustainable economy while also protecting and even restoring the natural environment?

CONCLUSION

Canada is one of the world's wonders. Against many odds, Canadians through the centuries have constructed a society that, for the most part, is prosperous and tolerant, progressive and civil. The torch is thus passed to future generations to continue the great Canadian experiment into the 21st century.

KEY TERMS

democracy
Human Development Index

CRITICAL THINKING QUESTIONS

1. Which countries do you think are good comparatives with Canada?

2. What do we mean by development?

3. Does development in one area of society always mean development in another area?

4. Is democracy compatible with economic inequality?

5. What do you think Canada will be like in 2050?

RECOMMENDED READINGS

Bell, Daniel. 1996. *The Cultural Contradictions of Capitalism*, 20th anniversary ed. New York: Basic Books.
Bell's book remains a classic in sociology, arguing that capitalism brings about cultural changes that, in turn, destroy capitalism's underpinnings.
Bello, Walden. 2002. *Deglobalization: Ideas for a New Economy*. London: Zed Books.
Bello's book questions globalization and suggests new ways of thinking about localism and sustainable development.
Galbraith, John Kenneth. 1997. *The Great Crash 1929*. Boston: Mariner.
Written by Canada's greatest contribution to the economics profession, Galbraith's account of the 1929 crash is humorous, concise, and remarkably current in explaining some of the reasons for market instability.
Macpherson, C.B. 1965. *The Real World of Democracy*. The Massey Lectures, 4th series. Toronto: CBC Enterprises.
Perhaps Canada's greatest political theorist, Macpherson in this book details the contradictions inherent in the term "liberal democracy."
Osberg, Lars (ed.). 2003. *The Economic Implications of Social Cohesion*. Toronto: University of Toronto Press.
This book provides essential readings on the importance of social cohesion and social capital for a successful economy.

RELATED WEBSITES

American Central Intelligence Agency (CIA)
www.cia.gov/library/publications/the-world-factbook/

This agency was established in 1947 as a civilian intelligence agency of the United States government. As such, it gathers a huge amount of information, much of which can be found on its site.

International Labour Organization (ILO)
www.ilo.org/global/lang--en/index.htm

This is a United Nations organization that deals with labour issues.

United Nations' Human Development Report Office
http://hdr.undp.org/en/
This United Nations office is housed in New York.

APPENDIX 1
CANADIAN FEDERAL ELECTION RESULTS SINCE CONFEDERATION

	Conservatives	Liberals				Other	Total
1867	101	80					181
1872	103	97					200
1874	73	133					206
1878	137	69					206
1882	139	71					210
1887	123	92					215
1891	123	92					215
1896	88	118				7	213
1900	81	132					213
1904	75	139					214
1908	85	133				3	221
1911	133	86				2	221
1917	153	82					235
			Progressives				
1921	50	116	69			4	235
1925	116	99				30	245
			United				
1926	91	116				38	245
1930	137	91				17	245
			CCF	**Social Credit**			
1935	39	171	7	17		11	245
					New Democracy		
1940	39	170	8		10	10	245
	Progressive Conservatives						
1945	67	125	28	13		12	245
1949	41	190	13	10		8	262
1953	51	171	23	15		5	265
1957	112	105	25	19		4	265
					Liberal Labour party		
1958	208	48	8		1		265
			NDP				
1962	116	99	19	30		1	265
1963	95	129	17	24			265
					Ralliement Créditistes		
1965	97	131	21	5	9	2	265
1968	72	155	22		14	1	264

1972	107	109	31	15		2	264
1974	95	141	16	11		1	264
1979	136	114	26	6			282
1980	103	147	32				282
1984	211	40	30			1	282
1988	169	83	43				295
				Reform	Bloc Québécois		
1993	2	177	9	52	54	1	295
1997	20	155	21	60	44	1	301
				Canadian Reform	Conservative Alliance		
2000	12	172	13	66	38		301
	Conservatives						
2004	99	135	19		54	1	308
2006	124	103	29		51	1	308
2008	143	77	37		49	2	308

Source: 1997-2008 general election results adapted from Elections Canada, available at: http://www.elections.ca/intro.asp?section=p as&document=index&lang=e.
1867-1997 election results adapted from the Library of Parliament, "Electoral Results by Party," available at: http://www2.parl.gc.ca/ parlinfo/Compilations/ElectionsAndRidings/ResultsParty.aspx?Language=E.

CANADIAN PRIME MINISTERS, GOVERNMENTS, AND MAJOR POLICIES SINCE CONFEDERATION

Prime Minister	Party	Dates of Administration	Major Policies/Events
Sir John A. Macdonald	C	July 1867–Nov. 1873	Confederation: Red River Rebellion; Manitoba, British Columbia, and Prince Edward Island join Canada
Alexander Mackenzie	L	Nov. 1873–Oct. 1878	Supreme Court of Canada established; Intercontinental Railway completed; first Indian Act passed
Sir John A. Macdonald	C	Oct. 1878–June 1891	National Policy; the North-West Rebellion; Louis Riel hanged
Sir John J.C. Abbott	C	June 1891–Nov. 1892	
Sir John S. Thompson	C	Dec. 1892–Dec. 1894	
Sir Mackenzie Bowell	C	Dec. 1894–Apr. 1896	
Sir Charles Tupper	C	Apr. 1896–July 1896	Manitoba School Act; Klondike Gold Rush; Boer War; Free Trade Election (lost)
Sir Wilfrid Laurier	L	July 1896–Oct. 1911	First World War; Conscription Crisis; income tax introduced
Sir Robert L. Borden	C	Oct. 1911–Oct. 1917	War ends; White women gain federal vote; Winnipeg General Strike
Sir Robert L. Borden	U	Oct. 1917–July 1920	
Arthur Meighen	U	July 1920–Dec. 1921	King-Byng Constitutional Affair
W.L. Mackenzie King	L	Dec. 1921–June 1925	
Arthur Meighen	C	June 1926–Sept. 1926	Great Depression begins; Cairine Wilson appointed Canada's first woman senator
W.L. Mackenzie King	L	Sept. 1926–Aug. 1930	Statute of Westminster; Co-operative Commonwealth Federation founded; Regina riot; Social Credit elected in Alberta
Richard B. Bennett	C	Aug. 1930–Oct. 1935	Second World War; beginning of welfare state; second Conscription Crisis; CCF elected in Saskatchewan
W.L. Mackenzie King	L	Oct. 1935–Nov. 1948	Korean War
Louis St. Laurent	L	Nov. 1948–June 1957	
John G. Diefenbaker	PC	June 1957–Apr. 1963	Avro Arrow cancelled; Canadian Bill of Rights; Status Indians gain vote
Lester B. Pearson	L	Apr. 1963–Apr. 1968	Maple Leaf flag; medicare
Pierre E. Trudeau	L	Apr. 1968–June 1979	Bilingualism; multiculturalism, the FLQ Crisis; capital punishment abolished; PQ elected
Charles Joseph Clarke	PC	June 1979–March 1980	
Pierre E. Trudeau	L	March 1980–June 1984	Quebec Referendum; National Energy Program; the Constitution Act, 1982
John N. Turner	L	June 1984–Sept. 1984	Free Trade Agreement: Meech Lake Accord; Charlottetown Accord and Referendum; Goods and Services Tax (GST); Oka Crisis
Martin Brian Mulroney	PC	Sep. 1984–June 1993	First female prime minister
Kim Campbell	PC	June 1993–Oct. 1993	North American Free Trade Agreement; Quebec Referendum; Clarity Act; 9/11 attacks; Canadian military involvement in Afghanistan War
Jean Chrétien	L	Oct. 1993–Nov. 2003	
Paul Martin	L	Nov. 2003–Feb. 2006	Gomery Inquiry; same-sex marriage becomes law
Stephen Harper	C	Feb. 2006–	GST cuts; increased military spending; recognition of Quebec "nation"; start of major world economic crisis

Legend: C = Conservative; L = Liberal; U = Unionist; PC = Progressive Conservative

Source: *Canadian Encyclopedia On-Line*. Used by permission from the Canadian Encyclopedia ©2008 Historica Foundation of Canada, http://www.thecanadianencyclopedia.com/index.cfm?PgNm=TCE&Params=A1ARTA0006474

REFERENCES

Abel, Kerry. 1993. *Drum Songs: Glimpses of Dene History*. Montreal and Kingston: McGill-Queen's University Press.

Abella, Irving, and Harold Troper. 1982. *None Is Too Many: Canada and the Jews in Europe, 1933–1948*. Toronto: Lester and Orpen Dennys.

Abrams, Philip. 1988. "Notes on the difficulty of studying the state." *Journal of Historical Sociology* 1(1): 58–89.

Adams, Howard. 1989. *Prison of Grass: Canada from a Native Point of View*, 2nd ed. Saskatoon: Fifth House Publishers.

_____. 1999. *Tortured People: The Politics of Colonization*, rev. ed. Penticton: Theytus Books.

Adams, Michael. 1998. *Sex in the Snow*. Toronto: Penguin.

Adema, Willem, and Maxine Ladaique. 2005. "Net social expenditure, 2005 edition." *OECD Social, Employment, and Migration Working Papers* 29. Paris: OECD.

Aitken, Hugh G.J. 1959. "The changing structure of the Canadian economy." In H.G.J. Aitken (ed.), *The American Economic Impact on Canada*, 3–35. Durham: Duke University Press.

Albrow, Martin. 1997. *The Global Age: State and Society beyond Modernity*. Stanford: Stanford University Press.

Alford, B.W.E. 1996. *Britain in the World Economy Since 1880*. London: Longman.

Alfred, Gerald R. 1995. *Heeding the Voices of Our Ancestors: Kahnawake Mohawk Politics and the Rise of Native Nationalism*. Toronto: Oxford University Press.

Alfred, Taiaiake. 2005. *Wasâse: Indigenous Pathways to Action and Freedom*. Peterborough: Broadview Press.

Allison, Derek. 1983. "Fourth world education in Canada and the faltering promise of Native teacher education." *Journal of Canadian Studies* 18(3): 102–119.

Anderson, Benedict. 1983. *Imagined Communities*. London: Verso.

Angus, Murray. 1991. *And the Last Shall Be First: Native Policy in an Era of Cutbacks*. Toronto: NC Press.

Antone, Eileen M. 2000. "Empowering Aboriginal views in Aboriginal education." *Canadian Journal of Native Education* 24(2): 92–101.

Asch, Michael. 2000. "Self-government in the New Millennium." In J. Bird, L. Land, and M. McAdam (eds.), *Nation to Nation: Aboriginal Sovereignty and the Future of Canada*, 65–73. Toronto: Irwin.

Baer, D., E. Grabb, and W. Johnston. 1993. "National character, regional culture, and the values of Canadians and Americans." *Canadian Review of Sociology and Anthropology* 30(1): 13–36.

Baker, Maureen. 1996. "Social assistance and the employability of mothers: Two models from cross-national research." *The Canadian Journal of Sociology* 21(4): 483–504.

Baldwin, Gordon C. 1967. *How Indians Really Lived*. New York: G.P. Putnam's Sons.

Baldwin, John R., and Guy Gallatly. 2005. *Global Links: Long-Term Trends in Foreign Investment and Foreign Control in Canada, 1960 to 2000*. Statistics Canada, Cat. 11-622-MIE, no. 08. Ottawa: Statistics Canada.

Baldwin, John R., and Walong Gu. 2004. *Trade Liberalization: Export Market Participation, Productivity Growth, and Innovation*. Statistics Canada Cat. no. 11-F0027-MIE. Ottawa: Statistics Canada.

Balikci, Asen. 1970. *The Netsilik Eskimo*. Garden City: The American Museum of Natural History.

Balthazar, Louis. 1993. "The faces of Quebec nationalism." In D. Taras, B. Rasporich, and E. Mandel (eds.), *A Passion for Identity: An Introduction to Canadian Studies*, 92–107. Scarborough: Nelson Canada.

_____. 1997. "Quebec and the ideal of federalism." In M. Fournier, M. Rosenberg, and D. White (eds.), *Quebec Society: Critical Issues*, 45–60. Scarborough: Prentice-Hall Canada.

Barber, Benjamin. 1996. *Jihad vs. McWorld*. New York: Ballantine.

Barman, Jean, Yvonne Hébert, and Don McCaskill. 1986. "The legacy of the past: An overview." In J. Barman, Y. Hébert, and D. McCaskill (eds.), *Indian Education in Canada*, vol. I: *The Legacy*, 1–22. Vancouver: UBC Press.

Barron, F. Laurie, and Joseph Garcea. 1999. "The genesis of urban reserves and the role of governmental self-interest." In F.L. Barron and J. Garcea (eds.), *Urban Indian Reserves: Forging New Relationships in Saskatchewan*, 22–52. Saskatoon: Purich.

Battiste, Marie. 2000. *Reclaiming Indigenous Voice and Vision*. Vancouver: UBC Press.

Battiste, Marie, and James (Sa'ke'j) Youngblood Henderson. 2000. *Protecting Indigenous Knowledge and Heritage*. Saskatoon: Purich.

Bauch, Hubert. 2006. "Quebec 'nation' debate divides French, English: Poll." *Montreal Gazette* (November 11), http://www.canada.com/topics/news/national/story.html?id=23ba4837-5854-458d-b513-0c2d2d0b5ea3&k=50919

Bear Heart. 1998. *The Wind Is My Mother: The Life and Teachings of a Native American Shaman*. New York: Berkley Books.

Beattie, Owen, and John Geiger. 1987. *Frozen in Time: Unlocking the Secrets of the Franklin Expedition*. Saskatoon: Western Producer Prairie Books.

Bell, Daniel. 1961. *The End of Ideology*. Glencoe: The Free Press.

_____. 1993. "The third technological revolution: And its possible socioeconomic consequences." In K. Finsterbusch and J. Schwartz (eds.), *Sources: Notable Selections in Sociology*, 351–365. Guilford: Dushkin.

_____. 1996. *The Cultural Contradictions of Capitalism*, 20th anniversary ed. New York: Basic Books.

Bell, Edward, 1993. *Social Classes and Social Credit*. Montreal and Kingston: McGill-Queen's University Press.

Bellamy, Donald, and Allan Irving. 1981. "Pioneers." In J. Turner and F. Turner (eds.), *Canadian Social Welfare*, 27–46. Don Mills: Collier Macmillan Canada.

Bello, Walden. 2002. *Deglobalization: Ideas for a New Economy*. London: Zed Books.

Bercuson, David, and Barry Cooper. 1991. *Deconfederation: Canada without Quebec*. Toronto: Key Porter Books.

Berger, Carl. 1976. *The Sense of Power: Studies in the Ideas of Canadian Imperialism 1867–1914*. Toronto: University of Toronto Press.

Bernard, Paul. 1996. "Canada as a social experiment." *The Canadian Journal of Sociology* 21(2): 245–258.

Berton, Pierre. 1958. *The Klondike Fever: The Life and Death of the Last Great Gold Rush*. New York: Knopf.

_____. 1980. *The Invasion of Canada, 1812–1813*. Toronto: McClelland & Stewart Ltd.

_____. 1988. *The Arctic Grail*. Markham: Penguin.

_____. 1991. *The Great Depression, 1929–1939*. Toronto: Penguin.

Bird, John, Lorraine Land, and Murray McAdam (eds.). 2000. *Self-Government in the New Millennium: Nation to Nation: Aboriginal Sovereignty and the Future of Canada*. Toronto: Irwin Publishing.

Bissoondath, Neil. 1994. *Selling Illusions: The Cult of Multiculturalism in Canada*. Toronto: Penguin.

Black, Conrad. 1977. *Duplessis*. Toronto: McClelland & Stewart.

Blumer, Herbert. 1969. *Symbolic Interactionism: Perspective and Method*. Englewood Cliffs: Prentice-Hall.

Bobiwash, A. Rodney. 1997. "Native urban self-government and the politics of self-determination." In F. Sanderson and H. Howard-Bobiwash (eds.), *The Meeting Place: Aboriginal Life in Toronto*, 84–94. Toronto: Native Canadian Centre.

Boldt, Menno. 1993. *Surviving as Indians: The Challenge of Self-Government*. Toronto: University of Toronto Press.

Bone, Robert M. 1988. "Cultural persistence and country food: The Case of the Norman Wells Project." *The Western Canadian Anthropologist* 5: 61–79.

_____. 1992. *The Geography of the Canadian North: Issues and Challenges*. Toronto: Oxford University Press.

_____. 2000. *The Regional Geography of Canada*. Toronto: Oxford University Press.

Bouchard, Gérald, and Charles Taylor. 2008. *Fonder L'Avenir: Le Temps de la Conciliation*. Quebec: Gouvernement du Quebec.

Bourgault, Pierre. 1991. *Now or Never: Manifesto for an Independent Quebec*. Toronto: Key Porter Books.

Bowler, Arthur. 1993. "Introduction." In A.D. Gilbert, G.M. Wallace, and R.M. Bray (eds.), *Reappraisals in Canadian History: Pre-Confederation*, 291–309. Scarborough: Prentice-Hall Canada Inc.

Boyer, Robert, and Daniel Drache (eds). 1996. *States against Markets*. London: Routledge.

Bradley, Paul G., and G. Campbell Watkins. 2003. "Canada and the U.S.: A seamless energy border?" *The Border Papers*, no. 178, April. Toronto: C.D. Howe Institute.

Brascoupé, Simon. 2000. "Aboriginal peoples' vision of the future: Interweaving traditional knowledges and new technologies of the heart." In D. Long and O.P. Dickason (eds.), *Canadian Aboriginal Issues*, 411–432. Toronto: Harcourt Canada.

Braz, Albert. 2003. *The False Traitor: Louis Riel in Canadian Culture*. Toronto: University of Toronto Press.

Brimelow, Peter. 1986. *The Patriot Game*. Toronto: Key Porter Books.

Brodie, Janine. 1990. *The Political Economy of Canadian Regionalism*. Toronto: Harcourt Brace Jovanovich Canada.

Brody, Hugh. 1987. *Living Arctic: Hunters of the Canadian North*. Vancouver: Douglas & McIntyre.

Brookes, Sonia. 1991. "The persistence of Native educational policy in Canada." In J.W. Friesen (ed.), *The Cultural Maze: Complex Questions on Native Destiny in Western Canada*, 163–180. Calgary: Detselig.

Brown, Wallace. 1993. "Victorious in defeat: The American Loyalists in Canada." In A.D. Gilbert, G.M. Wallace, and R.M. Bray (eds.), *Reappraisals in Canadian History: Pre-Confederation*, 241–250. Scarborough: Prentice-Hall Canada.

Brunelle, Dorval. 1999. "Free trade illusions in Quebec." *Le Monde Diplomatique* (April), 15.

Brunet, M. 1993. "The British conquest and the decline of the French-Canadian bourgeoisie." In A.D. Gilbert, G.M. Wallace, and R.M. Bray (eds.), *Reappraisals in Canadian History: Pre-Confederation*, 198–215. Scarborough: Prentice-Hall Canada.

Brym, Robert J. 2008. "Politics and new movements." In R.J. Brym (ed.), *New Society*, 5th ed., 464–486. Toronto: Nelson.

Brym, Robert J., and R. James Sacouman (eds.), 1979. *Underdevelopment and Social Movements in Atlantic Canada*. Toronto: New Hogtown Press.

Buckley, Helen. 1993. *From Wooden Ploughs to Welfare: Why Indian Policy Failed in the Prairie Provinces*. Montreal and Kingston: McGill-Queen's University Press.

Burbach, Roger, Orlando Nunez, and Boris Kagarlitsky. 1997. *Globalization and Its Discontents*. London: Pluto Press.

Cairns, Alan C. 2000. *Citizens Plus: Aboriginal Peoples and the Canadian State*. Vancouver: UBC Press.

Cajete, Gregory. 1994. *Look to the Mountain: An Ecology of Indigenous Education*. Durango: Kivaki Press.

Calgary Herald. 2001. "Abuse award insulting." *Calgary Herald* (July 14): A9.

Campbell, Bruce, and Ed Finn. 2006. *Living with Uncle*. Toronto: James Lorimer.

Canadian Encyclopedia. 1985. *Canadian Encyclopedia*, 1st ed. Edmonton: Hurtig.

_____. 1999. *Year 2000 Edition*. Toronto: McClelland & Stewart.

Canadian Global Almanac 2000. 1999. *A Book of Facts*. Toronto: Macmillan.

Cardinal, Harold. 1969. *The Unjust Society: The Tragedy of Canada's Indians*. Edmonton: Hurtig.

_____. 1977. *The Rebirth of Canada's Indians*. Edmonton: Hurtig Publishers.

Careless, J.M.S. 1970. *Canada: A Story of Challenge*. Toronto: Macmillan and Company.

Carlson, Leonard. 1981. *Indians, Bureaucrats, and the Land: The Dawes Act and the Decline of Indian Farming*. Westport: Greenwood Press.

Carr, Edward H. 1990. *What Is History?* Markham: Penguin Books.

Carter, Sarah. 1993. *Lost Harvests: Prairie Indian Reserve Farmers and Government Policy*.

Montreal and Kingston: McGill-Queen's University Press.

Catton, William R., and Riley E. Dunlap. 1980. "A new ecological paradigm for post-exuberant sociology." *American Behavioral Scientist* 24(1): 15 47.

Chalmers, J.W. 1974. "Marguerite Bourgeoys, Preceptress of New France." In R.S. Patterson, J.W. Chalmers, and J.W. Friesen (eds.), *Profiles of Canadian Educators*, 4–20. Toronto: D.C. Heath.

Chiste, Katherine Beaty. 2005. "Getting tough on crime the Aboriginal way: Alternative justice initiatives in Canada." In D. Newhouse, C. Voyageur, and D. Beavon (eds.), *Hidden in Plain Sight: Contributions of Aboriginal Peoples to Canadian Identity and Culture*, 218–232. Toronto: University of Toronto Press.

Chodos, Robert, and Eric Hamovitch. 1991. *Quebec and the American Dream*. Toronto: Between the Lines.

Chomsky, Noam. 2001. *9–11*. New York: Seven Stories Press.

Chorney, Harold. 1989. *The Deficit and Debt Management: An Alternative to Monetarism*. Ottawa: Canadian Centre for Policy Alternatives.

Citizenship and Immigration Canada. 1996. "Citizenship and immigration statistics 1996." Cat. No. MP22-/1996. Ottawa: Citizenship and Immigration Canada.

_____ . "Facts and figures 2008 – immigration review: Permanent and temporary residents." http://www.cic.gc.ca/english/resources/statistics/facts2008/permanent/index.asp

Clark, Samuel D., J. Paul Grayson, and Linda M. Grayson. 1975. *Prophecy and Protest: Social Movements in Twentieth-Century Canada*. Toronto: Gage.

Clarkson, Stephen. 1985. *Canada and the Reagan Challenge*. Toronto: Lorimer.

_____ . 2002a. *Uncle Sam and Us: Globalization, Neoconservatism, and the Canadian State*. Toronto: University of Toronto Press.

_____ . 2002b. "What Uncle Sam wants...." *Globe and Mail* (December 2): A13.

_____ . 2008. *Does North America Exist?* Toronto: University of Toronto Press.

Clarkson, Stephen, and Christina McCall. 1990. *Trudeau and Our Times*, vol. 1: *The Mag-nificent Obsession*. Toronto: McClelland & Stewart.

Clement, Wallace. 1975. *The Canadian Corporate Elite*. Toronto: McClelland & Stewart.

_____ . (ed.). 1997. *Understanding Canada: Building on the New Canadian Political Economy*. Montreal and Kingston: McGill-Queen's University Press.

Clement, Wallace, and Glen Williams. 1989. *The New Canadian Political Economy*. Montreal and Kingston: McGill-Queen's University Press.

Clerici, Naila. 1999. "The Cree of James Bay and the construction of their identity for the media." In Michael Behiels (ed.), *Futures and Identities*, 143–165. Montreal: Association for Canadian Studies.

Cline, Michael S. 1975. *Tannik School: The Impact of Education on the Eskimos of Anaktuvuk Pass*. Anchorage: Alaska Methodist University Press.

Coates, Ken S., P. Whitney Lackenbauer, William R. Morrison, and Greg Poelzer. 2008. *Arctic Front: Defending Canada in the Far North*. Toronto: Thomas Allen.

Cohen, Andrew. 1990. *A Deal Undone: The Making and Breaking of the Meech Lake Accord*. Vancouver: Douglas & McIntyre.

Cohen, Stewart J. 1997. "What if and so what in Northwest Canada: Could climate change make a difference to the future of the Mackenzie Basin?" *Arctic* 50(4): 293–307.

Collins, Randall. 1982. *Sociological Insight: An Introduction to Non-Obvious Sociology*. Oxford: Oxford University Press.

Colombo, John Robert. 1994. *Colombo's All-Time Great Canadian Quotations*. Toronto: Stoddart.

Condon, Richard G. 1987. *Inuit Youth: Growth and Change in the Canadian Arctic*. Newark: Rutgers University Press.

Conrad, Margaret, Alvin Finkel, and Cornelius Jaenen. 1993. *History of Canadian Peoples: Beginnings to 1867*. Toronto: Copp Clark Pitman.

Conway, John. 1994. *The West: The History of a Region in Confederation*. Toronto: James Lorimer and Company.

_____ . 1997. *Debts to Pay*. Toronto: James Lorimer and Company.

Cook, Ramsay. 1995. *Canada, Quebec, and the Uses of Nationalism*, 2nd ed. Toronto: McClelland & Stewart.

Cooke, Martin, and Daniéle Bélanger. 2006. "Migration theories and First Nations mobility: Towards a systems perspective." *Canadian Review of Sociology and Anthropology* 43(2): 141–165.

Cornellier, Manon. 1995. *The Bloc*. Toronto: James Lorimer and Company.

Cornish, George H. 1881. *Encyclopedia of Methodism in Canada*. Toronto: Methodist Book and Publishing Company.

Coulombe, Pierre A. 1998. "Quebec in the federation." In M. Westmacott and H. Mellon (eds.), *Challenges to Canadian Federalism*, 187–197. Scarborough: Prentice-Hall Canada.

Courchene, Thomas. 1997. *The Nation State in a Global/Information Era: Policy Challenges*. Kingston: John Deutsch Institute for the Study of Economic Policy, Queen's University.

_____ . 1998. *From Heartland to North American Region State: The Social, Fiscal, and Federal Evolution of Ontario*. Toronto: University of Toronto Press.

Couture, Claude. 1998. *Paddling with the Current: Pierre Elliott Trudeau, Etienne Parent, Liberalism, and Nationalism in Canada*. Edmonton: University of Alberta Press.

Couture, Joseph E. 1991. "The role of Native elders: Emergent issues." In J.W. Friesen (ed.), *The Cultural Maze: Complex Questions on Native Destiny in Western Canada*, 201–218. Calgary: Detselig Enterprises.

_____ . 2008. "First Nations say no but gov't continues to persist with offer." *Saskatoon SAGE* (August 8): 1.

Creighton, Donald. 1970. *Canada's First Century, 1867–1967*. Toronto: Macmillan of Canada.

Cross, Ronald, and Hélène Sévigny. 1994. *Lasagna: The Man behind the Mask*. Vancouver: Talonbooks.

Crowe, Keith J. 1974. *A History of the Original Peoples of Northern Canada*. Montreal: Queen's University Press.

Cruikshank, Julie. 1998. "Discovery of gold on the Klondike: Perspectives from oral tradition." In J.S.H. Brown and E. Vibert (eds.), *Reading beyond Words: Contexts for Native History*. Toronto: Broadview Press.

Curtis, James, Edward Grabb, and Neil Guppy. 1999. *Social Inequality in Canada: Patterns, Problems, and Policies*. Scarborough: Prentice-Hall Allyn and Bacon Canada.

Dahrendorf, Ralf. 1958. "Toward a theory of social conflict." *Journal of Conflict Resolution* 2: 170–183.

Davis, Wade. 2009. *The Wayfinders. Why Ancient Wisdom Matters in the Modern World*. Toronto: House of Anansi Press.

Deloria, Vine, Jr. 1995. *Red Earth, White Lies: Native Americans and the Myth of Scientific Fact*. New York: Schribner.

Dene of the NWT. 1975. *The Dene: Land and Unity for the Native People of the Mackenzie Valley*. Brampton: Charters.

Denis, Claude. 1989. "The genesis of American capitalism: An historical inquiry into state theory." *Journal of Historical Sociology* 2(4): 328–356.

_____ . 1993. "Quebec-as-distinct-society as conventional wisdom: The constitutional silence of Anglo-Canadian sociologists." *Canadian Journal of Sociology* 18(3): 251–270.

_____ . 1997. *We Are Not You: First Nations and Canadian Modernity*. Peterborough: Broadview Press.

Denton, Frank. 1983. "The labour force." *Historical Statistics of Canada*, 2nd ed. Ottawa: Statistics Canada.

Deutsch, Karl W. (ed.). 1980. *Politics and Government: How People Decide Their Fate*. Boston: Houghton Mifflin

Diamond, Jared. 2005. *Collapse: How Societies Choose to Fail or Succeed*. New York: Viking.

Dickason, Olive Patricia. 1984. *The Myth of the Savage and the Beginnings of French Colonialism in the Americas*. Edmonton: University of Alberta Press.

_____ . 2002. *Canada's First Nations: A History of Founding Peoples from Earliest Times*. Toronto: McClelland & Stewart.

_____ . 2006. *A Concise History of Canada's First Nations*. Toronto: Oxford University Press.

Dickinson, John, and Brian Young. 2003. *A Short History of Quebec*, 3rd ed. Montreal and Kingston: McGill-Queen's University Press.

Dilthey, Wilhelm. 1961. *Pattern and Meaning in History*. London: Harper and Row.

Dion, Joseph F. 1979. *My Tribe: The Crees.* Calgary: Glenbow Museum.

Dobbin, Murray. 2008. "Afghanistan transforms Canada: To play junior partner to empire, we've militarized our identity." *The Tyee* (August 11): http://thetyee.ca/Views/2008/08/11/Afghan-Can/

Doern, B., and B.W. Tomlin. 1991. *Faith and Fear: The Free Trade Story.* Toronto: Stoddart.

Drache, Daniel. 1995. "Introduction: Celebrating Innis: The man, the legacy." In D. Drache (ed.), *Staples, Markets, and Cultural Change. Selected Essays,* xiii–lix. Montreal and Kingston: McGill-Queen's University Press.

Driedger, Leo. 1991. *The Urban Factor: Sociology of Canadian Cities.* Oxford: Oxford University Press.

Dubuc, Alain. 2001. *The Lafontaine-Baldwin Lecture: Canadian Nationalism.* www.operation-dialogue.com/lafontaine-baldwin/e/2001_article_gm_dubuc.html

Dufour, Christian. 1990. *A Canadian Challenge: Le defi quebecois.* Halifax: Oolichan Books and the Institute for Research on Public Policy.

Dumond, Don E. 1977. *The Eskimos and Aleuts.* London: Thames and Hudson.

Duncan, Sarah J. 1971. *The Imperialist.* Originally published in 1904. Toronto: McClelland & Stewart.

Dunn, Christopher. 1995. *Canadian Political Debates.* Toronto: McClelland & Stewart.

Dunning, John. 1983. "Changes in the level and structure of international production: The last one hundred years." In M. Casson (ed.), *The Growth of International Business,* 84–139. London: George Allen and Unwin.

Durkheim, Emile. 1964. *The Division of Labor in Society.* Originally published in 1893. New York: The Free Press.

_____ . 1978. *Elementary Forms of Religious Life.* Originally published in 1912. London: George Allen and Unwin.

Dyck, Rand. 1998. *Canadian Politics,* concise ed. Toronto: Nelson.

Dyer, Gwynne. 2008. *Climate Wars.* Toronto: Random House Canada.

Dymond, Bill, and Michael Hart. 2003. "Canada and the global challenge: Finding a place to stand." *The Border Papers* 180 (March). Toronto: C.D. Howe Institute.

Easterbrook, W.T., and Hugh G.J. Aitken. 1988. *Canadian Economic History.* Toronto: University of Toronto Press.

Eccles, W.J. 1993a. "The French forces in North America during the Seven Years War." In A.D. Gilbert, G.M. Wallace, and R.M. Bray (eds.), *Reappraisals in Canadian History: Pre-Confederation,* 162–174. Scarborough: Prentice-Hall Canada Inc.

_____ . 1993b. "The society of New France, 1680's-1760." In A.D. Gilbert, G.M. Wallace, and R.M. Bray (eds.), *Reappraisals in Canadian History: Pre-Confederation,* 40–48. Scarborough: Prentice-Hall Canada.

Echenberg, Havi, and Hilary Jensen. 2008. *Defining and Enumerating Homelessness in Canada.* Ottawa: Library of Parliament, Social Affairs Division PRB 08-30E.

Edmonton Journal. 1999a. "Bloc's new Quebecer lives most fully in French," (September 12): A7.

_____ . 1999b. "Sovereignty support lowest since '95." *Edmonton Journal* (September 19): A7.

_____ . 1999c. "Exports jumped under free trade says bank study," (June 2): A3.

_____ . 2000a. "House passes Clarity Act," (March 16): A6.

_____ . 2000b. "Quebecers federal gov't's top fans, poll shows," (January 15): A6.

_____ . 2000c. "New confederacy aims to restore Blackfoot Nation," (August 13): A8.

_____ . 2001. "The death of a diocese." (December 16): D4.

_____ . 2002. "Younger Quebecers shrug at sovereignty," (November 6): A6.

_____ . 2007. "Canada's Inuit facing 'cultural genocide,' says Arctic expert," (November 23).

_____ . 2008. "Separatism dormant but not forgotten: Survey," (June 2): A5.

Esping-Andersen, Gösta. 1990. *The Three Worlds of Welfare Capitalism.* Princeton: Princeton University Press.

Fairchild, Henry Pratt (ed.). 1967. *Dictionary of Sociology and Related Sciences.* Totowa: Littlefield, Adams, and Company.

Fairclough, Norman. 1989. *Language and Power: Language in Social Life.* London: Longman.

Fanon, Frantz. 1968. *The Wretched of the Earth.* New York: Grove Press.

Ferguson, Niall (ed.). 2003. *Virtual History: Alternatives and Counterfactuals.* London: Pan Books.

_____. 2004. *Colossus: The Price of America's Empire.* New York: Penguin.

Fettes, Mark, and Ruth Norton. 2000. "Voices of winter: Aboriginal languages and public policy in Canada." In M.B. Castellano, L. Davis, and L. Lahache (eds.), *Aboriginal Education: Fulfilling the Promise,* 29–54. Vancouver: UBC Press.

Fidler, Richard. 2006. "'Québécois nation'? Harper fuels an important debate." *Global Research* (December 22): http://www.globalresearch.ca/index.php?context=va&aid=4244.

Findley, L.M. 2000. "Foreword." In M. Battiste (ed.), *Reclaiming Indigenous Voice and Vision,* ix–xiii. Vancouver: UBC Press.

Finkel, Alvin. 1989. *The Social Credit Phenomenon in Alberta.* Toronto: University of Toronto Press.

_____. 1997. *Our Lives: Canada after 1945.* Toronto: Lorimer.

Finnie, Richard. 1940. *Lure of the North.* Philadelphia: David McKay Company.

_____. 1948. *Canada Moves North.* Toronto: Macmillan Company of Canada.

Fisher, A.D. 1981. "A colonial education system: Historical changes and schooling in Fort Chipewyan." *Canadian Journal of Anthropology* 2(1): 37–44.

Flanagan, Thomas. 1977. "Louis Riel: Insanity and prophecy." In H. Palmer (ed.), *The Settlement of the West,* 15–36. Calgary: Comprint.

_____. 2000. *First Nations? Second Thoughts.* Montreal and Kingston: McGill-Queen's University Press.

Fleras, Augie. 2007. *Unequal Relations: An Introduction to Race, Ethnic, and Aboriginal Dynamics in Canada,* 5th ed. Toronto: Pearson Canada.

Fleras, Augie, and Jean Leonard Elliott. 1992. *The Nations within: Aboriginal-State Relations in Canada, the United States, and New Zealand.* Toronto: Oxford University Press.

Food Banks Canada. 2009. *Hunger Count 2008: A Comprehensive Report on Hunger and Food Bank Use in Canada.* Toronto: Food Banks Canada.

Forbes. 2003. "Special report: The world's richest people." http://www.forbes.com

_____. 2008. "Special report: The world's billionaires." http://www.forbes.com

Fossum, Jon-Erik. 1997. *Oil, the State, and Federalism: The Rise and Demise of Petro-Canada as a Statist Impulse.* Toronto: University of Toronto Press.

Foucault, Michel. 1973. *Madness and Civilization: A History of Insanity in the Age of Reason.* New York: Vintage Books.

_____. 1977. *Power/Knowledge: Selected Interviews and Other Writings 1972–1977,* C. Gordon (ed.). New York: Pantheon.

_____. 1980. *The History of Sexuality,* vol. 1: *An Introduction.* New York: Vintage.

Fournier, Marcel. 2001. "Quebec sociology and Quebec society: The construction of a collective identity." *Canadian Journal of Sociology* 26(3): 333–347.

Fournier, Marcel, Michael Rosenberg, and Deena White (eds.). 1997. *Quebec Society: Critical Issues.* Scarborough: Prentice-Hall Canada.

Fox, John, Robert Andersen, and Joseph Dubonnet. 1999. "The polls and the 1995: Quebec referendum." *The Canadian Journal of Sociology* 24(3): 411–424.

Fox, Terry, and David Long. 2000. "Struggles within the circle: Violence, healing, and health on a First Nations reserve." In D. Long and O.P. Dickason (eds.), *Visions of the Heart: Canadian Aboriginal Issues,* 2nd ed., 271–301. Toronto: Harcourt Canada.

Francis, Daniel. 1997. *National Dreams: Myth, Memory, and Canadian History.* Vancouver: Arsenal Pulp Press.

Francis, R. Douglas, Richard Jones, and Donald B. Smith. 1988. *Origins: Canadian History to Confederation.* Toronto: Holt, Rinehart, and Winston of Canada.

Frank, Andre Gunder. 1975. *On Capitalist Underdevelopment.* Bombay: Oxford University Press.

Fraser, Blair. 1967. *The Search for Identity: Canada: Postwar to Present.* Toronto: Doubleday Canada Ltd.

Frideres, James S., and Rene R. Gadacz. 2001. *Aboriginal Peoples in Canada: Contemporary Conflicts,* 6th ed. Scarborough: Prentice-Hall Canada.

Fried, Jacob. 1969. "Boom towns ... Must they bust?" In M. van Steensel (ed.), *People of the Light and Dark*, 38–42. Ottawa: Department of Indian Affairs and Northern Development.

Friesen, Jean. 1986. *Magnificent Gifts: The Treaties of Canada with the Indians of the Northwest, 1869–70*. Series 5, vol. 1, 41–51. Ottawa: Transactions of the Royal Society of Canada.

Friesen, John W. 1983. *Schools with a Purpose*. Calgary: Detselig.

_____. 1991. "Introduction: Highlights of western Canadian Native history." In J.W. Friesen (ed.), *The Cultural Maze: Complex Questions on Native Destiny in Western Canada*, 1–22. Calgary: Detselig.

_____. 1993. *When Cultures Clash: Case Studies in Multiculturalism*, 2nd ed. Calgary: Detselig.

_____. 1995. *You Can't Get There from Here: The Mystique of Plains Indians' Culture & Philosophy*. Dubuque: Kendall/Hunt.

_____. 1996. *The Riel/Real Story: An Interpretive History of the Métis People of Canada*, 2nd ed. Ottawa: Borealis Press.

_____. 1997. *Rediscovering the First Nations of Canada*. Calgary: Detselig.

_____. 1998. *Sayings of the Elders*. Calgary: Detselig.

_____. 1999. *First Nations of the Plains: Creative, Adaptable, and Enduring*. Calgary: Detselig.

_____. 2005. *First Nations in the Twenty-first Century: Contemporary Educational Frontiers*. Calgary: Detselig.

_____. 2008. *Western Canadian Native Destiny: Complex Questions on the Cultural Maze*. Calgary: Detselig.

Friesen, John W., and Virginia Lyons Friesen. 2004. *We Are Included: The Métis People of Canada Realize Riel's Vision*. Calgary: Detselig.

Frisby, David, and Derek Sayer. 1986. *Society*. London: Ellis Horwood/Tavistock.

Fukuyama, Francis. 1992. *The End of History and the Last Man*. New York: The Free Press.

Furniss, Elizabeth. 1995. *Victims of Benevolence: The Dark Legacy of the Williams Lake Residential School*. Vancouver: Arsenal Pulp Press.

Gagnon, Lysiane. 2000. "The October Crisis: Singular anomaly." *The Beaver* 80(5): 6–7.

Gairdner, William. 1990. *The Trouble with Canada*. Toronto: Stoddart.

Galbraith, John Kenneth. 1969. *The New Industrial State*. Boston: Houghton Mifflin.

_____. 1997. *The Great Crash 1929*. Boston: Mariner.

Gardner, Dan. 2002. "The first casualty of Hollywood ... is truth." *Edmonton Journal* (February 9): A16.

Geddes, John. 2000. "Northern son." *Maclean's* 114(17): 16–21.

Gibbins, Roger. 1979. *Prairie Politics and Society: Regionalism in Decline*. Toronto: Butterworths.

Gibson, Gordon. 1994. *Plan B: The Future of the Rest of Canada*. Vancouver: The Fraser Institute.

Giddens, Anthony. 1984. *The Constitution of Society: Outline of the Theory of Structuration*. Cambridge: Polity Press.

_____. 1987. "Structuralism, post-structuralism, and the production of culture." In A. Giddens and J. Turner (eds.), *Social Theory Today*, 195–223. Stanford: Stanford University Press.

Giffen, Naomi Musmaker. 1930. *The Roles of Men and Women in Eskimo Culture*. Chicago: University of Chicago Press.

Gilbert, Martin. 1991. *The Second World War*. New York: Holt.

Gingras, Yves, and Jean-Philippe Warren. 2006. "A British connection? A quantitative analysis of the changing relations between American, British, and Canadian sociologists." *The Canadian Journal of Sociology* 31(4): 509–522.

Gitlin, Todd. 2001. "The ordinariness of American feelings." *Open Democracy* (October 9): http://www.opendemocracy.net/conflict-us911/article_105.jsp

Globe and Mail. 2002. "Allophones hike use of French in Quebec, census figures show." *Globe and Mail* (December 11): A7.

Goddard, John. 1991. *Last Stand of the Lubicon*. Vancouver: Douglas & McIntyre.

Goffman, Erving. 1961. *Asylums*. Garden City: Anchor Books.

Gonzalez, Roberto J. 2001. "Lynne Cheney-Joe Lieberman group puts out a Blacklist." *San Jose Mercury News* (December 13).

Gordon, Charles. 2002. "What's playing at the cinema?" *Edmonton Journal* (February 10): A14.

Gordon, Walter. 1966. *A Choice for Canada: Independence or Colonial Status?* Toronto: McClelland & Stewart.

Government of Canada. 1963. *A Preliminary Report of the Royal Commission on Bilingualism and Biculturalism.* Ottawa: Queen's Printer.

_____. 1969. *The White Paper.* Statement of the Government of Canada on Indian Policy. Published under the Authority of the Honourable Jean Chrétien, Minister of Indian Affairs and Northern Development. Ottawa: Indian Affairs Branch.

_____. 1979. *A Future Together: Observations and Recommendations of the Task Force on Canadian Unity.* Ottawa: Minister of Supply and Services.

_____. 1982. *The Canadian Constitution.* Ottawa: Public Works.

_____. 2008. *Report of the Independent Panel on Canada's Future Role in Afghanistan.* Ottawa: Public Works.

Government of Quebec. 2008. *Building the Future: Abridged Report of the Bouchard-Taylor Commission.* http://communiques.gouv.qc.ca/gouvqc/communiques/ME/Mai2008/22/c3134.html

Government of the United States. 2002. *The National Security Strategy of the United States of America.* Washington: Government of the United States.

Goyder, John. 1993. "The Canadian syndrome of regional polarities: An obituary." *Canadian Review of Sociology and Anthropology* 30(1): 1–12.

Grabb, Edward. 2000. "Defining moments and recurring myths: Comparing Canadians and Americans after the American Revolution." *Canadian Review of Sociology and Anthropology* 37(4): 373–420.

Grabb, Edward, Douglas Baer, and James Curtis. 1999. "The origins of American individualism: Reconsidering the historical evidence." *The Canadian Journal of Sociology* 24(4): 511–534.

Grabb, Edward, and James Curtis. 2005. *Regions Apart: The Four Societies of Canada and the United States.* Toronto: Oxford University Press.

Granatstein, Jack. 1996. *Yankee Go Home? Canadians and Anti-Americanism.* Toronto: HarperCollins Publishers.

Grant, Agnes. 1996. *No End of Grief: Indian Residential Schools in Canada.* Winnipeg: Pemmican Publications.

Grant, George. 1965. *Lament for a Nation.* Toronto: McClelland & Stewart.

Gray, John. 1994. *Lost in North America: The Imaginary Canadian in the American Dream.* Vancouver: Talonbooks.

Gregg, Allan. 2005. "Quebec's final victory." *The Walrus* (February): 50 61.

Gregoire, Lisa. 2007. "People of the Delta." *Canadian National Geographic* 127(3): 42–58.

GRES. 1997. "Immigration and ethnic relations in Quebec: Pluralism in the making." In M. Fournier, M. Rosenberg, and D. White (eds.), *Quebec Society: Critical Issues,* 95–122. Scarborough: Prentice-Hall Canada.

Gresko, Jacqueline. 1986. "Creating little dominions within the dominion: Early Catholic Indian schools in Saskatchewan and British Columbia." In J. Barman, Y. Hébert, and D. McCaskill (eds.), *Indian Education in Canada,* vol. 1: *The Legacy,* 88–109. Vancouver: UBC Press.

Griffiths, Rudyard. 2008. *We're Prying French and English Canada Apart.* Ottawa: The Dominion Institute.

Grunwald, Michael. 2002. "Security fears have U.S. and Canada rethinking life on the border." *Guardian Weekly* (January 10–16): 29.

Gwyn, Richard. 1996. *Nationalism without Walls: The Unbearable Lightness of Being Canadian.* Toronto: McClelland & Stewart.

Haig-Brown, Celia. 1993. *Resistance and Renewal: Surviving the Indian Residential School.* Vancouver: Tillacum Library.

Hall, D.J. 1977. "Clifford Sifton: Immigration and settlement policy, 1896–1905." In H. Palmer (ed.), *The Settlement of the West,* 60–85. Calgary: Comprint Publishing Company.

Halliday, W.M. 1935. *Potlatch and Totem and the Recollections of an Indian Agent.* London: J.M. Dent and Sons.

Hamelin, J. 1993. "What middle class?" In A.D. Gilbert, G.M. Wallace, and R.M. Bray (eds.), *Reappraisals in Canadian History:*

Pre-Confederation, 215–223. Scarborough: Prentice-Hall Canada.

Hanks, Lucien M., Jr., and Jane Richardson Hanks. 1950. *A Study of the Blackfoot Reserve of Alberta*. Toronto: University of Toronto Press.

Hanohano, Peter. 1999. "The spiritual imperative of Native epistemology: Restoring harmony and balance to education." *Canadian Journal of Native Education* 23(2): 206–219.

Harrison, Trevor. 1995. *Of Passionate Intensity: Right-Wing Populism and the Reform Party of Canada*. Toronto: University of Toronto Press.

_____. 1996. "Class, citizenship, and global migration: The case of the Canadian Business Immigration Program." *Canadian Public Policy* 22(1): 7–23.

_____. 1999. "Globalization and the trade in human body parts." *Canadian Review of Sociology and Anthropology* 36(1): 21–36.

_____. 2000. "The changing face of Prairie politics: Populism in Alberta." *Prairie Forum* 25(1): 107–122.

_____. 2002. *Requiem for a Lightweight: Stockwell Day and Image Politics*. Montreal: Black Rose.

_____. 2005. "Introduction." In T. Harrison (ed.), *The Return of the Trojan Horse and the New World (Dis)Order*. Montreal: Black Rose.

_____. 2007. "Anti-Canadianism: Explaining the deep roots of a shallow phenomenon." *International Journal of Canadian Studies* 35: 217–240.

Hawthorn, Harry B. 1966/67. *A Survey of the Contemporary Indians of Canada*, Part I and II. Ottawa: Indian Affairs.

Heilbroner, Eric. 1992. *Twenty-First Century Capitalism*. Concord: Anansi.

Hemberger, Suzette. 1993. "Constitution." In J. Krieger (ed.), *The Oxford Companion to Politics of the World*, 189–190. Oxford: Oxford University Press.

Henderson, James (Sákéj) Youngblood. 2000. "Postcolonial ledger drawing: Legal reform." In M. Battiste (ed.), *Reclaiming Indigenous Voice and Vision*, 57–76. Vancouver: UBC Press.

Henderson, Robert (ed.). n.d. *A Soldier's Account of the Campaign on Quebec, 1759*. Taken from *A Journal of the Expedition up the River St. Lawrence*, originally published in 1759. Manotick: The Discriminating General.

Henlin, Calvin. 2006. *Dances with Dependency: Indigenous Success through Self-Reliance*. Vancouver: Orca Spirit Publications and Communications.

Heron, Craig, and Robert Storey. 1986. "On the job in Canada." In C. Heron and R. Storey (eds.), *On the Job*, 3–46. Montreal and Kingston: McGill-Queen's University Press.

Hiller, Harry. 1987. "The foundation and politics of separation: Canada in comparative perspective." *Research in Political Sociology* 3: 39–60.

Hobsbawm, Eric. 1992. *Nations and Nationalism Since 1780*, 2nd ed. Cambridge: Cambridge University Press.

_____. 1995. *Age of Extremes. The Short Twentieth Century 1914–1991*. London: Abacus.

Hofstadter, Richard (ed.). 1958. *Great Issues in American History*, vol. I: *1765–1865*. New York: Vintage Books.

Hofstadter, Richard, William Miller, and Daniel Aaron. 1957. *The United States: The History of a Republic*. Englewood Cliffs: Prentice-Hall.

Honan, William. 1998. "Historians warming to games of 'What if?'" *New York Times* (January 7): B7.

Hood, Duncan. 2008. "How Canada stole the American dream." *Maclean's* (July 7): 51–54.

Horowitz, Gad. 1966. "Conservatism, liberalism, and socialism in Canada: An interpretation." *Canadian Journal of Economic and Political Science* 32: 143–171.

Horsman, Reginald. 1993. "On to Canada: Manifest Destiny and United States strategy in the War of 1812." In A.D. Gilbert, G.M. Wallace, and R.M. Bray (eds.), *Reappraisals in Canadian History: Pre-Confederation*, 272–291. Scarborough: Prentice-Hall Canada.

House, John D. 1978. *The Last of the Free Enterprisers*. Toronto: MacMillan of Canada.

Howard, V. 1999. "Unemployment relief camps." *The Canadian Encyclopedia*, Year 2000 ed. Toronto: McClelland & Stewart.

Hufbauer, Gary C., and Jeffrey J. Schott. 2004. "The prospects for deeper North American integration." *The Border Papers* 195 (January). Toronto: C.D. Howe Institute.

Hum, Derek. 1983. *Federalism and the Poor: A Review of the Canada Assistance Plan.* Toronto: Ontario Economic Council.

Huntington, Samuel P. 1996. *The Clash of Civilizations and the Remaking of World Order.* New York: Touchstone.

Hylton, John H. 1999. "Future prospects for Aboriginal self-government in Canada." In J.H. Hylton (ed.), *Aboriginal Self-Government in Canada*, 432–455. Saskatoon: Purich.

Ibbitson, John. 2001. *Loyal No More: Ontario's Struggle for a Separate Destiny.* Toronto: HarperCollins.

_____ . 2009. *Open and Shut: Why America Has Barack Obama, and Canada Has Stephen Harper.* Toronto: McClelland & Stewart.

Igartua, Jose E. 2006. *The Other Quiet Revolution: National Identities in English Canada, 1945–1971.* Vancouver: UBC Press.

Ignatieff, Michael. 1993. *Blood and Belonging: Journeys into the New Nationalism.* Toronto: Penguin.

_____ . 2009. *True Patriot Love: Four Generations in Search of Canada.* Toronto: Viking.

Indian and Northern Affairs Canada. 1996. *Highlights from the Report of the Royal Commission on Aboriginal Peoples: A Word from Commissioners.* http://www.ainc-inac.gc.ca/ap/pubs/rpt/rpt-eng.asp

Indian Chiefs of Alberta. 1970. *Citizens Plus: A Presentation by the Indian Chiefs of Alberta to the Right Honourable P.E. Trudeau, Prime Minister and the Government of Canada*, a.k.a. "The Red Paper." Edmonton: Indian Association of Alberta.

Innis, Harold. 1956. "Great Britain, the United States, and Canada." In M.Q. Innis (ed.), *Essays in Canadian Economic History*, 394–412. Toronto: University of Toronto Press.

_____ . 1962. *The Fur Trade in Canada.* Toronto: University of Toronto Press.

_____ . 1995. "Recent trends in Canadian-American relations." In D. Drache (ed.), *Staples, Markets, and Cultural Change: Selected Essays*, 262–270. Montreal and Kingston: McGill-Queen's University Press.

Irwin, R. Stephen. 1994. *The Indian Hunters.* Blaine: Hancock House.

Ives, John W. 1990. *A Theory of Northern Athapaskan Prehistory.* Boulder: Westview Press.

Jackson, Andrew. 1999. "From leaps of faith to lapses of logic." *Policy Options* (June): 12–18.

Jaenen, Cornelius. 1986. "Education for francization: The case of New France in the seventeenth century." In J. Barman, Y. Hébert, and D. McCaskill (eds.), *Indian Education in Canada*, vol. I: *The Legacy*, 45–63. Vancouver: UBC Press.

James, Lawrence. 1997. *The Rise and Fall of the British Empire.* London: Abacus.

Jaszi, Oszkar. 1961. *The Dissolution of the Habsburg Monarchy.* Originally published in 1929. Chicago: University of Chicago Press.

Jennings, Jesse D. 1978. *Ancient Native Americans.* San Francisco: W.H. Freeman and Company.

Jensen, Joan. M. 1988. *Passage from Indian: Asian Indian Immigrants in North America.* New Haven: Yale University Press.

Jessop, Bob. 1993. "Towards a Schumpeterian workface state? Preliminary remarks on post-Fordist political economy." *Studies in Political Economy* 40: 7–39.

Johnson, Andrew, and Andrew Stritch. 1997. *Canadian Public Opinion: Globalization and Political Parties.* Toronto: Copp Clark.

Johnson, Chalmers. 2006. *Nemesis: The Last Days of the American Republic.* New York: Holt.

Johnson, William. 1999. "Ottawa must wake Quebecers from secessionist dream." *Edmonton Journal* (September 17): A17.

Johnston, Basil. 1995. *The Manitous: The Spiritual World of the Ojibway.* Toronto: Key Porter Books.

Johnston, Charles M. (ed.). 1964. *The Valley of the Six Nations: A Collection of Documents on the Indian Lands of the Grand River.* Toronto: University of Toronto Press.

Johnston, Darlene. 1989. *The Taking of Indian Lands in Canada: Consent or Coercion?* Saskatoon: University of Saskatchewan Native Law Centre.

Josephy Jr., Alvin M. 1968. *The Indian Heritage of America.* New York: Alfred A. Knopf.

Keegan, John. 1990. *The Second World War.* New York: Penguin.

Kelly, W.E. 1997. "Canada's Black defenders." *The Beaver* 77(2): 31–34.

Kendall, Diana, Jane L. Murray, and Rick Linden. 2007. *Sociology in Our Times*, 4th Canadian ed. Toronto: Nelson.

Keohane, Robert O. 2002. "The globalization of informal violence: Theories of world politics, and the 'liberalism of fear.'" *Dialogue IO* (Spring): 29–43.

Kerr, Clark, J.T. Dunlop, F H. Harbison, and C.A. Meyers. 1964. *Industrialism and Industrial Man*, 2nd ed. New York: Oxford University Press.

Kerstetter, Steven. 2002. *Rags and Riches: Wealth Inequality in Canada*. Ottawa: Canadian Centre for Policy Alternatives.

King, A. Richard. 1967. *The School at Mopass: A Problem of Identity*. New York: Holt, Rinehart, and Winston.

Kirkness, Verna J. 1998a. "The critical state of Aboriginal languages in Canada." *Canadian Journal of Native Education* 22(1): 93–107.

_____ . 1998b. "Our peoples' education: Cut the shackles; cut the crap; cut the mustard." *Canadian Journal of Native Education* 22(1): 10–15.

Knuttila, Murray. 2002. *Introducing Sociology: A Critical Perspective*. Toronto: Oxford University Press.

Knuttila, Murray, and Wendee Kubik. 2000. *State Theories: Classical, Global, and Feminist Perspectives*. Halifax: Fernwood.

Korten, David. 1995. *When Corporations Rule the World*. San Francisco: Berrett-Koehler.

Krahn, Harvey, Trevor Harrison, Michael Haan, and William Johnston. 2009. "Social capital and democratic political engagement." *International Journal of Contemporary Sociology* 46(1): 51–76.

Krahn, Harvey, Graham Lowe, and Karen Hughes. 2007. *Work, Industry, and Canadian Society*, 5th ed. Toronto: Nelson.

Krotz, Larry. 1990. *Indian Country: Inside Another Canada*. Toronto: McClelland & Stewart.

Kulchyski, Peter. 2005. *Like the Sound of a Drum: Aboriginal Cultural Politics in Denendeh and Nunavut*. Winnipeg: University of Manitoba Press.

Kurth, James. 1993. "Military-industrial complex." In J. Krieger (ed.), *The Oxford Companion to Politics of the World*, 587–588. Oxford: Oxford University Press.

La Haye, Laura. 1993. "Mercantilism." In D.R. Henderson (ed.), *The Fortune Encyclopedia of Economics*, 534–538. New York: Warner Books.

Lairson, T.D., and D. Skidmore. 1997. *International Political Economy: The Struggle for Power and Wealth*. Toronto: Harcourt Brace.

Lane, Jan-Erik, and Svante O. Ersson. 1994. *Politics and Society in Western Europe*. London: Sage.

Langer, W.L. 1948. *An Encyclopedia of World History*. Boston: Houghton Mifflin Company.

Laurendeau, Andre. 1985. "The conditions for the existence of a national culture." In H. D. Forbes (ed.), *Canadian Political Thought*, 255–269. Toronto: Oxford University Press.

Laviolette, Gontran. 1991. *The Dakota Sioux in Canada*. Winnipeg: DLM Publications.

Laxer, Gordon. 1989. *Open for Business: The Roots of Foreign Ownership in Canada*. Toronto: Oxford University Press.

_____ . (ed.). 1991. *Perspectives on Canadian Economic Development*. Toronto: Oxford University Press.

_____ . 1992. "Distinct status for Quebec: A benefit to English Canada." *Constitutional Forum* 3(3): 57–61.

_____ . 1995. "Social solidarity, democracy, and global capitalism." *Canadian Review of Sociology and Anthropology* 32(3): 287–314.

_____ . 2000. "Surviving the Americanizing right." *Canadian Review of Sociology and Anthropology* 37(1): 55–76.

_____ . 2001. "Alternatives to secession." In C. Couture (ed.), *In Search of a Community: Globalization and the Canadian National Identity*.

_____ . 2010. "Superpower, middle power, or satellite? Canadian energy and environmental policy." In N. Hynek and D. Bosold (eds.), *Canada's Foreign and Security Policy: Soft and Hard Strategies of a Middle Power*, 138–161. Toronto: Oxford University Press Canada.

Laxer, Gordon, and John Dillon. 2008. *Over a Barrel: Exiting from NAFTA's Proportionality Clause*. Edmonton: Parkland Institute.

Laxer, Gordon, and Trevor Harrrison (eds.). 1995. *The Trojan Horse: Alberta and the Future of Canada*. Montreal: Black Rose.

Laxer, James. 2004. *The Border*. Toronto: Anchor.

Leger Marketing. 2008. *Referendum Voting Intentions in Quebec. legermarketing.com/documents/ intvote/IVREFEN_quebec.pdf*

Lekachman, Robert. 1966. *The Age of Keynes.* New York: Random House.

Lemmen, Don, and Fiona Warren. 2004. *Climate Change Impacts and Adaptation: A Canadian Perspective.* Ottawa: Government of Canada.

Lethbridge Herald. 2007. "Foreign takeovers concern Canadians." *Lethbridge Herald* (September 7): B6.

Levitt, Kari. 1970. *Silent Surrender: The Multinational Corporation in Canada.* Toronto: Macmillan of Canada.

Li, Peter. 1996. *The Making of Post-war Canada.* Toronto: Oxford University Press.

Lian, Jason Z., and David Ralph Matthews. 1998. "Does the vertical mosaic still exist? Ethnicity and income in Canada, 1991." *The Canadian Review of Sociology and Anthropology* 35(4): 461–482.

Lincoln, Kenneth. 1985. *Native American Renaissance.* Berkeley: University of California Press.

Lipset, Seymour M. 1968a. *Agrarian Socialism: The Co-operative Commonwealth Federation in Saskatchewan.* Garden City: Doubleday.

_____ . 1968b. *Revolution and Counter-revolution.* New York: Basic Books.

_____ . 1986. "Historical conditions and national characteristics." *Canadian Journal of Sociology* 11(2): 113–155.

_____ . 1990. *Continental Divide.* New York: Routledge.

_____ . 1996. *American Exceptionalism: A Double-Edged Sword.* New York: W.W. Norton.

Lipsey, Richard. 2000. "The Canada–US FTA: Real results versus unreal expectations." *World Economic Affairs* (Autumn): 29–32.

Lovelock, James. 2009. *The Vanishing Face of Gaia: A Final Warning.* London: Allen Lane.

Lowe, Graham S. 1987. *Women in the Administrative Revolution.* Toronto: University of Toronto Press.

Lower, Arthur R.M. 1977. *Colony to Nation: A History of Canada.* Toronto: McClelland & Stewart.

Lower, J. Arthur. 1983. *Western Canada: An Outline History.* Vancouver: Douglas & McIntyre.

Luffman, Jacqueline, and Deborah Sussman. 2007. "The Aboriginal labour force in Western Canada." *Perspectives on Labour and Income* 8(1) (January). *www.statcan.gc.ca/pub/75-001-x/10107/4096795-eng.htm*

Lyon, John Tylor. 1998. "'A picturesque lot': The Gypsies of Peterborough." *The Beaver* 78(5): 25–30.

Macdonald, David, and Stephen Staples. 2008. *The Cost of the War and the End of Peacekeeping: The Impact of Extending the Afghanistan Mission.* Ottawa: The Rideau Institute, October.

Mackenzie, Hugh. 2009. *Banner Year for Canada CEOs: Record High Pay Increase.* Ottawa: Canadian Centre for Policy Alternatives, January.

Maclean's. 1990. "Uncertain future," (July 2): 22–25.

_____ . 1999. "The vanishing border," (December 20): 20–49.

_____ . 2000. "Trudeau: His Life and Legacy." A Special Commemorative Edition.

_____. 2002. "Why so cranky?" (December 30): 24–36.

MacLennan, Hugh. 1974. *The Rivers of Canada.* Toronto: Macmillan of Canada.

_____ . 1998. *Two Solitudes.* Toronto: Stoddart.

MacMillan, Margaret. 2008. *The Uses and Abuses of History.* Toronto: Viking.

Macpherson, C.B. 1965. *The Real World of Democracy.* The Massey Lectures, 4th Series. Toronto: CBC Enterprises.

Macpherson, Don. 2000. "Sovereignty non-movement." *Edmonton Journal* (November 2): A14.

Macrory, Patrick. 2002. "NAFTA Chapter 19: A successful experiment in international trade dispute resolution." *The Border Papers* 168 (September). Toronto: C.D. Howe Institute.

Makela, Kathleen, 1999. "Legal and jurisdictional issues of urban reserves." In L.F. Barron and J. Garcea (eds.), *Urban Indian Reserves: Forging New Relationships in Saskatchewan,* 78–95. Saskatoon: Purich.

Manchester, William. 1992. *A World Lit Only by Fire: The Medieval Mind and the Renaissance.* Boston: Little, Brown.

Mann, Michael. 2008. "American empires: Past and present." *Canadian Review of Sociology* 45(1): 7–50.

Marchak, M. Patricia. 1988. *Ideological Perspectives on Canada.* Toronto: McGraw-Hill Ryerson.

Marchildon, Gregory. 1995. "From Pax Britannica to Pax Americana and beyond." In C. Doran and E. Babby (eds.), *Being and Becoming Canada: The Annals of the American Academy of Political and Social Science* 538: 151–169.

Margolis, Eric. 2008. "Time to face facts in Afghanistan." *Toronto Star* (October 6).

Marker, Michael. 2000. "Economics and local self-determination: Describing the clash zone in First Nations education." *Canadian Journal of Native Education* 24(1): 30–44.

Marquis, Greg. 2000. *In Armageddon's Shadow: The Civil War and Canada's Maritime Provinces*. Kingston and Montreal: McGill-Queen's University Press.

Marsden, William. 2007. *Stupid to the Last Drop: How Alberta Is Bringing Environmental Armageddon to Canada (and Doesn't Seem to Care)*. Toronto: Alfred A. Knopf.

Martin, Ged. 1993a. "The influence of the Durham Report." In A.D. Gilbert, G.M. Wallace, and R.M. Bray (eds.), *Reappraisals in Canadian History: Pre-Confederation*, 437–448. Scarborough: Prentice-Hall Canada Inc.

_____. 1993b. "History as science or literature: Explaining Canadian Confederation." In A.D. Gilbert, G.M. Wallace, and R.M. Bray (eds.), *Reappraisals in Canadian History: Pre-Confederation*, 543–570. Scarborough: Prentice-Hall Canada.

Martin, Lawrence. 1982. *The Presidents and Prime Ministers*. Markham: Paper Jacks.

_____. 1993. *Pledge of Allegiance: The Americanization of Canada during the Mulroney Years*. Toronto: McClelland & Stewart.

_____. 1999. "Canada was on brink of civil strife just four years ago." *Edmonton Journal* (April 10): A19.

_____. 2008. "In case you haven't noticed, there's a new unity in the land." *The Globe and Mail* (July 24): A13.

Marx, Karl. 1977a. "The Communist manifesto." In D. McLellan (ed.), *Karl Marx: Selected Writings*. Oxford: Oxford University Press.

_____. 1977b. "Theses on Feuerbach." In D. McLellan (ed.), *Karl Marx: Selected Writings*, 156–158. Oxford: Oxford University Press.

_____. 1977c. "The eighteenth brumaire of Louis Napoleon." In D. McLellan (ed.), *Karl Marx: Selected Writings*, 300–325. Oxford: Oxford University Press.

Massey, Don, and Patricia N. Shields. 1995. *Canada: Its Land and People*, 2nd ed. Edmonton: Reidmore Books.

Mayes, Hubert G. 1999. "Resurrection: Tolstoy and Canada's Doukhobors." *The Beaver* 79(5): 39–44.

Maynard, Jean-Pierre. 2007. "A comparison of GDP per capita in Canada and the United States from 1994 to 2005." Statistics Canada, Cat. 11-624-MIE, no. 016. Ottawa: Statistics Canada.

McCall-Newman, Christina. 1982. *Grits: An Intimate Portrait of the Liberal Party*. Toronto: Macmillan of Canada.

McCallum, John. 1991. "Agriculture and economic development in Quebec and Ontario until 1870." In G. Laxer (ed.), *Perspectives on Canadian Economic Development*, 10–20. Toronto: Oxford University Press.

McCue, William Westaway. 1999. "Crossing the line." *The Beaver* 79(1): 16–21.

McDonald, Kevin. 1994. "Globalisation, multiculturalism and rethinking the social." *Australian-New Zealand Journal of Sociology* 30(3): 239–247.

McDonnell, R.F., and R.C. Depew. 1999. "Self-government and self-determination in Canada: A critical commentary." In J.H. Hylton (ed.), *Aboriginal Self-Government in Canada*, 352–376. Saskatoon: Purich.

McDougall, John. 1903. *In the Days of the Red River Rebellion*. Toronto: William Briggs.

McGaa, Eagle Man (ed.). 1990. *Mother Earth Spirituality: Native American Paths to Healing Ourselves and Our World*. New York: HarperCollins.

_____. 1995. *Native Wisdom: Perceptions of the Natural Way*. Minneapolis: Four Directions Publishing.

McKie, Craig. 1994. "A history of emigration from Canada." *Canadian Social Trends* 35: 26–29.

McMillan, Alan, D. 1995. *Native Peoples and Cultures of Canada*, 2nd ed. Vancouver: Douglas & McIntyre.

McPherson, James. 1998. "Quebec whistles Dixie." *Saturday Night* (March): 13–14, 18, 20, 22–23, 72.

Meekison, J. Peter. 1993. "Canada's quest for constitutional perfection." *Constitutional Forum* 4(2): 55–59.

Meili, Dianne. 1991. *Those Who Know: Profiles of Alberta's Elders*. Edmonton: NeWest Press.

Melling, John. 1967. *Right to a Future: The Native Peoples of Canada*. Toronto: T.H. Best Printing Co.

Mercredi, Ovide, and Mary Ellen Turpel. 1993. *In the Rapids: Navigating the Future of First Nations*. Toronto: Viking Press.

Merkur, Daniel. 1991. *Powers Which We Do Not Know: The Gods and Spirits of the Inuit*. Moscow: University of Idaho Press.

Merriam-Webster, Incorporated. 2003. *Merriam-Webster's Collegiate® Dictionary*, 10th ed. Springfield: Merriam-Webster. www.Merriam-Webster.com.

Merritt, Christopher B. 1996. *Free Trade: Neither Free nor about Trade*. Montreal: Black Rose.

Merton, Robert. 1968. *Social Theory and Social Structure*. New York: The Free Press.

Miliband, Ralph. 1969. *The State in Capitalist Society*. New York: Basic Books.

Miller, Alan D. 1988. *Native Peoples and Cultures of Canada*. Vancouver: Douglas & McIntyre.

Miller, Carman. 1999. "Canada's first war." *The Beaver* 79(5): 6–7.

Miller, J.R. 1987. "The irony of residential schooling." *Canadian Journal of Native Education* 14(2). 3–14.

_____. 2000. *Skyscrapers Hide the Heavens: A History of Indian-White Relations in Canada*, 3rd ed. Toronto: University of Toronto Press.

Mills, C. Wright. 1956. *The Power Elite*. Oxford: Oxford University Press.

_____. 1961. *The Sociological Imagination*. New York: Grove Press.

Mills, Sean. 2005. "Modern, postmodern, and post-postmodern." *The Beaver* (April–May): 11–12.

Milne, Seumas. 2008. "Civilian dead are a trade-off in Nato's war of barbarity." *Guardian Weekly* (October 16).

Mittelman, J.H. 1996. "The dynamics of globalization." In J.H. Mittelman (ed.), *Globalization: Critical Reflections*, 1–19. International Political Economy Yearbook, vol. 9. London: Lynne Rienner Publishers.

Moffett, Samuel E. 1972. *The Americanization of Canada*. Originally published in 1908. Toronto: University of Toronto Press.

Momatiuk, Yva, and John Eastcott. 1995. "'Nunavut' means 'Our Land.'" *Native Peoples* 9(1): 42–48.

Monahan, Patrick. 1995. *Cooler Heads Shall Prevail: Assessing the Costs and Consequences of Quebec Separation*. Toronto: C.D. Howe Institute.

Montgomery, Charles. 2007. "When mountains crumble." *Canadian National Geographic* 127(3): 68–78

Moore, Christopher. 1997. *1867: How the Fathers Made a Deal*. Toronto: McClelland & Stewart.

_____. 2000. "Colonization and conflict: New France and its rivals (1600–1760)." In Craig Brown (ed.), *The Illustrated History of Canada*, 105–188. Toronto: Key Porter Books.

Morissette, Rene, and Xuelin Zhang. 2001. "Experiencing low income for several years." *Perspectives* (Summer): 25–35. Cat. no. 75-001-XPE. Ottawa: Statistics Canada.

Morrow, Ray. 1994. "History of sociological theory." In W. Meloff and D. Pierce (eds.), *An Introduction to Sociology*, 1–22. Scarborough: Nelson.

Morton, Desmond. 1997. *A Short History of Canada*. Edmonton: Hurtig Publishers.

_____. 2000. "1900: A new century begins." *The Beaver* 79(6): 23–29.

Morton, William Lewis. 1970. "The Battle at Grand Coteau, July 13 and 14, 1851." In D. Swainson (ed.), *Historical Essays on the Prairie Provinces*, 45–59. Toronto: McClelland & Stewart.

Mowat, Farley. 1952. *People of the Deer*. Toronto: McClelland & Stewart.

Nakhaie, M. Reza. 1997. "Vertical mosaic among the elites: The new imagery revisited." *The Canadian Review of Sociology and Anthropology* 34(1): 1–24.

Naylor, R.T. 1975. *The History of Canadian Business 1867–1914*, 2 vols. Toronto: Lorimer.

Nemni, Max, and Monique Nemni. 2006. *Young Trudeau: 1919–1944: Son of Quebec, Father of Canada*. Toronto: Douglas Gibson.

Nevitte, Neil. 1996. *The Decline of Deference*. Peterborough: Broadview Press.

Newman, Peter C. 1998. *Empire of the Bay: The Company of Adventurers That Seized a Continent*. Toronto: Penguin Books.

_____. 1999. "The year of living dangerously." *Maclean's* (December 20): 51–56.

Nikiforuk, Andrew. 2008. *Tar Sands: Dirty Oil and the Future of a Continent*. Vancouver: Greystone.

Norrie, Ken, and Douglas Owram. 1996. *The History of the Canadian Economy*, 2nd ed. Toronto: Harcourt Brace and Company, Canada.

O'Hara, Jane. 2000. "Abuse of trust." *Maclean's* 113(26): 16–21.

Ohmae, Ken'ichi. 1990. *The Borderless World: Power and Strategy in the Interlinked Economy*. New York: Harper Business.

_____. 1995. *The End of the Nation State: The Rise of Regional Economies*. New York: The Free Press.

Olsen, Gregg. 2002. *The Politics of the Welfare State: Canada, Sweden, and the United States*. Oxford: Oxford University Press.

Orchard, David. 1998. *The Fight for Canada*, 2nd ed. Westmount: Robert Davies Multimedia Publishing Inc.

Organisation for Economic Co-operation and Development (OECD). 2007. *OECD in Figures 2007 Edition*. Paris: OECD.

Orum, Anthony M., and John G. Dale. 2008. *Political Sociology: Power and Participation in the Modern World*, 5th ed. Oxford: Oxford University Press.

Orwell, George. 2008. *1984*. Toronto: Penguin.

Osberg, Lars (ed.). 2003. *The Economic Implications of Social Cohesion*. Toronto: University of Toronto Press.

Osborn, Kevin. 1990. *The Peoples of the Arctic*. New York: Chelsea House.

Ouellet, Fernand. 1993. "The 1837/38 rebellions in Lower Canada as a social phenomenon." In A.D. Gilbert, G.M. Wallace, and R.M. Bray (eds.), *Reappraisals in Canadian History: Pre-Confederation*, 356–379. Scarborough: Prentice-Hall Canada.

Palmer, Howard. 1982. *Patterns of Prejudice: A History of Nativism in Alberta*. Toronto: McClelland & Stewart.

Palmer, R.R., with Joel Colton. 1957. *A History of the Modern World*. New York: Alfred A. Knopf.

Panitch, Leo. 1977. *The Canadian State: Political Economy and Political Power*. Toronto: University of Toronto Press.

_____. 1981. "Dependency and class in Canadian political economy." *Studies in Political Economy* 6: 7–33.

Panitch, Leo, and Sam Gindin. 2003. *Global Capitalism and American Empire*. London: Merlin.

Panitch, Leo, and Donald Swartz. 1988. *The Assault on Trade Union Freedoms: From Consent to Coercion Revisited*. Toronto: Garamond.

Paquet, Gilles. 1997. "States, communities, and markets: The distributed governance scenario." In T.J. Courchene (ed.), *The Nation State in a Global/Information Era: Policy Challenges*. Kingston: Queen's University Press.

Parenti, Michael. 1995. *Against Empire*. San Francisco: City Lights Books.

Parsons, Talcott. 1951. *The Social System*. Glencoe: The Free Press.

Parti Québécois. 1994. *Quebec in a New World: The PQ's Plan for Sovereignty*, R. Chodos (trans.). Toronto: James Lorimer and Company.

Pauls, Syd. 1984. "The case for band-controlled schools." *Canadian Journal of Native Education* 12(1): 31–37.

Pentland, Clare. 1991. "The transformation of Canada's economic structure." In G. Laxer (ed.), *Perspectives on Canadian Economic Development*, 296–310. Toronto: Oxford University Press.

Perley, David G. 1993. "Aboriginal education in Canada as internal colonialism." *Canada Journal of Native Education* 20(1): 118–128.

Persson, Diane. 1986. "The changing experience of Indian residential schooling: Blue Quills, 1931–1970." In J. Barman, Y. Hébert, and D. McCaskill (eds.), *Indian Education in Canada, vol. I: The Legacy*, 150–167. Vancouver: UBC Press.

Petitot, Father Emile. 1999. *Among the Chiglit Eskimos*, E. Otto Höhn (trans.). Edmonton: Boreal Institute for Northern Studies.

Pevere, Geoff, and Greig Dymond. 1996. *Mondo Canuck: A Canadian Pop Cultural Odyssey*. Scarborough: Prentice-Hall.

Piven, Frances Fox. 2007. "The neoliberal challenge." *Contexts* 6(3): 13–15.

Plain, Fred. 1988. "A treatise on the rights of the Aboriginal peoples of the continent of North America." In M. Boldt and J.A. Long (eds.), *The Quest for Justice: Aboriginal Peoples and Aboriginal Rights*, 31–40. Toronto: University of Toronto Press.

Ponting, J. Rick. 1986. "Relations between bands and the Department of Indian Affairs: A case of internal colonialism." In J.R. Ponting (ed.), *Arduous Journey: Canadian Indians and Decolonization*, 84–111. Toronto: McClelland & Stewart.

_____. 1997a. "Getting a handle on recommendations of the Royal Commission on Aboriginal Peoples." In J.R. Ponting (ed.), *First Nations in Canada: Perspectives on Opportunity, Empowerment, and Self-Determination*, 445–472. Toronto: McGraw-Hill Ryerson Limited.

_____. 1997b. "The socio-demographic picture." In J.R. Ponting (ed.), *First Nations in Canada: Perspectives on Opportunity, Empowerment, and Self-Determination*, 68–114. Toronto: McGraw-Hill Ryerson Limited.

Ponting, J. Rick, and Linda J. Henderson. 2005. "Contested visions of First Nations governance: Secondary analysis of federal government research on the opinions of on-reserve residents." *Canadian Ethnic Studies* 37(1): 63–86.

Porter, John. 1965. *The Vertical Mosaic*. Toronto: University of Toronto Press.

Potts, Karen, and Leslie Brown. 2008. "Becoming an anti-oppressive researcher." In M. Webber and K. Bezanson (eds.), *Rethinking Sociology in the 21st Century*, 50–59. Toronto: Canadian Scholars' Press Inc.

Poulantzas, Nicholas. 1973. *Political Power and Social Classes*, T. O'Hagan (trans.). London: New Left Books.

Pratt, Larry, and Garth Stevenson (eds.). 1981. *Western Separatism: The Myths, Realities, and Dangers*. Edmonton: Hurtig.

Purich, Donald. 1986. *Our Land*. Toronto: James Lorimer.

_____. 1992. *The Inuit and Their Land*. Toronto: Lorimer and Company.

Ralph, Diana S., André Régimbald, and Nérée St-Ama (eds.). 1997. *Open for Business, Closed to People: Mike Harris's Ontario*. Halifax: Fernwood.

Ramonet, Ignacio. 2001. "The changing face of separatism." *Le Monde diplomatique* (February): 1.

Ramos, Howard. 2006. "What causes Canadian Aboriginal protest? Examining resources, opportunities, and identity, 1951–2000." *Canadian Journal of Sociology*, 31(2): 211–234.

Ray, Arthur J. 1974. *Indians in the Fur Trade: Their Role as Trappers, Hunters, and Middlemen in the Lands Southwest of Hudson Bay, 1660–1870*. Toronto: University of Toronto Press.

Rea, K.J. 1968. *The Political Economy of the Canadian North*. Toronto: University of Toronto Press.

Reid, Scott. 1992. *Canada Remapped*. Vancouver: Pulp Press.

Resnick, Philip. 1991. *Toward a Canada Quebec Union*. Montreal and Kingston: McGill-Queen's University Press.

_____. 2000. *The Politics of Resentment: B.C. Regionalism and Canadian Unity*. Vancouver: UBC Press.

_____. 2005. *The European Roots of Canadian Identity*. Peterborough: Broadview Press.

Resnick, Philip, and Daniel Latouche. 1990. *Letters to a Quebecois Friend*. Montreal and Kingston: McGill-Queen's University Press.

Rice, James, and Michael Prince. 2000. *Changing Politics of Canadian Social Policy*. Toronto: University of Toronto Press.

Richards, John, and Larry Pratt. 1979. *Prairie Capitalism: Power and Influence in the New West*. Toronto: McClelland & Stewart.

Rickman, H.P. 1961. "General introduction." In W. Dilthey's *Pattern and Meaning in History*, 11–63. London: Harper Row Publishers.

Riesman, David, with Reuel Denney and Nathan Glazer. 1950. *The Lonely Crowd: A Study of the Changing American Character*. New Haven: Yale University Press.

Rioux, Marcel. 1978. *Quebec in Question*. Toronto: James Lorimer and Company.

_____. 1993. "The development of ideologies in Quebec." In D. Taras, B. Rasporich, and E. Mandel (eds.), *A Passion for Identity: An Introduction to Canadian Studies*, 72–91. Scarborough: Nelson Canada.

Robbins, Richard H. 2008. *Global Problems and the Culture of Capitalism*, 4th ed. Toronto: Pearson.

Roberts, Joseph K. 1998. *In the Shadow of Empire: Canada for Americans.* New York: Monthly Review Press.

Robin, Martin. 1991. *Shades of Right: Nativist and Fascist Politics in Canada, 1920–1940.* Toronto: University of Toronto Press.

———. 1993. "British Columbia: The company province." In D. Taras, B. Rasporich, and E. Mandel (eds.), *A Passion for Identity: An Introduction to Canadian Studies.* Scarborough: Nelson Canada.

Romanow, Roy. 2006. "A house half built." *The Walrus* (June): 48 54.

Romney, Paul. 1999. *Getting It Wrong: How Canadians Forgot Their Past and Imperilled Confederation.* Toronto: University of Toronto Press.

Ross, Rupert. 1992. *Dancing with a Ghost: Exploring Indian Reality.* Markham: Reed Books.

Rotstein, Abraham. 1978. "Is there an English-Canadian nationalism?" *Journal of Canadian Studies* 13: 109–118.

Rubin, Jeff. 2009. *Why Your World Is about to Get a Whole Lot Smaller.* Toronto: Random House.

Rudmin, Floyd. 1993. *Bordering on Aggression.* Hull: Voyageur Publications.

Rummel, R.J. 1994. *Death by Government.* New Brunswick: Transaction.

Russell, Dan. 2000. *A People's Dream: Aboriginal Self-Government in Canada.* Vancouver: UBC Press.

Ryan, Joan. 1995. *Doing Things the Right Way: Dene Traditional Justice in Lac La Martre, NWT.* Calgary: Arctic Institute of North America.

Said, Edward. 1993. *Culture and Imperialism.* New York: Vintage Books.

Sassan, Saskia. 2001. "Governance hotspots: Challenges we must confront in the post-September 11 world." Social Science Research Council. http://essays.ssrc.org/sept11/essays/sassen.htm

Saul, John Ralston. 1997. *Reflections of a Siamese Twin: Canada at the End of the Twentieth Century.* Toronto: Penguin Books.

———. 2008. *A Fair Country: Telling Truths about Canada.* Toronto: Viking.

Saul, S.B. 1969. *The Myth of the Great Depression 1873–1896.* London: The Macmillan Press.

Savoie, Donat (ed.). 1970. *The Amerindians of the Canadian North-West in the 19th Century, as seen by Émile Petitot: The Loucheux Indian,* vol. II. Ottawa: Northern Science Group, Department of Indian Affairs and Northern Development.

Sawatsky, John. 1991. *Mulroney: The Politics of Ambition.* Toronto: Macfarland, Walter, and Ross.

Sayer, Derek. 1987. *The Violence of Abstraction: The Analytic Foundations of Historical Materialism.* Oxford: Basil Blackwell.

Schlesinger, Arthur, Jr. 1997. "Has democracy a future?" *Foreign Affairs* 76(5): 2–12.

Schouls, Tim. 2003. *Shifting Boundaries: Aboriginal Identity, Pluralist Theory, and the Politics of Self-Government.* Vancouver: UBC Press.

Schultz, Marylou, and Miriam Kroeger (eds.). 1996. *Teaching and Learning with Native Indians: A Handbook for Non-Native American Adult Educators.* Phoenix: Adult Literacy and Technology Resource Center.

Schwartz, Bryan, 1986. *First Principles, Second Thoughts: Aboriginal Peoples, Constitutional Reform, and Canadian Statecraft.* Montreal: Institute for Research on Public Policy.

Scott, John, and Gordon Marshall. 2005. "Post-structuralism." In J. Scott and G. Marshall, *Oxford Dictionary of Sociology,* 510–512. Oxford: Oxford University Press.

Scott-Brown, Joan. 1991. "Native land claims." In J.W. Friesen (ed.), *The Cultural Maze: Complex Questions on Native Destiny in Western Canada,* 97–110. Calgary: Detselig.

Scowen, Reed. 1999. *Time to Say Goodbye: The Case for Getting Quebec out of Canada.* Toronto: McClelland & Stewart.

Sicherman, Harvey. 2007. "Virtue, interests, and works in American foreign policy." *Society* 44(6): 113–119.

Sikotan (Flora Zaharia), and Mikai'sto (Leo Fox). 1995. *Kitomahkitapiiminnooniksi: Stories from Our Elders,* vol. 1. Kainaiwa Board of Education. Edmonton: Donahue House Publishing.

Sikotan (Flora Zaharia), Mikai'sto (Leo Fox), and Omahksipootaa (Marvin Fox). 2003. *Kitomahkitapiiminnooniksi: Stories from Our*

Elders, vol. 4. Kainaiwa Board of Education. Edmonton: Donahue House Publishing.

Silver, A.I. 1997. *The French-Canadian Idea of Confederation 1864–1900*, 2nd ed. Toronto: University of Toronto Press.

Silver, Jim. 1996. *Thin Ice: Money, Politics, and the Demise of an NHL Franchise*. Halifax: Fernwood.

Skocpol, Theda. 1979. *States and Social Revolutions*. Cambridge: Cambridge University Press.

Slair, Leslie. 2002. *Globalization: Capitalism and its Alternatives*. Toronto: Oxford University Press.

Smith, David, Peter MacKinnon, and John Courtney (eds.). 1991. *After Meech Lake: Lessons for the Future*. Saskatoon: Fifth House.

Smith, Donald. 1998. *Beyond Two Solitudes*. Halifax: Fernwood.

Smith, Goldwin. 1971. *Canada and the Canadian Question*. Originally published in 1891. Toronto: University of Toronto Press.

Smith Q.C., Melvin H. 1995. *Our Home OR Native Land? What Government Aboriginal Policy Is Doing to Canada*. Toronto: Stoddart.

Snow, Chief John. 1977. *These Mountains Are Our Sacred Places: The Story of the Stoney Indians*. Toronto: Samuel Stevens.

_____ . 1988. "Identification and definition of our treaty and Aboriginal rights." In M. Boldt and A. Long (eds.), *The Quest for Justice: Aboriginal Peoples and Aboriginal Rights*, 41–46. Toronto: University of Toronto Press.

_____ . 2005. *These Mountains Are Our Sacred Places: The Story of the Stoney People*. Calgary: Fifth House.

Sprague, D.N. 1988, *Canada and the Métis, 1869–1885*. Waterloo: Wilfred Laurier University Press.

Srebrnik, Henry F. 1998. "The radical 'second life' of Vilhjalmur Stefansson." *Arctic* 51(1): 58–60.

Stabler, Jack. 1989. "Dualism and development in the Northwest Territories." *Economic Development and Cultural Change* 37(4): 805–840.

Stacey, C.P., and Norman Hillmer. 1999. "World War II." *The Canadian Encyclopedia*, 2551–2553. Toronto: McClelland & Stewart.

Stanford, Jim. 2006. "Modelling North American integration: Pushing the envelope of reality." In B. Campbell and E. Finn (eds.), *Living with Uncle*, 151–182. Toronto: James Lorimer.

Stanley, George F.G. 1975. *The Birth of Western Canada: A History of the Riel Rebellion*. Originally published in 1936. Toronto: University of Toronto Press.

Staples, Steven, and William Robinson. 2008. *More Than the Cold War*. Ottawa: The Rideau Institute.

Statistics Canada. 1983. *Historical Statistics of Canada*. Cat. no. 11-516. Ottawa: Statistics Canada.

_____ . 1992. *The Nation*. Cat. no. 93-333. Ottawa: Statistics Canada.

_____ . 2001a. Canada Year Book. Cat. no. 11-402. Ottawa: Statistics Canada.

_____ . 2001b. "Aboriginal people in Canada." Canadian Centre for Justice Statistics profile series, Cat. no. 85F0033MIE2001001. Ottawa: Statistics Canada.

_____ . 2003. "Earnings of Canadians: Making a living in the new economy." *2001 Census: Analysis Series*. Cat. no. 96F0030XIE2001013. http://www.statcan.gc.ca/bsolc/olc-cel/olc-cel?lang=eng&catno=97-563-X2006001

_____ . 2006a. "Population by mother tongue, by province and territory." *2006 Census*. http://www40.statcan.gc.ca/l01/cst01/demo11a-eng.htm

_____ . 2006b. "Total income groups (23) in constant (2005) dollars, age groups (7A), highest certificate, diploma or degree (5) and sex (3) for the population 15 years and over of Canada, provinces, territories, census metropolitan areas and census agglomerations, 2000 and 2005–20% Sample." *2006 Census*, http://www12.statcan.ca/english/census06/.

_____ . 2006c. *Canada's Farm Population: Agriculture-Production Linkage Data for the 2006 Census*. Cat. no. 95-633-XWE. Ottawa: Statistics Canada

_____ . 2007a. Citizenship, place of birth, sex, and immigrant status and period of immigration for the population of Canada, provinces, territories. Census metropolitan areas and census agglomerations, 2006 census." *2006 Census of Population*. Cat. no. 97-557-XCB2006008. Ottawa: Statistics Canada.

_____ . 2007b. *Canada Year Book 2007*. Ottawa: Statistics Canada.

_____ . 2007c. "Study: The new underground economy of resources." *The Daily* (October 11).

_____ . 2008a. *Earnings and Incomes of Canadians Over the Past Quarter Century, 2006 Census.* Cat. no. 97-563-X. Ottawa: Statistics Canada.

_____ . 2008b. "Farm population." *Canada at a Glance 2008*, Table 35. Ottawa: Statistics Canada.

_____ . 2008c. "Aboriginal Population Profile, 2006 Census." http://www.statcan.gc.ca/

Stearns, P.N. 1975. *European Society in Upheaval*, 2nd ed. New York: Macmillan Publishing Company.

Steckley, John I., and Bryan D. Cummins. 2008. *Full Circle: Canada's First Nations*, 2nd ed. Toronto: Pearson Education Canada.

Steele, James, and Robin Mathews. 2006. "Canadianization revisited: A comment on Cormier's 'The Canadianization movement in context.'" *The Canadian Journal of Sociology* 31(4): 491–508.

Stefansson, Vilhjalmur. 1921. *The Friendly Arctic*. New York: Macmillan.

——— . 1938. *Unsolved Mysteries of the Arctic*. New York: Collier.

Stein, Janice Gross, and Eugene Lang. 2007. *The Unexpected War: Canada in Kandahar.* Toronto: Viking.

Stern, Nicholas. 2007. *The Economics of Climate Change: The Stern Review.* Cambridge: Cambridge University Press.

Strange, Susan. 1996. *The Retreat of the State*. Cambridge, U.K.: Cambridge University Press.

Stubbs, R., and G.R.D. Underhill (eds.). 1994. *Political Economy and the Changing Global Order*. Toronto: McClelland & Stewart.

Surtees, R.J. 1969. "The Development of a Reserve Policy in Canada." *Ontario Historical Society* LXI: 87–99.

Suzuki, David. 1992. "A personal foreword: The value of Native ecologies." In P. Knudtson and D. Suzuki, *Wisdom of the Elders*, xxi–xvi. Toronto: Stoddart.

Swedberg, Richard. 1990. *Economics and Society*. Princeton: Princeton University Press.

Tajfel, Henri, and John C. Turner. 1986. "The social identity theory of intergroup behavior." In S. Worchel and W.A. Austin (eds.), *Psychology of Intergroup Relations*, 7–24. Chicago: Nelson-Hall.

Taylor, Charles. 1993. *Reconciling the Solitudes*. Montreal and Kingston: McGill-Queen's University Press.

Taylor, J. Garth. 1974. *Netsilik Eskimo Material Culture: The Roald Amundsen Collection from King William Island*. Oslo: Universitetsforlaget.

Teeple, Gary. 2000. *Globalization and the Decline of Social Reform: Into the Twenty-First Century*, 2nd ed. Toronto: Garamond.

Tennant, Paul. 1988. "Aboriginal rights and the Penner Report on Indian self-government." In M. Boldt and A. Long (eds.), *The Quest for Justice: Aboriginal Peoples and Aboriginal Rights*, 321–332. Toronto: University of Toronto Press.

Thomas, Lewis H. 1977. "A judicial murder: The trial of Louis Riel." In H. Palmer (ed.), *The Settlement of the West*, 37–59. Calgary: Comprint.

Thompson, Dale. 1995. "Language, identity, and the nationalist impulse: Quebec." In C. Doran and E. Babby (eds.), *Being and Becoming Canada: The Annals of the American Academy of Political and Social Science* 538: 69–82.

Time. 2009. *Almanac 2009.* Chicago: Time Inc.

Titley, E. Brian. 1992. "Red Deer Industrial School: A case study in the history of Native education." In N. Kach and K. Mazurek (eds.), *Exploring Our Educational Past*, 55–72. Calgary: Detselig.

Tobias, John L. 1977. "Indian reserves in Western Canada: Indian homelands or devices for assimilation?" In D.A. Muise (ed.), *Approaches to Native History in Canada*, 89–103. Ottawa: National Museum of Man Mercury Series.

_____ . 1983. "Protection, civilization, assimilation: An outline history of Canada's Indian policy." In Ian A.L. Getty and Antoine Lussier (eds.), *As Long as the Sun Shines and Water Flows: A Reader in Canadian Native Studies*, 39–55. Vancouver: UBC Press.

Tompkins, Joanne. 1998. *Teaching in a Cold and Windy Place*. Toronto: University of Toronto Press.

Tönnies, Ferdinand. 1957. *Community and Society*, C.P. Loomis (ed. and trans.). Originally published in 1887. New York: Harper and Row.

Treasury Board of Canada Secretariat. 2005. *Canada's Performance 2005: The Government of Canada's Contribution*, http://www.tbs-sct. gc.ca/report/govrev/05/cp-rc-eng.asp

Trent, John E. 1995. *The 1995 Quebec Referendum: A Practical Guide*. Ottawa: Dialogue Canada.

Trigger, Bruce G. 1969. *The Huron: Farmers of the North*. New York: Holt, Rinehart, and Winston.

Trofimenkoff, Susan. 1993. "For whom the bell tolls." In A.D. Gilbert, G.M. Wallace, and R.M. Bray (eds.), *Reappraisals in Canadian History: Pre-Confederation*, 380–392. Scarborough: Prentice-Hall Canada.

Trudeau, Pierre. 1996. *Against the Current: Selected Writings 1939–1996*, G. Pelletier (ed.). Toronto: McClelland & Stewart.

Turk, James L., and Allan Manson (eds.). 2007. *Free Speech in Fearful Times: After 9/11 in Canada, the U.S., Australia, and Europe*. Ottawa: Canadian Association of University Teachers.

Turner, Joanne. 1981. "The historical base." In J. Turner and F. Turner (eds.), *Canadian Social Welfare*, 49–57. Don Mills: Collier Macmillan Canada.

Turp, Daniel. 1993. "Solutions to the future of Canada and Quebec after the October 26th referendum: Genuine sovereignties within a novel union." *Constitutional Forum* 4(2): 47–49.

Ugbor, Kez O. 1994. "Social stratification." In W. Meloff and D. Pierce (eds.), *An Introduction to Sociology*, 97–121. Scarborough: Nelson.

Ungar, Sheldon. 1991. "Civil religion and the arms race." *Canadian Review of Sociology and Anthropology* 28(4): 503–525.

United Nations. 2007a. *United Nations Intergovernmental Panel on Climate Change*. New York: United Nations.

_____. 2007b. *Human Development Index 2006*. New York: United Nations Human Development Research Office.

United States Census Bureau. 2009. *Top Trading Partners—Total Trade, Exports, Imports: Year-to-Date December 2008*. http://www.census. gov/foreign-trade/statistics/highlights/top/ top0812yr.html

Valaskakis, Kimon, and Angeline Fournier. 1995. *The Delusion of Sovereignty: Would Independence Weaken Quebec?* Montreal: Robert Davies Publishing.

Vallee, Frank. 1971. "Eskimos of Canada: A minority group." In Jean Elliott Leonard (ed.), *Native Peoples*, 75–88. : Prentice-Hall of Canada.

Vallières, Pierre. 1971. *White Niggers of America*. Toronto: McClelland & Stewart.

van den Berghe, Pierre. 1992. "The modern state: Nation-builder or nation-killer?" *International Journal of Group Tensions* 22: 191–208.

van Kirk, Sylvia. 1999. *Many Tender Ties: Women in the Fur Trade Society 1670–1870*. Winnipeg: Watson and Dwyer.

Waite, P.B. 1997. "In Loyalist Ontario: A schoolboy's recollections, 1930–1933." *The Beaver* (February–March): 12–13.

Wall, Denis. 2000. "Aboriginal self-government in Canada: The cases of Nunavut and the Alberta Métis settlements." In D. Long and O.P. Dickason (eds.), *Visions of the Heart: Canadian Aboriginal Issues*, 2nd ed., 143–166. Toronto: Harcourt Canada.

Wallerstein, Immanuel. 1997. "World-systems analysis." In A. Giddens and J. Turner (eds.), *Social Theory Today*, 309–324. Stanford: Stanford University Press.

Wanner, Richard A. 1999. "Expansion and conscription: Trends in educational opportunity in Canada, 1920–1994." *Canadian Review of Sociology and Anthropology* 36(3): 409–442.

Warry, Wayne. 1998. *Unfinished Dreams: Community Healing and the Reality of Aboriginal Self-Government*. Toronto: University of Toronto Press.

_____. 2007. *Ending Denial: Understanding Aboriginal Issues*. Peterborough: Broadview Press.

Waters, Malcolm. 1994. "Introduction: A world of difference." *Australian-New Zealand Journal of Sociology* 30(3): 229–234.

Watkins, Melville. 1963. "A staple theory of economic growth." *Canadian Journal of Economics and Political Science* 29(2): 80–100.

_____. 1991. "The 'American system' and Canada's National Policy." In G. Laxer (ed.), *Perspectives on Canadian Economic Development*, 148–157. Toronto: Oxford University Press.

_____. 1997. "Canadian capitalism in transition." In W. Clement (ed.), *Understanding*

Canada: Building on the New Canadian Political Economy, 19–42. Montreal and Kingston: McGill-Queen's University Press.

Wax, Murray, Rosalie Wax, and Robert V. Dumont (eds.). 1964. "Formal Education in an American Indian Community." *Social Problems*, SSSP Monograph: 1–126.

Weaver, Andrew. 2008. *Keeping Our Cool: Canada in a Warming World*. Toronto: Viking.

Weaver, Jace (ed.). 1998. *Native American Religious Identity: Unforgotten Gods*. Maryknoll: Orbis Books.

Webber, Jeremy. 1994. *Reimagining Canada*. Montreal and Kingston: McGill-Queen's University Press.

Weber, Max. 1958. *From Max Weber: Essays in Sociology*, H. Gerth and C.W. Mills (eds.). New York: Oxford University Press.

Weller, Christian E., Robert E. Scott, and Adam S. Hersh. 2001. *The Unremarkable Record of Liberalized Trade*. Washington: Economic Policy Institute.

Westfall, William. 1993. "On the concept of region in Canadian history and literature." In D. Taras, B. Rasporich, and E. Mandel (eds.), *A Passion for Identity: An Introduction to Canadian Studies*, 335–344. Scarborough: Nelson Canada.

Whitaker, Reg. 1987. "Neo-conservatism and the state." *Socialist Register*. London: The Merlin Press.

_____ . 1991. *Canadian Immigration Policy Since Confederation*. Ottawa: Canadian Historical Association.

White, Deena. 1997. "Quebec state and society." In M. Fournier, M. Rosenberg, and D. White (eds.), *Quebec Society: Critical Issues*, 17–44. Scarborough: Prentice-Hall Canada.

Whyte, Donald. 1992. "Sociology and the constitution of society: Canadian experiences." In W. Carroll, L. Christiansen-Ruffman, R. Currie, and D. Harrison (eds.), *Fragile Truths: 25 Years of Sociology and Anthropology in Canada*, 313–319. Ottawa: Carleton University Press.

Widdis, Randy. 1997. "American-resident migration to Western Canada at the turn of the twentieth century." *Prairie Forum* 22(2): 237–261.

Wilensky, Harold. 1975. *The Welfare State and Equality: Structural and Ideological Roots of Public Expenditures*. Berkeley: University of California Press.

Wilson, C. Roderick, and Carl Urion. 1995. "First Nations prehistory and Canadian history." In R.B. Wilson, and C.R. Morrison (eds.), *Native Peoples: The Canadian Experience*, 2nd ed. Toronto: McClelland & Stewart.

Wilson, Roger (ed.). 1976. *The Land That Never Melts: Auyuittuq National Park*. Ottawa: Minister of Supply and Services.

Winks, Robin. 1998. *The Civil War Years: Canada and the United States*, 4th ed. Montreal and Kingston: McGill-Queen's University Press.

Wiseman, Nelson. 1993. "The pattern of Prairie politics." In D. Taras, B. Rasporich, and E. Mandel (eds.), *A Passion for Identity: An Introduction to Canadian Studies*, 456–470. Nelson Canada.

Wissler, Clark. 1923. *Man and Culture*. New York: Thomas Crowell

Witt, Norbert. 1998. "Promoting self-esteem, defining culture." *Canadian Journal of Native Education* 22(2): 260–273.

Wittington, Michael. 1985. "Political and constitutional development in the NWT and Yukon: The issues and the interests." In M. Wittington, (ed.), *The North*, 53–108. Toronto: University of Toronto Press.

Wonders, William. 1993. "Canadian regions and regionalisms: National enrichment or national disintegration?" In D. Taras, B. Rasporich, and E. Mandel (eds.), *A Passion for Identity: An Introduction to Canadian Studies*, 345–366. Scarborough: Nelson Canada.

Woodsworth, J.S. 1972. *Strangers within Our Gates*. Originally published in 1909. Toronto: University of Toronto Press.

Wright, Eric Olin. 1985. *Classes*. London: Verso.

Wright, Ronald. 1993. *Stolen Continents: The New World through Indian Eyes*. Toronto: Penguin.

Wuttunee, William I.C. 1971. *Ruffled Feathers: Indians in Canadian Society*. Calgary: Bell Books.

Wynn, Graeme. 2000. "On the margins of empire 1760–1840." In Craig Brown (ed.), *The Illustrated History of Canada*, 189–278. Toronto: Key Porter Books.

Yazzie, Robert. 2000. "Indigenous peoples and post-colonial colonialism." In M. Battiste (ed.), *Reclaiming Indigenous Voice and Vision*, 39–49. Vancouver: UBC Press.

York, Geoffrey. 1989. *The Dispossessed: Life and Death in Native Canada*. Toronto: Lester and Orpen Dennys.

Young, Robert A. 1995. *The Secession of Quebec and the Future of Canada*. Montreal and Kingston: McGill-Queen's University Press.

———. 1998. "Quebec succession and the 1995 referendum." In M. Westmacott and H. Mellon (eds.), *Challenges to Canadian Federalism*, 112–126. Scarborough: Prentice-Hall Canada.

Zinn, Howard. 1995. *A People's History of the United States 1492–Present*. New York: Harper Perennial.

COPYRIGHT ACKNOWLEDGEMENTS

Table 5.2: "Percent of Anglophone and Francophone Respondents Viewing Various Groups as Nations within Canada, 2006," adapted from Jedwab, Jack, "Canada: Nation of Nations?," The Association for Canadian Studies, available at: http://www.acs-aec.ca/oldsite/CurrentEvent/Face%20the%20Nations%20_2_.pdf. Reprinted with permission.

Chapter Six
Opening Photo Copyright © istockphoto.com/stock-photo-2897885-ambush.php

Chapter Seven
Opening Photo Copyright © istockphoto.com/stock-photo-1903696-going-for-a-ride.php
Table 7.1: "Immigration to Canada 1852–2006," adapted from the Citizenship and Immigration Canada publications *Citizenship and Immigration Statistics 1996*, "Table G2,"Catalogue no. MP22-1/1996; *Citizenship and Immigration Statistics 2003*, Catalogue no. C&I 291-07-02E, pp. 3; and *Facts and Figures 2008 Immigration Overview: Permanent and Temporary Residents*, available at http://www.cic.gc.ca/English/resources/statistics/facts2008/permanent/index.asp. Copyright © Citizenship and Immigration Canada. Adapted and reproduced with the permission of the Minister of Public Works and Government Services Canada, 2010.
Table 7.2: "Canadian Rural and Urban Population, 1871–2006 (in thousands)," adapted from the Statistics Canada publications *Historical Statistics of Canada*, Cat. 11-516-XWE, 1983, Series A67-69 and A75-77; *Population and Dwelling Counts (On-line)* available at http://www12.statcan.ca/english/census01/products/standard/popdwell/Table-UR-PS.cfm; *Canada at a Glance 2008*, Catalogue no. 12-581-XWE, Table 35, "Farm Population"; and *Canada's Farm Population: Agriculture-Population Linkage Data for the 2006 Census* Catalogue no. 95-633-XWE, Table 1, available at: http://www.statcan.gc.ca/ca-ra2006/agpop/article-eng.htm. Copyright © Statistics Canada. Reprinted with permission.
Box 7.2: "The Six Elements of Scientific Management," adapted from Krahn, Harvey, Lowe,

Graham, and Karen Hughes, *Work, Industry, and Canadian Society*, 5th ed. (Toronto: Nelson, 2007), 237. Copyright © 2007 Nelson Education Ltd. Reproduced with permission. www.cengage.com/permissions.

Chapter Eight
Opening Photo Copyright © quickpixels.com/Store/Prodimages/DFR6265_QP.jpg
Table 8.1: "Experienced Labour Force 15 Years and over by Occupation (Censuses 1991 and 2006)," adapted from the Statistics Canada publication *2006 Census of Population*, available at http://www40.statcan.gc.ca/l01/cst01/labor44-eng.htm. Copyright © Statistics Canada. Reprinted with permission.
Table 8.2: "Immigrant Status and Period of Immigration and Place of Birth, 2001 (total and percent)," adapted from the Statistics Canada publication *2001 Census*, "Immigrant Status and Period of Immigration (10A) and Place of Birth of Respondent (260) for Immigrants and Non-permanent Residents, for Canada, Provinces, Territories, Census Metropolitan Areas and Census Agglomerations, 2001 Census - 20% Sample," Catalogue no. 97F0009XCB2001002. Copyright © Statistics Canada. Reprinted with permission.
Table 8.3: "Canadian Population, by Place of Birth, and Province/Territory of Residence, 2006 (in percent)," adapted from the Statistics Canada publication *2006 Census of Population,* "Citizenship (5), Place of Birth (35), Sex (3), and Immigrant Status and Period of Immigration (12) for the Population of Canada, Provinces, Territories. Census Metropolitan Areas and Census Agglomerations, 2006 Census—20% Sample Data"(table) topic-based tabulation, Catalogue no. 97-557-XWE2006008, Ottawa; released December 4, 2007. Copyright © Statistics Canada. Reprinted with permission.
Table 8.4: "Population of Canada's 33 Census Metropolitan Areas (2006), 1996, 2001, and 2006," adapted from the Statistics Canada publication *Canada Year Book 2007,* "Table 24.3," Catalogue no. 11-402-XIE. Copyright © Statistics Canada. Reprinted with permission.

Chapter Fourteen

INDEX